Better Criticism

Ten Commandments for a Dying Art

For 20 years, from 1993 to 2013, **Chris Tookey** was the film critic for the *Daily Mail*, the UK's best-selling mid-market daily newspaper. He was also film critic for the world's most popular online newspaper, *Mail Online*. In 2013, he won the award Arts Reviewer of the Year from the London Press Club. Other jobs have included TV & film critic for the *Sunday Telegraph*, TV critic for the *Daily Telegraph* and theatre critic for the *Mail on Sunday*. He has written features and reviews for *Prospect*, the *Sunday Times*, *Observer*, *European*, *Books & Bookmen* and *National Review*. He is a prolific broadcaster, interviewer and interviewee on radio and TV, has presented *Back Row* and *The Film Programme* for Radio 4, and has worked in television and theatre (fringe, regional and West End), as a writer, composer, director and producer. His books on criticism are *The Critics' Guide to Movies, Named & Shamed: The World's Worst and Wittiest Movie Reviews from Affleck to Zeta-Jones, Tookey's Turkeys, Tookey's Talkies* and *Better Criticism: Ten Commandments for a Declining Art.*

Better Criticism

Ten Commandments for a Dying Art

Chris Tookey

Arena Books

First published in 2017 by Arena Books

Arena Books
6 Southgate Green
Bury St. Edmunds
IP33 2BL

www.arenabooks.co.uk
Distributed in America by Ingram International, One Ingram Blvd.,
PO Box3006, La Vergne, TN 37086-1985, USA.

Chris Tookey
Better Criticism *Ten Commandments for a dying Art*
    British Library cataloguing in Publication Data. A Catalogue record of this
    book is available from the British Library.

ISBN-13   978-1-911593-10-2
BIC classifications:- DS, AN, AP, APF, DSA, DSB, GT, DD, DN, DNJ.
Printed and bound by Lightning Source UK

Cover design
by Jason Anscomb
Typeset in
Times New Roman

FOREWORD
The Ten Commandments of Criticism

One of the most popular, smug and inane observations of the last few years is "everyone's a critic".

Looked at superficially, criticism is in rude health. There is a huge amount of it, and it's more available than ever. Just turn on your computer. On subjects from films to food, hotels to video games, music to theatre, art exhibitions to zoos, reviews are everywhere – and not only in the democratic, freedom-loving west.

There is, of course, an awful lot to be said in favour of increasing the range of people who criticise. There is no reason why reviewing should be the preserve of a metropolitan, white, male elite, as it has been in the past – though let's not *exclude* metropolitan white males, who should be allowed their voices as well. Everyone has the right to criticise, and it lies at the base of our other democratic freedoms. Our ability to assemble, vote and speak freely all depend on our right to express opinions.

Look deeper, though, and the news is far from good. Most professional critics of the arts, especially in America and the UK, will tell you (truthfully) that paid reviewing is under threat. Editors are culling most – sometimes all – of their best critics. In the academic world, balanced criticism is being driven out, in favour of weird and wacky dogma. Especially on the internet but also in newspapers and magazines, there's more *bad* criticism than ever before – needlessly rude, ill-judged, poorly expressed or bigoted, and sometimes all four.

There are "reviews" that are not reviews at all, but paid-for marketing tools or uncritical hagiography by friends and relations of the artist (and sometimes by the artist himself). Corruption in the field of reviewing is rife. Bad is driving out good.

Even in such havens of free speech as Western Europe and America, the story of criticism over the last few years has been a shocking tale of sackings, corruption, suicides, murders and editorial stupidity. Good, honest critics are an endangered species.

In our universities, "critical theory" has disgraced real criticism, by seeking to place the critic above other creators, and viewing all creation through a prism laid down by Hard Left dogma, based on race, gender or environmental activism. Emanating from universities and academic publishing is an unappetising aroma of intellectual snobbery, assuming that structuralism (or whatever doctrine is currently fashionable) is the only way to look at art.

In the wonderfully simple world of critical theory, the villains of our age are authority, capitalism, Christianity, conservatism, convention, ethnocentrism, the family, global warming, heredity, hierarchy, loyalty, morality, nationalism, patriarchy, patriotism, sexual restraint and tradition. Any cultural artifact that seeks to justify any of these things is quite simply wrong.

This leads to "clubland reviewing", the kind of criticism that reflects little more than the writer's anxiety to belong to a like-minded association of reviewers. This approach is especially rife at the BBC, where TV and radio producers alike seem to feel that any reviewing panel should consist of a token left-wing feminist, a left-winger from an ethnic minority and a left-wing gay man or woman. This, think the producers, will produce a balanced discussion. It produces the opposite, of course, by leaving out the vast majority of people and rendering them silent - which is why hardly anyone bothers to watch such programmes or listen to them. Between them, the token critics will cover all the bases of political correctness but ensure that the viewers will receive virtually no information on whether the play, book or film being discussed is worth the effort of seeing. This is part of the madness of our times.

One of my purposes in this volume is to do something that has not been attempted before. I want to praise and encourage *good* criticism that comes from a multiplicity of standpoints – criticism that is sensitive, informed, entertaining, useful and (above all) honest.

Let's not forget, either, that in many countries it's very hard to be an honest critic. Dissent is unpopular in all authoritarian societies. Speaking out is punishable by persecution, imprisonment and even execution.

On the night of March 22, 1980, in La Paz, the most famous film critic in Bolivia, Luiz Espinal, was kidnapped, tortured for hours, and murdered. His corpse was abandoned outside the city, where a peasant found it at dawn on the following day.

Besides being a film critic, Espinal directed the TV programme *In Flesh and Blood*, in which he tackled themes such as prisons, political violence, prostitution, drugs and guerrilla warfare.

Film criticism disappeared altogether from the press when the military took over, soon afterwards. The Bolivian Association of Film Critics, which Espinal had helped found in 1979, ceased to exist.

Colonel Luis Arce Gomez, who was rumoured to be responsible for Espinal's execution, became minister of the interior under the military regime. The government turned into an agent for a multi-million dollar cocaine trade.

Espinal may not be well known outside Bolivia, but he was a critic who deserves to be remembered for his courage in defending his democratic beliefs. Months before he was assassinated, he denounced the impending dictatorship each week in the pages of the weekly magazine *Aqui*. He may not have guessed that he would be its first victim – but if he did, that did not stop him from writing what he knew was the truth.[1]

In Russia under Vladimir Putin[2], expressions of dissent all too often result in premature death. The Russian journalist Anna Politkovskaya[3] was gunned down in October 2006 after criticising Putin. Coincidentally, or perhaps not, her execution took place on Putin's birthday.

Politkovskaya foresaw her own assassination, saying "People sometimes pay with their lives for saying aloud what they think. In fact, one can even get killed for giving me information. I am not the only one in danger. I have examples that prove it."[4]

The phenomenon that gave her grounds for optimism was the internet:

"We are hurtling back into a Soviet abyss, into an information vacuum that spells death from our own ignorance. All we have left is the internet, where information is still freely available. For the rest, if you want to go on working as a journalist, it's total servility to Putin. Otherwise, it can be death, the bullet, poison, or trial — whatever our special services, Putin's guard dogs, see fit."[5]

A week after Politkovskaya's shooting, former Russian spy Alexander Litvinenko[6] accused Putin of sanctioning her murder. Just two weeks later, Litvinenko was poisoned in London with a lethal dose of radioactive polonium. The main suspect in the case, a former officer of the Russian Federal Protective Service (FSO), Andrey Lugovoy, remains in Russia. As a member of the Duma, he enjoys immunity from prosecution. But even before he was elected to the Duma, the British government tried to extradite him without success.

Litvinenko was in no doubt about who had ordered his execution. He had recently written two books, *Blowing Up Russia: Terror from Within* (2002) and *Lubyanka Criminal Group* (2002), in which he and former KGB member Yuri Felshinsky accused the Russian secret services of staging the Russian apartment bombings and other terrorist acts in order to bring Vladimir Putin to power. They also claimed that Putin had been personally involved in organised crime, including covering up drug traffic from Afghanistan.[7]

Historian Robert Conquest[8] reviewed *Blowing Up Russia: Terror from Within* in the *Guardian,* noting that "it has taken Litvinenko's murder for the book to appear in this updated edition." He added that it was "as vivid a condemnation of the Putin regime as has yet been written."[9]

From his hospital deathbed, Litvinenko sent a defiant message to Putin:

"You may succeed in silencing me, but that silence comes at a price. The howl of protest from around the world will reverberate, Mr Putin, in your ears for the rest of your life."[10]

In 2015, yet another of Putin's most outspoken critics, Boris Nemtsov[11], was shot and killed by four bullets in the back. Putin's ally Ramzan Kadyrov, Chechnya's president, immediately blamed the crime on "western spy agencies". The muck-raking website Lifenews.ru, which has close links to Putin's former spy agency, the FSB, announced that Nemtsov was paying the price for his colourful love life. It noted that at the time of his murder, he was walking past the Kremlin with a Ukrainian model.[12]

It would seem a good deal more probable that he was murdered for his opposition to Putin's regime, and in particular its secret war in Ukraine, that had resulted in more than 6,000 deaths. Nemtsov had already described Putin's annexation of Crimea as "illegal". In the weeks before his death, Nemtsov expressed fears that Putin would have him killed.[13]

Let Luke Harding of the *Guardian* take up the story:

"Hours before his murder, moreover, Nemtsov said he had 'documentary' proof that undercover Russian soldiers were fighting and dying in eastern Ukraine. It was an assertion borne out by a steady flow of coffins returning in the dead of night from the war zone in Donetsk and Luhansk. According to his friend Ilya Yashin, Nemtsov was preparing an explosive essay on the subject. Nemtsov had written dissenting pamphlets before. One of them, *Putin: A Reckoning*, accused Russia's president and his circle of massive personal corruption. Another targeted Yuri Luzhkov, Moscow's former mayor, later toppled. But this new one went to the heart of the Kremlin's big lie. At the weekend, police seized Nemtsov's hard drives. There seems little prospect his last polemic will now ever be published."[14]

Nor is Putin's Russia an isolated example of a merciless, homicidal dictatorship bent on suppressing criticism. In China, dissidents are routinely locked up on charges such as "spreading counterrevolutionary propaganda", "inciting counterrevolutionary activities", "disturbing public order", "defection to the enemy" and "treason".[15]

I could fill another book with their names and individual stories. Writers who have fallen foul of the Chinese Communist system and been imprisoned for expressing criticisms of the regime have included the historian Bao Zunxin, Cai Lujun, Chen Pokong, He Depu (for inciting subversion on the internet), Jiang Lijun, Liao Yiwu (who bravely wrote a poem called *Massacre* about Tiananmen Square), Lu Jiamin, Shi Tao, Yuan Hongbing and Zeng Jinyan.[16]

In his book *The Slaughter: Mass Killings, Organ Harvesting, and China's Secret Solution to Its Dissident Problem* (2014), investigative journalist Ethan Gutmann[17] has alleged that Chinese dissidents are routinely rounded up and executed so that doctors can harvest their organs for transplantation. Needless to say, the book has been banned in China.

Even more bizarre reports have come from North Korea. Former guards who defected from Prison Camp No. 22, a labour camp in Hoeryong County, North Korea, revealed to human rights groups that human vivisection and experiments with biological and chemical weapons were routine there.

An August 2013, a report from the Washington-based Committee for Human Rights in North Korea (HRNK) called for an inquiry into the fate of 20,000 former prisoners of Camp 22. In 2012, the camp population was reported by Radio Free Asia (RFA) to have diminished suddenly from an estimated 30,000 to 3,000. RFA's sources, who were undercover North Koreans, revealed that most of the prisoners had starved to death. In September 2013, the *Washington Post* editorial board wrote about the disappearance of the camp: "Thousands of prisoners seem to have evaporated into thin air — perhaps via Camp 22's crematoria."

A former Camp 22 guard, Ahn Myong-chol, testified before Congress, published a memoir, and spoke out about North Korea's mass atrocities to various media, declaring he was doing so in penance for having once been part of the DPRK's inhuman system. He told NBC News in 2003:

"They trained me not to treat the prisoners as human beings. If someone is against socialism, if someone tries to escape from prison, then kill him. If there's a record of killing any escapee, then the guard will be entitled to study in the college. ... Beating and killing is an everyday affair. They are not treated as human beings; they are just like dogs or pigs."

A 2004 BBC documentary report featured interviews with North Korean camp survivors and Camp 22's former head of security, Kwon Hyu, who confessed to the crime of extermination and other crimes against humanity. He and an escaped victim confirmed that prisoners of conscience had been used as guinea pigs for biological and chemical weapon experiments over several decades, on a systematic scale.[18]

Kim Jong-Un (1983 -) succeeded his father Kim Jong-Il as Supreme Ruler of North Korea in 2011. He has carried out purges within his own government of anyone he believes may be disloyal, up to and including his own close relatives. He had his uncle, Jang Sung-Taek, executed by machine gun, along with members of Jang's family. These include Jang's sister Jang Kye-sun, her husband and ambassador to Cuba, Jon Yong-jin, and Jang's nephew and ambassador to Malaysia, Jang Yong-chol. The nephew's two sons were also killed.[19] At the time of Jang's removal it was announced that "the discovery and purge of the Jang group... made our party and revolutionary ranks purer."[20]After his execution on 12 December 2013, state media warned that the army "will never pardon all those who disobey the order of the Supreme Commander."[21]

On 7 March 2013, North Korea threatened the United States with a "pre-emptive nuclear attack". Its supreme leader has also revealed plans to conduct nuclear strikes on Los Angeles and Washington, D.C.[22]

In *The Interview*, a Hollywood comedy, Seth Rogen and James Franco play Americans who are enlisted by the C.I.A. to try to assassinate Kim. In

June 2014, North Korea promised to unleash a "merciless countermeasure" should the film be shown.[23]

When the film's production company, Sony Pictures, suffered an embarrassing breach of its internal computer network only weeks before the movie's December release, the North Korean government in Pyongyang was widely blamed.[24]

On a more serious note, there are said to be about 120,000 political prisoners in North Korea. Such is the level of repression that we don't even know their names. Even the United Nations, which is notoriously slow to condemn dictators, voted overwhelmingly in November to recommend that he and the rest of North Korea's leadership be hauled before the International Criminal Court, in The Hague, and tried for crimes against humanity.[25]

Persecution of critics and other dissidents does not exist only under dictatorship. With the rise of extremist Islamic movements, cartoons of the Prophet Muhammad bring the artists not only death threats, but also assassination. Most notoriously, journalists and cartoonists working for the Parisian satirical magazine *Charlie Hebdo* were massacred by French Jihadi gunmen, causing worldwide condemnation. [26]

Several writers have received *fatwas*, or death sentences, merely for questioning the Islamic faith. There are too many examples to list them all, but here are three lesser-known examples.

In 1993, Bangladeshi fundamentalists proclaimed a fatwa against Taslima Nasreen in 1993, after she wrote newspaper columns critical of the treatment of women under Islam. The next year she wrote *Lajja* (Shame) which described the abuse of women and minorities. Again there were death threats, and the Bangladeshi authorities confiscated her passport. She fled the country via Calcutta, was granted asylum in Sweden, lived in Paris, and finally went to India. Even in India, she was ordered by the Indian government to leave the city of Kolkata after riots there, and had to move to Delhi.

In March 2007, an Indian Muslim group called the All India Ibtehad Council offered a 500,000 rupees bounty for her decapitation. The president of the Council, Taqi Raza Khan stated that "Taslima has put Muslims to shame in her writings. She should be killed and beheaded and anyone who does this will get a reward from the council."[27]

In an interview given on September 30, 2002, for the American TV programme 60 Minutes, American Southern Baptist pastor and televangelist Falwell said: "I think Muhammad was a terrorist. I read enough by both Muslims and non-Muslims, [to decide] that he was a violent man, a man of war." The highly immoderate response of Iranian cleric Mohsen Mojtahed Shabestari, was to issue a fatwa calling for Falwell's murder, saying he was a "mercenary and must be killed."[28]

In 2010, an Australian imam called Feiz Mohammed called for Dutch politician Geert Wilders to be decapitated, after Wilders compared the *Quran* to *Mein Kampf*, stating that "the book incites hatred and killing and therefore has no place in our legal order."[29] It may be doubted whether calling for Wilders to be hated and killed was the most sensible response to his accusation.

In Malaysia, Muslim clerics were reported in 2015 to have issued no fewer than 1,500 *fatwas* condemning anyone attracted to such nefarious western practices as celebrating Valentine's Day or Halloween. Other crimes deserving death sentences were putting on dog shows or practising yoga.[30] So in Malaysia you don't even have to criticise anything to receive a fatwa.

Many fatwas have been treated in the west with scornful derision or dismissed as mere posturing, but they are in fact quite serious. Easily the most notorious was the 1989 fatwa against Salman Rushdie by the Iranian Ayatollah Khomeini, for Rushdie's novel *The Satanic Verses*. In 1991, Rushdie's Japanese translator, Hitoshi Igarashi, was stabbed to death in Tokyo, and his Italian translator was beaten and stabbed in Milan. In 1993, Rushdie's Norwegian publisher William Nygaard was shot and severely injured in an attack outside his house in Oslo. Thirty-seven guests died when their hotel in Sivas, Turkey was burned down by locals protesting against Rushdie's Turkish translator, Aziz Nesin. In 1998 Iran stated it was no longer pursuing Rushdie's death; however, that decree was reversed in 2005 by Ayatollah Ali Khamenei. Rushdie is still in fear of his life, but alive.

Others have not been so fortunate. In February 2015, American critic and blogger Avjit Roy, who had been promoting secular views in books and on the internet, was dragged from a bicycle rickshaw and hacked to death in a Dakha street in Bangladesh by fanatics wielding meat cleavers.[31] His wife, Rafida Bonya Ahmed, suffered head injuries and lost a finger. "While Avijit and I were being ruthlessly attacked, the local police stood close by and did not act," Rafida told Reuters.[32]

A month later, a second blogger, 27 year-old Wasjiqur Rahman, was stabbed to death in Dakha, after writing in favour of atheism and against religious fundamentalism.[33]

Most recently, there have been the activities of extreme Muslim fundamentalists, operating mainly, but not exclusively, in Syria and Iraq. Fanatics from Islamic State, or Isis, are continuing to murder many thousands of people, not for any crime but for not sharing their radical Muslim beliefs.

Isis is not the only organisation to blame in the Middle East. Under the brutally theocratic judicial system of Saudi Arabia, criticising the king is banned. Liberals are flogged and dissidents tortured. Women cannot travel without a man's permission.

There are too numerous victims to mention, but Khaled Johani was jailed for calling for democracy. Raif Badawy was flogged for opening an online liberal forum. Hamza Kashgari was imprisoned for daring to question Islam on Twitter. Abdul Hamid Al Fakki had his head chopped off for sorcery. Amina bint Nasser was beheaded for being a witch. Manal al Sharif was imprisoned for being a woman driver.[34]

Dozens of people are beheaded every month by the Saudi authorities. But, according to Human Rights Watch, the U.S. maintains a "deafening silence" on human rights violations by Saudi Arabia, because Saudi Arabia is its key ally in the region.[35]

Iran, too, is notorious for its intolerance of criticism. The methods of its theocratic government include blanket censorship of all media, jamming of foreign satellite TV broadcasts, and the closing down of dissident newspapers and magazines. A new 2016 Law on Political Crimes criminalized all expression deemed to be "against the management of the country and its political institutions and domestic and foreign policies" and made "with intent to reform the affairs of the country without intending to harm the basis of the establishment". Common Iranian punishments include floggings, blindings and amputations. These are sometimes carried out in public.[36]

Also in 2016, Turkey's Islamic President Recep Tayyip Erdogan used the excuse of a failed coup against him to imprison more than 40,000 people, dismiss nearly 90,000 civil servants and close down at least 184 media outlets. 118 journalists were sent to prison without trial.[37]

Hard-line anti-Islamic governments have been just as sensitive to criticism. In Tajikistan, a 2016 law declared that "insulting the leader of the nation" was a criminal offence. In November of that year, the independent newspaper *Nigoh* and website Tojnews announced their closure because "conditions no longer exist for independent media and free journalism". [38]

Secular rulers can be every bit as monstrous as religious ones. Take Zimbabwe under Robert Mugabe[39]. The Human Rights Forum in Harare, a coalition of 10 groups, including the Amani Trust, Amnesty International and the Catholic Commission for Justice and Peace, published a damming report on Mugabe's regime in August, 2001:

"The rule of law has been replaced by rule by thugs. Armed militias roam the countryside assaulting people whose sole 'crime' is to support the opposition party. The victims receive little or no protection from the law enforcement agencies; worse, members of these agencies sometimes participate in the assaults. To retain power in the face of increasing opposition, Mugabe has been prepared to subvert the democratic process, the independence of the judiciary, the freedom of the press, and the professional neutrality of the police and the army. He has deliberately stirred up violence, race hatred and political intolerance, and he has brought economic destitution to his country."[40]

Mr Mugabe and his ministers have repeatedly issued public death threats against their opponents. The late defence minister, Moven Mahachi, told a rally in 2000 that "we will move door to door, killing... I am the minister responsible for defence. Therefore, I am capable of killing".[41]

In June 2001, the foreign minister, Stan Mudenge, told trainee teachers: "As civil servants, you have to be loyal to the government of the day. You can even be killed for supporting the opposition, and no one would guarantee your safety."[42]

Small wonder, then, that Robert Mugabe has banned western critics of his regime from Zimbabwe. Only after his death – and perhaps not even then - can we expect full exposure of his murderous activities against those who have dared to criticise him.

The United States of America has long been regarded – by friends and enemies alike - as a bastion of free speech, but even here there are worrying signs of dictatorial tendencies. When President Donald Trump attacks credible news sources such as the BBC, CNN, *New York Times, Daily Mail, LA Times, New York Daily News* and *Guardian* as purveyors of "fake news" and calls them the "enemy of the American people," he appears anxious to smear anyone who presents opinions or facts that diverge from his own view of reality.

Damian Collins, Conservative MP and chairman of the Culture, Media and Sport Parliamentary Committee, shares Trump's dislike of deceptive journalism but told the Huffington News:

"We need to fight for a clear definition of fake news. This term should be restricted for news stories that are entirely fake, or where the key part of the story has been made up. It is pernicious for politicians like Donald Trump to use the term 'fake news' to include any piece of journalism that they disagree with. This deliberately blurs the lines, and suggests that fake news is in the eye of the beholder, rather than being something that can be clearly defined. When people then rightly call out websites that are pushing out fake news stories, the challenge could come back that all news organisation engage in fake news, so what's the difference? This is dangerous."[43]

This kind of authoritarianism in the face of legitimate criticism appears to be on the increase around the world. It has often needed bravery to stand up and be counted; and never more so than today.

The British restaurant and TV critic Adrian Gill expressed this need succinctly when he wrote:

"Freedom of speech is what all other human rights and freedoms balance on. That may sound like unspeakable arrogance when applied to restaurant reviews or gossip columns. But that's not the point. Journalism isn't an individual sport like books and plays; it's a team effort. The power of the press is cumulative. It has a conscious human momentum. You can – and probably do – pick up bits of it and sneer or sigh or fling them with great force at the dog. But together they make up the most precious thing we own."[44]

Despite the low reputation of criticism and the poor quality of too many of its practitioners, it is a noble calling; and we – especially those of us in the west - have become far too complacent and sluggish when it comes to recognising its importance.

The right to free and honest expressions of opinion is a universal one, and it lies at the foundation of every other liberty.

THE FIRST COMMANDMENT
Thou Shalt Expect To Be Criticised Thyself

Beware of The Scrunts

Critics are routinely reviled and deeply despised - and not only for their overuse of alliteration.

When told of a proposal that there should be a university chair for music criticism, the orchestra conductor Sir Thomas Beecham[45] responded tersely "if they must have one, I think it should be an electric chair."[46]

At the Annual Dinner of the Critics' Circle in 1922, the playwright and author Sir James (J.M.) Barrie[47] hinted that he too had entertained homicidal thoughts towards critics. Cheerily addressing the assembled reviewers as "scum", he mused:

"How easy it would be to follow a critic or two to their office on a first night and give them a sudden push as a bus came along. But I dare say you are all rather nippy at the kerbside."[48]

There are plenty of people, especially in the creative fields, who would happily prescribe the death penalty for reviewers who have maligned them. You can tell this from the way critics are portrayed in books, plays and movies. They're a bad lot.

In Joseph Mankiewicz's film *All About Eve*[49], the sharp-tongued reviewer Addison DeWitt, based on real-life theatre critic George Jean Nathan[50], turns out to be a criminal blackmailer.

In Douglas Hickox's black comedy film *Theatre of Blood*[51], drama critics representing the seven deadly sins are gleefully murdered in a variety of spectacular ways. The first victim is hacked to death by tramps, in a reenactment of *Julius Caesar*. The next is speared, and his corpse is dragged behind a horse, like Hector in *Troilus and Cressida*. Other deaths include drowning, decapitation, electrocution by hair curlers and – perhaps most memorably - being made to eat one's 'babies' (when an effeminate, gluttonous critic, played by Robert Morley, is force-fed his pet poodles).

In John Updike's story *Bech Noir*[52], the author writes with enthusiasm of literary critics being terrorized and culled by a vengeful writer. One is poisoned; one is driven to suicide; a third is asphyxiated when his oxygen supply is turned off; another is crushed to death under the wheels of a New York subway car.

In M. Night Shyamalan's film *Lady In The Water*[53], a know-it-all literary and film critic (played by the diminutive, bespectacled and splendidly cold Bob Balaban) is killed and eaten by scrunts (don't ask – imagine rabid wart-hogs from outer space). This was widely interpreted as Mr Shyamalan taking revenge on reviewers who had been insufficiently reverent about his previous film, *The Village*[54]. Unfortunately, the critic character's supercilious complaints about cinematic clichés, laboured exposition and unrealistic dialogue were even more applicable to *Lady in the Water* than they had been to *The Village*.

The critics bit back by being beastly about all M. Night Shyamalan's subsequent films - a succession of turkeys including *After Earth*[55] ("It's impossible to take this movie seriously, certainly not as seriously as it takes itself" - Peter Rainer, *Christian Science Monitor*), *The Last Airbender*[56] ("an insult to anyone with a triple-digit I.Q." - James Berardinelli, *ReelViews*) and *The Happening*[57] ("a load of shite" - Robbie Collin, *News of the World*).

Oh dear. I suppose that means we'll all end up being eaten by scrunts.

Expect To Be Hated

I have spent most of my professional life as a critic – of music, books, television, theatre and movies. I was paid to watch movies for 28 years,[58] was Chairman of the British Film Critics' Circle for five of them[59], and was voted Arts Reviewer of the Year in 2013.[60] My reviews have been read by millions of people all over the planet.[61] All the same, look me up on the internet and you will find that I am, in some people's opinion at least, the Worst Critic in the World.[62]

Internet bloggers have claimed – without producing a shred of evidence - that I never like movies based on comic strips[63], or action movies[64], or movies that aren't in a foreign language[65], or movies that are in a foreign language.[66] It is also claimed that I hate any film that doesn't promote wholesome Christian values.[67] None of this is even slightly true.[68]

At least one actor hates me. Former film actor and self-confessed crack-addict[69] Danny Dyer once denounced me on a DVD commentary track[70] as a "nonce", which I understand is a prison term for someone who sexually interferes with children. That's the same Danny Dyer who held down a job as agony columnist on the lads' mag *Zoo*, until he went too far with his advice to one reader that he disfigure his ex-girl-friend, so that no one else would fancy her.[71] The last film I reviewed of his, *Run for Your Wife*, made just £602 on its first weekend, averaging £67 per screen.[72] The last time I looked, he was in the TV soap *EastEnders*.[73]

I have been accused many times on the internet – anonymously, needless to say - of being a paedophile and a couple of times of bestiality.[74] Needless to say, none of these accusations has the slightest basis in reality.[75]

My undesirable reputation as a pervert came about after a review I wrote of *Kick-Ass*, which complained that the film purveys "a perniciously sexualised view of children and glorifies violence, especially knife and gun crime". I called attention to the sexual overtones in the deliberately

Never Dies, and a piece in which he questioned the commercial success of another musical, *Legally Blonde*:

"I blogged about the fibs people were telling about how many seats it had sold and I got a lot of responses saying I didn't know what I was talking about, but also saying I should go away and die. It's the anonymity of the web that allows people to say these things."[92]

Coveney acknowledges that we are all entitled to our opinion, but says that the mere expression of an opinion "is not criticism". He regards the fans of certain musicals as the most vicious bloggers. He is often accused of being "up himself", and replies:

"Well, I answer, it is because I am a professional. It is my life and has been my whole career. I don't think that just having opinions is so valuable. You need a sense of historical memory. I am sure there will be online critics who have this, but not everybody."[93]

Andrew Lloyd-Webber points out that the ethics of bloggers are not nearly as refined or reliable as professional critics. Whereas critics will wait for the press night to praise or condemn a musical, bloggers will lay into the first preview:

"It's a very worrying situation for anyone who's opening any kind of play or musical. I dread to think what anybody would have said about the first preview of *Cats* or, frankly, *Les Misérables*, which was a huge undertaking and wasn't right at the beginning."[94]

David Benedict, *Variety*'s theatre critic, points out that word-of-mouth has gone viral, but that "bloggers are dealing in unfettered opinions. True criticism is analysis, and it gives you an understanding of the form. Ideally, a critic doesn't just tell you something didn't work; they tell you why."[95]

Andrew Keen, author of the book *The Cult of the Amateur*, laments the fact that "today a book or play is treated like a car that you might want to buy". He believes that the world of professional criticism is in crisis:

"There is a general rebellion against the cultural critic... The web is a platform for that rebellion, but it is also the cause of it. There is something in online culture that lends itself to rebellion."[96]

There's another good reason why critics' tastes differ from those of the general public, as the acerbic American theatre and film critic John Simon pointed out in 1982:

"The critic is primarily concerned with how much lasting, artistic value there is in a film; the paying customer is principally interested in having a good time... The critic's apparent negativism sets him off from the happy-go-lucky (or, better, eager-to-be-happy) crowd, and makes him look intolerant, mean and deserving of isolation... Let a critic say that a movie the reader loved is worthless (which, of course, never means more than 'worthless to the critic', but somehow always gets misconstrued), and the reader feels insulted and threatened: 'This man considers me to be an idiot.'

And then, either insultedly, 'I am not an idiot!' or intimidatedly, 'My God! *Am* I an idiot?' So the tough critics end up being rejected, not merely with indignation or scorn, but actually with hate and fear, which condemn him to greater aloneness. No help for this."[97]

Are Critics Human?

The word "critic" comes from Greek word "kritikos" which means "able to discern", which is in turn derived from the word "krites", meaning a person who offers reasoned judgment or analysis, value judgment, interpretation or observation. Sometimes you'd never guess that the word has such a respectable pedigree, for scornful attacks on critics are far from new. Critics have long been reviled as ignorant parasites, even by those with good reason to be grateful to them.

Alexander Woollcott, a former drama critic of the *New York Times*, was candid about the number of his enemies, saying "If I were found dead with a dagger through my heart, the next morning three hundred actors would be arrested on suspicion of murder."[98]

Playwright Brendan Behan, a convicted bomber for the IRA during his impetuous twenties and a notoriously belligerent drunk, likened critics to eunuchs in a harem:

"They know how it is done, they've seen it done every day, but they are unable to do it themselves."[99]

That strikes me as more than a little ungrateful to Kenneth Tynan, who had the balls to support Mr Behan when hardly anyone else would. The young critic of the *Observer* gave the Irishman's breakthrough play *The Quare Fellow* a crucial boost in 1956 by writing that the playwright was fulfilling the Irish duty to "save the English theatre from inarticulate glumness". [100]

Tynan's less well-known successor at the *Observer*, Mervyn Jones, also helped to make a hit of the Irishman's play *The Hostage* in 1959. Sadly, Mr Behan died of drink in 1964 before he could pen any penitent thank-you letters to the splendidly thrusting, virile critics who had helped fund his drink habit.

Another angry young man, but one who lived long enough to become a bad-tempered old fart, was John Osborne. He hated all reviewers with a passion. "Asking a working writer what he thinks about critics," he snarled, "is like asking a lamppost what it feels about dogs."[101]

This too strikes me as unfair to Mr Tynan, who - however much in person he may have resembled a pampered pooch fresh from the poodle parlour - was the only critic to see the merits of Osborne's patchy theatrical debut, *Look Back in Anger*. There can be little doubt, even if Mr Osborne never chose to acknowledge the fact, that without Tynan's timely rave Mr essay called *The Quintessence of Ibsenism*[129], which reads today as Shaw's own, passionately argued theatrical credo. It was only after encountering Ibsen's work as a critic that Shaw found the courage - and the ability - to try and emulate him as a creator. In short, teaching as a critic gave George Bernard Shaw the impetus to do, as a dramatist.

Revenge of The Artists

Artists of all kind are entitled to ignore professional reviewers or, indeed, the public, if all they care about is self-expression. Mozart[130] claimed "I pay no attention whatever to anybody's praise or blame. I simply follow my own feelings."[131]

Lesser geniuses, especially in the so-called popular arts, may take a more populist or commercial approach. Walt Disney[132] said "we are not trying to entertain the critics. I'll take my chances with the public."[133]

It is hardly surprising, however, that some creative artists, injured by critical barbs, have taken umbrage at those who have hurt them. The Victorian poet Alfred, Lord Tennyson[134] famously described critic John Churton Collins (1848-1908) as "a louse in the locks of literature."[135] That is much quoted as a witticism about critics, but it is not an altogether fair description of John Churton Collins.

Collins had a distinguished career as a journalist, essayist and lecturer, publishing learned volumes on the artist Sir Joshua Reynolds, Dryden, Voltaire, Swift and Rousseau. He was instrumental, for better or for worse, in pioneering the study of English within British universities, and in 1904 was appointed to the chair of English Literature at the new University of Birmingham. So he wasn't only a parasite.

The maligned Collins incurred Tennyson's hatred with three articles in the magazine *Cornhill*, which were republished in book form as *Illustrations of Tennyson* in 1891. Collins wrote that Tennyson's verse was guilty of "commonplace thought" and "commonplace sentiment". The critic also dared to point out that the poet was indebted to various sources, ancient and modern, though Collins stopped well short of accusing Tennyson of plagiarism.

His tone was, by modern standards, deferential:

"It would be absurd and presumptuous to conclude that the analogies which have been traced between the ideas and expressions of Lord Tennyson and those of other poets and writers were in all, or indeed in most cases, deliberate or even conscious imitations. In his own noble words, we moderns are 'the heirs of all the ages.'"

The Poet Laureate was notoriously sensitive about adverse criticism, however, and chose to ignore the numerous passages in Collins' work that praised the poet's rhythm and imagery. So nowadays Collins is unjustly remembered only for Tennyson's cruelly ungracious description of him.

The playwright David Mamet[136] wrote equally scathingly of the influential New York critics Frank Rich[137] and John Simon[138] that they were "the syphilis and gonorrhoea of the theatre."[139]

Mamet's feud with John Simon ran and ran. In 2005, Mamet penned a premature celebration of Simon's departure from theatre criticism: "I have just heard that John Simon has been fired from the post he long disgraced at *New York Magazine*. In his departure he accomplishes that which during his tenure eluded him: he has finally done something for the American Theatre."[140] In 2008, Mamet returned to that theme, lambasting Simon - who was still writing theatre reviews professionally - for his "stunning amalgam of superciliousness and savagery".[141]

Simon was by no means an uncritical admirer of Mamet's work. In 2008, Simon wrote:

"That Mamet can write, he proved early in *Sexual Perversity in Chicago* and recently in *Romance*. But in between, things became iffy, hairy, and sometimes just plain poor. Mamet's procedure is fracture of the language. He may start with sentences, which become shorter and shorter, and tend to devolve into sentence fragments. Forthwith they may be reduced to mere words, which, in turn, are apt to break off into forlorn syllables, sometimes single vowels or consonants interrupted by another speaker. Often there are only pauses, but those, to be sure, are bequests from Harold Pinter, like so many other questionable devices drawn by Mamet from that insalubrious well."[142]

But Simon's judgments of Mamet mellowed over the years. Ironically, it was Simon who leapt to the defence of Mamet's much-panned play *Race* (2009) at the Ethel Barrymore Theatre. Though it was described as "a bewildering muddle" by the *New York Post*[143], "slick but hollow" by *Variety*[144] and "smug cynicism" by the *Financial Times*[145], Simon gave it a complimentary review, calling it "a high-voltage melodrama that is unafraid to raise painful questions while dispensing prickly ideas and provocative dialogue amid steady suspense".[146]

Simon also found much to like in the 2009 Broadway revival of *Oleanna*, saying it "has lost none of its power to provoke."[147]

Mamet's opinion of Simon does not seem to have softened, however; of the two men, Mamet appears to be the more unreasonable hater.

Mamet's description of Frank Rich as a social disease is even more surprising, for the long-serving *New York Times* critic praised Mamet's *American Buffalo* as a "brilliant...violent vision of the dog-eat-dog jungle of urban American capitalism."[148] Rich acclaimed Mamet's *Glengarry Glen Ross* as "ferocious comedy and drama, a top American playwright in bristling form."[149] When Madonna appeared in *Speed-the-Plow* in 1988, she fellow-novelist D. H. Lawrence[189]. The author of *Lady Chatterley's Lover* sounded off about the depravity of Joyce's *Ulysses* in 1928, denouncing it as:

"The dirtiest, most indecent, most obscene thing ever written... My god, what a clumsy *olla putrida* James Joyce is! Nothing but old fags and cabbage-stumps of quotations from the Bible and the rest, stewed in the juice of deliberate, journalistic dirty-mindedness."[190]

You might expect a fellow-modernist such as Virginia Woolf[191] to be more appreciative of Joyce, but she wasn't. She called *Ulysses* "the work of a queasy undergraduate scratching his pimples".

Even writers who have suffered their own run-ins with unsympathetic critics cannot be relied upon to produce kindly critiques when asked for their own opinions. Here, for example, is Charles Dickens' merciless dissection of a play at the Theatre Royal, Haymarket, in December 1837:

"On Thursday night an original domestic drama (advertised in the bills as the work of one Frederick Lawrance) was produced at this house, and was received in play-bill phraseology with 'roars of laughter' – meeting, in short, with a reception which would have been most delightful to the author's feelings if the piece had been intended to be funny, but which (his intention apparently being that it should be very affecting) was calculated to awaken feelings of quite an opposite description in his mind – if he has such a thing about him, which we rather doubt."[192]

Dickens may well have been right to be contemptuous of Mr Lawrance's work, which was taken off after only two performances and has long since been forgotten. But even a versatile and highly creative man of the theatre such as Noel Coward[193] could be wrong in his estimation of genuine dramatic talent. Even though he never saw *Waiting for Godot* he read it and pronounced Samuel Beckett's work to be "pretentious gibberish, without any claim to importance whatever."

Theatre critic Irving Wardle recalls with a shudder the period when one much less witty playwright had a brief try-out as theatre critic on the *Observer*:

"For lazily opinionated arrogance and disregard of the critical basics (e.g. reporting on an actress's looks instead of her performance) it would be hard to beat the notices John Osborne wrote during his guest spell on the *Observer*."[194]

And it should be remembered that not all creative artists are intellectual powerhouses. Here, for example, is Gene Simmons[195] of the rock group Kiss, expressing his feelings about Shakespeare's musicality, his populism and rhythm:

"Shakespeare is shit. Absolute shit! He may have been a genius for his time, but I just can't relate to that stuff. 'Thee' and 'thou' - the guy sounds like a faggot. Captain America is classic because he's more entertaining."[196]

The obvious conclusion is that being an artist - of whatever quality - does not necessarily qualify one to be a critic of sound judgment and measured expression.

Indeed, anyone who thinks at all seriously about criticism must realise that it cannot and should not be left to practitioners. To say that only poets should judge the work of other poets is as stupid as saying that a judge shouldn't sentence murderers if he has never committed a murder. Judging and doing are separate skills. A fine poet may also be a fine critic of poetry. But he might not be. And a truly rotten poet might turn out to be an excellent critic.

Michael Coveney, former theatre critic for the *Financial Times, Observer* and the *Daily Mail*, is scornful about the view that you have to have done something if you are going to criticise it:

"It's an odd notion that someone who writes about football should have played in the Premier League in order to be an authentic critic. The best football writers - Geoffrey Green, Brian Glanville, James Lawton - had no such experience. And anyone who watches exceptional ex-football players such as Alan Shearer or Michael Owen pontificate on television knows instantly that they cannot string two or three words together, let alone a few paragraphs."[197]

That's a bit tough on Shearer[198] and Owen[199]. And for my money, some of the most revealing pundits on football have been ex-players Alan Hansen[200], Andy Gray[201] and (now) Gary Neville[202]. But Coveney has a point. And it's worth remembering that two of the most analytical football managers of recent years, Arsene Wenger[203] and Jose Mourinho[204], weren't much cop as players.

There is much to be said for the view that many critics don't know how to create artistically, and that mitigates their credibility. There's an old Native American proverb, to the effect that "Don't judge any man until you have walked two moons in his moccasins."

But creation and criticism are two skills rarely found in the same person. As Dr Samuel Johnson once wrote:

"You may abuse a tragedy, though you can not write one. You may scold a carpenter who has made you a bad table, though you can not make a table. It is not your trade to make tables."[205]

Threats Of Death And Violence

Most creative people want to be critiqued. They may not enjoy hearing negative things about their work, but – especially years later – they know very well that not everything they've done has been of imperishable greatness. And, contrary to received opinion, creative people are often appreciative of good reviews.

to tear your guts out and serve them to my dog! That review of yours cost me hundreds of thousands of pounds! Probably millions! I had to close a whole damn restaurant. I could lose my entire business. Dozens of people could lose their jobs. I could end up on the STREET!' 'Well,' I said, sliding sideways out of his grip and straightening my tie. 'I suggest you open a better restaurant next time.' And I slipped out by the back door, after first leaving an enormous tip, which I always do in these situations because I hate to cause a rumpus."[251]

Another food Critic, A.A. Gill, was forcibly chucked out of a Chelsea restaurant by its chef, Gordon Ramsay, after a less than complimentary review.[252] When asked in 2007 whether he had mellowed towards his enemies, Ramsay told the interviewer "Food critics? Love 'em. I'll happily agree at my cost to do all the canapés at their funerals free of charge."[253]

The doyen of American wine critics, Robert M. Parker, says he too has been attacked and received death threats - though he also claims he has had two French château owners offer him the sexual favours of their daughters, which has certainly never happened to me. Jacques Hebrard, the manager of one vineyard, Chateau Cheval Blanc, was so outraged at Parker's evaluation of one of his wines that he demanded Parker re-taste it. When the critic returned, Hebrard's dog attacked him. Parker says that when he requested a bandage to stop the bleeding from his leg, the wine-grower, who had stood by and watched the attack impassively, merely gave Parker a copy of his offending newsletter. For his part, the Frenchman denies that his dog ever drew blood. But it's obvious that Mr Parker's review did - at least figuratively.[254]

Acerbic TV reviewer Victor Lewis-Smith, of the *Evening Standard*, happily recalls comedian/actor/presenter/ former crackhead Craig Charles[255] threatening to throw him through a plate glass window. This was all the more ironic, since Mr Charles had only recently been heading up an advertising campaign against, er, bullying.[256]

Lewis-Smith also waxes nostalgic[257] about a man with the splendidly actorish name of Addison Cresswell, volunteering to hurl the critic into a car crusher. Before he was able to carry out any such attack, however, Mr Cresswell died of a heart attack after snorting cocaine at a Christmas party. So the car crusher has had to wait.[258]

Film critic Mark Kermode also has his enemies:

"I've been threatened professionally, physically and legally; in person and in print; online and on the phone. I have been shot at, shouted at and sworn at. I have been stalked by post, by email, by voicemail. I have been banned, barred and blacklisted from screenings, festivals and venues. I have had arsey American lawyers yelling at me in the middle of the night and coke-addled Groucho Club habitués swearing at me in the middle of the day. I have been the target of obscene videos and outrageously defamatory remarks posted online by the unwell, the unhinged and the unnamed. I have been cartooned and caricatured, imitated and insulted – in words and pictures. All in a day's work."[259]

The kindly and almost supernaturally emollient film reviewer Barry Norman recalls the time John Wayne threatened to knock him out, and had to be physically restrained by his minders while calling Barry a "Goddam pinko liberal".[260]

Barry also had an interesting, near-physical encounter with Australian movie star Mel Gibson at a Hollywood party when Mel insisted belligerently that he was at least as tall as Barry (who is 6 foot). Mel is 5 foot 9. Maybe Mel was confusing height with stature. But then everyone looks down on critics.[261]

Critics need to be able to take a lot of shit, sometimes literally. Graham Greene recalled this lesson in 1972, long after he had retired as a film critic:

"On one occasion, I opened a letter to find a piece of shit enclosed. I have always – though probably incorrectly – believed that it was a piece of aristocratic shit, for I had made cruel fun a little while before of a certain French *marquis*. Thirty years later in Paris at a dinner of the *haute bourgeoisie* I sat opposite him and was charmed by his conversation. I longed to ask him the truth, but I was daunted by the furniture."[262]

Even the less well-bred do this. Aspiring television critics should be warned that reality TV celebrity Sharon Osbourne[263] likes to take revenge on reviewers by sending them boxes of her own excrement (though daughter Kelly Osbourne claims that sometimes they contained hers or her brother's). In 2013, Sharon admitted she had been doing this for years.

"The last turd? Three... no, four years ago, when the first review came out of *The Osbournes*. The journalist said something about my kids being fat and how unappealing that was. I said, 'I heard you've got an eating disorder. Eat this.' I've done it for an awfully long time. I suppose I find it funny. I mean, I don't just do it to *anybody*. They have to have done something really *bad*."[264]

I hardly need to spell out the message for any would-be critic, whether you're planning to be as punctiliously polite as Barry Norman or as relentlessly rude as Victor Lewis-Smith.

Prepare to be hated and even physically attacked by people who become over-excited under the influence of drink, drugs or their own celebrity. Develop a thick skin, so you can take criticism as well as dish it out. If you want easy popularity, do something else. Anything else.

And these days it's probably a sensible idea to avoid making disparaging references to the Prophet Mohammed.

newspaper that has the reputation of being Right-wing. But it is the lot of any honest critic to be vilified unfairly.

The only negative review of my book *Tookey's Turkeys* was written anonymously by someone calling himself "theediscerning", who turned out to be one John Lloyd, an obscure local film reviewer living in Leicester. His one-star review ran counter to all the other four or five-star reviews. He dismissed *Tookey's Turkeys* as "a collection of vitriolic cinema write-ups from a bloke who used to work for the *Daily Mail* – and it shows." He proceeded to accuse me of plagiarism, writing from a homophobic standpoint, and prejudice against the disabled.

When I discovered his email address and challenged him over his groundless claim that I had copied "the historical mistakes sections off IMDB", he admitted that this was a false accusation but made no attempt to withdraw it.

His "review" also claimed, without any basis in truth, that I made "repeated use of the word 'gay' as an insult." Unfortunately for him there is not a single instance in the book of my using "gay" as an insult. On the other hand, I looked up the word "homophobic" and found myself using the adjective to describe five films I disliked (*Hostel, I Now Pronounce You Chuck and Larry, Nixon, 300* and *Anatomy of Hell*). Perhaps he thought I was using "homophobic" as a compliment.

Another bizarre claim in his review was that I was guilty of "whingeing on in a completely UKIP style". I searched in vain for any reference by me to curbing immigration or leaving the European Union, the two policies with which UKIP is principally associated. I imagine Mr Lloyd erroneously thought I must be a UKIP supporter because I wrote for the *Daily Mail*, but as I pointed out to him in my email that paper consistently supports the Conservative Party, not UKIP. Again, he made no attempt to withdraw his accusation.

He also disliked my describing certain characters as "retarded" and interpreted that as indicating prejudice against the disabled. I used the word about a minor character in *Gigli* and the anti-heroes of *The Human Centipede II* and *Norbit*. In all three cases, I was using the term inoffensively (so I thought) to describe people who were intellectually backward, slow on the uptake and, in politically correct language, "intellectually challenged" or "developmentally disabled". I had no idea that the word "retarded" had become taboo. I've received no complaints before from many millions of readers, or indeed from anyone disabled.

In other words, Mr Lloyd's review was inaccurate and libellous. Perhaps I should have sued him, but on the whole I thought it better just to ignore him.

Of course it can be scary to find that by expressing an opinion you have angered people who don't know you and who will stop at nothing to discredit you with unfounded accusations. But, as Sir Winston Churchill[269] said, "You have enemies? Good. That means you've stood up for something, some time in your life."[270]

THE SECOND COMMANDMENT
Thou Shalt Experience The Thing Thou Art Reviewing

The Perils of Cutting Corners

You need to have experienced the thing you are criticising. This second commandment may seem too obvious to be stated, but how many of us at school tried to save time in an essay crisis by ignoring the primary source – the play, novel or poem, say – and merely read the articles about it? I bet most of us would plead "guilty" to that, but it's simply not permissible when you're a professional reviewer.

It breaks the unwritten law that you shouldn't lie to your readers. Besides, it's unfair to the creative artists involved, and it precludes the possibility of your finding something in it that no one else has. Many newspapers would regard this kind of absenteeism as a sacking offence.

Chicago Sun-Times journalist Paige Wiser was fired after her *Glee Live!* concert review mentioned a song that wasn't performed and described another that she didn't see.

At least she had the honesty to admit her dishonesty. "I'm at fault," she said. "I do understand what a big deal this was. I am ashamed, and it's just a matter of making bad decisions when you're exhausted." Wiser, who had been with the *Sun-Times* for 17 years, explained what happened:

"I was told my kids' cutesy reactions would be welcome, so I brought along my 6- and 7-year-old. Jack nearly decapitated himself falling off his seat, and Audrey started murmuring "I'm going to throw up" 10 songs into the set. I made her stick it out for three more songs, saying "This is Mommy's job!" but she looked so green I finally shoved the half-full cotton candy bag at her to throw up in, and hustled her out of there. What I should have done was written that I had to leave early, but I didn't want to let the paper down, so I tried to make the review seem complete by including the encore Friday that I'm familiar with. Big mistake. I didn't see it there, so it was a lie."[271]

Sun Times editor-in-chief Don Hayner told his readers that "accuracy and honesty in reporting are essential parts of the promise we make to our readers. We regret the incident and apologize."[272]

Daily Mirror theatre critic Matthew Wright[273] learned not to lie, to his own professional and his newspaper's financial cost.

Wright's "review" of American actor David Soul in a 1998 play called *The Dead Monkey* cost the paper £30,000 in damages, plus legal costs estimated at £150,000.

Wright had claimed that only 45 people were at the performance on a Monday evening and that he had never seen a worse play in the West End.

It was shown that not only had he not attended the play himself - a freelance had been there on his behalf - but also that it was factually incorrect.

The performance in question had been seen by about 130. Soul commented at the time:

"I stand really strong on the side of fair comment and opinion about the theatre. I think it's a cornerstone of the theatre but you have to see the play, you have to be there, you have to have the facts."[274]

Amen to that. It is a sign of the times that the case did not ruin the offending journalist's career, though he does appear to have slithered further downmarket. Since 2000, Wright has been the host of the topical discussion series *The Wright Stuff*, which airs on weekday mornings on Channel 5. In 2011, Wright joined the *Daily Star Sunday* as a columnist, but was dropped by the newspaper in 2012. In 2013, Wright took part in the thirteenth series of *I'm a Celebrity...Get Me Out of Here!*. He was the fourth participant to be eliminated. In April 2014, Wright appeared on *Celebrity Juice*, where he sucked Marmite from an elderly man's nipples and licked marmalade out of his belly button.[275]

Film guides are often put together by people who have neither the time nor the inclination to go back to the original sources, i.e. watch the film. A particularly outrageous example of this came when, in his guide to films, Elkan Allen[276] gave two contrasting reviews to the westerns *Ride the High Country* and *Guns in the Afternoon*. Unfortunately for his credibility, these were two titles for the same movie.

My faith in *Halliwell's Film Guide* was shaken when I looked up one of my favourite movies, the little-seen *Queen of Hearts* (1989), to discover the following review:

"[It's an] odd but ultimately unsatisfactory mix of fantasy and reality, contrasting Italian warmth and British cool to the detriment of both."

There is absolutely no attempt in the film to make any such contrast. The verdict could only have been written by someone who never saw the film.[277]

I would also take with several pinches of salt listings reviews of films on TV. There was a time when these were written by the newspapers' film critics – I remember spending many hours labouring away on my reviews, paring them down to a single sentence – but nowadays employing real critics to do the job is considered unnecessarily expensive. Instead, the "reviews" are usually cut-and-pasted by low-ranking staff members or interns from publicity material, with star ratings that wildly overrate the films' viewability. I remember reading one rave for *Garfield: The Movie*, clearly written by a fan of Bill Murray (he provided Garfield's voice) and blithely unaware that in the whole of the film there's barely a laugh in it.

William Hurt repressing his emotions, Robert Duvall in a cowboy hat, anything involving a child who has been mute since a parent or pet died, and any pair of zanily mismatched detectives or bank robbers... I, Libby, am a Movie-leptic. I only hope that my frank confession will stop the shame and encourage others to seek counselling, especially those who haven't regained consciousness since watching *Maurice*."[286]

Serial Offenders

When it comes to critics claiming to have viewed films they hadn't seen, one of the most unrepentant offenders was Pauline Kael[287], routinely held up ever since her 70s heyday as the "perfect" film critic by her numerous acolytes. Her first published review was an attack on a film called *Salt of the Earth* (1954), made by a self-confessed Communist, director Herbert Biberman[288]. Surprisingly for a critic who later held firmly left-wing views, her critique was stridently anti-Communist, doubtless to fit in with the McCarthyite flavour of the times. Her "review" quoted, verbatim, many lines of dialogue that were not in the film, but were in the script. She not only wasn't fired but saw fit to republish it in her collection *I Lost It at the Movies* - with no corrections.[289]

Ironically, the much-maligned (by the Left) critic of the *New York Times*, Bosley Crowther, wrote that "an unusual company made up largely of actual miners and their families plays the drama exceedingly well."[290] Kael, on the other hand, opined without bothering to see the piece in question that it was "as clear a piece of Communist propaganda as we have had in many years."[291]

Despite this attempt to ingratiate herself with the prevailing conservative culture of the 1950s, it was not until 13 years later - 1967, when she was 48 - that Kael managed to find a steady, paying job as a critic for the *New Yorker*. She adopted the much safer stance of a political left-winger and carefully kept to that identity for the rest of her career.

Other breakers of the Second Commandment have been "celebrity critics" – usually radio and TV presenters - being paid handsomely to lend their name to (almost invariably glowing) reviews of films they had not seen. These critiques were, in fact, ghost-written by real journalists. At the end of the year, some of these no-show celebrities even had the effrontery to demand pay rises for continuing not to do their job.

I would name names, but such "critics" tend to be litigious and have usually made those who deal with them – or write books and articles in their name - sign gagging clauses, in order to ensure that even in a court of law the truth will never come out. Never mind – they know who they are, and most people actively involved in paid criticism also know their names.

The one person who has owned up to not writing the film reviews that appeared under his byline is Richard Bacon, a "celebrity critic" whose main claim to fame is that he succeeded in getting himself fired in 1988 from the BBC children's programme *Blue Peter* for cocaine abuse. This minor embarrassment served only to raise his media profile, and his jack-the-lad persona enabled him to land jobs such as presenting *The Big Breakfast* on Channel Four (which earned him the dubious accolade "The Alan Partridge of breakfast television"). Since then he has had shows on Capital, XFM and Radio Five.

In his autobiography, all too accurately entitled *A Series of Unrelated Events (2013)*, Mr Bacon is surprisingly frank about cutting corners as a film critic, first for the downmarket *Sunday People* and then the lads' magazine *Loaded*. In both positions, he proudly contends not only that he did not see the films he was reviewing, but also that the person he got to write the reviews for him didn't bother to watch them either.

This seems to me an abuse of power. Almost as disturbing as the fact that Mr Bacon felt no responsibility towards his readers and the people who had made the films he was meant to be reviewing is the apathy of the editors who employed him and must have known he was not fulfilling a film critic's most basic function, which is to see the bloody film.

THE THIRD COMMANDMENT
Thou Shalt Be Honest

Conflicts of Interest

One major reason why professional criticism has fallen into disrepute is the rise and rise of the "quote whore". These are writers or broadcasters who praise pieces of work that ought not to be praised, and act as unofficial PR men and women, whether from sheer lack of taste or because they are being paid to express opinions they do not really hold. As the French novelist Gustave Flaubert once remarked, "You need a high degree of corruption or a very big heart to love absolutely everything."[292]

Quote whores have been with us since at least the eighteenth century, though not under that name. The playwright Richard Brinsley Sheridan[293] satirized the breed in his farce *The Critic* (first produced in 1779), where the playwright impresario Mr Puff invites theatre reviewers Dangle and Sneer to a rehearsal of his terrible new play *Spanish Armada*.

Mr Puff is not a critic himself, but a corruptor of critics. He boasts to Sneer that he is "a Professor of the Art of Puffing". He has taught critics and advertisers how to exaggerate so they may "enlay their phraseology with variegated chips of exotic metaphor" and "crowd their advertisements with panegyrical superlatives."

One of the British Critics' Circle's rules, specifically aimed to counter this kind of behaviour, was formulated in 1928. It states that members performing press agent or publicity work will be suspended. It still stands, though as far as I know it has never been enforced.

Mark Adams, for example, operated for four years as both film critic for the *Sunday Mirror* and as a writer for the trade press organ *Screen International*. It was Alexander Walker's perception that this kind of thing led to a conflict of interest that made him resign from the Critics' Circle in 1964.

Mark would doubtless claim that writing for the trade press does not destroy his impartiality. It would be fair to say, however, that he is the kindliest national film critic of the present day, especially when it comes to British product. Even without having seen *Sex Lives of the Potato Men* (2004), he raved about it to his readers:

"[Johnny] Vegas and [Mackenzie] Crook are a sleazy dream-team and brilliantly cast as the soft-core spud men... After several pints and a curry it could be the lads' film of the year."[294]

Contrary to Adams' confident prediction, it turned out to be one of the year's most notorious flops and more of a nightmare than a dream. Catherine Shoard in the *Sunday Telegraph* described it as "less a film than an appetite suppressant".[295] David Gritten in the *Daily Telegraph* wrote "this vile, grubby little film must surely be the year's worst."[296] James Christopher in the *Times* called it "a masterclass in film-making ineptitude, a squalid waste of lottery money, and an inexcusable gaffe by the British Film Council."[297]

Alone among his colleagues, Adams described the British film *Malice in Wonderland* (2009), which he had seen, as "stylish and engaging".[298] Peter Bradshaw in the *Guardian* captured the prevailing critical view that it was "pointless and heavy-handed".[299] David Jenkins in *Time Out* complained "Quite apart from the fact that it mistakes sexism and homophobia for sardonic liberal rib-tickling, even at 80 minutes, the film feels like a brash, crass and boneheaded music promo that's been stretched to breaking point."[300]

Another British film, *St Trinian's 2: The Legend of Fritton's Gold* (2009) inspired an astonishingly favourable reaction from Adams. He raved that it was "fun, frothy and frantic... rollicking good fun".[301] Other critics did not share his good humour. Nicholas Barber in the *Independent on Sunday* called it "an interminable, headache-inducing time-waster".[302]Robbie Collin snarled in the *News of the World* that "this jaw-droppingly hopeless sequel deserves to be packed off for a one-way exchange trip to Columbine".[303] Ray Bennett of the *Hollywood Reporter* said it was "strident, clumsy and pointless".[304]

Yet another home-grown comedy, *Holy Water* (2010), found favour with the *Sunday Mirror*. "A good-natured comedy romp," stated Adams. "Strong cast," he added.[305] Yet again, he found himself in a minority of one. Peter Bradshaw wrote in the *Guardian* that it was "fantastically depressing, unfunny and embarrassing."[306] Dave Calhoun in *Time Out* pointed out that it "doesn't raise a single laugh".[307]

Arguably the worst British film of the lot, *Love's Kitchen* (2011), also received Adams' unhesitating support. He called it "a nicely-staged British rom-com, which features a brief cameo from Gordon Ramsay. Dougray Scott is charming as the gruff chef who finds love (for both cooking and a sultry critic who's nicely played by Claire Forlani) at his new country restaurant. An unpretentious film with a fine cast."[308]

That's not how any other critic saw it. Henry Fitzherbert in the *Sunday Express* called it "astonishingly amateur and awful".[309] Peter Bradshaw introduced it to *Guardian* readers with the following: "Here is a new British film with an eternal, timeless kind of embarrassing awfulness... a script so poisonously naff it could have been bred in a Porton Down petri dish."[310] Anthony Quinn wrote in the *Independent* "The cast perform as if they had never acted before in their lives. Gordon Ramsay, who has never acted before, can't even do a convincing impersonation of himself."[311]

Not only British films have received Adams' dodgy seal of approval. For him, the Garry Marshall portmanteau comedy *Valentine's Day* (2010) was "the ultimate date movie for Valentine's Day."[312]

That may be how the film's publicists would have liked the film to be received, but critics on both sides of the Atlantic savaged it.

Manohla Dargis in the *New York Times* called it "grim grim grim... a disaster: cynically made, barely directed, terribly written."[313] Roger Ebert pointed out that *"Valentine's Day* is being marketed as a Date Movie. I think it's more of a First-Date Movie. If your date likes it, do NOT date that person again. And, if you like it, there may not be a second date."[314]

Peter Bradshaw summed up the near-unanimous British response to the film, calling it "a brutal St Valentine's Day massacre of comedy, of love, of believable human emotion... It makes *Love Actually* look like *Citizen Kane*."[315]

Adams ploughed another lonely furrow with his raves for two of 2011's most expensive blockbusters. He raved about *Transformers 3: Dark Side of the Moon* as "a fantastic feast of all-action entertainment... The first big summer blockbuster is one worth catching."[316]

Virtually every reputable critic disagreed. In the *Chicago Tribune*, Michael Phillips panned it as "a work of ineffable soullessness and persistent moral idiocy".[317] Roger Ebert called it "a visually ugly film with an incoherent plot, wooden characters and inane dialogue. It provided me with one of the more unpleasant experiences I've had at the movies."[318]

Zack Snyder's blockbuster *Sucker Punch* also found little favour with the vast majority of critics. In the *Daily Mail*, I called it "soul-suckingly putrid... It seems to have been made for 12 year-old boys by a sad middle-aged man whose only experience of life is from violent comics, shoot-'em-up video games and online pornography".[319]

Mark Kermode described the film on Radio 5 as "the most boring, ploddingly put together, infantile, crass, adolescent, stupid, chauvinistic twaddle that I've sat through in a very, very long time." James Berardinelli, of the website *ReelViews*, admitted "I walked out of this movie in a state of depression. Depressed that so much technical bravura could be thrown away. Depressed that someone mistook this empty, nihilistic sketch for a substantive and meaningful project. Depressed that I had been bamboozled into paying $10 to be subjected to it. At least, however, I understood the meaning of the title. I had been sucker punched."[320]

Only one prominent critic disagreed. Mark Adams hailed it as "stylish, sexy and seriously cool, *Sucker Punch* is a knockout."[321]

Then there are the showbiz writers who, from time to time, are misrepresented - or misrepresent themselves - as film critics. One of the most conspicuous of these was my own colleague, Baz Bamigboye of the *Daily Mail*. Baz was and is an experienced showbiz news journalist and gossip writer, reliant on his numerous influential contacts for tip-offs and hot leads. He is offered advance previews of many films, long before the national critics. Publicists and distributors alike are delighted when Baz "puffs" some production and are rightly confident that he will not abuse their trust.

The result is that Baz has many "scoops" and an early access that many national critics would envy. However, as a critic, Baz is not what you would call reliable. His view that *Bean* (1997) was "the ultimate funny movie, 89 minutes of absolute hilarity"[322] was not widely shared. And his opinion that Anthony Minghella's mediocre thriller *Breaking and Entering* (2006) was a "modern masterpiece"[323] was equally wide of the mark.

Baz's early access to *The Golden Compass*, based on Philip Pullman's children's classic *Northern Lights*, led him to rave that it was "big-screen entertainment at its best"[324], a view out of step with every critic who saw it after him. Similarly, when Baz attended an early screening of Richard Curtis's disappointing and historically inaccurate account of pirate radio, *The Boat That Rocked*, and roared the instruction "Get on board and rock on!"[325] few critics - or members of the public - obeyed.

Baz's Oscar predictions have been especially bizarre. He was fond of Jude Law, saying that he gave "the performance of his career" in *Breaking and Entering*[326]. He delivered the even more startlingly perverse verdict on Michael Caine and Jude Law in Kenneth Branagh's universally panned *Sleuth* that they were "at the top of their game", giving "masterclass performances."[327]

His opinion that in *The Boys Are Back* (2009) Clive Owen was "at the top of his game here giving a performance of Oscar stature"[328] turned out to be anything but prophetic. Equally dodgy was his judgment that the flop musical *Nine* "is a sparkling ten... I predict *Nine* will be garlanded with multiple Oscar and Bafta nominations. *Bellissimo!*"[329]

Most surprising of all, unless you knew that he had personal reasons for desiring a *rapprochement* with Madonna after she had sued the *Daily Mail* for something Baz had written about her previously, was Baz's lonely endorsement of her disastrous account of the relationship between Edward VIII and Wallis Simpson. *W.E.* (2011). "One of the most compelling love stories in history!" raved Baz. "Whatever your feelings about Ms Ciccone, it's impossible to refute that her film brings to the screen one of the most compelling love stories in history."[330]

When I described it in my review a few weeks later as "a colossal, narcissistic bore",[331] the *Daily Mail* legal department - obviously rattled by their previous litigious encounter with Madonna - phoned me in the middle of the night - the only time in 20 years that they did so - to ascertain that I was not being "unfair". I assured them that I would be far from alone in my opinion. Nor was I.

Philip French in the *Observer* called it "laughable"[332] Peter Bradshaw in the *Guardian* found it "fantastically wooden".[333] In the *Daily Telegraph*, Robbie Collin's verdict was "stultifyingly vapid".[334]

I've always admired Baz's work ethic and enthusiasm. On the other hand, it is pretty obvious that his judgments of quality are not exactly trustworthy, affected as they are by his need to ingratiate himself with his many contacts.

Baz's role as a showbiz journalist means that he takes great pains to avoid confrontation with stars, and tries to cosy up to them whenever possible, in order to gain "exclusives". The same goes for directors, producers and publicists. The very qualities that make him an effective showbiz reporter nullify his reliability as a critic.

Jonathan Ross's judgment was disastrously affected by his desire to endear himself to the interviewees on his film programme for the BBC. So he gave absurdly favourable reviews to Demi Moore in *Striptease*[335] and Tom Cruise in *Vanilla Sky*,[336] not to mention raves for movies whose makers he knew, or just happened to be appearing on his show that week.

Take his rave review for *Final Cut*, an abject British thriller starring several of Ross's friends from the "Primrose Hill set", such as Jude Law and Sadie Frost. Ross described their efforts as "fresh and original... unbelievably entertaining... definitely worth watching."[337]

That was distinctly at odds with his fellow-critics, who penned some of the year's most virulent brickbats. Alexander Walker wrote in the *Evening Standard* that the film was "a nasty, ugly, banal affair... These thespians are toxic."[338] Cosmo Landesman in the *Sunday Times* agreed, calling it "one long and witless scene of gross laddish self-indulgence after another. They wanted to do a Mike Leigh and have ended up creating one long Jeremy Beadle wind-up. And what terrible acting, too!"[339]

I wrote that it was "puerile rubbish, all too obviously semi-improvised by the participants, almost all of whom ill-advisedly play characters with the same names as themselves. This is one of those movies that appears to be inexplicable in rational terms. The most charitable interpretation is that those involved were so high, either on their own self-importance or on some of the substances sniffed so energetically during the film, that they forgot they were making it for anyone outside their immediate circle. Luckily for them, it's so horrendous that virtually no one else will see it."[340]

Another example of Ross's untrustworthiness came when he raved about a new British comedy, *Lesbian Vampire Killers*, starring Matthew Horne and James Corden from TV's *Gavin and Stacey*. Ross appeared on most of the ads with his claim that it was "bloody fang-tastic!"[341]

Anyone who attended the film on his recommendation may have noticed that his description bore little relation to the film itself. Tim Robey of the *Daily Telegraph* wrote "there's as much not to like as you might find in a 20 year-old can of rancid minestrone at the back of your mum's larder". James Christopher in the *Times* called it "profoundly awful".[342] Philip French noted in the *Observer* that it was "badly directed, poorly acted, witlessly scripted".[343] I described it as "the most half-witted British comedy since *Sex Lives of the Potato Men* – lewd, loutish laddism at its worst."[344]

Whilst appearing on the comedy panel show *The King is Dead* in September 2010, even the star of the movie Corden admitted that the film was "a pile of shit" and said the film would be too harsh a punishment for prisoners being held at Guantanamo Bay. He has since described the film as "quite embarrassing". That's a long way from "bloody fang-tastic".

The BBC gave Jonathan Ross the opportunity to become a respected, scrupulous film critic in the tradition of Barry Norman. Unfortunately, Ross became nothing of the sort.

The former film critic for the *Daily Star*, Alan Frank, who worked concurrently as a publicist for films on Channel 4, cannot be accused of soft-pedalling when he dislikes a movie, but openly acknowledges the problem of writing reviews at the same time as being active in the publicity business:

"I spent 14 years as a press writer for Channel 4 lying through my teeth, and there's no way around it. I don't think anything critics say has the slightest bit of influence on the box office anyway. A publicist once said to me, 'When I have a film to release, I just buy a positive quote from a men's mag'. You just have to look at some film magazines and their advertising budgets to understand why bad films get good quotes."[345]

In 2012, Tom Sutcliffe – a television reviewer and former Arts Editor of the *Independent* - acknowledged his own failure as outgoing President of the Critics' Circle to counter such conflicts of interest:

"We seem to be in danger in the UK of reverting to the late 18th century world of which Sheridan wrote so sublimely in his comedy *The Critic*. My biggest failure is not to have made even one small step towards getting the Circle to set down what it thinks about the routine corruption to which the business of criticism is these days all too prone. Our rulebook should say that our members must be seen to be independent and incorrupt, that they will not review work by individuals and institutions with whom they are associated or for whom they are working."[346]

Sutcliffe went on to mention three critics by name:

"Of course a critic like John Allison who edits (and part owns) *Opera* magazine and is also chief music critic of the *Sunday Telegraph* is free to damn Glyndebourne productions, as he sometimes does, and the fact that he edits the Glyndebourne programme each year does not remove his independence. But I well recall that my dear old colleague Edward Greenfield used to go to Salzburg as guest of various record companies and review their artists *in the Guardian* - promoting Herbert von Karajan for example. Just because a star is famous does not mean praising them is exonerated from being corrupt... Of course Ted thought he was independent. But professional critics must be seen to be free of taint. Ed Seckerson, who was interviewing artists the ENO [English National Opera] was employing, and who rarely found fault with ENO work, was eventually a few months back removed from his *Independent* critic's role by the arts editor there."[347]

Quote Whores

The art critic Brian Sewell[348] was of the opinion that the British art scene is infested with critics who have divided loyalties or are hellbent on ingratiating themselves with the powers that be. He was especially brutal about the pretensions and worthlessness of commentators he sees as compromised, who gush over such concessions to the avant-garde as the Turner Prize. He laid into them with gusto in 2003:

"We must treat the Prize only as an entertainment; on our television sets we shall again watch poor gabblingly inarticulate Matthew Collings [an artist, academic, curator, critic and broadcaster] struggle wearily to appear to take it seriously, and in the general debate we shall, yet again, suffer the opinions of sub-celebrities who have no status in this matter - Janet Street-Porter and her ilk certainly among them - working themselves into a froth or treating the Prize as an event as theologically significant as the second coming of Christ. The sane, however, will see it as they see a pantomime - as a not too onerous obligation to adolescent children who will not be shocked by the obscenities. Let us rejoice in its clowning and leave support and indignation to poor souls without a sense of humour."[349]

Brian Dillon, another art critic, makes a similar, more personal point:

"Criticism pays badly. The entirely independent critic is almost unheard of: you moonlight as curator, editor, academic, broadcaster. Asked to corral your own enthusiasms into the space of a single show, how can you not let slip your allegiances, your debts, your affiliations?"[350]

However dodgy the art scene may be, the most notorious quote whores tend to be in the world of film. Back in 1997, Roger Ebert warned that they were multiplying like locusts:

"In the old days, movies ads simply stated their bold claims. 'Passion! Adventure! Excitement! The Most Thrilling Adventure of the Decade!' These days the ad guys figure such claims are more convincing if they come in quotes and were allegedly said by 'critics.' As a rule of thumb, any critic quoted in an ad more than a week before the movie opens is a quote whore - unless he works for a monthly or weekly publication with an early deadline, or actually made his statement in print or on the air. Legitimate critics do not supply quotes directly to publicists, nor do they scoop their own reviews by sharing the highlights before publication day."[351]

The movie industry is one of the biggest in America, and they are not above some extremely dubious business practices. Sony Pictures once had to offer a $5 refund to all Americans who saw films that had been advertised using quotes from film critic David Manning, of the Ridgefield Press. The reason was that Manning didn't exist – he was an invention of the studio.[352]

The glowing reviews attributed to Manning included tributes for *A Knight's Tale* in which Australian actor Heath Ledger was praised (prematurely) as "this year's hottest new star!" and for Rob Schneider's abysmal comedy *The Animal* which was hailed as "another winner!" Equally upbeat endorsements were used in advertising copy for the creatively challenged *Hollow Man* and *Vertical Limit.* [353]

That little misadventure cost Sony $1.5 million, and two employees were suspended.[354] But it didn't stop Sony from misrepresenting two of the employees in their marketing department as "fans" in a testimonial ad for their movie *The Patriot.*[355]

Sony is far from the only studio that engages in dishonest advertising. According to a 2002 article in the *Los Angeles Times*, contributions to message boards promoting films could be traced back via their IP addresses to studios including Universal and Paramount.[356]

Another way executives publicize their pictures is to fly certain journalists to press junkets where they meet the stars and are expected to provide adulatory quotations for the marketing campaign. Sometimes the studios even supply critics with pre-written quotes. This enables the journalist to have his or her name on TV, along with the organisation he represents.[357]

Does money change hands? It's hard to say. But it's no secret that the studios place ads with periodicals that support their films, and fail to support ones that don't. And they offer exclusives to journalists who they think will support their product. It's a classic case of "you scratch my back, I'll scratch yours."

Editorial Pressure

Many critics have felt pressure from their editors to change a star rating or even an entire opinion about a piece of art or entertainment. I am no exception.

I was hired for the *Daily Mail* by Sir David English, but he soon handed over to his designated successor, Paul Dacre. I had my first dispute with the new Editor-in-Chief in June 1995, two years after my arrival at the *Mail*, over my favourable 5-star review of Quentin Tarantino's *Pulp*

Fiction.[358] I received a phone call from one of the editor's deputies, Robin Esser, who told me that although neither he nor Dacre had seen the movie, Dacre was concerned about the amount of violence in it, and would like me to tone down my enthusiasm.

I pointed out to Esser that I had been hired for my critical judgment, and that I was happy to stand or fall by it. I told him that *Pulp Fiction* was one of the outstanding films of the year (it had just won the top prize at Cannes and went on to be nominated for Best Picture at the Oscars) and would probably win the Academy Award for Best Original Screenplay (which it did). I said that my reputation, such as it was, depended on how ready I was to recognise talent when I saw it, and I argued that *Pulp Fiction* was in fact quite moral in its approach to criminality and violence, as Dacre should himself recognise if he actually went to see it.

My piece went in as I had written it. However, Dacre punished me by publishing a feature-length piece by Mary Kenny, the day after my review appeared, condemning the film and, by implication, me for saying that the film was not only harmless but excellent.[359] It was hard to tell from Ms Kenny's piece whether she had seen the film or not, but it certainly toed the editorial line put to me by Mr Esser.

By way of further punishment, Dacre removed my film column from the full-colour middle pages of the newspaper, even though the film review illustrations looked much worse in black and white. I also couldn't help but notice that whenever space was at a premium over the next few months my film and video reviews were cut ruthlessly to make way for adverts.

Two months later, in August 1995, I had another dispute, this time over the obscure horror film *Funny Man* (about a serial-killing jester) which I reviewed in two scornful sentences:

"Since it is British, I wish I could find something positive and uplifting to say about this nasty, abysmally acted, unfunny, formulaic slasher flick. I can't."[360]

Mr Esser phoned me up again, more apologetically and less menacingly than the first time, to say that the producer of *Funny Man* was a friend of the then Lord Rothermere (father of the current one). Couldn't I find anything nice to write about it?

I told him that the only kindness was to dismiss *Funny Man* as briefly as I had done, since any longer review would have dwelt far more cruelly on its shortcomings. I assured him that it wouldn't receive a single positive review from my national press colleagues (it didn't). Esser told me that he would regretfully have to leave it off my film page, and he would pen a neutral listing for the film elsewhere in the paper. I said that was his editorial prerogative, but I drew the line at making myself look a fool. I refrained from saying that I didn't see it as my job to sacrifice my own integrity in order to toady to friends of the proprietor, but he may have got that message.

A decade later, I had a more serious run-in with an editor, or at any rate one of his lackeys. I had become extremely disappointed when the long-promised launch of a larger Arts section of the Friday newspaper, *Friday First*, was guided – or I would argue misguided - by the tastes of Martin Clarke (now editor of *Mail Online*) and "Arts Editor" Heather McGlone – towards celebrity gossip and away from in-depth analysis. Although the mock-up of the first issue contained a feature ostensibly written by me, I was never approached to write a single in-depth feature, and the pages were filled with salacious gossip and the kind of celebrity fawning you would expect to see in *Hello!* or *OK! Magazine*.

My situation took a turn for the considerably worse with the move of Clarke to *Mail Online* and the arrival at the newspaper of Paul Field, a former *Sun* journalist and failed editor of America's scandal sheet the *National Enquirer*, who took it into his head to bully me in September 2011 over a review I had written of *I Don't Know How She Does It*. This was a film based on Allison Pearson's best-selling novel of 2002, and not a good one. Like most leading critics, I gave it a 1-star rating out of 5.

Mr Field rang me up to say that my review was "unacceptable" and "could not be used". When I inquired why, he told me that the Editor-in-Chief, Mr Dacre, had only recently dismissed Ms Pearson from her high-profile position as columnist for the paper, and that he had been extremely upset when *Private Eye* had revealed the acrimonious nature of their parting.

He said that "everyone" would assume that my review had been dictated by Mr Dacre, and interpret it as an act of editorial malice. If I wanted to keep my job, I must write a more favourable review.

I told him that my duty as a critic was to tell the truth, not rewrite the truth as if I were the Editor-in-Chief's PR man. I said I was hardly alone in my analysis of the film being dated and unfunny – at the screening I attended, hardly anyone laughed during the entire 89 minutes. I did, however, promise to look at the piece again and remove anything that could be construed, however mistakenly, as personally insulting to Ms Pearson.

I didn't find anything insulting in my review, but as a concession I did insert a favourable description of Ms Pearson's novel as "widely acclaimed on publication for its accurate, supportive portrait of working mothers".

When my review appeared, it had been brutally cut without my consent - and so ineptly that it made no sense at all. Still less did the little copy that did appear reflect my lowly rating of 1 star. I responded by writing on Facebook to readers of my internet website that if they wanted to read what I really thought about the film, they should read not the version printed in the *Daily Mail*, but the one on my website.[361]

A day later, I received an extremely abusive phone call from Mr Field, in which he called me the Editor-in-Chief's favourite expletive to his employees, "a cunt". He had read my Facebook entry and told me I was going the right way about losing my job. At the end of a tirade that lasted at least twenty minutes, he warned I would "hear more about this". It was the most menacing phone call I have ever received, unless you count a death threat from the IRA.

So shocked was I that he – and presumably the Editor-in-Chief – would over-react to such an extent over, first, a harmless and accurate review and, second, a statement of simple fact, that I did remove my comment from my Facebook page. I have learned since that Mr Field did, indeed, attempt to have me fired after this event, but that it never came to anything. Mr Field was soon moved sideways in the editorial hierarchy and vanished.[362]

Another moment of truth for me came when Heather McGlone asked me to write a feature for the weekend magazine commending the National Movie Awards (2007-2011), which was to be held at the Royal Festival Hall and broadcast on ITV and presented by the actor James Nesbitt. The winners of the awards were to be decided by a popular vote. Since she'd never asked me to write anything for her before - although her title was Arts Editor - I agreed to write the piece, but when I found out more about the event, the more questionable it seemed.

For Best Comedy of the Year, *Juno* won the award, which was certainly an honourable contender. However, the nominees were a rum lot: *Sex and the City* (New Line), *St Trinian's* (Ealing) and *The Love Guru* (Paramount Pictures). Nowhere to be seen were much funnier films such as *In Bruges, Ghost Town, Burn After Reading* or *Tropic Thunder*.

It was particularly astonishing that *The Love Guru* was nominated for both Best Comedy and Best Performance (Mike Myers). Its nomination in either category was hilariously inappropriate. Hated by the critics, it wasn't liked by the public either. It won the *Village Voice*'s poll of its readers as Worst Film. It also won awards at the Razzies, triumphing as Worst Picture, Worst Actor and Worst Screenplay. It was nominated for worst supporting actor (Ben Kingsley and Jessica Alba) and worst director (Marc Schnabel). The Oklahoma Film Critics Circle Awards named it as the "obviously worst film" of 2008.

Among the other questionable nominees for Best Action/ Adventure, suggesting influence by big film companies rather than popularity, was an abysmal sequel, *The Mummy: Tomb of the Dragon Emperor* (Universal Pictures)

So I found myself instructed to commend an awards ceremony where, clearly, the nominations had been decided either by someone's tasteless whim or the big movie companies and bore no relation either to popular success or artistic worth. I did my best, but I fear my sardonic tone - I was inspired by Terry Wogan's bitter-sweet coverage of the Eurovision Song Contest - may not have gone down well with the powers that be. I was never asked to cover the ceremony again.

Barry Norman did it the following year, and he managed to toe the popular line "Hey what do critics know?", though with obvious difficulty regarding some of the unlikelier nominees and winners; the worst of the *Twilight* movies, *New Moon*, managed to win one of the awards, to widespread incredulity. I don't think Barry was asked to cover it again either.

Former *Sunday Times* film editor George Perry also admits to editorial pressure being exerted upon him, but not in any systematic way:

"*Private Eye* suggested that *Sunday Times* writers had to plug 20th Century Fox films and Sky TV come what may, but I can categorically deny it. I never saw any such instruction. However, editor's whim was different. I was rung one night by the section editor who was concerned that my review of *A Fish Called Wanda* was too negative. I had been perturbed by the fact that its director was the great Charlie Crichton of Ealing comedies such as *Hue and Cry* and *The Lavender Hill Mob*. [Ealing boss Sir Michael] Balcon would never have allowed dogs or goldfish to be murdered in the cause of comedy, but I took most serious objection to the ending which had Otto clawing from the outside at a window of a taxiing jumbo jet, then being flattened into wet cement by a steam roller, without coming to any harm. Both situations were impossible. It turned out the ending had been devised by Cleese with Iain Johnstone, a great friend of Andrew Neil, then editor of the *Sunday Times*, who I was told was expecting a favourable review. I did a hasty rewrite because if I had not done so it would not just have been me who would have been in deep ordure. I think that counts as editorial interference, but with hindsight I must admit it's possible Neil never knew about it. His acolytes spent their lives running scared of his disgraceful irascibility."[363]

After Mark Shenton's summary dismissal from the *Sunday Express*, the theatre critic claimed that on one occasion his review of the stage musical *Rock Of Ages* had been replaced with a "much more positive review from an in-house journalist". Shenton said he suspected this might have been because the show's head of PR was a former *Sunday Express* music editor.[364]

He also claimed he was asked to "amend" a rating of another musical, *Scrooge*, from three stars to five. Shenton agreed to change the rating to four stars. He said: "If I had refused to amend the ratings I think I would have been disciplined".

Jay Rayner can recall only one moment when he was placed under editorial pressure:

"What did happen once was the deputy editor of the *Observer*, Roger Alton, came to me and said 'A mate of mine has got a restaurant'. I said 'Roger, we're straying into dangerous territory here. What do you want me to do? I'll go and if it's brilliant I'll write about it, and if it's not I won't bother.' As it turned out, it wasn't brilliant or crap. It was mediocre, and so I never wrote about it."[365]

Rayner says that clumsy attempts at bribery do take place, which he disregards:

"There's an awful lot of stupidity. Chefs send me extra dishes, and I always send them back. I only want to eat the food I've ordered. Or they increase the size of the portion. I could see that everyone else was getting two sardines and I was given three. Or they offer me a free bottle of wine. Or they leave stuff off the bill. I won't have any of that."[366]

Charles Spencer (for many years a reviewer for the *Daily Telegraph*), once summed up the essential obligations of a theatre critic: "Arrive sober, stay awake, stay to the end and don't take a bribe unless it is big enough to allow you to retire in comfort for the rest of your life. My own price, should anyone be interested, is £1.25 million in used twenties."[367]

Presumably he was joking about the last bit. However, recent events at the *Telegraph* have suggested that the line of demarcation between advertising and editorial - so rigorously adhered to in my day, and in Spencer's - may no longer be as clear as it should be.

At the *Telegraph*, Tim Robey's star rating on the family film *Despicable Me 2* had its 2-star rating changed to 3 stars on the orders of Andrew Pettie, Head of Arts and Entertainment at the *Telegraph* Group.[368] That may not sound like much of a change, but actually it's a big one. Normally, a 2-star review is a discouragement (which is how Robey's review reads[369]), while a 3-star review is a recommendation. Not many children's films score above 3 stars, which makes a 3-star rating all the more important in that particular genre.

The alteration was made, apparently, in order to appease the advertising department of the *Telegraph*, which feared a loss of ads from Universal. It may also have been made in order to save editorial embarrassment, as the following day's Review supplement contained four pages of gushing, paid-for "advertorial" about the animation.[370]

In 2015, the *Daily Telegraph*'s chief political commentator Peter Oborne resigned, saying that he felt commercial considerations were affecting editorial output. Oborne called the newspaper's suppression of stories about the HSBC bank a "form of fraud on its readers". He also claimed that *The Telegraph's* coverage of stories about the UK supermarket chain Tesco, the shipping company Cunard and the pro-democracy protests in Hong Kong had also been influenced by commercial considerations.[371]

Shortly after Oborne's resignation, the Guido Fawkes website received a leaked memo sent by Sony to the *Telegraph*'s 'Create' department, which produced sponsored content. Stuart Williams, the Deputy Managing Director of Sony Pictures, thanked them for their "unique" "integrated... editorial and paid for" content. Williams has confirmed that Sony received "support across editorial, promotions and media" as part of "the partnership with the *Telegraph*" on the film *Fury*. The last line of his memo is particularly damning:

"From our side we are really delighted with how the partnership with the *Telegraph* on *Fury* has turned out. We were very pleased last year with *Captain Phillips* with yourselves and this has taken it to a new level. The activity and support across editorial, promotions and media has been truly outstanding and the enthusiasm, creative thinking and hard work by all the team has made it such a success. We look forward to seeing some of the numbers on the impact of the activity online. We were also really pleased you came on board as a partner at the LFF for the regional screenings and streaming, we hope you also felt this was a successful addition for you too. It really made it a complete partnership on the campaign. I do think the *Telegraph* are unique in being able to offer a really integrated solution that genuinely works in editorial and paid for activity."[372]

Incidentally, the *Telegraph* review of *Fury* described it as "astonishing" and "gripping" drama that "brings us as close to an understanding of war as cinema can".[373] *Captain Phillips* was hailed as a "triumph of solid, professional and sometimes inspired film crafts, deserving of all the plaudits that come its way".[374]

There was an outcry against the *Telegraph* over this issue, but it would be naïve to imagine that making editorial adjustments to please advertisers (and potential advertisers) is endemic to magazines and newspapers.

William Russell, former film critic for the *Glasgow Herald*, is careful not to name names, but knows – as do most other critics – that the practice is widespread and, on many magazines and newspapers, dominant:

"So many critics moderate what they have to say in light of whatever deal their publication has made for star interviews – one can hardly dismiss as 'poor' something the interviewee has been claiming was a wonderful experience to make. This is common in film magazines and in colour supplements. One week the colour supplement raves about the new film from X – brave is the critic who next week says the new film, performance or whatever is not much good. Also, I am not sure critics should do interviews. It colours their judgment and they should never get too close to the people whose work they write about. They are not their friends."[375]

So please don't underestimate the extent to which any critic nowadays has to fight to protect his or her integrity.

As critics become worse and worse paid and have to take other jobs in order to keep themselves and their families, more are bound to compromise whatever principles they have and take on roles that compromise their honesty. More people will be willing to kiss the hand that feeds them and take money or free publicity from the very organisations they are supposed to be criticising.

From my limited contact with foreign critics, I would judge that the situation for critics in countries other than Britain and America is even more dire. I have been assured by a Japanese reviewer, who not surprisingly wishes to remain anonymous, that critics in his country are routinely expected to line up to praise product that has been made by their employers' corporate interests and to belittle their rivals.

With globalisation, the crisis in honest criticism is going viral. So I would make this plea from my heart: don't become the kind of critic that is rightly reviled and mistrusted. Without honesty and integrity, a critic's opinions are worthless.

THE FOURTH COMMANDMENT
Thou Shalt Appreciate As Well As Find Fault

The Uses of Abuse

Richard Nixon's Vice-President Spiro T. Agnew[376] once described critics as "nattering nabobs of negativism."[377] Yes, that's the Vice-President who had to resign over charges of tax fraud, extortion, bribery and conspiracy. Later, he paid the state of Maryland nearly $270,000 after a civil suit made bribery allegations against him. So it's easy to see why Spiro might have been a tad sensitive to criticism.

But it's a common accusation against reviewers that they dwell unduly on the negative. There's a reason for this. Most of the art that critics experience is bad art.

Maureen Ryan, TV Critic on the *Huffington Post*, believes this is an unchanging phenomenon:

"To be well-versed in the field I cover, I try to watch most of the new scripted fare that comes down the pike, and the truth is, a good percentage of new shows are bad. That's not a knock on television; that's just an acknowledgement of the common sense rule that 80 to 90 percent of anything in any entertainment medium is derivative, boring or inept."[378]

Observer and Radio 5 film critic Mark Kermode agrees:

"Whenever I'm asked what qualification one needs to become a movie reviewer I always reply that a tolerance for watching *Fred: The Movie* without screaming is best, because the surest way to find employment is to review the films no one else wants to watch. Perhaps this is why so many film critics complete their apprenticeship of good sandwiches and terrible films with a finely honed ability to be nasty about movies but almost no experience of how to say anything nice. After all, what's there to be nice about?"[379]

Graham Linehan is well known as a comedy writer and director, the talented creator of sitcoms *Father Ted* and *Black Books*. He is less well-known as a critic, mainly because he gave it up in disgust:

"I used to be a film and music journalist, and wrote for different magazines in the 1990s. I still love music, but the experience destroyed my enthusiasm for film. The problem with being a film critic is that most films are crap. You have to sit through so many awful ones that any enjoyment is sucked out, and then when a good one comes along you tend to overpraise it."[380]

Kenneth Tynan famously gave up reviewing films after only a year, complaining about "the vast advertising techniques that ensure a mass audience" for films he regarded as rubbish.[381]

Even earlier, Wolcott Gibbs informed readers of the *New Yorker* "99% of the moving pictures exhibited in America are so vulgar, witless and dull that it is preposterous to write about them in any publication not intended to be read while chewing gum".[382] The year he wrote that was 1944, a year when Hollywood gave us *Double Indemnity*, *Laura* and *To Have and Have Not*, all regarded today as classics. What would he make of a time when *Transformers* movies and the comedies of Adam Sandler are hits?

Novelist and critic Howard Jacobson is unrepentant about his notoriously bleak view of the world (one collection of his essays is called *Whatever It Is, I Don't Like It*):

"Why is dissatisfaction taken to be a mark of failing powers and patience, when it might just as easily be understood as a proper judgment on a foolish world?"[383]

Most critics compensate for their suffering by having a good rant about something really, really bad. Joe Queenan has written some of the most entertaining hatchet jobs in movie criticism. Even if you don't agree with his verdict on *The English Patient*, it's hard not to enjoy his one-liner: "The problem with *The English Patient* is that to enjoy it, you have to be either English or patient."[384]

He has a particular horror of Christmas movies, even the classics:

"Christmas movies come in four basic varieties: the cuddly, the cloying, the cretinous and the cute. *It's a Wonderful Life*, a putatively heartwarming story about a small-time banker with a heart of gold, manages to combine all four elements, as it inexplicably lionises a lunkheaded ninny who risks the financial health of his community by making a series of bad loans to people who are in no position to repay them. Particularly unsuitable for holiday viewing this year, the 1947 Frank Capra classic should really be called *It's a Wonderful Subprime Life*. *A Christmas Carol*, in any of its myriad manifestations, perpetuates the myth that the obscenely rich can be made to see the error of their ways and rehabilitated, even though anyone who has ever had to deal with the obscenely rich knows that this is not true."[385]

Queenan believes the evidence is mounting that most people in the movie industry are morons:

"Movies often look great but their plots are cretinous. Their plots, in fact, are sub-cretinous. Not even a scintilla of intelligence is present in a film such as *Swing Kids*, the 1993 offering that dealt with the plight of twentysomething Benny Goodman fans starved for thrills in Nazi Germany. Films such as *Indian Summer* (a *Big Chill* with more moose) radiated an incandescent stupidity that had an almost otherworldly quality to it. Movies such as *A Stranger Among Us* seriously expected intelligent audiences to believe that the cerebrally inoperative Melanie Griffith could just sort of blend in with the Brooklyn Hassidim and nobody would notice - the way

Shaquille O'Neill could just kind of disappear into the crowd at a Shriners' Convention. The people who made these movies were almost criminally stupid."[386]

There is a place for negative criticism. A critic's job is to analyze, judge and evaluate – which means he must be at liberty to give bad news as well as good. After all, you wouldn't think much of a doctor who failed to warn you that you were overweight, drank too much and had high blood pressure. The critic's job is not to "puff", sell tickets or endear himself to the creators of art, their financial masters or indeed his own bosses. The critic's job is to tell the truth as he or she sees it.

In a radio debate about criticism, the playwright Simon Gray complained to *Guardian* theatre critic Michael Billington that a dramatist with a new play is as vulnerable as a mother with a new baby. She wouldn't like it if she took her baby to the park and people poked their noses into the pram and criticised the baby's legs for being too short or its nose too long. Fine, said Billington. But, once you start charging people up to £50 a time for a glimpse of a new infant, you must expect public comment.[387]

When one of May Sarton's novels was panned in *The New York Times Book Review* in the late 1970s, she says that she curled up into a fetal ball for months. She detailed her martyrdom at the hands of the critics in a 1980 book full of self-pity, entitled, *Recovering: A Journal.* "I felt," Sarton wrote, "like a deer shot down by hunters."

Reviewing the book, Paul Fussell reacted like the critic he was. "The deer does not," he told her, "emerge from the privacy and silence of the woods, come to the edge, wag its antlers at the hunters and invite them to take some shots."[388]

It must be admitted that several critics have built a reputation on being abrasive to the point of abusive. Charlie Brooker's *Guardian* column is a case in point. Brooker is charmingly modest about his limitations:

"I was never a proper critic. A 'proper critic' is an intellectually rigorous individual with an encyclopaedic knowledge of their specialist subject and an admirably nerdy compulsion to dissect, compare and analyze each fresh offering in the field – not in a bid to mindlessly entertain the reader, but to further humankind's collective understanding of the arts. True critics are witty rather than abusive, smart rather than smart-arsed, contemplative rather than extrovert."[389]

All the same, Brooker's rants about television and the movies were often funny and perceptive. Here he is on the *High School Musical* series of Disney films:

"As an embittered cynic, I should be programmed to vomit all over the screen at the mere sight of this, but instead, I find it strangely moving. You see, as I stare into their happy smiling faces filled with naive *joie de vivre*, I know they're just blissfully unaware of the crushing despair that awaits them as they venture into adulthood. The myriad disappointments, the yawning chasms of pain, the slow gnawing descent into physical decay, the sheer unrelenting horror of it all."[390]

Charlie Brooker is equally entertaining about the *Twilight* series of movies, aimed predominantly at impressionable teenage girls:

"In some quarters the films and books are lauded for their wholesome message, which is weird considering Bella is essentially deciding whether she'd rather shag a bat or a wolf. She's got zero interest in honest-to-goodness human-on-human action. No. It's magic farmyard creatures or nothing for her."[391]

Finally, here's Brooker's verdict on the *Transformers* movies:

"The second *Transformers* movie came out this year. I didn't fight for a ticket. I'd caught the first one by accident. It was like being pinned to the ground while an angry dishwasher shat in your face for two hours. Any human dumb enough to voluntarily sit through a second helping of that unremitting fecal spew really ought to just get up and leave the planet via the nearest window before their continued presence does lasting damage to the gene pool."[392]

Critic Mark Kermode is at his best when ranting about films he detests. My favourite Kermode rant was about *Sex and the City 2* on BBC Radio 5. He calls it "ghastly, putrid and vomit-inducing", "consumerist pornography" and "a vile and pernicious slice of imperialist propaganda which celebrates misogyny, belittles non-Americans, insults audiences and wallows in greed, avarice and bulimic vomit".

One reason I'm not quoting more of that here is that you can easily watch it in full on YouTube[393], and there happens to be an even funnier rant about *Sex and the City 2*, written by Lindy West for the Seattle magazine *The Stranger*. The whole of her piece can be found on the internet, and the climax of her diatribe is an account of how the supposedly feminist heroines of the movie solve the thorny problem of sexism in the Middle East:

"Abu Dhabi is crawling with Muslim women — and not one of them is dressed like a super-liberated diamond-encrusted fucking clown!!! Oppression! OPPRESSION!!! This will not stand. Samantha, being the sexual revolutionary that she is, rages against the machine by publicly grabbing the engorged penis of a man she dubs 'Lawrence of My-Labia.' When the locals complain (having repeatedly asked Samantha to cover her nipples and *mons pubis* in the way of local custom), Samantha removes most of her clothes in the middle of the spice bazaar, throws condoms in the faces of the angry and bewildered crowd, and screams, "I AM A WOMAN! I HAVE SEX!" Thus, traditional Middle Eastern sexual mores are upended and sexism is stoned to death in the town square. At sexism's funeral (which takes place in a mysterious, incense-shrouded chamber of international sisterhood), the women of Abu Dhabi remove their black robes and veils to reveal — this is not a joke — the same hideous, disposable, criminally expensive shreds of cloth and feathers that hang from Carrie et al.'s emaciated goblin shoulders. Muslim women: Under those craaaaaaay-zy robes, they're just as vapid and obsessed with physical beauty and meaningless material concerns as us! Feminism! Fuck yeah! If this is what modern womanhood means, then just fucking veil me and sew up all my holes. Good night."[394]

No one is going to pretend such rants are models of subtlety or in-depth analysis; but they do serve to show that negative reviews are often more enjoyable than positive critiques, and it is one of the duties of critics to entertain their readers.

Where most negative critics use the bludgeon, Libby Gelman-Waxner (feminine *alter ego* of gay screenwriter Paul Rudnick) prefers the stiletto. Here she is on the *Twilight* series:

"Like every female on earth, I'm on my fifth viewing of *Breaking Dawn*. Because when Robert Pattinson and Kristen Stewart gaze at each other, their passion is so intense that it's like they're trying to pass kidney stones through their foreheads... And of course I adore Taylor Lautner as Jacob the hunky werewolf, because when he learns that Kristen's pregnant, it takes him a long moment of deep thinking before he turns to Robert and yelps, 'You did this!' And as a special bonus, there's even a new character named Renesmee, because what girl doesn't yearn to sound like a new prescription drug for acid reflux?"[395]

This is Libby's equally no-nonsense verdict on *Titanic:*

"I just saw *Titanic,* which is a $200 million film about a real-life disaster at sea, but according to Hollywood Logic, none of the actual passengers was interesting enough, so the writer-director had to invent a *Romeo and Juliet*-style fictional couple to heat up the catastrophe. This seems a tiny bit like giving Anne Frank a wacky best friend, to perk up that attic."[396]

It is undoubtedly true that the easiest way to make a name as a critic is to be a vituperative one. In the USA, fearless pans helped make Judith Crist a household name in the 1960s and 1970s. Roger Ebert once said that Crist's TV appearances inspired him to become a film critic. In 2008, he still remembered the impact that Judith Crist had in 1963.

"Judith Crist changed everything at the *New York Herald-Tribune* when she panned *Cleopatra* and was banned from 20th Century-Fox screenings. There was a big fuss, and suddenly every paper hungered for a 'real' movie critic."[397]

Crist may not have been the most fiercely analytical of critics – and the same can be said of Mark Kermode, Libby Gelman-Waxner and Charlie Brooker – but she was an early exponent of the entertaining bad review.

The Japanese-American feminist Michiko Kakutani has made her reputation as the leading American literary critic of the modern day with an array of withering put-downs over three decades of writing for the *New York Times*. The author Nicholson Baker said that one of her reviews "was like having my liver taken out without anaesthesia."[398] David Foster Wallace told friends that after she reviewed one of his books he hid in his room for two days and cried.[399] She described Martin Amis's *The Second Plane* as "weak" and "risible". Nick Hornby's *A Long Way Down* was, to her, a "cringe-making excuse for a novel," and "a maudlin bit of tripe". Jonathan Franzen's memoir, *The Discomfort Zone*, was dismissed as "an odious self-portrait of the artist as a young jackass."[400]

In return, Franzen called her "the stupidest person in New York City" and "an international embarrassment". Salman Rushdie says she's a "weird woman who seems to feel the need to alternately praise and spank". After reading a review that called one of his books "silly, self-important and at times inadvertently comical", Norman Mailer called her "a one-woman kamikaze". He said he didn't know what had "put the hair up her immortal Japanese ass" and that the only reason the *Times* didn't fire her was because she was "a twofer", being "Asiatic" and "feminist".[401]

For me, she has a tendency to be hyperbolic, especially about some less than stellar writers. She even went as far as comparing Donna Tartt to Euripides.[402] But whether you always agree with her or not, Kakutani is a well-respected critic. In 1998, she was awarded a Pulitzer Prize for her "fearless and authoritative" journalism.

Restaurant critic Jay Rayner is the modern master of the negative restaurant review. Here's Jay on the Buddha Bar, on London's Victoria Embankment: "There is just enough light by which to read the pan-Asian menu, which was a shame, because it meant we could order."[403]

Rayner is honest about why he writes pans:

"What I write has to be entertaining and a compelling read, it's not about the finer points of cooking. There are people out there who know more about food than I do, but reading their stuff is pure Mogadon - it puts you to sleep... People like reviews of bad restaurants. No, scratch that. They adore them, feast upon them like starving vultures who have spotted fly-blown carrion out in the bush for the first time in weeks. They like to claim otherwise, of course. Readers of restaurant reviews like to present themselves as private arbiters of taste; as people interested in the good stuff. I'm sure they are. I'm sure they really do care whether the steak was served au point as requested, whether the jus showed that joyful accident of technique and good taste. Whether the soufflé had achieved a certain ineffable lightness. And yet, when I compare dinner to bodily fluids, the room to an S&M chamber in Neasden (only without the glamour or class) and the bill to an act of grand larceny, why, then, the baying crowd is happy... Every time I disembowel a place, they feel I am taking revenge on that particular restaurant for all the truly shitty meals theory themselves have had anywhere."[404]

Rayner admits that writing negative reviews is easier than penning a positive one:

"The language of the overwhelmingly positive can be a strain. Before you know it you are lurching into accounts of angels' kisses; of the delicate flapping of butterfly wings against your downed cheek; of silken bed linen and sun-dappled glades and fey-eyed kittens. The meals can be satisfying, the writing about them a quick route to acuter nausea."[405]

Giles Coren is another expert at the rude restaurant review. When he started out, he deliberately set out to be the food world's answer to car critic Jeremy Clarkson. He once told the Oxford University newspaper *Cherwell* about his first volume of vicious reviews:

"I decided to call my book *Anger Management for Beginners* and to make the unifying theme anger and ranting, and outbursts, in a slightly half-arsed imitation of Clarkson. Now, I'm a much better writer than Clarkson, I'm a much more educated, reasonable, and liberal human being than Clarkson. He's a far more brilliant media personality than I am: he's very funny, very accessible, he has all sorts of exciting opinions that the common man is likely to be terribly interested in. I don't. I'm just an over-educated snob. I thought that if I could persuade people I'm a bit like Clarkson then maybe they'd buy my book. It worked up to a point."[406]

Coren is happy to admit that he enjoys being offensive. In 2011, he wrote in the *Spectator*:

"Rudeness has been good to me over the years. And while I, like most people on the threshold of middle age, deplore our society's ongoing descent into vulgarity, and believe that politeness is, and must remain, the grease that keeps the wheels of the nation turning, I am here to tell you that being very, very rude to the right people, at the right time, can be extraordinarily satisfying, not to mention spiritually elevating, professionally effective and lucrative beyond imagining."[407]

Coren regards his finest hour as his demolition of the Bombay Bicycle Club restaurant chain:

"'The food was terrible,' I wrote. 'Six or seven bowls of brown cloacal waste, studded with amorphous protein chunks. The sick of an infant who lives on Dairylea Lunchables. Why cubed? The meat here was always slices of chicken, big pieces on the bone, skin, fat, all that. Now it's rhomboids from giant rectangular chickens reared on Mars and cut by machines undreamt of in Bernard Matthews's most foetid nightmares.' Within a week, the branch was gone; in a couple of months, the entire chain."[408]

Coren admits that he may, at times, have been obnoxious:

"I used to be so angry. I wasn't happy unless jobs were lost, reputations were ruined and 'closed' notices were up in the window by the end of the week. I remember reading an interview in the *Financial Times* with the owner of a restaurant I'd just panned, in which he declared that 'Giles Coren's review cost me £150,000,' and thinking, 'Is that all?'"[409]

In 2015, he claimed he had matured from being an angry young man and wondered what went wrong in his early days as a reviewer:

"How did I get that way? I was once such a nice child. I honestly think it was the job. I had become mean and stupid and deliberately hurtful because that is what is expected of restaurant critics. Of critics in general. The successful ones, the only ones anyone had heard of, were the bastards. So I went totally bastard. So much simpler to write that way. It's just much easier to be funny when you're being mean. But the meanness is like a horrible growing disease that infects everything it touches (I'm not going to say 'a cancer', because it's not that bad). All those dark, angry critics, they're not happy. And nor was I. My inbox was always full of emails saying, 'We went to a really crap restaurant on Sunday, bad food, bad service, terrible music… you simply MUST go and write about it!' But why would anybody deliberately go to a bad restaurant? What sort of system is that for living a life? Gradually, I began to ask myself if there were not another way."[410]

Now, Coren tries to be constructive, and he doesn't think that's being presumptuous:

"I do it all the time. In my line of work it is important. Remember I am not criticising anything remotely akin to art (whatever some arsehole uneducated chefs might think). I am criticising businesses, so they probably want the benefit of my experience. And if they don't, they should."[411]

Anthony Burch made his name as a video games reviewer, but when he started developing games for a living he realised how callously ignorant he had been of the processes and people involved:

"I *still* don't like any of those games I negatively reviewed when I was a blogger, but I'm far less likely to be a hostile asshole about them. Don't get me wrong: I still believe that negative reviews are absolutely important to the medium, but I no longer take joy in ripping apart a game I didn't like *just* to prove that I'm smarter than its creators in some way. Criticism is generally more about your readers than the creators — when I gave *Twilight Princess* a 4/10 for *Destructoid*, I was trying to warn people from spending their money on it more than I was trying to stick it to Nintendo. But it can be easy, in that relationship, to miss the fact that when you shit on a developer, you're shitting on actual human beings. Human beings with lives, feelings, passions and (if they're anything like me) significant self-esteem problems. It probably, in other words, wouldn't have killed me to be a little goddamn nicer."[412]

At least one other angry young man has repented his early ways. Literary critic Martin Amis admitted in his Preface to *The War Against Cliché* that with the onset of middle age he, too, has mellowed:

"Enjoying being insulting is a youthful corruption of power. You lose your taste for it when you realise how hard people try, how much they mind, and how long they remember. Angus Wilson and William Burroughs nursed my animadversions - and no doubt the animadversions of others - to the grave."[413]

The American literary critic Gore Vidal, who can be pretty splenetic himself, has no time for negative book critics, whom he calls "literary gangsters":

"The literary gangster's initial problem is a poignant one: how to be noticed? How to occupy a turf of one's own? Having been for a quarter-century an observer of the scene, with a special interest in literary crime... I would suggest, right off, that the apprentice criminal write the following on the lid of his typewriter: Today's reader is not interested in analysis but opinion, preferably harsh and unexpected.... Needless to say, the more violent and *ad hominem* the style, the more grateful his readers will be. Americans like to be told who to hate."[414]

Not so Simple Simons and Destructive Criticism

John Simon is undoubtedly the most notorious of these *ad hominem* critics. He is often held up as representing all that's worst in negative criticism, mainly because he frequently insults the way actors look, whether or not this is relevant to their performance. For example, he wrote of Liza Minnelli in *Lucky Lady*:

"Age cannot wither, nor make-up stale, her infinite sameness... She is herself a perfect *ménage a trois* in which lack of talent, lack of looks, and lack of a speaking voice cohabit blissfully. [Director Stanley] Donen sensibly concentrates on her best feature, her legs, but he unfortunately can't wrap them around her face." [415]

Diana Rigg was especially mortified by Simon's merciless review of her when she appeared nude in *Abelard and Heloise*:

"She is built like a brick basilica with inadequate flying buttresses and suggests neither intense womanliness nor outstanding intellect."

Most notoriously, Simon wrote of Barbra Streisand in *What's Up Doc* that she "looks like a cross between an aardvark and an albino rat surmounted by a platinum-coated horse bun".[416]

Simon's fellow critic Roger Ebert, whom Simon regularly rebuked not so much for his physical shortcomings but for his low intellect and vulgar tastes, wrote in his memoir *Life Itself*, "I feel repugnance for the critic John Simon, who made it a specialty to attack the way actors look. They can't help how they look, any more than John Simon can help looking like a rat."[417]

John Simon could be unnecessarily cruel, but occasionally he perceived weaknesses that few other critics dared to do - as, for example, in his review of Gena Rowlands' tendency to over-emote in *A Woman Under the Influence* (1974):

"As Isabel, Gena Rowlands lets it all hang out ubiquitously and continually; if feelings were laundry, she'd be the city of Naples."[418]

He could also be witty. When English comedian Norman Wisdom came to Broadway in a play, Simon wrote, "If this be Norman Wisdom, give me Saxon folly."

It's also hard not to warm to the elegance of Simon's prose when, for example, he attacked director (and former critic) Peter Bogdanovich's decision to cast his girl-friend in the atrocious film musical *At Long Last Love*, which proved conclusively that she could neither sing nor dance:

"Cybill Shepherd, Mr B's inamorata, plays a poor little snotty rich girl with a notion of sophistication that is underpassed only by her acting ability. (I will not even sully my pen by making it describe her singing and dancing.) If it weren't for an asinine superciliousness radiating from her, Miss Shepherd would actually be pitiable, rather like a kid from an orphanage trying to play Noel Coward. In fact, she comes across like one of those inanimate objects, say, a cupboard or a grandfather clock, which is made in certain humorous shorts to act, through trick photography, like people. Well, Bogdanovich is truly in love with Miss Shepherd, so one cannot call his slapping her into the lead of almost every one of his films the casting-couch approach; yet even those crude old-time producers who did have the crassness to use that method at least had the good sense to cast the girl, not the couch."[419]

I have much less time for another *ad hominem* critic (if, indeed, he can be called a critic), Simon Cowell[420]. He made a reputation for himself on a succession of series – *Pop Idol, American Idol, The X Factor* and *Britain's Got Talent* – by insulting people, mostly amateurs, who had clearly been chosen very carefully by his researchers to come on and be humiliated. Here are a few of Cowell's most popular put-downs:

"You have the personality of a handle."[421]

"You have just invented a new form of torture."[422]

"Shave off your beard and wear a dress. I think you'd be a great female impersonator."[423]

"I don't think any artist on earth can sing with that much metal in your mouth anyway. You have so much metal in your mouth. That's like a bridge."[424]

The last quotation has received the most press attention, because that target of Cowell's vitriol committed suicide.

The press portrayed the two events as linked, but the truth was a little more complex than that. For a start, there was a considerable lapse of time between Paula Goodspeed appearing on *American Idol* in 2005 and her suicide, at the age of 30, in 2008.

Also, she appears to have been less upset by Cowell's insult than by the comments of another judge on the programme, the usually anodyne Paula Abdul, who said after Goodspeed's offkey rendition of *Proud Mary* "that's not a great thing... I'm speechless. I don't know what to say and not in a good way."[425]

Goodspeed, who had admitted on her MySpace.com page that she had a crush on Abdul, turned out to have had a history of turning up outside Abdul's Los Angeles home and "disturbing the peace". She was found dead of a drugs overdose in her car, parked a few doors away from Abdul's house. Prescription pills, along with CDs and pictures of Abdul, were also found in the vehicle. The license plate on her car read "ABL LV", an abbreviation of "Abdul Love", and a photo of Abdul was hanging from the rear-view mirror.[426]

So, on this particular death, Cowell is probably blameless (although, as one of the producers, he was partially responsible for choosing Ms Goodspeed as a contestant in the first place and holding her up to ridicule). But, given the number of nutters with access to guns in America, it's amazing that Cowell has not fallen foul of one of them and become an involuntary martyr to freedom of speech.

Needless to say, I would regret that happening. I am all for honest criticism, and I wouldn't mind so much if any of Cowell's insults were witty. The trouble is that virtually all of them are destructive. Since, quite clearly, most of Cowell's victims have been selected for being several sandwiches short of a full picnic if not downright delusional, his cruel reactions strike me as tantamount to making fun of the handicapped, or shooting proverbial fish in a barrel. I am also unpleasantly reminded of early Christians being thrown to the lions in the Coliseum for the edification of a bloodthirsty Roman crowd.

The same thought has evidently occurred even to Cowell, for he admitted to his Britain's Got Talent co-panellist Piers Morgan on ITV1's *Morgan's Life Stories:*

"There's many, many times where I've watched the show back and I'm absolutely appalled... You become part of a mob and when you watch the show back you realise that you've gone too far."[427]

Quite.

Those who most dislike destructive criticism will often say that the destructive critic should try to be more "objective". Indeed, one of the first things most journalists are taught is to be "objective". The more objective a reporter is, the more credible he will be. His job is to give the reader the facts and some background. If two journalists disagree on the facts, the likelihood is that eventually one will be proved wrong.

However, criticism isn't like that. A critic is more like an opinionated columnist than a journalist. A good critic will give a truthful account of the facts (perhaps a brief account of the story premise and the talent involved) but is also expected to give a subjective account of his reactions, to place it in context artistically, morally, socially and/or politically.

Two critics may drastically disagree about the merits of a play or film, but neither is necessarily "wrong". A good critic will enable readers to think critically about the subject, and will help them decide whether it is worth their time and money to attend the particular work of art.

Critics have responsibilities. They should try to be fair, and recognise that they may not be the ideal audience for a particular work of art, or indeed a whole genre. They shouldn't dismiss work without giving valid reasons for such an assessment. Constructive criticism is not a contradiction in terms.

Joseph Addison (1672-1719) was an outstanding critic who was at his peak in the age of Queen Anne. (He was also a poet, playwright and politician.) His major contributions to criticism appeared in his new magazine *The Spectator*, which he founded with his friend Richard Steele, and *The Tatler*, which Steele set up by himself. Through these essays, he satirized literature, society and the arts, but in a kindlier fashion than his contemporaries Jonathan Swift, Alexander Pope, Daniel Defoe and John Dryden. Writing in 1712, he advocated constructive rather than destructive criticism:

"One great mark, by which you may discover a critic who has neither taste nor learning, is this, that he seldom ventures to praise any passage in an author which has not been before received and applauded by the public, and that his criticism turns wholly upon little faults and errors... A true critic ought to dwell rather upon excellencies than imperfections, to discover the concealed beauties of a writer, and communicate to the world such things as are worth their observation."[428]

Destructive criticism may sometimes be justified, but even here critics should have respect for the creative process. Flippancy and rudeness purely in order to show off can have unpleasant consequences for creators who may have devoted months or even years to a project. Nasty theatre and restaurant reviews have been known to close down projects and put people out of work. Hatchet jobs should only be attempted if they are truly warranted.

Critics should also be wary not to be used by their editors as character assassins. Towards the end of my time at the *Daily Mail*, I was approached by one of the features editors to write a hatchet job on Emma Watson[429], still best known as Hermione in the Harry Potter movies. The idea had come from an editorial conference, he said.

I asked what she had done wrong to deserve this treatment, and he replied that her last few films had been rubbish, and she deserved "pulling down a peg or two". I pointed out that although I had disliked her last film, the apocalyptic comedy *This is the End* for being, as I put it, "the death throes of intelligent comedy", she was a very peripheral character and not responsible for the film's laziness, smugness and stupidity. Though I hadn't admired *Bling Ring*, Sofia Coppola's celebration of gormless teenagers who broke into the homes of Hollywood stars in 2008-9 as a perverted kind of celebrity-worship, Watson had been the best thing in it. I also said that she had shown a gift for comedy and pathos in her previous film, *The Perks of Being a Wallflower*, which I had liked very much. The upshot is that, foolishly or not, I turned down more than a thousand pounds because I didn't wish to write a hatchet job of someone I didn't feel deserved character assassination. I was never invited to write another feature for the *Daily Mail*.

Camilla Long rose from journalistic obscurity thanks to hatchet jobs on Rachel Cusk, Julie Burchill and Carole Middleton. The last of these largely consisted of snobbish comments on the royal *arriviste*'s working-class background. I am indebted to *Burke's Peerage* for the information that Camilla herself is descended on her mother's side from one Henry Pelham-Clinton, 4th Duke of Newcastle (1785-1851). She attended Oxford High School and Corpus Christi College, Oxford - unlike Carole Middleton, who attended a state school in Southall, Middlesex, and became an air hostess, much to Ms Long's amusement.

The winner in 2010 of the British Press Awards "Interviewer of the Year (broadsheet)", Long now writes film reviews for the *Sunday Times* of unparalleled personal savagery, and appears to have few scruples, if any, about being used by her editors as an attack dog.

Her journalistic assault on Richard Dawkins, for example, centred not on his arguments in favour of atheism, but on his personal appearance. "Richard Dawkins," she reported, "has an extremely unfortunate face". Then she complained about his "nibbly little voice", "tiny teeth" and even his "crumpled tie". And she derided the 70 year-old's 'forgetful' memory. The piece epitomized sneeriness.[430]

Three years earlier, she interviewed UKIP leader Nigel Farage, whom she dismissed as "pretty odious, a shifty saloon-bar lizard."[431] She began the interview by scorning the fact that, having had cancer, he has only one testicle. This struck some readers as a low blow. One pointed out that she would not have dared to sneer at a woman who had lost a breast.

Let Gawain Towler, Farage's press officer, take up the story behind the interview:

"On Friday, just after Farage had delivered a barnstormer of a speech at the Milton Keynes conference I received a phone call. It was Camilla Long.

'Look Gawain', she said, 'I am really sorry to ask you this but the editors have told me to'.

'What's that?' I said.

'They want me to ask which one of his balls was removed after his cancer.'

You want odious? I would suggest even asking that question is pretty bloody impertinent and cheap, and I told her so, but she persisted. So I agreed to ask, but told her not to expect a particularly forthcoming answer.

When I asked Farage, he was, unusually for him, somewhat put out, but after saying that he though it a cheap shot he then he recovered his normal poise.

'Tell her if she is so bloody interested that she can come over and check herself.'

So I called her back and told her, both that he felt is tawdry, but if she must then that is his comment.

Or as she puts it...

'Two days later when I call his press officer to confirm which testicle he had removed. Farage has just given his party conference speech and is in high spirits. 'Tell her to come and find out, ha-ha-ha!' he shouts over the din.'

So do tell me, concludes Gawain Towler in his blog, "*who* is vile and odious?"[432]

When he was TV critic on the *Evening Standard*, Victor Lewis-Smith struck me as sometimes going too far with his *ad hominem* criticisms, which were not only personally abusive but boringly repetitive. Oddly enough, one of his victims was just starting out as an abrasive critic himself. Giles Coren still hasn't forgiven him.

When I asked Giles "what do you think is the worst fault of some professional critics", he gave a surprisingly frank reply:

"Vanity, pompousness, mendacity. We are all guilty of it sometimes. I would never name another critic. Yes I would: Victor Lewis Smith. In his time as television critic he pursued a relentless assault on my entire family. Writing the same piece, filled with the same jokes, many times over several years. I don't know why. Possibly my father [*Punch* editor Alan Coren] didn't give him a job forty years ago or something. But he was vile to me and my dad and sister [the writer and broadcaster Victoria Coren Mitchell]. I in fact complained myself (I was a kid, not yet a critic) to his editor Max Hastings (when he was vile not about me but about Nigella Lawson in the last weeks of her first husband's life, my friend John Diamond). Hastings wrote me the sort of letter that now editors write in my own defence. When

VLS was fired for being utterly shit and poisonous he ended up writing restaurant reviews for the *Guardian*, which he again used to take up cudgels against me. I think using a responsible position as a critic to pursue personal vendettas is heinous."[433]

The Art of the Hatchet Job

Peter Fuller was a British art critic and magazine editor who was appointed art reviewer of the *Daily Telegraph* in 1989. His career was cut short by death in a car accident on the M4 motorway in Berkshire on 28 April 1990, at the age of only 42. An expert on Ruskin, he was widely recognised as one of the most opinionated and accomplished critics in England.[434]

Although he could be a constructive critic, he was also in his element as a destructive one. He had a particular hatred of the work of Gilbert and George, whom he saw as both aesthetically and spiritually ugly:

"Their work is without any sense of touch, aesthetic sensitivity, nuance or tradition. Indeed, they have repeatedly expressed their antagonism towards 'elitism', and would not appear to have been influenced by any of the great art of the West. Their colours clash and jostle with all the glaring smoothness of billboards; and their space is literally flat and superficial. These large, gaudy montages incessantly refer to their narcissistic preoccupations with each other, with alcohol, and with young boys."[435]

Fuller analyses the themes within their work with scarcely concealed contempt:

"Their images cannot rise above their obsessive preoccupation with urban violence, lumpen philistinism, sexual products and organs, and personal depravity A peculiarly ugly series of the later 1970s, composed out of black-and-white and red-coloured photographs, incorporating reproductions of graffiti, was presented with titles like *Prostitute Poof, Cock VD, Bollocks We're All Angry, Bent Shit Cunt, Smash the Reds, Bugger, Queer*, and *Prick Ass*. The latter shows their heads separated by an image of the crucified Christ; the top of the picture is inscribed with the scrawled word 'Prick', and the bottom with "Ass'. In the centre, there are red-coloured photos of the inner city, and at the edges shots of a derelict down-and-out."[436]

Fuller concludes his description with a wry comment on the arts establishment's reverence for the two "artists" (when calling them artists, he invariably places inverted commas around the word, to designate doubts as to whether they deserve the title):

"Gilbert and George won the Turner Prize in 1986, an annual award of £10,000, made under the auspices of the Tate Gallery to the individual(s) who, in the opinion of the jury, has done the most for art in Britain in the previous twelve months."[437]

Clive James wrote a perceptive essay in 2013, pointing out one important difference between British and American literary criticism:

"America does polite literary criticism well enough. And how: there is a new Lionel Trilling on every campus. But America can't do the bitchery of British book reviewing and literary commentary. In Britain, the realm of book reviewing is still known as Grub Street though the actual Grub Street vanished long ago. But its occasionally vicious spirit lives on; one of the marks of Grub Street is that the spleen gets a voice. Ripping somebody's reputation is recognised blood sport. Shredding a new book is a kind of fox hunting that is still legal today. Such critical violence is far less frequent in America. Any even remotely derogatory article in an American journal is called 'negative,' and hardly any American publication wants to be negative. In America, consensus is considered normal and controversy is confusing."[438]

Like me, James sees the value of "destructive" criticism and prefers the British tradition.

The Hatchet Job of the Year prize was set up in 2011 by the Britain-based *Omnivore* website to "raise the profile of professional book critics and to promote integrity and wit in literary journalism". It is given to the "writer of the angriest, funniest, most trenchant book review" of the past year, "not to punish bad writing, but to reward good and brave and funny and learned reviewing."

"Book reviews are, in the main, too fawning and dull," says site editor Anna Baddeley, and she's right. The prize each year is a golden hatchet and a year's supply of potted shrimp.[439]

In 2011, Adam Mars-Jones took the award for his smooth assassination in the *Observer* of Michael Cunningham's novel *By Nightfall*.[440]

Mars Jones particularly hated the author's misuse of language:

"At the very least, shouldn't a writer try to shield the kettle of language from further cracks by knowing the meanings of the words he uses?"[441]

Camilla Long won the 2012 award for her merciless panning of Rachel Cusk's *Aftermath*, an account of how divorce led to her life falling apart.[442]

Aftermath, according to Long, "is crammed with mad, flowery metaphors and hifalutin creative-writing experiments", including "hectic passages on Greek tragedy" in which she compares herself with Clytemnestra and Oedipus.

But Long mainly dislikes Cusk's tendency to overdramatise: "can a tray of vol-au-vents really be 'steeped in rejection'? In Cusk's world, even the canapes are victims."

Long also notes the galloping self-obsession of the book: "we have acres of poetic whimsy and vague literary blah, a needy, neurotic mandolin solo of reflections on child sacrifice and asides about drains".[443]

I must admit that had I been a judge in 2012, I would have given the award to Zoe Heller, for her hilarious hatchet job on Salman Rushdie's characteristically vain memoir *Joseph Anton.*[444]

Her 2,600-word essay criticised him for his self-aggrandizing prose, written "in a de Gaulle-like third person", and the "lordly nonchalance with which Rushdie places himself alongside Lawrence, Joyce and Nabokov in the ranks of literary merit... one would hope that when recollecting his emotions in freedom and safety, he might bring some ironic detachment to bear on his own bombast. Hindsight, alas, has had no sobering effect on Rushdie's magisterial *amour propre*. An unembarrassed sense of what he is owed as an embattled, literary immortal-in-waiting pervades his book."

Heller's cheerfully *ad hominem* approach also takes in Rushdie's imperious attitude to women:

"In a close-run contest between Marianne Wiggins (number two) and Padma Lakshmi (number four), it is the latter who emerges as the worst of the spousal bunch. Rushdie presents her as the Marion Davies to his William Randolph Hearst — an erotically beguiling but fundamentally vapid gold digger, whose selfish ambitions as a model, actress, and TV host have, in the end, 'nothing to do with the fulfillment of his deepest needs.' The final revelation of her shallowness comes in the wake of September 11 when Rushdie, grieving and shaken and feeling the need to connect with loved ones, calls her in Los Angeles and finds her 'doing a lingerie shoot.' Rushdie's shuddering *hauteur* at this moment may strike the reader as a bit rich, coming from a man who spends much of his memoir recalling encounters with pop stars, *Playboy* bunnies, and 'hot' pop-star girlfriends in the breathless style of a young Austen character writing up her first visit to the pump rooms at Bath. But Rushdie would have us understand that his copious accounts of nightclubbing with celebrities are the record of a doughty man's will to survive, of his commitment to a moral duty... If he hadn't been out there, frugging with Padma at Moomba, the terrorists would have won, you see."

Heller ends with a lethal sideswipe at Rushdie's pretentiousness:

"The job of literature, he instructs us in the final pages of this memoir, is to encourage 'understanding, sympathy and identification with people not like oneself...to make the world feel larger, wider than before.' Some readers may find, by the end of *Joseph Anton*, that the world feels rather smaller and grimmer than before. But they should not be unduly alarmed. The world is as large and as wide as it ever was; it's just Rushdie who got small."

In 2013, A.A. Gill won the Golden Hatchet of the Year award with his slicing and dicing job on Morrissey's egotistical autobiography called, er, *Autobiography*[445]:

"There are many pop autobiographies that shouldn't be written. Some to protect the unwary reader, and some to protect the author. In Morrissey's case, he has managed both. This is a book that cries out like one of his maudlin ditties to be edited. But were an editor to start, there would be no stopping. It is a heavy tome, utterly devoid of insight, warmth, wisdom or likeability. It is a potential firelighter of vanity, self-pity and logorrhoeic dullness. Putting it in *Penguin Classics* doesn't diminish Aristotle or Homer or Tolstoy; it just roundly mocks Morrissey, and this is a humiliation constructed by the self-regard of its victim."[446]

However, my favourite was Craig Brown's devastating dissection of *Distant Intimacy: A Friendship in the Age of the Internet*, by Frederic Raphael and Joseph Epstein.[447] Brown begins with an explanation of who the authors are:

"Frederic Raphael is a British author who peaked in the Seventies, and remains best known for his hit 1976 television series *The Glittering Prizes*. Joseph Epstein is an American author and essayist who – he tells us in his introduction – was once described by an editor as 'the American Frederic Raphael'. This might have caused others to punch that editor but Epstein was, he says, 'much pleased by this remark'."

Brown tells of how these two authors began emailing each other each week, with a view to publishing the results:

"The first thing to be said about their exchanges is how extraordinarily unpleasant they are, almost as though they were trying to make it into the *Guinness Book Of Records* under a section called *Authors, Most Bilious*. It is all a bit like watching a tennis match, but instead of the competitors bashing balls to and fro, they prefer to bash authors and artists more successful than themselves. Not a paragraph goes by without the expression of a fresh loathing. Epstein hates, in no particular order, the director Mike Nichols ('wealthy creep'), Arthur Miller, Walter Cronkite (a 'dope, a jerk'), Edward Albee, Ernest Hemingway ('stupid'), Steven Spielberg, George Clooney, Robert Redford, William Styron, Salman Rushdie, Joyce Carol Oates, Colm Toibin, David Hockney, Don DeLillo, Seamus Heaney."

The list of Raphael's hates is even longer:

"In strict alphabetical order, Raphael hates Kingsley Amis ('the worst influence on the English novel since the war'), Julian Barnes, Saul Bellow, Alan Bennett ('carefully preserves the lineaments of the local lower-middle class provinciality which he seems to have done everything possible to leave behind'), A.S. Byatt, Alan Clark, Jesus Christ ('he never said anything that one wished one had said oneself, did he?'), Richard Dawkins,

Sebastian Faulks, Christopher Hitchens ('lazy, facile'), Alan Hollinghurst, Michael Holroyd ('gleams with renown and self-importance'), Michael Ignatieff ('the smoothies' smoothy')... Enough! On reflection, it might be quicker to list everyone Raphael loves, a roll-call that begins with R for Raphael and ends, a little abruptly, with R for Raphael. Freddie, as he signs himself, is, it emerges, his own best friend. 'I still write like a man who never wanted to do anything else much, except make love, of course, and a name, I guess,' he says. He also notes that 'I find that I am able to hold an audience better now than ever' and recalls that 'Stanley Donen did once say to me that I was the most talented man he had ever met'. His faults are few and far between, though he does at one point confess, boastfully, that 'I have sometimes been accused of 'moral courage' .'"

Any review written with humour, verve and accuracy is to be commended as long as the motive is pure: to tell the unvarnished truth, rather than to settle old scores.

How Far is Too Far?

The most notorious case of a journalist being sued for libel over unfair personal criticism was Liberace's lawsuit in 1959 against William Connor, "Cassandra" of the *Daily Mirror*, for implying in a 1956 column that the flamboyant American was homosexual.[448]

Perhaps Connor was, by modern standards, homophobic; but it is hard not to admire the energy of his diatribe against the celebrity pianist:

"He reeks with emetic language that can only make grown men long for a quiet corner, an aspidistra, a handkerchief, and the old heave-ho. Without doubt, he is the biggest sentimental vomit of all time. Slobbering over his mother, winking at his brother, and counting the cash at every second, this superb piece of calculating candy-floss has an answer for every situation. Nobody since Aimee Semple MacPherson has purveyed a bigger, richer and more varied slag-heap of lilac-covered hokum. Nobody anywhere ever made so much money out of high speed piano playing with the ghost of Chopin gibbering at every note. There must be something wrong with us that our teenagers longing for sex and our middle-aged matrons fed up with sex alike should fall for such a sugary mountain of jingling claptrap wrapped up in such a preposterous clown."[449]

The key passage in Connor's critique was that Liberace was "the summit of sex - the pinnacle of masculine, feminine, and neuter... a deadly, winking, sniggering, snuggling, chromium-plated, scent-impregnated, luminous, quivering, giggling, fruit-flavoured, mincing, ice-covered heap of mother love."[450]

After a six-day hearing, during which Liberace lied about being homosexual (which he was) and claimed that he had never taken part in homosexual acts (which he had), the jury found for him. He was awarded a then-record £8,000 in damages (in today's money, about half a million pounds).[451]

In Liberace's defence, it is worth bearing in mind that in those days homosexuality was still illegal, and he must have felt that a certain amount of hypocrisy was essential if he was to retain his predominantly female, middle-aged fanbase. Other homosexuals, from Noel Coward to W. Somerset Maugham, were equally keen to disguise their sexuality. Liberace died aged 67 in 1987, of an Aids-related illness.

The Liberace case showed very clearly the hatred of the popular press amongst the judiciary (whose approach to the case was almost comically skewed against popular newspapers) and the public.

Liberace's counsel, Gilbert Beyfus, claimed that the slander of Liberace was only the tip of the iceberg that constituted this "venal, reckless journalist". He called Connor "a literary assassin who dips his pen in vitriol, hired by this sensational newspaper to murder reputations and hand out sensational articles on which its circulation is built." Through Liberace, the English court had the chance to redress all these transgressions. "Here's a piano player," Beyfus proclaimed, "giving these people a chance to fight back."[452]

The message rings loud and clear across five decades: hardly anyone likes a critic, especially if he is taking on someone popular and uttering unpalatable truths.

In 1985, a British actress called Charlotte Cornwell – best known for her leading role in the TV series *Rock Follies* – successfully sued the *News of the World* and its professionally bitchy television reviewer Nina Myskow for libel,[453] when Myskow claimed in a 1983 review of a show named, ironically enough, *No Excuses*:

"As a middle-aged star all Miss Cornwell has going for her is her age. She can't sing, her bum is too big and she has the sort of stage presence that jams lavatories. Worst she belongs to that arrogant and deluded school of acting which believes that if you leave off your make-up (how brave, how real) and SHOUT A LOT, it's great acting. It's ART. For a start, dear, you look just as ugly with make-up, so forget that. And as for ART? In the short sharp words of the series, there is just one reply. It rhymes."[454]

The defence of fair comment was used, but failed. Counsel for the critic suggested that the courts were "not the place to deal with someone's sense of grievance that another person has been rude in print about their bottom". The court disagreed. Two juries (the case went to a retrial) came to the conclusion that Myskow's invective was immoderate. The decisive factor was that there had previously been bad feeling between the two women, and so the piece was judged to be malicious.

Anyone keen on emulating Ms Cornwell ought to be aware, however,

that although she was awarded £11,500 in damages she ended up at least
£70,000 out of pocket because of costs incurred in bringing the case to
court.[455] And the unwished for consequence of her litigation is that she will
forever be remembered not for the quality of her acting, but for the size of
her bum.

In 1996, the actor-director-writer Steven Berkoff triumphed in another
high-profile court case, when a majority of judges found that he had been
defamed by the *Sunday Times* columnist Julie Burchill.[456]

In a review of *The Age of Innocence* in January 1994, Burchill
described film directors "such as Stephen Berkoff" as "notoriously hideous
looking people". In November of the same year, reviewing Kenneth
Branagh's *Frankenstein*, she described "the creature" as "a lot like Stephen
Berkoff, only marginally better looking". When Mr Berkoff sued for libel,
Ms Burchill and Times Newspapers Ltd applied for the proceedings to be
dismissed on the grounds that to call a person "hideously ugly" was not
defamatory.

In its majority judgment of 1996, the Court of Appeal held that words
might be defamatory even though they neither imputed disgraceful conduct
to the plaintiff nor any lack of skill or efficiency in the conduct of his
business or profession, if they held him up to contempt, scorn or ridicule or
tended to exclude him from society. Although insults which did not
diminish a man's standing were not sufficient to found an action for libel or
slander, the words used had to be considered in the light of all surrounding
circumstances.

It would be open to a jury to conclude that, in their context, the
remarks about Mr Berkoff gave the impression that he was not merely
physically unattractive in appearance but actually repulsive. To say that of
someone in the public eye, such as an actor, was capable of lowering his
standing in the estimation of the public and of making him an object of
ridicule.[457]

Lord Justice Millett dissented, judging that Mr Berkoff's claim was as
frivolous as Ms Burchill's article:

"Chaff and banter are not defamatory, and even serious imputations
are not actionable if no one would take them to be meant seriously. The
question, however, is how the words would be understood, not how they
were meant, and that issue is pre-eminently one for the jury. So, however
difficult it may be, we must assume that Miss Julie Burchill might be taken
seriously. The question then is: is it defamatory to say of a man that he is
'hideously ugly'? Mr Berkoff is a director, actor and writer. Physical beauty
is not a qualification for a director or writer. Mr Berkoff does not plead that
he plays romantic leads or that the words complained of impugn his
professional ability. In any case, I do not think that it can be defamatory to
say of an actor that he is unsuitable to play particular roles... If I have

appeared to treat Mr Berkoff's claim with unjudicial levity it is because I find it impossible to take it seriously. Despite the views of my brethren, who are both far more experienced than I am, I remain of the opinion that the proceedings are as frivolous as Miss Burchill's article. The time of the court ought not to be taken up with either of them."[458]

For what it's worth, I'm with Lord Justice Millett on this one. It's highly doubtful that calling someone ugly would be actionable defamation under U.S. law. And anyone who takes any of Julie Burchill's random opinions with anything other than a pinch of salt is clearly delusional.

Writing for the New Law Journal in 2013, legal journalist James Wilson takes a similar line to mine:

"With due respect to the other judges, it is impossible to disagree with Millett. Burchill was obviously writing in a sardonic and flippant tone. Even had she been serious, the appropriate response would have been 'so what'?... Putting the case at its highest, it amounted to a complaint that 'Julie Burchill called Steven Berkoff ugly'. That was not the sort of dispute that called for the attention of the expensive and scarce resource of the law courts. Instead it was a Primary School-level insult that should have been treated accordingly. Nearly two decades on, the controversy does not seem to have affected either party. Berkoff has continued to have a successful acting and directing career. Burchill has maintained her abrasive ways: earlier this year, she attracted controversy with an article pouring scorn on what she saw as oversensitivity by transgender spokespeople (or "dicks in chicks' clothing" as she called them). The Press Complaints Committee declined to censure her, stating that it 'did not address issues of taste and offence'. Neither should the libel courts."[459]

In 2013, American film critic Rex Reed managed to escape being sued for libel or defamation, but was widely abused on the internet for his review of *Identity Thief*, in which he described leading actress Melissa McCarthy as a "female hippo" and "tractor-sized". Reed also described her career as a study in "being obese and obnoxious with equal success."[460]

I can see why some people found Reed's review ugly and tasteless. Criticising an actor's appearance when it is irrelevant to his or her performance does smack of sadism.

As a presenter on Radio 4's *The Film Programme* and as a print journalist, I have interviewed several young movie stars who were suffering quite clearly from anorexia and/or bulimia. I am sure this was because they didn't want to be pilloried in the media (or on the internet) for being overweight or (horrors!) having cellulite. And don't get me started on those older actors, of both sexes, who have ruined their looks – and their ability to express emotion with their faces – thanks to misconceived plastic surgery aimed at giving them eternal youth.[461] So I try not to make personal comments in a review unless they are relevant to someone's ability to play a part.

The trouble is that vis-à-vis Ms McCarthy, Reed told an unwelcome truth. I referred to her none too kindly in my own review of *Identity Thief* as "the fat, aggressive loudmouth from *Bridesmaids*" and pointed out that her behaviour in the movie was more unpleasant than amusing:

"One running 'gag' has the heroine punching male victims in the throat; this is meant to be hilarious, even though it's potentially fatal. Projectile vomiting is, needless to say, laugh-out-loud funny, as is nauseatingly foul language and the leading lady having casual, adulterous sex in a crummy motel with an equally overweight cowboy... The extreme obesity of the leading lady is exaggerated one moment, forgotten the next. She runs a couple of yards and is out of breath. A few hours later, she is able to carry our hero half a mile or more. None of it makes sense."[462]

In the *Guardian*, Peter Bradshaw also questioned the leading actress's comedic abilities:

"Almost every single one of her scenes looks like an outtake."[463]

The inconvenient truth is that Ms McCarthy's fatness, coarseness and repellent behaviour were her calling card or – in modern parlance – her unique selling point. And many would share Rex Reed's opinion that her alleged talent and versatility are negligible. In his 2014 review of *Tammy*, which McCarthy not only starred in but wrote with her husband Ben Falcone, Reed explains his contempt for the actress and her works:

"It's a rambling, pointless and labored attempt to cash in on Ms. McCarthy's fan base without respect for any audience with a collective IQ of 10. And it's about as funny as a liver transplant. With all due respect, I bow to her ability to pander to the lowest instincts of her groupies by making box office obesity profitable. So, fool that I am, I went to *Tammy* hoping for the best and ready to give Ms. McCarthy every benefit of the doubt. What I got was one hour and 36 minutes of farting, belching, snoring, and the kind of violence a sadist would perpetrate against someone in a wheelchair. One thing you gotta admit: however amiable and attractive she might be in real life, the star makes no attempt to beautify herself onscreen. Nothing she's ever done before will prepare you for what she looks like here, with swollen feet, tag-sale clothes and hair that resembles a nesting place for field mice. Working as a shuffling, nose-picking waitress for a greasy junk-food chain called Topper Jack's and looking like she's been wolfing down most of the grease all by herself, she gets sacked, wrecks her Toyota when she broadsides a deer, and returns home to find her cheating husband cooking dinner for a new bedmate (the over-employed Toni Collette). Tammy moves out, announces to her mother (Allison Janney) she's leaving town, and hits the road. Susan Sarandon is hopelessly miscast as the drunken nymphomaniac grandmother with $6,700 in cash and a battered Cadillac who decides to go with her. The preposterous, generation-gap road trip that follows is no *Thelma and Louise*."[464]

Reed has a point when he writes that McCarthy's movies are remarkably repetitive:

"The purpose of every Melissa McCarthy movie is the same: Take the most repulsive loser you can conjure up and make her sympathetic and lovable, proving you can find beauty in anything if you look hard enough. This one fails to even do that. Instead of following any kind of linear narrative, the script limps from one phony vignette to the next, linked only by a different road sign. Without structure, trajectory or logic, the result becomes tragically boring. In the chaos, I applaud the star — not for any discernible talent, but for sheer stamina. Her entire performance — if you can call it that — consists of being slapped, slugged, dumped in various lakes and rivers, and bounced off walls and pavements like a big rubber Shmoo doll. She isn't smart, imaginative or creative enough to be a real female clown, like Lucille Ball. Nothing that resembles a fresh approach to slapstick farce ever engages the mind or the eye. Instead she recycles every fatso cliché from John Candy to Totie Fields, which only turns the viewer cynical. This movie is so bad it almost makes me take back everything I said about *Identity Thief* and *The Heat*."[465]

Charles Spencer, one time theatre critic of the *Daily Telegraph*[466], nowadays best remembered for his description of Nicole Kidman on stage as "pure theatrical Viagra",[467] was – to my mind – rightly accused of sexism when he ungallantly remarked of Maureen Lipman in *A Little Night Music* that she was "a wildly unlikely *grande horizontale*", adding that she was too "angular" to have slept her way through the royal families of Europe.[468]

Maureen's stylish response was to write to him, listing several women who had managed to attract royals - including Wallis Simpson, Dorothy Jordan and Camilla Parker Bowles – who hadn't possessed the looks of Helen of Troy either. She made her point, though I don't think Spencer ever apologized.[469]

In opera circles, there was a huge outcry after allegedly "sexist" reviews by several male critics of Tara Erraught's Octavian in *Der Rosenkavalier*. Rupert Christiansen in the *Daily Telegraph* wrote that though the Irish mezzo-soprano sang beautifully she was "dumpy of stature" with "costuming [that] makes her resemble something between Heidi and Just William". Michael Church in the *Independent* also referred to her as "dumpy". Andrew Clark in the *Financial Times* described her as "a chubby bundle of puppy-fat", Andrew Clements in the *Guardian* called her "stocky", Richard Morrison in the *Times* described her as "unbelievable, unsightly and unappealing".[470]

The reaction was swift – especially from women in the opera world. "Clearly overt sexism is still rife," said opera singer Jennifer Johnston. Another soprano, Elisabeth Meister, inquired: "What on earth does your body size have to do with how well you can sing?" Music journalist Elizabeth Davies complained: "Some pretty shocking casual sexism in the opera world this morning".[471]

Christiansen put up a spirited, and to my mind convincing, defence of his criticism:

"Octavian is a young nobleman, conceived by Strauss and his librettist Hofmannsthal as a Principal Boy-type and most successfully incarnated in the past by taller or more strapping mezzo-sopranos such as Anne Sofie von Otter or Sarah Connolly who can play the gender-bending game to great effect."[472]

Christiansen pointed out that opera is not only a musical medium:

"Opera is a visual as well as an aural experience, a form of theatre: it may be 75 per cent about the voice, but it is also 25 per cent about the ability to act well and create a convincing character. Fat and thin can be equally beautiful, but one has to make an audience believe. There are times when physical absolutes make this impossible: one would not cast a skeletally thin man as Falstaff or an elderly lady as Juliet, and in my opinion (and that of the majority of my colleagues), Miss Erraught's Octavian, with all its virtues, falls on the wrong side of dramatic plausibility. She simply fails to make it credible that she would be having an affair with the Marschallin, fighting a duel with Ochs or captivating Sophie with her manly bravado. As a critic, I must not only reserve but defend the right to comment on the visual aspects of a performance, and that includes germane matters of personal appearance, whether the singer concerned is male or female. I have never traded in gratuitous insults or cheap mockery, but in the theatre I am not reviewing a CD and therefore cannot ignore 25 per cent (or whatever figure you may want to put on it) of what constitutes a musical drama... I am a critic, not a cheerleader."[473]

Though widely admired as a novelist and a film critic, Graham Greene was not above making *ad hominem* comments. Reviewing a scene in *High, Wide and Handsome*, in which Irene Dunne sang to a farm horse, Greene wrote unkindly that the actress could be identified as "the one without the white patch on her forehead."[474]

But his most notorious *ad hominem* review was of Shirley Temple[475]. Greene had previously, in a review of *Captain January* (1936), written that the appeal of the 8 year-old child star "seems to rest on a coquetry quite as mature as Miss (Claudette) Colbert's and an oddly precocious body as voluptuous in grey flannel trousers as Miss (Marlene) Dietrich's."[476]

Greene created a bigger furore – ending his own, highly distinguished career as a film critic and financially ruining the magazine for which he wrote - with his review of *Wee Willie Winkie* a year later, in which he mischievously analyzed Temple's sex appeal:

"Infancy is her disguise, her appeal is more secret and more adult. Already two years ago she was a fancy little piece (real childhood, I think, went out after *The Littlest Rebel*). In *Captain January* she wore trousers with the mature suggestiveness of a Dietrich: her neat and well-developed rump twisted in the tap-dance: her eyes had a sidelong searching coquetry. Now in *Wee Willie Winkie*, wearing short kilts, she is completely totsy. Watch her swaggering stride across the Indian barrack-square: hear the gasp of excited expectation from her antique audience when the sergeant's palm is raised: watch the way she measures a man with agile studio eyes, with dimpled depravity. Adult emotions of love and grief glissade across the mask of childhood, a childhood that is only skin-deep. It is clever, but it cannot last. Her admirers - middle-aged men and clergymen - respond to her dubious coquetry, to the sight of her well-shaped and desirable little body, packed with enormous vitality, only because the safety curtain of story and dialogue drops between their intelligence and their desire."[477]

Twentieth Century Fox successfully sued him and his publication *Night and Day* for libel, claiming that Greene had effectively accused the studio of "procuring" Temple for "immoral purposes" and had implied that she played deliberately to "a public of licentious old men, ready to enjoy the fine flavour of such an unripe, charming little creature".[478]

According to the autobiography of Greene's close friend, the cinema pioneer Alberto Cavalcanti:

"Thanks to vigilant, quick-witted friends, Graham was warned that the Americans producing the film had introduced a writ of libel against him, meaning that not only would the backers of *Night and Day* pay a large fine [in the event, the magazine went out of business], but he, Graham himself, faced a prison sentence. The only solution was to find a country without extradition. They chose Mexico and our poor Graham went away very quickly indeed. Very likely Shirley Temple never learned that it was partly thanks to her that, during his exile, Graham Greene wrote one of his best books [*The Power and The Glory*]."[479]

Greene's "crime" was mainly honesty. There was indeed a sexual component to Shirley Temple's appeal, as she herself was to realise after a much too close encounter with MGM executive Arthur Freed, the producer and head of MGM's legendary musical department. In her 1988 autobiography, she reveals that Freed exposed himself to her:

"Best known as producer of the blockbusting *The Wizard of Oz*, Freed was rumoured in some adult circles to have an adventuresome casting couch. At the time I knew none of this, not would I have recognised such furniture even when sitting on one. To visit an executive of such stature was enough to send my spirits soaring. 'I have something made for just

you,' he continued, fumbling in his lap. 'You'll be my new star!'...
Obviously, Freed did not believe in preliminaries. With his face gaped in a
smile, he stood up abruptly and executed a bizarre flourish of clothing.
Having thought of him as a producer rather than an exhibitor, I sat bolt
upright... Not twelve years old, I still had little appreciation for masculine
versatility and so dramatic was the leap between schoolgirl speculation and
Freed's bedazzling exposure that I reacted with nervous laughter. Disdain
or terror he might have expected, but not the insult of humour. 'Get out!' he
shouted, unmindful of his disarray, imperiously pointing to the closed door.
'Go on, get out!'"[480]

Another child star of Hollywood's so-called golden era, Judy Garland,
had an even closer encounter with Freed's boss at MGM, Louis B. Mayer.
He started groping her in his office, telling her as he put a hand on her left
breast that she "sang from the heart". I often thought I was lucky I didn't
sing from another part of my anatomy, she quipped. When she found the
courage to tell him to back off, he wept in shame."[481]

Like all the best *ad hominem* reviewers, Greene had a serious point; he
was calling attention to the morality – or lack of it – that lay not far beneath
the surface of Hollywood.

By the time *Bugsy Malone* was released in 1976, critics were allowed
to be far more frank about paedophile tendencies in movies. Pauline Kael in
the *New Yorker* called attention to these in her review of Alan Parker's
musical, in which children play gangsters and their molls:

"The almost pornographic dislocation, which is the source of the
film's possible appeal as a novelty, is never acknowledged, but the camera
lingers on a gangster's pudgy, infantile fingers or a *femme fatale's* soft little
belly pushing out of her tight satin dress, and it roves over the pubescent
figures in the chorus line."[482]

Robert Asahina in the *New Leader* described it as "a movie that is
about as offensive as any I have lately seen. *Village Voice* columnist Arthur
Bell has called it 'the first film for gay children'. My own feeling is that it
will probably be less attractive to gay children than to pederasts."[483]

In the *National Review*, John Simon was characteristically direct:

"The film's gimmick is to turn the kids into appallingly realistic scale
models of full-grown brutes and trollops for the amusement of whom, I
wonder? Pederasts and child molesters certainly, who may find something
deliciously provocative about tots got up as delinquent adults; some
backward children, no doubt, who think this film exalts them; and adults
benighted enough to perceive this offal as a lovable masquerade... On top of
its other troubles, *Bugsy* is a musical, with songs by Paul Williams, not one
bar of which strikes me as music. Worse yet, the songs are dubbed in by
adult voices, many if not all belonging to Williams himself. This makes the
transitions from speech to song perfectly ludicrous, and has the further

depressing effect of suggesting that the very mouths of these children have been violated... Now, what could Alan Parker & Company do for an encore? The history of the Campfire Girls performed entirely by androgynous Oriental giants? A movie about horse racing with all the horses played by kangaroos? The life of Albert Einstein in which Einstein is portrayed by a dog postsynched by Paul Williams? An all-male, all-nude *Romeo and Juliet* with songs by David Bowie? In a world where *Bugsy Malone* can get a G rating, anything goes."[484]

So how far is too far? Libby Gelman-Waxner's review of Demi Moore's performance in *We're No Angels* may seem like a personal attack on Moore's acting ability – and it is – but it's also about Hollywood's objectification of women:

"In this movie, Demi Moore plays a poverty-stricken mother during the Depression who prostitutes herself in the dead of winter on the Canadian border, all to help her deaf-mute toddler. Demi first appears in the film taking a topless sponge bath in front of an open window, and throughout she wears mostly sleeveless house dresses with plunging necklines. She always looks fresh and gorgeous, and you expect the other people in the movie to call her Demi and ask about her baby with Bruce Willis; Demi knows that being poor really means turtlenecks and clogged pores, but why bum out the audience? She has clearly studied frontier pouting and shameless hair tossing with Ali McGraw and Christie Brinkley, and she may in fact be the first actress to use movies as a steppingstone to modelling."[485]

Similar thoughts lay behind Ms Gelman-Waxner's tongue-in-cheek review of Nicole Kidman's appearance in *Days of Thunder*:

"Nicole Kidman plays Tom's girlfriend, and like most surgeons, she has lots of frizzy hair in her eyes and wears tight white pantsuits to the track."[486]

Gelman-Waxner was also quick to spot the questionable ethics beneath Julia Roberts' Oscar-nominated turn as a prostitute in *Pretty Woman*:

"*Pretty Woman* is basically a recruiting poster for prostitution as an alternative to grand school or even dating. I'm thinking of telling my adorable six year-old daughter, Jennifer, to rethink her plans for Harvard Law and just head straight for a push-up bra and a big shoulder bag."[487]

My advice to any aspiring critic would be to consider the effect of your review on the people you are criticising. Actors are people too. In her autobiography, *My Story*, film star Ava Gardner was disarmingly honest about how much she had been hurt by criticism:

"Don't think for a minute that bad publicity and endless criticism don't leave their claw marks on everyone concerned. Your friends try to cheer you up by saying lightly, 'I suppose you get used to it, and ignore it.' You try. You try damned hard. But you never get used to it. It always wounds and hurts."[488]

However, personal invective has a place in reviewing, especially when the victim really, really deserves it. Here's Rod Liddle in the *Times*, savaging Piers Morgan for attention-seeking behaviour on the TV show *Morgan & Platell*:

"Amanda Platell, one suspects, might be a rather good interlocutor, but we don't hear much of her because Piers Morgan is hopping up and down all over the place like a demented kangaroo with Tourette's and a bad case of self-obsession."[489]

And this is Charlie Brooker in the *Guardian*, criticising the same show and disliking Platell even more than Morgan:

"It's hard trying to work out which of the two hosts you'd like to smack in the cakehole first. Morgan spends the entire time looking twice as smug as a man who's just learnt to fellate himself. Yet miraculously it's moon-faced putty-nose Platell who snatches first place in the punchability stakes, because there's something about her that suggests she thinks she's gorgeous and pouting. It's a bit like watching a drunken old spinster pinching the waiter's arse at a wedding reception. Still, there is one remarkable side effect to all this, it is the first political show where the politicians are far the most likable people in the studio."[490]

Clive James was famous for his descriptive put-downs. Among his best was his evocation of Dame Barbara Cartland's appearance:

"Twin miracles of mascara, her eyes looked like the corpses of two small crows that had crashed into a chalk cliff."[491]

And Clive wrote an unforgettable one-line description of Arnold Schwarzenegger:

"He looks like a brown condom stuffed with walnuts."[492]

Ban this kind of "abuse" and you'd be censoring some of the most memorable criticism of all time. And it's been going on for years.

Here's W.S. Gilbert (of Gilbert and Sullivan fame) on an actor he detested, Sir Herbert Beerbohm Tree[493]:

"Do you know how they are going to decide the Shakespeare-Bacon dispute? They are going to dig up Shakespeare and dig up Bacon; they are going to set their coffins side by side. And they are going to get Tree to recite Hamlet to them and the one who turns in his coffin will be the author of the play."[494]

Cyril Connolly wittily satirized the tendency of George Orwell to be over-earnest: "He reduced everything to politics... He would not blow his nose without moralizing on conditions in the handkerchief industry."[495]

The normally courteous Dilys Powell greeted the news of Joan Crawford's Oscar with unconcealed disbelief:

"So they gave Joan Crawford an Academy Award for her performance in *Mildred Pierce*... I suppose it is possible to admire her exhibition, through the trying circumstances of this film, of iron-faced imperturbability. Myself, I found the range of expression with which she greeted divorce, death, remarriage, financial ruin and murder so delicate as to approximate to indifference."[496]

One of America's finest film critics, James Agee, reviewing *Out of the Past* in 1947, elegantly captured the unappealing side of Robert Mitchum:

"His curious languor, which suggests Bing Crosby supersaturated with barbiturates, becomes a brand of sexual complacency that is not endearing."[497]

Big-star egotism does need exposing from time to time. In my review of *Jack Reacher* (2012), I decided that Tom Cruise's wrongness for the part warranted *ad hominem* comment:

"In Lee Child's 17 novels, Jack is a hulking, muscular 6 foot 5. Tom Cruise is not. It's inadvertently hilarious to see Cruise beating up people much bigger and younger than he is – like watching an ageing chihuahua mauling a pack of rottweilers...The gorgeous and talented Rosamund Pike has a non-role that requires her to be captured by bad guys and look adoringly at Cruise's finely toned physique. She gets the biggest laugh in the film when she tells Cruise to put his shirt on; I think her line was written to show she was getting hot and bothered by his unclothed manliness, but she delivers it more subversively, as though rebuking him for his vanity. I wonder if he noticed."[498]

I shouldn't imagine Tom Cruise was unduly perturbed by my review, if he bothered to read it, and even if he was I wouldn't regret writing it. Too many stars are insulated from reality by an entourage of yes-people. But critics should bear in mind that they are critics, not murderers of other people's reputations. In 1990, Broadway producer Rocco Landesman made a pertinent comment on why so many people feel uncomfortable around John Simon:

"You have to make important differences between critics and assassins. There are important differences between John Simon and Sirhan Sirhan. Sirhan Sirhan is in prison."[499]

How to Avoid Being Sued

The easiest way to avoid being sued is to check your facts. As long as you do this, anything else you write deserves to be permissible as "fair comment".

But here are two cautionary tales. On 1 November 2008, Lynn Barber wrote a panning review in the *Daily Telegraph* of a book called *Seven Days in the Art World* by Sarah Thornton, a sociologist and writer on contemporary art for *The Economist*.

Despite Barber's review, the book became an international hit. Another critic, Ben Lewis for the *Sunday Times*, praised it as "excellent, vivid, wittily written" and called it "the best book yet about the modern art boom."[500]

Of course, Lynn Barber was entitled to her contrary opinion - especially as she is a respected journalist, a five times winner at the British Press Awards and a famously merciless interviewer of those she feels deserve a hatchet job.[501]

On this occasion, however, she used her position as book reviewer for a major national broadsheet to launch an extremely personal attack on Thornton, matronising her as "a decorative Canadian... with a seemingly limitless capacity to write pompous nonsense".[502]

Barber claimed that Thornton had lied when she said that she had interviewed Barber for the book. Barber also wrote that Thornton had promised "copy approval" to those she had interviewed.[503]

Unfortunately for Barber's credibility, there were records that Sarah Thornton had indeed interviewed her by telephone for over 30 minutes. Even Barber's own appointment diary noted the interview.[504]

Nor did Barber have any convincing explanation of why, if no interview had taken place, Thornton might have promised her "copy approval". Nor could Barber provide evidence that Thornton had granted her interviewees copy approval.[505]

Sarah Thornton alleged that Barber's intent was to "kill the book", either out of personal malice or because three of the other interviewees in her book had been uncomplimentary about Barber as a judge of the Turner Prize for modern art.[506]

In 2011, when the matter finally came to court, she pointed out an unpleasant characteristic of British journalism: "being nasty appears to be the easiest way to get ahead in the UK newspaper world. Fair-mindedness and objectivity are perceived as boring."[507]

The *Daily Telegraph* admitted in April 2009 that the interview allegation was false and that Ms Thornton had never offered her interviewees copy approval.[508] But the falsehoods lingered online, and Thornton sought legal representation to clear her name. The judge found in her favour, fining the newspaper £65,000.[509]

The *Telegraph*'s PR woman stated after the court case that the ruling would have "adverse implications for freedom of expression".[510] But when, as here, journalist A misrepresents the facts in order to attack journalist B, the issue is not freedom of speech. It is whether journalist A has the right to spread a malicious falsehood. The *Telegraph*'s reaction was an ineffectual cover-up for its failure to do the right thing.

In his ruling, Mr Justice Tugendhat made it clear that Thornton v *The Telegraph* was not about a critic's right to pen a panning review. It was about the need to get your facts right – even in a book review.[511] Moreover, if you are going to accuse someone of being a liar, as Barber unwisely did,[512] you had better have your facts straight. And if you do make a factual error, you'd better own up as quickly as possible. As Ms Thornton's senior barrister Ronald Thwaites QC said, "telling lies is not a human right".[513]

My second cautionary tale is about when, even though you may technically be in the right, it may still be ill-advised to sue a critic for libel. In 2014, the world's most famous female architect Zaha Hadid[514] sued the *New York Review of Books*, claiming that architecture critic Martin Filler in his review of Rowan Moore's book *Why We Build* was defamatory.[515] Hadid's lawyers demanded a retraction of the review, which they claimed had caused Hadid "severe emotional and physical distress."[516]

Hadid's lawsuit did result in an apology from Filler. He posted a retraction admitting that his review had confused the number of deaths involved in all construction in Qatar in 2012-13 (almost 1,000) with the number of deaths on Hadid's own Al Wakrah stadium, a venue for the 2022 FIFA World Cup (at that point zero, since building had not started).[517]

However, Hadid's lawsuit had the undesired effect of calling attention to her apparently unfeeling comment that it wasn't her duty to solve the issues of working conditions in Qatar, which had formed the basis of Filler's criticisms. Before the lawsuit, Filler's allegations were confined to readers of the *New York Review of Books*. After the lawsuit, his claims travelled around the world.

Anna Kats, writing for the visual arts website *Blouin ArtInfo*, called the lawsuit "a disturbing, if not absurdly comical, measure of her social consciousness." Kats pointed out that construction workers across the Gulf are regularly exposed to rather more serious forms of such distress while toiling to realise the formal whimsies of many a lauded architect. If Hadid was truly troubled by Filler's statements, she could use her position of authority to do something about their suffering, and her own."[518]

Paul Goldberger in *Vanity Fair* agreed:

"When unhappy subjects of criticism sue the critics who criticise them they rarely come through it looking anything other than spoiled and self-absorbed."[519]

Although Martin Filler was factually mistaken in saying that workers had died on Hadid's project, construction hadn't even begun on her stadium, and deaths on the project look all too likely in the light of Qatar's other construction projects, so the probability is that his opinion will prove in the long run to be well-founded. Perhaps most pertinently, Anna Kats points out that Hadid's lawsuit is terrible public relations:

"Instead of pursuing initiatives that would ensure worker safety and drastically distinguish her construction site from prevalent working conditions for laborers in Qatar, Zaha Hadid pillories the press."[520]

Restaurant critic Jay Rayner, nicknamed "Acid Rayner" for the vitriolic nature of his reviews, explains why he doesn't fear being threatened with lawsuits:

"I know the laws of libel. I know the difference between fair comment ('The soup tasted like it came from a packet, which is remarkable given they must have made it themselves') and a blatant untruth ('The soup came from a packet')."[521]

Rayner may have escaped lawsuits, but Italy's leading restaurant critic, Eduardo Raspelli of the newspaper *La Stampa*, was not so lucky. In May 2003, he was sued for $15 million by McDonald's, after he described their food as "gastronomically repellent" and their hamburgers as "rubbery". He also said their chips were "obscene" and tasted like "cardboard."[522]

McDonalds executives said they had spent $26 million to promote themselves in Italy and were suing for defamation. The lawyer for McDonalds said: "What he said harmed my client's reputation, and it is completely false. We have the proof that McDonald's uses nothing but the finest ingredients, and we will go through this point by point."[523]

The Italian judge told the two parties to come to terms outside the court. Nothing more was heard of the case.[524] Nevertheless, as a result of McDonald's legal action, Raspelli's criticisms were republished around the world.

In the *Guardian*, food critic Jay Rayner went to a branch of McDonald's close to London home and wrote an even more savage review than Mr Raspelli's:

"First I put the slimy grey puck of a burger into my mouth and yes, Mr Raspelli, it is indeed rubbery, but so much worse than that. The thing leaked hot, greasy, salty water into my mouth. Next the bun, whose third ingredient after flour and water is sugar. It was floppy and burnt. Finally, there was a vicious bile-esque back taste to the sauce. So far, so disgusting. On to the chips. Cardboard, yes, but fatty cardboard - and after half a minute any crispness sagged away. Next I tried one of the new dishes recently introduced as part of its 'Ever Changing New Tastes' campaign. Chicken Selects are breaded strips of chicken breast, and are a truly remarkable example of fast-food science. Although they are clearly pieces of breast, they taste of chicken not at all. They taste of salt. And then the worst item of all, a pasta and feta-cheese salad in a lemon and olive-oil dressing. After this one I needed counselling: floppy pasta, cheese-like chalk dust and a syrupy dressing packed with sugar. I studied the ingredients. In the olive-oil dressing, glucose syrup comes ahead of the oil. I only ate this because I was being paid to do so."[525]

In 2004, Shepherd's Restaurant in Westminster, London, said they were considering taking restaurant critic Matthew Norman to court, and described his article in the *Sunday Telegraph* as a "vituperative diatribe" containing "wrong, unfair and defamatory allegations".[526]

Norman had described the restaurant, with perhaps a hint of hyperbole, as "the "eighth circle of hell": "The decor was "fake, dreary, cheap and pompous"; the vinaigrette with his cold asparagus was "an insipid, feckless mayonnaise" that made him wish he had had Hellman's; and the crab and brandy soup reminded him of Saddam Hussein's alleged weapons of mass destruction:

"When I say... that were it found in a canister buried in the Iraqi desert, it would save Tony Blair's skin, I exaggerate only slightly".[527]

That threatened lawsuit never materialized, and Matthew Norman's colourfully negative review received much more coverage throughout the media when it might easily have passed unnoticed, had it been confined to the relatively small readership of the *Sunday Telegraph.*

Caroline Workman was sued for writing a one-star review of Ciaran Convery's Belfast restaurant Goodfellas in *The Irish News* in 2000. The review described the staff as unhelpful, the cola as flat, and the chicken marsala as "so sweet as to be inedible".[528]

Ms Workman assured the jury that her review was "completely honest." The jury didn't believe her, however, and awarded damages of £25,000 plus costs.

Restaurant critic Matthew Norman described the jury verdict as "very worrying news: "You really cannot overstate the imbecility of a libel jury: what we really need now is a sustained campaign against our ludicrous libel laws." [529]

Fortunately for free speech and *The Irish News*, the jury's verdict was overturned by the Court of Appeal, which ruled that the original jury had been misdirected on whether the critic's opinions were defensible as fair comment.[530]

The most bizarre case of a restaurant critic being sued occurred in 2004, when restaurant-owner Phil Roman sued *Dallas Morning News* food reviewer Dotty Griffith for her favourable review of his new Dallas restaurant, Il Mulino.

Ms Griffith awarded the restaurant four stars out of five for food, but Romano challenged her judgment in the light of her criticisms: "With what she said about Il Mulino, I shouldn't have gotten any stars."

Griffith's problem is that she made a series of unwise factual allegations, claiming that the risotto was partially cooked in advance and then finished to order (the lawsuit called this a "scandalous accusation");

that the Spaghetti Bolognese and Penne with Tomato Vodka Sauce were overwrought with butter (according to Romano, there was no butter in the recipe); and that the Porcini-stuffed Ravioli with Champagne Truffle sauce "whispered of Gorgonzola" (Romano denied the presence of Gorgonzola in the dish).[531]

Five months later, Romano dropped his lawsuit when the *Dallas Morning Herald* agreed to re-review his establishment in 2006.[532] Sadly, Il Murino closed in the summer of that year, and almost simultaneously Dotty Griffith retired after 36 years on her local paper.[533]

In 2007, the *Philadelphia Inquirer* was sued after a three-sentence condemnation of Chops Restaurant in Bala Cynwyd, Pennsylvania by food critic Craig LaBan. The review praised the crab cake but described the meal overall as "expensive and disappointing, from the soggy and sour chopped salad to a miserably tough and fatty strip steak."[534]

The resulting libel lawsuit was 16 pages long. Interestingly, it did not dispute that the steak was abysmal. Rather, it said that the journalist "ate a steak sandwich without bread, not a strip steak, and therefore had, and has, no personal knowledge of the quality of the Chops strip steak."[535]

Later, it turned out that the dish in question had not been a steak sandwich but "steak frites" (according to the restaurant's own bill) which rather undermined the lawsuit.[536] The case was settled out of court, after which all parties responded to questions with a terse "No comment". The restaurant closed at the end of June 2013.[537]

In America, very few lawsuits against food critics have amounted to anything. Freedom of speech is guaranteed under the constitution, and judges of every political stripe support it.

When a food critic christened a restaurant dish "Trout à la green plague" the judge's ruling was that "An ordinarily informed person would not infer that these entrees were actually carriers of communicable diseases."

When a reviewer wrote "The fish on the Key West platter tasted like old ski boots" the judge also recognised that this was a joke: "Obviously, that was hyperbole used to indicate that the reviewer found the fish to be dry and tough."

When a restaurant critic recommended "Bring a can of Raid if you plan to eat here" the judge ruled this joke about food hygiene was also permissible: "The techniques of humour and ridicule are protected."[538]

Infamously, one lawsuit against a food critic not only materialized, it resulted in serious damages being paid.

In 2003, *Sydney Morning Herald* critic Matthew Evans gave an eatery called Coco Roco an unfavourable review, calling it "a bleak spot on the culinary landscape," and making observations like "the texture is scary" and "flavours jangle like a car crash." Six months later, the restaurant Coco closed, along with its sister-bistro Roco. The owners filed a defamation suit, claiming that the review had failed to point out that the review had been of Coco, not Roco – although, in fact, Evans had referred in his critique to the fact that there were two eateries at the one location and that he was reviewing Coco, the more expensive one.[539]

In his judgment Justice Harrison said: "I accept Mr Evans' description of the parmesan cheese, the hard sorbet, the dry pork and the sherry-scented white sauce with apricots, the wilting and yellow salad leaves, the starchy lentils, the sticky sweet below-average broth and the overcooked, flavourless potatoes as some examples of poor quality food. A seafood foam that tasted like reflux could not be excluded from this group."[540]

Nevertheless, John Fairfax Publications, owners of the *Sydney Morning Herald*, were successfully sued, and had to pay the restaurant damages of $80,000. A decade-long legal battle eventually cost Fairfax more than $600,000 in damages. Restaurateurs Aleksandra Gacic, Ljiljana Gacic and Branislav Ciric were awarded $623,526 in damages and interest. The moral seems to be: if you want to be an honest critic, don't work in Australia.[541]

Political Correctness Rules OK

One of the things that baffled me for a time when I was a working critic was how isolated I often seemed to be. When, for example, *Braveheart* (1995) came out, I could appreciate why so many people liked it. Handsomely photographed and edited with panache, *Braveheart* would have been worth seeing for its battle sequences alone. Thrillingly shot, they showed not only the horror of war, but also the rush of adrenaline which accompanies it.

Unfortunately, as a former historian I was also able to spot how untruthful the film was. For example, in order to generate a feelgood ending, it devoted an amazing amount of screen time to Wallace's alleged affair with Isabella (Sophie Marceau), wife to the future Edward II. In the film, minutes before Wallace's execution, she taunted the dying Edward I with the news that she is to bear Wallace's son - so Wallace's ultimate triumph would be to father the King of England's heirs.

Hmm. Wallace was executed on August 23rd 1305; Edward I died almost two years later, on July 7th 1307; and Isabella bore her first child - the future Edward III - on November 13th, 1312. Even if we assume that Isabella conceived by Wallace on the eve of his execution, this would make her pregnancy - at seven years, two and a half months - the longest in history.

A bigger and more significant distortion was that the English were portrayed - as in most recent Hollywood films - as vicious imperialists and unmitigated bad guys. Edward Longshanks was portrayed as a greedy tyrant - a cartoon caricature of the real Edward I, who could certainly be cruel (though would a 13th century King have lasted long if he wasn't?), but was also one of the founding fathers of Parliament and the rule of law.

For a three-hour epic, the message in *Braveheart* was disappointingly simple-minded. The issues were reduced to two slogans - Freedom good, Tyranny bad; and Scottish good, English bad.

The "feelgood" postscript suggested that Scotland under Robert Bruce - inspired by the glorious example of Wallace - won its freedom after Bannockburn in 1314. A more truthful postscript might have been that it meant freedom for Scotland to suffer under Bruce's son David II, one of the worst rulers in the history of the British Isles, who ruined his country with his extravagance and futile raids into England, and sold out the independence of Scotland by offering the succession to Edward Longshanks's grandson.

I concluded my *Daily Mail* review with this:

"Braveheart is, in fact, part of that limp-liberal tradition which assumes that Imperialism and Colonialism are invariably bad, while 'freedom-fighters' are honourable, family-loving chaps with no personal axe to grind. I can't help remembering that among recent so-called 'freedom-fighters' have been such charmers as Mao, Pol Pot and Gerry Adams, while among the most notorious imperialists of history have been Thucydides, Sir Francis Bacon and Disraeli. I know who I'd rather be ruled by."[542]

When I wrote that in 1995, I had no idea what the other critics would write about *Braveheart*. I imagined that quite a few others would share my reservations about the film's naïve view of history. But no.

Caryn James in the *New York Times* praised it as "one of the most spectacular entertainments in years."[543] Ian Nathan of *Empire* magazine commended its "rip-roaringly good story-telling". William Leith, in the *Mail on Sunday*, called it "a terrific movie... designed to pump you into a state of high emotion."[544]

Roger Ebert did remark wryly that "the concept of personal freedom was a concept not much celebrated in 1300, but it doesn't stop Gibson from making it his dying cry... Gibson is not filming history here, but myth."[545] However, I found I was the only critic on either side of the Atlantic who, on the film's release, challenged its cavalier disregard for historical truth.

A similar degree of inhibition also seemed to affect most critics' response to Michael Moore's documentary *Bowling for Columbine* (2002). His film posed an important and deadly serious question: why do the USA's gun-related deaths outnumber Canada's each year by an astonishing 11,000 to 165?

Moore found an easy target in America's National Rifle Association, with its assumption that every true American's responsibility is to own a gun. The trouble with blaming the NRA is that gun ownership in Canada is no lower than it is in America; yet Canadians don't go round killing nearly so many of their fellow citizens.

So Moore also blamed America's rulers for setting a bad example with a foreign policy that assumes might is right. He then had a go at capitalism and "white racism" for instilling fear in white people of civil disorder and black people.

Needless to say, he made no attempt to differentiate between cases where America could reasonably be shown to be aggressive, and where it had used violence in its own defence or against ethnic cleansing, as part of NATO. And Moore chose to ignore the inconvenient fact that capitalism is hardly confined to America, and doesn't cause so many gun-related deaths elsewhere.

Moore was also careful not to attempt a breakdown of the numerous American deaths into those which are drug-related, or investigate the extraordinary growth in black-on-black violence which underlies American crime statistics.

In order to increase the effectiveness of his emotional blackmail, Moore seized on some notorious killings of children, especially the massacre at Columbine High School, in which two teenage students murdered 12 of their fellows and one teacher, and another in Moore's hometown of Flint, Michigan, when a black 6 year-old boy shot a little white girl of similar age - whether accidentally or out of malice, we were never told.

Here again, sloppiness and ideological blinkers prevented Moore from investigating the details of the cases. He tried to ascribe the Columbine tragedy, for example, to the school's proximity to Lockheed Martin, which manufactured missiles, but failed to mention the surely more relevant fact that the two teenage student killers were high on drugs when they murdered their fellow pupils. And, in his eagerness to blame the six year-old girl's death on welfare cuts, he chose to ignore the fact that the 6 year-old boy's uncle had left a loaded gun around the house.

Once again, I was surprised to find that the vast majority of critics couldn't be bothered to question Moore's tactics or his assumptions. It won virtually unanimous critical praise, along with the Oscar as best documentary. Yet the film's principal merit, as far as I could see, was that it told people on the Left exactly what they wanted to hear about the American Right.

In the same year, 2004, I read the other reviews of Walter Salles's *The Motorcyle Diaries* and wondered if I was the only critic with a memory.

The film was a long, rambling but beautifully shot road movie romanticising two young Argentinian medics who went on a tour of South

America in 1952 on a decrepit motorcycle. It was a cute, lightweight account of their adventures, in which the leading man, a fragile asthmatic (played by South America's most photogenic actor, Gael Garcia Bernal), saved a puppy, collided with a cow, fell off the bike a lot and became aware – at a curiously late age, for he was supposed to be 23 - that there are a lot of poor people in South America.

And what do you think this nice young man - who looked like a sun-kissed, tousle-haired matinee idol - did with the rest of his life? Did he become a doctor serving the poor? Did he, perhaps, return to Buenos Aires and become a social worker? Did he spend the rest of his life helping lepers? No, of course he didn't. For if he had, producer Robert Redford and Walter Salles would never have bothered to make a film about his early life.

No, he became Che Guevara, a Stalin-worshipping, mass-murdering, Communist leader who helped to destroy industry, society and the rule of law in Cuba, became a remarkably incompetent guerrilla in the Congo and Bolivia, and in 1967 was executed by the Bolivian army (with CIA help) at the age of 39, before he could do too much damage anywhere else in the world.

Rather than produce any hint of what drove such a man to Stalinism, mass murder and the delusion that he had the right to kill anyone who disagreed with him, Walter Salles gave us a simplistic-to-the-point-of-idiocy view of Che as a handsome young man whose eyes welled up at the sight of injustice.

Salles and his writer Jose Rivera depicted a kindly young idealist who wouldn't hurt a fly and is so smiley he wouldn't look out of place in a boy band; yet only two years after the film ends, the 25 year-old Guevera wrote to his aunt after seeing the United Fruit Company's holdings in Costa Rica, "I have sworn before a picture of our old, much lamented comrade Stalin that I will not rest until I see these capitalist octopuses annihilated." In a letter to another aunt, he signed himself "Stalin II".

Salles made no attempt to chronicle the process by which Che's anger at the mistreatment of the "proletariat" turned to hatred. "I feel my nostrils dilate," he wrote in the diaries, "savouring the acrid smell of gunpowder and blood, of the enemy's death."

Only four years after the film ends, Guevara was a commander in Castro's military campaign to overthrow President Batista of Cuba. When he became Castro's second-in-command, Che not only ordered thousands of executions without trial, he even carried out some of them himself. "To send men to the firing squad, judicial proof is unnecessary," Che announced. "These procedures are an archaic bourgeois detail. This is a revolution! And a revolutionary must become a cold killing machine motivated by pure hate."

This adorable young man also pioneered Cuba's system of prison camps, founding the first gulag at Guanahacabibes, which he filled with those he described as "people who have committed crimes against revolutionary morals". These included harmless dissidents and social "deviants", such as homosexuals, Jehovah's Witnesses and even people who played loud music. It is a pleasing irony that many who worship the idealized Guevara would have been the first to have been imprisoned or executed by him, had they ever met.

As head of Cuba's National Bank and Minister for Industry, posts for which he was spectacularly unqualified, Che imposed a system of Stalinist central planning that brought economic devastation to his adopted country, which continues to this day and has sent thousands of Cubans into exile.

Yet Walter Salles's film chose to portray Che as a kindly humanitarian. By excluding everything that was despicable about the man and then announcing in a closing caption that he was, in effect, murdered by the CIA, Salles strove to aggrandize this icon of the Left as a kindly, selfless young man who died heroically for his beliefs.

Unsurprisingly, critical reaction to the movie was overwhelmingly positive, across the political spectrum. Jason Solomons in the left-leaning *Observer* pronounced it "a triumph". Cosmo Landesman in the centre-right *Sunday Times* called it "a joy." Even Baz Bamigboye in the right-wing *Daily Mail* raved that it was "a stunning movie."

In the UK, there were two honourable exceptions. Jenny McCartney in the right-wing *Sunday Telegraph* saw through the cultural and political subterfuge:

"Salles' reluctance even to hint at a more complicated reality means that, despite its enormous aesthetic charms, this film has the sentimental soul of a dim-wittted adolescent."

Much to his credit, Peter Bradshaw swam against the tide of political culture within the *Guardian* by pointing out that the film left an awful lot out, and was:

"A sentimentalisation of Che himself, for whom this film contrives the slightly humdrum climax of swimming heroically between two islands of the leper colony. We see our young hero struggling with his asthma, which is treated with old-fashioned glass hypodermics of adrenaline. These are said to have given Che his ferocious rages: an unlovely side to his personality, and surely a part of his revolutionary temperament, but quite absent from this film."[546]

A similar critical response took place in the United States, with the vast majority of critics praising the film, and a very small minority pointing out the film's blatant political bias.

Roger Ebert – whose political views were Liberal Democrat – spotted what lay behind the movie's critical success:

"The movie is receiving devoutly favorable reviews. They are mostly a matter of Political Correctness, I think; it is uncool to be against Che Guevara. But seen simply as a film, *The Motorcycle Diaries* is attenuated and tedious."[547]

Braveheart, Bowling for Columbine and *The Motorcycle Diaries* are just three of many, many examples where most critics were too scared, ignorant or left-wing to challenge the film-makers' assumptions. There is a fashionable view of critics that they are hidebound by something called "political correctness", but the truth is that most critics' fear of raising their heads above the invisible parapet and running the risk of being criticised themselves has its roots in something far deeper and more insidious... Oh dear, I can put it off no longer. Let's talk about critical theory.

The Weird and Wacky World of Critical Theory

The novelist and critic Martin Amis [548] claims, not altogether convincingly, that he and his pals (including Julian Barnes[549], Christopher Hitchens[550] and Craig Raine[551]) talked of little else but Critical Theory when Martin worked on the *Times Literary Supplement* in the 1970s[552]. My own memory of knowing these people at Oxford[553] consists of everyone getting seriously drunk and then trying to remember the lyrics of Buddy Holly[554] songs but hey, maybe they dumbed themselves down when I was around.

In my three decades as a reviewer of music, books, theatre, television and film, mingling with reviewers of every level of IQ from genius to well below igloo temperature, I've never heard a single working critic mention or discuss Critical Theory. They were all too busy being critics.

Whenever I read books on Critical Theory – and, in a spirit of masochistic self-improvement, I must have ploughed through virtually all of them – I'm struck by how remote they are from the practical realities of getting a job as a critic and keeping it.

Critical theory has its roots in several traditions, but predominantly in Marxism. In the Soviet Union, Communists were dogmatic critics of all art. "Art," wrote the Russian constructivist Alexander Rodchenko, "has no place in modern life... Every cultured modern man must wage war against art, as against opium."[555]

In 1993, the French Marxist poet Louis Aragon wrote:
"The universe must hear
a voice shouting the glory of materialistic dialectics
marching on its feet on its thousands of feet
shod in military boots
on its feet magnificent as violence
holding out its host of arms bearing weapons

to the image of victorious Communism
Glory to materialist dialectics
And glory to its incarnation
The Red
Army."[556]

Decades later, after the collapse of Russian Communism, few intellectuals in the West are as enthusiastic about Communism, yet vestiges of that old arrogance towards artists remains. The famous literary critic George Steiner[557], interviewed in 1994, reminded his colleagues that critics had lost their humility. He blamed this on the rise of academic critical theory, which placed the critic above the creator:

"Today we're told there is critical theory, that criticism dominates — deconstruction, semiotics, post-structuralism, postmodernism. It is a very peculiar climate, summed up by that man of undoubted genius, Monsieur Derrida, when he says that every text is a 'pretext.' This is one of the most formidably erroneous, destructive, brilliantly trivial wordplays ever launched. Meaning what? That whatever the stature of the poem, it waits for the deconstructive commentator; it is the mere occasion of the exercise. That is to me ridiculous beyond words...The notion that students today read second- and third-hand criticism of criticism, and read less and less real literature, is absolutely the death of the normal naive and logical order of precedence."[558]

Although Steiner has had many an argument with the American literary critic Harold Bloom[559], both believe the literary critic should retain a proper humility towards original texts, especially when they are of the highest quality.

"The proper attitude to take," says Bloom, "toward Shakespeare, toward Dante, toward Cervantes, toward Geoffrey Chaucer, toward Tolstoy, toward Plato — the great figures — is indeed awe, wonder, gratitude, deep appreciation. I can't really understand any other stance in relation to them. I mean, they have formed our minds."[560]

Though an academic and a literary critic, Bloom is dismissive of many modern academic approaches to literature:

"To a rather considerable extent, literary studies have been replaced by that incredible absurdity called cultural studies which, as far as I can tell, are neither cultural nor are they studies. But there has always been an arrogance, I think, of the semi-learned. We have this nonsense called Theory with a capital T, mostly imported from the French and now having evilly taken root in the English-speaking world. And that, I suppose, also has encouraged absurd attitudes toward what we used to call imaginative literature... Throughout the English-speaking world, the wave of French theory was replaced by the terrible mélange that I increasingly have come to call the School of Resentment — the so-called multiculturalists and feminists who tell us we are to value a literary work because of the ethnic background or the gender of the author."[561]

To Bloom, the important things for a critic is to examine the text with care and, if possible, sympathy. For him, the dogma of modern critical theory are anathema:

"What theory did the great critics have? Critics like Dr. Samuel Johnson or William Hazlitt? Those who adopt a theory are simply imitating somebody else. I believe firmly that, in the end, all useful criticism is based upon experience. An experience of teaching, an experience of reading, one's experience of writing — and most of all, one's experience of living. Just as wisdom, in the end, is purely personal."[562]

Novelist and critic Geoff Dyer[563] wrote an interestingly splenetic piece about the way academic criticism has driven itself up a blind alley, in the form of his 1998 book *Out of Sheer Rage: In The Shadow of D.H. Lawrence*. He describes his own final year at university (he attended Corpus Christi, Oxford studying English):

"In my final year at university there was a great deal of fuss about course reform. Instead of ploughing through everything from Beowulf to Becket, academics like Terry Eagleton were proposing a 'theory' option. I didn't know what theory was but it sounded radical and challenging. Within a few years 'theory', whatever it was, had achieved a position of dominance in English departments throughout Britain. Synoptic works of theory were pouring from the presses. Fifteen years down the line these texts still appear radical and challenging except in one or two details, namely that they are neither radical nor challenging."[564]

Philosopher and critic Roger Scruton[565] laments the rise of "gender studies and other forms of essentially ideological confrontation with the modern world."[566] Scruton believes that such activism poses as free inquiry, but is in fact nothing of the sort:

"The whole defining nature of philosophy is that you start from free inquiry and you don't actually know what you're going to come up with as a result of your arguments. To think that you have to have the conclusion prior to the investigation is effectually to say that this is a form of indoctrination."[567]

He points out that "feminist studies" in universities work from a premise that is highly controversial, but largely unexamined by its practitioners:

"It's quite clear that the feminist position is not accepted by everyone in the world around us, that it isn't something that you have to have as a premise for your worldview if we are to see the world in which we live as it is. It's not like the morality which tells us 'Thou shalt not kill' and so on. And there is a kind of a closing of the mind that has happened here which excludes those that disagree with a particular position. And considering that some of those are highly intelligent people who don't just wallow in their own prejudices, this is obviously a threat to our academic freedom... I think what has happened is that new subjects, or new disciplines, so called, have come into being which... require adherence to a particular conclusion."[568]

Scruton argues that subjects such as English and art history grew from the desire to teach young people the difference between beauty and kitsch, real feeling and phoney sentiment, depth and superficiality:

"Conservatives often complain about the politicization of the universities, and about the fact that only liberal views are propagated or even tolerated on campus. But they fail to see the true cause of this, which is the internal collapse of the humanities. When judgment is marginalized or forbidden nothing remains save politics. The only permitted way to compare Jane Austen and Maya Angelou, or Mozart and Meshuggah, is in terms of their rival political postures. And then the point of studying Jane Austen or Mozart is lost. What do they have to tell us about the ideological conflicts of today, or the power struggles that are played out in the faculty common room?"[569]

Scruton believes – and I agree with him – that a revolution is needed within universities to salvage the humanities:

"The true conservative cause, when it comes to the universities, ought to be the restoration of judgment to its central place in the humanities. And that shows how difficult a task the recapture of the universities will be. It will require a confrontation with the culture of youth, and an insistence that the real purpose of universities is not to flatter the tastes of those who arrive there, but to present them with a rite of passage into something better."[570]

Critical theorists often try to deny the triumph of capitalism over socialism by describing western economies as "late capitalist", thus implying that their demises are to be expected around the next historical corner.

Marxism is alive and well in universities, especially in the areas known as "cultural studies" or "critical theory". Instead of positing old-school Marxist class warfare, the neo-Marxists regard bourgeois "culture" (however they define it) as inherently oppressive and the proletariat (another ever-changing concept tied up with race, gender, sexuality and any other hobbyhorse the theorist cares to ride) unfairly dispossessed.

They agree with Antonio Gramsci[571] that cultural hegemony is the means to class dominance, and with Gyorgy Lukacs[572] who believed that the existing culture must be destroyed. It was Lukacs who, in 1923, founded the Institute of Social Research at Frankfurt University in Germany. This institute, modeled on the Marx-Engels Institute in Moscow, broke up with the rise of the Nazis and diffused around the world, but mainly in American universities.

In the 1960s, their views became popular, largely as a reaction to the Vietnam war, and some members of the "Frankfurt school" such as Herbert Marcuse[573] became famous. Marcuse echoed Mao's concept of cultural revolution:

"One can rightfully speak of a cultural revolution, since the protest is directed toward the whole cultural establishment, including morality of existing society."[574]

It was Marcuse who invented the catchphrase "Make love, not war." He was adopted as the intellectual guru of the hippie movement. For Marcuse, the only answer to the problem of fascism was communism. "The Communist Parties are, and will remain, the sole anti-fascist power," he declared. For this reason, he urged Americans not to be too hard on the totalitarian experiments of their communist enemies, asserting that "the denunciation of neo-fascism and Social Democracy must outweigh denunciation of Communist policy."[575]

In his book *Intellectual Morons*, Daniel J. Flynn compares Marcuse's views on labour with those of Marx:

"Marx argued against the exploitation of labour; Marcuse, against labour itself. Don't work, have sex. This was the simple message of *Eros and Civilisation*, released in 1955. Its ideas proved to be extraordinarily popular among the fledgling hippie culture of the following decade. It provided a rationale for laziness and transformed degrading personal vices into virtues. This elevation of laziness included self-conscious rejection of the 'work' of keeping oneself clean. Thus, Marcuse argued that those who returned to a more primitive state must reject personal hygiene and experience the freedom of embracing a 'body unsoiled by plastic cleanliness.'"[576]

Marcuse also argued that traditional ideas of tolerance – the notion, for example, that you should not imprison, torture or execute those of whose views you disapprove – were something he called "repressive tolerance". Marcuse wished to replace these laissez-faire attitudes with something he called "liberating tolerance". This involved being sternly hostile to anything perceived as coming from the Right, while bending over backwards to empathise with the struggle of anyone perceived as oppressed, such as women, blacks, homosexuals and immigrants. In other words, Marcuse and his followers have attempted to turn intolerance into a virtue.

Nowadays, this intolerance is often known as "political correctness" and regarded as something of a joke. Nevertheless, the imposition of political correctness is of huge importance to the hard-line Left. Marcuse frankly believed in shifting the balance between Right and Left by restraining the liberty of the Right.

Instead of the old notion of tolerance, which accepted that some values and viewpoints were wrong-headed but needed to be tolerated, there grew up a new and obviously barmy belief on the Left that all values and viewpoints are equally legitimate – except, of course, any notion that runs counter to whatever notions are currently fashionable on the Left.

Marcuse's views have not only lingered on, they dominate the academic Left. In 2014, John Agresto, a former president of St John's College in Santa Fe, warned that liberal arts are "dying", because they are so out of touch with reality. He argued that critical theory was, paradoxically, discouraging truly critical thinking in students. He spoke in favour of an older mode of instruction, which involved not so much preaching and converting as instilling critical thinking skills. He wanted students to ask questions and see a variety of answers, and not to be led towards one particular point of view. He added that it doesn't matter that Dante and Homer are "dead white males", and he denied that bringing Shakespeare to students is an "ethnocentric act".[577]

Mr Agresto's words, unsurprisingly, fell on deaf ears. In the wonderfully simple world of critical theory, the villains of the piece are authority, capitalism, Christianity, conservatism, convention, ethnocentrism, the family, global warming, heredity, hierarchy, loyalty, morality, nationalism, patriarchy, patriotism, sexual restraint and tradition. Any cultural artifact that can be construed as advocating any of these things is quite simply wrong.

Good guys are dedicated to concepts such as "tolerance" and "diversity", though for some reason these concepts do not extend to anyone who subscribes to any of the core values that are considered villainous. Anyone using the wrong word or phrase must be denounced as racist, sexist, or homophobic. Especially in academic and increasingly in media circles, offences of this kind are sackable. Elsewhere, the invention of "hate crimes" leads to people serving jail sentences for their political thoughts.

Roger Scruton points to four beliefs that are widely held by intelligent people, but now effectively forbidden on American campuses:

"(1) The belief in the superiority of Western culture; (2) The belief that there might be morally relevant distinctions between sexes, cultures, and religions; (3) The belief in good taste, whether in literature, music, art, friendship, or behaviour; and (4) The belief in traditional sexual mores. You can entertain those beliefs, but it is dangerous to confess to them, still more dangerous to defend them, lest you be held guilty of 'hate speech' — in other words, of judging some group of human beings adversely. Yet the hostility to these beliefs is not founded on reason and is never subjected to rational justification. The postmodern university has not defeated reason but replaced it with a new kind of faith — a faith without authority and without transcendence, a faith all the more tenacious in that it does not recognise itself as such."[578]

Critical theory pretends to be non-judgmental but is really the opposite. The Leftist orthodoxy is that all cultures are equal and that judgment between them is absurd. However, it simultaneously argues a contradictory belief - that Western culture and the traditional curriculum are racist, ethnocentric, patriarchal and well beyond the pale of political acceptability. In other words, they presuppose the very universalist vision that they declare to be impossible.

Multi-culturalism affects to be non-judgmental but is quick to call anyone who expresses doubts about one religion or culture as opposed to another, as "racist". The multicultural ideal thus turns into a form of intellectual apartheid. All criticism of minority cultures is censored out of public debate. Small wonder that members of disaffected minorities quickly conclude that it is possible to reside in a European state as an "enemy within" and still enjoy all the rights and privileges that are the reward of citizenship.

The intellectual climate that I grew up in is radically different from the present one, and – as more critics emerge from universities – it is as well to remember the strengths of the old ways, and the dangers of the new ones. In the old days, a student could emerge from a course as a conservative, socialist or liberal and still be able to demonstrate the knowledge that his or her course had imparted. To that extent, the courses were apolitical.

In the new climate, many courses are proudly political, built around an agenda and designed to indoctrinate in one direction, and to close minds in any other. Some will claim that the old ways were themselves repressive, but – as Scruton has written – western civilisation has, in fact, rewarded dissidence rather than forbidden it:

"Think of those vociferous critics of Western civilisation such as the late Edward Said and the ubiquitous Noam Chomsky. Said spoke out in uncompromising and, at times, even venomous terms on behalf of the Islamic world against what he saw as the lingering outlook of Western imperialism. As a consequence, he was rewarded with a prestigious chair at a leading university and countless opportunities for public speaking in America and around the Western world. The consequences for Chomsky have been largely the same. This habit of rewarding our critics is, I think, unique to Western civilisation. The only problem with it is that, in our universities, things have gone so far that there are no rewards given to anyone else. Prizes are distributed to the left of the political spectrum because it feeds the ruling illusion of those who award them: namely, that self-criticism will bring us safety, and that all threats come from ourselves, and from our desire to defend what we have."[579]

One of the worst aspects of critical theory as a political force is that its champions see no need to be practical, or positive. The best way to destroy western culture and capitalism is *not* to suggest an alternative. Except in the broadest sense of describing what they're against (patriarchy, prejudice, sexism, etc), critical theorists say it can't be done, that we can't imagine a truly free society.

For them, Critical Theory is about criticising as destructively as possible, so that the current order can be brought down. Ostensibly humanitarian messages are employed to show why capitalism must be destroyed. The Left's view of the Right is that anyone who disagrees with left-wing thinking is evil. This is a markedly different view of the Right's view of the Left, which is that those on the Left are mistaken.

Presumably, once the Right has been routed, a new non-racist, non-sexist, pro-gay, pro-green utopia will miraculously spring into being, though theorists seem unable or reluctant to say how. Let us hope that one of their first acts in office will not be to send anyone who disagrees with their principles to prison, or the gas chamber. But anyone who has studied the teachings of Pol Pot in Cambodia may notice disturbing similarities.

In Praise of Constructive Criticism

Contrary to many people's beliefs, criticism is as much about appreciation as it is about finding fault. Criticism can be useful, constructive and even creative. As Abraham Lincoln[580] remarked, "He has a right to criticise, who has a heart to help."[581]

One of America's most celebrated essayists, Ralph Waldo Emerson, wrote:

"Criticism should not be querulous and wasting, all knife and root-puller, but guiding, instructive, inspiring, a south wind, not an east wind."[582]

Former film editor of the *Sunday Times* George Perry regards Dilys Powell as the best critic he's ever known, partly because she was so quick to see good in a movie:

"Her wisdom was tempered with her extraordinary humanity. She had the ability to discern merit in the unlikeliest contexts. For instance she singled out the brief appearance of an unknown actor in a forgotten modest pot-boiler called *The Day they Robbed the Bank of England*. Her review helped Peter O'Toole land *Lawrence of Arabia*."[583]

Irving Wardle, former theatre critic of the *Times* and *Independent on Sunday*, argues that professional critics have a duty to try and find good in the things they witness, however easy it may be to do the opposite:

"Hostile notices are much easier to write; if only for the reason that hostility allows you to remain in command, and thus generates mental energy. Admiration puts you in a subordinate role - the artist has done something that is beyond you - which may reduce you to gushing drivel or tongue-tied paralysis. Hostility also appeals to mob opinion; you can hold the victim at arm's length and deliver the attack without divulging much of yourself. When it comes to praise, you have to expose your own values, thus laying yourself open to public derision."[584]

However, Wardle warns against advising practitioners on what they should be doing better:

"Prescriptive criticism goes wrong, and causes justified offence, when it seeks to instruct an artist on how he should have done his job... Whatever the meaning of 'constructive criticism', it does not mean hovering about, making helpful suggestions - at which point the professional commentator turns into the would-be artist. This kind of comment is not criticism: it is a bid to stage your own show."[585]

Humorist Stephen Potter[586] neatly twisted the knife into some literary critics' pretensions when he wrote ironically:

"Your function as a critic is to show that it is really you yourself who should have written the book, if you had had the time."[587]

Stephen Fry[588] has often poured scorn on critics for thinking they are "better" than the artists they are criticising. He finds it especially presumptuous when they offer constructive criticism. The critic he regards as especially annoying is TV reviewer Allison Pearson, whom he consigned to hellish oblivion in the comedy TV show *Room 101*, but I'd like to think he had me in mind for criticising his contribution to Kenneth Branagh's atrocious film of Mozart's *The Magic Flute*, of which I wrote:

"Stephen Fry may be a polymath, but on this evidence he is to lyric-writing what Stephen Sondheim is to quantity surveying. This is a shockingly inept libretto, lacking wit, intelligence or even basic competence. Fry attempts to rhyme girls and world, tease me with easy, and – ghastliest of all - dominion with wisdom. What's more, this diabolical torture goes on for 130 minutes. Aaaaaaaagh!"[589]

Despite Mr Fry's assertions to the contrary, I would argue that if reviewers do their job by pointing out the technical weaknesses of a work, suggesting which parts work less well than others, pointing out things that are missing or that have been included but should not have been, then artists should be able to learn from those reviews and produce better works in future.

It is also hard to resist pointing out when, say, a novel you love has been travestied by the miscasting of a single actor. The film I'm thinking of is *One Day* (2011), based on David Nicholls' word-of-mouth bestseller, which struck me as not only a charming, cleverly structured romcom but one of the most socially observant books about Britain in the last twenty years.

The central point of my movie review was that the film had been compromised by the miscasting of the talented young American actress Anne Hathaway in the lead:

"She's as awful here as she was terrific in *The Devil Wears Prada*. It's not so much that she can't do a Yorkshire accent, though this comes and goes from scene to scene; but the effort of maintaining an English accent of any kind utterly destroys her performance, much as it did her dire attempt to impersonate Jane Austen in *Becoming Jane*... Hathaway is far too slim and conventionally beautiful for the role, and should never have been cast in the first place. The same might have been said of Renee Zellweger in *Bridget Jones's Diary*, but she took steps to prepare, put on weight and de-glamorized herself. All Hathaway does is wear glasses and sport some unbecoming haircuts; it's never enough. On the page, Emma struck me as a potentially Oscar-winning role, one with whose insecurities and moments of self-destructive spikiness billions of women could identify. I imagined Anna Maxwell-Martin in the role – a Yorkshire-born actress you may have seen in the TV series *South Riding, North and South* and *Bleak House*. Hathaway just doesn't have the depth, sexual angst or sheer ability required to develop the role. It needed a young Judi Dench; it gets someone who reduces each scene she's in to TV sitcom. All the best scenes are ones where she's off-screen."[590]

Was my review presumptuous? Possibly. It was certainly too late to do anything about the casting of Anne Hathaway. But I hope that in pointing out the disastrous consequences of miscasting "bankable" American actors in roles that could be played far better by indigenous talent, I was being constructive and helping others to avoid making the same mistake; and I've found an awful lot of people who agreed with my analysis.

Another function of good, constructive criticism is to call people's attention to virtues they might otherwise have missed. It can encourage and publicize new talent. It can rediscover old talent.

It may even lead to action. Nigel Andrews of the *Financial Times* thinks this is what happened with Oliver Stone's *Alexander*:

"Several critics – including this one – said the essential problem of Oliver Stone's *Alexander* was its lousy structure. They/we pointed out ways in which the film could be better structured. Stone took the advice, or seemed to, when reissuing the film on the DVD. The same kind of thing can happen between a film's festival showing and its commercial release. The director can take on board the critical reaction at the festival and modify or re-edit."[591]

Constructive reviews can entertain. They can be witty and humorous. They can open eyes and broaden horizons. Just like good art, in fact. For me, two constructive critics of the past stand out: William Hazlitt and John Ruskin.

The Genius of Hazlitt

Although reasonable claims might be made for George Bernard Shaw, Oscar Wilde and Graham Greene, to my mind William Hazlitt is the finest writer ever to take to criticism. It is a pity he has fallen out of fashion.

His style of criticism – learned but subjective, and refusing to judge by a set of fixed rules – was indebted to Samuel Taylor Coleridge, the poet, who was also a fine critic with many illuminating observations about Shakespeare, Milton and Wordsworth. Coleridge and Hazlitt were the first critics to introduce psychology into literary criticism.

Hazlitt's classic sports review, *The Fight*, was nearly turned down for publication in the *New Monthly Magazine* of February 1822 as "a very vulgar thing". It's the finest piece Hazlitt ever wrote, combining the ebullience of Henry Fielding with the instinctive populism of Charles Dickens. It describes the boxing match between Tom Hickman, nicknamed "The Gas-man" and Bill Neate. It took place in Hungerford, Berkshire on 11 December 1821.

The whole essay, which I recommend every aspiring critic to read in full, brilliantly encapsulates Hazlitt's notion of reviewing as a kind of heightened, super-sensitive description:

"A genuine criticism should, as I take it, reflect the colours, the light and shade, the soul and body of a work."[592]

For Hazlitt, criticism was a creative act, and a living and enhancing part of our life as citizens. As he implies in his respect for the boxers in *The Fight*, the critic also has to be a pugilist, prepared to give and take blows.

Hazlitt's criticism covered many areas including politics and society, but his writing on the arts managed to be well-informed and wide-ranging. In all his writing he conveyed a commendable passion and support for creativity.

In the early nineteenth century, Hazlitt wrote with particular eloquence in praise of the artist Hogarth, whose reputation had been low since his death in 1764. The critic said his pictures "breathe a certain close, greasy, tavern air". Hazlitt maintained that beyond the comical there lurked a remarkable "power of invention" and a "wonderful knowledge of human life and manners."

Hazlitt praised Hogarth's "research, the profundity, the absolute truth and precision of the delineation of character; in the invention of incident, in wit and humour; in the life, in which they are 'instinct in every part', in everlasting variety and originality.... They stimulate the faculties as well as soothe them." [593]

Hazlitt justified his liking for Hogarth by guiding his readers through various works, especially *Marriage a la Mode, The Rake's Progress* and the *Election* series. It's an exemplary precursor to modern art criticism.

Hogarth also enthused about the energy of Renaissance painters:

"There is a gusto in the colouring of Titian. Not only do his heads seem to think - his bodies seem to feel. This is what the Italians mean by the *morbidezza* of his flesh-colour. It seems sensitive and alive all over' not merely to have the look and texture of flesh, but the feeling in itself. For example, the limbs of his female figures have a luxurious softness and delicacy, which appears conscious of the pleasures of the beholder... Michael Angelo's forms are full of gusto. They everywhere obtrude the sense of power upon the eye. His limbs convey an idea of muscular strength, of moral grandeur, and even of intellectual dignity, they are firm, commanding, broad, and massy, capable of executing with ease the determined purposes of the will."[594]

Hazlitt loved the theatre. His praise of Shakespeare was well-informed and articulate, especially about Shakespeare's tragedies:

"*Lear* stands first for the profound intensity of the passion; *Macbeth* for the wildness of the imagination and the rapidity of the action; *Othello* for the progressive interest and powerful alternations of feeling; *Hamlet* for the refined development of thought and sentiment. If the force of genius shown in each of these works, their variety is not less so."[595]

We are also indebted to Hazlitt for his vivid description of Mrs Siddons playing Lady Macbeth:

"We can conceive of nothing grander. It was something above nature. It seemed almost as if a superior order had dropped from a higher sphere to awe the world with the majesty of her appearance. Power was seated on her brow, passion emanated from her breast as from a shrine; she was tragedy personified. In coming on in the sleeping-scene, her eyes were open, but their sense as shut. She was like a person bewildered and unconscious of what she did. Her lips moved involuntarily; all her gestures were involuntary and mechanical. She glided on and off the stage like an apparition. To have seen her in that character was an event in every one's life, not to be forgotten." [596]

Hazlitt even dared to criticise the critics. He smartly summarized the way reviewers are apt to be ungenerous to those they regard as rivals, or who have appeared to disrespect them in the past. (Some things, regrettably, never change.) Hazlitt wrote of William Wordsworth:

"Had he been less fastidious in pronouncing sentence on the work of others, his own would have been received more favourably, and treated more leniently."[597]

It was left to Hazlitt to champion the much-maligned poet:

"There is little mention of mountainous scenery in Mr Wordsworth's poetry; but by internal evidence one might be almost sure that it was written in a mountainous country, from its bareness, its simplicity, its loftiness and its depth!"[598]

In the opening paragraph of his portrait of Wordsworth, Hazlitt praises him as a courageous experimental poet who rejects mythological figures and poetic diction:

"His style is vernacular: he delivers household truths. He sees nothing loftier than human hopes, nothing deeper than the human heart. This he probes, this he tampers with, this he poises, with all its incalculable weight of thought and feeling, in his hands, and at the same time calms the throbbing pulses of his own heart by keeping his eye ever fixed on the face of nature."[599]

William Hazlitt's last words – "Well, I've had a happy life"[600] – suggest that he was content with his life's work, as well he should have been. However, critics wishing to follow in his footsteps should be aware that he died in poverty in a Soho lodging house, aged only 52. His stomach was riddled with cancer, and he had two broken marriages behind him. His social reputation was in tatters after an ill-advised affair with a landlord's daughter half his age. His political reputation was little better, because he took the unpopular view that Napoleon was a great man who had remained commendably true to the principles of the French Revolution.

His landlady was so eager to rent out his room as quickly as possible that she hid his body under the bed as she showed around new, potential tenants.

A Limp-Wristed Fop? In Defence of Ruskin

To my mind, Mike Leigh's biopic of Britain's greatest Victorian artist, *Mr Turner*, was overpraised. It's a classic example of a film that impressed critics but disappointed audiences. That is borne out by its rating on the website *Rotten Tomatoes*. With critics, it rated a near-perfect 98%; with audiences, it rated an indifferent 60%.

It was called a "masterpiece" by most critics on both sides of the Atlantic. Weirdly, they didn't seem to notice Mike Leigh's facile sideswipe at them, via his characterization of John Ruskin, played in the movie by Joshua McGuire as a limp-wristed fop, a posturing nincompoop, speaking in a high, affected voice and pontificating arrogantly like Brian Sewell on helium, while Turner fixed him with a stolid stare and an air of imperturbable artistic superiority.

It was all too evident from their reviews that modern critics knew little more about John Ruskin than that he was a critic with a thing about pubic hair, being accustomed only to the frozen marble bodies of classical sculpture. Famously, his marriage to Effie Gray (commemorated in an equally misleading film named after her by Emma Thompson) was annulled on grounds of his impotence.

In Thompson's film, her off-screen husband Greg Wise played Ruskin as an austere ascetic, whose passions were reserved for the stones of Venice and the painting of the pre-Raphaelites. However, it is arguable that, far from being disgusted by his new bride's physicality, Ruskin became aware that she had married him for money, not love, after her father's bankruptcy; and when Effie sued for annulment on grounds of his impotency, Ruskin was too gentlemanly to raise an objection.

Whatever the peculiarities of his private life, Ruskin deserves admiration as the best art critic this country has ever produced and the selfless patron of the pre-Raphaelites and of J.M.W. Turner.

Ruskin celebrated Turner above all other artists. He wrote that his paintings "move and mingle among the pale stars, and rise up into the brightness of the illimitable heaven, whose soft, and blue eye gazes down into the deep waters of the sea for ever".

At first sight, Ruskin's love of Turner's impressionistic, whirling patterns of colour and the Pre-Raphaelites' obsessive attention to realistic detail may seem contradictory. Ruskin, however, believed that both styles of painting revealed God's work. He concocted a new, romantic theory of art – partly inspired by Wordsworth's poetry – that emphasized sincerity, intensity and imagination. His argument was that art does not merely imitate the natural world, it makes statements about it.

He was also the first English art critic to place individual works, both ancient and modern, in their social, political, economic, and intellectual contexts. He was far from a prudish conservative or a foppish aesthete; he was a revolutionary. As Arnold Hauser writes in his *Social History of Art*:

"Ruskin was the first person in England to emphasize the fact that art is a public concern and its cultivation one of the most important tasks of the state, in other words, that it represents a social necessity and that no nation can neglect it without endangering its intellectual existence. He was, finally, the first to proclaim the gospel that art is not the privilege of artists, connoisseurs and the educated classes, but is part of every man's inheritance and estate.... His influence was extraordinary, almost beyond description.... The purposefulness and solidity of modern architecture and industrial art are very largely the result of Ruskin's endeavours and doctrines."[601]

Ruskin loved Gothic art because of the way it escaped from the demands of economics and function, and represented the individual arts' love of ornament and creativity. He told his readers:

"Go forth again to gaze upon the old cathedral front where you have smiled so often at the fantastic ignorance of the old sculptors: examine once more those ugly goblins, and formless monsters, and stern statues, anatomiless and rigid; but do not mock at them, for they are signs of the life and liberty of every workman who struck the stone; a freedom of thought, and rank in scale of being, such as no laws, no charters, no charities can secure; but which it must be the first aim of all Europe at this day to regain for her children."[602]

Ruskin was not an uncritical lover of Gothic. Ruskin took detours on his daily walks in order to avoid seeing the striped red-brick Keble College, Oxford[603]; and he much preferred the modernistic architecture of King's Cross railway station to the ornately Gothic style of St Pancras station nearby.[604] Ruskin's mission was not so much to lay down laws of architecture as to enable his contemporaries to see art through his eyes. He was a great teacher. For example, when he was discussing how shadows look like in water, he writes:

"It is always to be remembered that, strictly speaking, only light objects are reflected and that the darker ones are seen only in proportion to the number of rays of light that they can send; so that a dark object comparatively loses its power to affect the surface of water, and the water in the space of a dark reflection is seen partially with the image of the object, and partially transparent. It will be found on observation that under a bank, suppose with dark trees above showing spaces of bright sky, the bright sky is reflected distinctly, and the bottom of the water is in those places not seen, but in the dark spaces of reflection we see the bottom of the water, and the colour of that bottom and of the water itself mingles with and modifies that of the colour of the trees casting the dark reflection."[605]

That kind of detailed observation elevates Ruskin to the status of a great critic. Indeed, one of his most prominent admirers, Oscar Wilde, maintained that John Ruskin raised the level of criticism to the status of an art. As far as Wilde was concerned, Ruskin's writing about art was often finer artistically than the work he was analyzing:

"Who cares whether Mr Ruskin's views on Turner are sound or not? What does it matter? That mighty and majestic prose of his, so fervid and so fiery-coloured in its noble eloquence, so rich in its elaborate symphonic music, so sure and certain, at its best, in subtle choice of word and epithet, is at least as great a work of art as any of those wonderful sunsets that bleach or rot on their corrupted canvases in England's Gallery."[606]

Whenever I read essays by Ruskin and Wilde, I am aware of creativity at work: analytical and artistic at the same time – with a near-magical ability to make us see things in a fresh and illuminating way. As Francois Mauriac wrote in 1961:

"A good critic is the sorcerer who makes some hidden spring gush forth unexpectedly under our feet."[607]

Developing Analytical Skills

I enjoy good wine and reckon I can tell good from bad. All the same, I would not regard myself as a wine connoisseur, still less a competent wine critic. When I went on a wine course led by Michael Schuster, it showed me how much I have to learn, and how inexperienced I was compared with him.

Michael Schuster is a wine taster, wine writer and wine teacher with over 25 years experience. He studied tasting in Bordeaux, where he gained the University Tasting Diploma, and in the early eighties he was instrumental in creating an award-winning wine retail business. His first book, *Understanding Wine* (Mitchell Beazley 1989) was translated into six languages and sold over 350,000 copies. His book *Essential Winetasting* (2000), won all three major wine book prizes in the UK in 2001.

I am equally happy to acknowledge the superior knowledge and taste of a contemporary of mine at Oxford, Jancis Robinson, whose *Oxford Companion to Wine* is the most comprehensive wine encyclopaedia in the world.

On an even higher level of fame, the American wine critic Robert M. Parker possesses what Andrew Edgecliffe-Johnson of the *Financial Times* describes as "the world's most prized palate". Max Lalondrelle, fine wine-buying director for Berry Bros & Rudd says: "Nobody sells wine like Robert Parker. If he turns around and says 2012 is the worst vintage I've tasted, nobody will buy it, but if he says it's the best, everybody will."

That is not to say that Mr Parker is infallible. In a public blind tasting of fifteen top wines from Bordeaux 2005, which he called "the greatest vintage of my lifetime", Parker failed to identify any of the wines, confusing left bank wines for right on several occasions. And Mr Parker allegedly exchanged cross words with Jancis Robinson after they differed over the merits of the 2003 vintage of Chateau Pavie.

I would not presume to judge which of the two has the finer palate. My own has not been trained to recognise the subtle variations that a Master of Wine would recognise at once. I also lack the necessary vocabulary, so I would probably resort to clichés in any attempt to describe my taste experiences.

In other words, when it comes to wine I am an amateur. I know what I like; but I would acknowledge the superior expertise of experts who have devoted a large part of their lives to the study and appreciation of wine.

On the matter of food, too, I am no expert. I have been to fine restaurants and appreciate good food, but I have many blind spots. I've never got on with the taste of bananas, for some reason. Also, my lack of expertise in the kitchen means that I don't know how most of the dishes I have enjoyed have ended up the way they have. My wife, a skilful cook, is far more knowledgeable than I am.

When I watch *Professional Masterchef* on TV, I am impressed with the quality of the finalists; but I wouldn't presume that I would be able to pass judgment on them with the skills that have been honed over many years by the professional cooks and critics who do judge them.

Despite being a former adman and a failed chef - his only attempt to run a restaurant was a hotel-restaurant in Buxton, Derbyshire that went bust - it is obvious from Charles Campion's writing that he is a knowledgeable food critic, who has honed his skills on the *Times, Independent* and the *Evening Standard*.

His fellow judge on *Professional Masterchef*, Jay Rayner, has an equally refined palate that has enabled him to become restaurant critic of *The Observer*. I can't compete with either as a food critic, and I wouldn't make the attempt.

Despite a tendency to write more about himself than the food he's eating, Giles Coren has also made a reputation for himself as restaurant critic for *The Times* since 1993 and was named Food and Drink Writer of the Year at the 2005 British Press Awards.

Both Coren and Rayner are entertaining writers who have tens of thousands of followers on Twitter. Good luck to them. Despite their reputations as incorrigible show-offs, both men possess an engaging mixture of exhibitionism and self-mockery. When I asked Giles what he thought was the best aspect of professional critics, he replied:

"Hard work, fairness, a willingness to travel. I display none of these attributes. But Marina O'Laughlin of the *Guardian* does. Which is why she is the best."[608]

With regard to food and drink, I suspect most people would be willing to acknowledge the superior taste of a connoisseur or expert. But when it comes to theatre and (especially) film, many people seem to think that one opinion is as good as any other. That is emphatically not true.

Opinions are valueless unless you can justify them in an articulate, cogent and convincing way. The most common failing of young critics is to believe that any strong expression of opinion is as good as any other. It isn't. A kneejerk opinion will always be less valuable than one based on experience.

It's important not just to come up with insights others don't have, but also to construct a persuasive argument about why you are right. Here, the academic literary tradition is of enormous value. It teaches about narrative, character and dialogue.

The critic Joseph Addison wrote in 1712 that the prime requisite for a good critic is "a clear and logical head", He went on to argue in favour of a classical education, since "there is not a Greek or Latin critic who has not shown, even in the style of his criticisms, that he was a master of all the elegance and delicacy of his native tongue."[609]

The study of History or Political Theory is a great way to develop analytical skills. It is no accident that many of the best professional critics have read English, History or Politics, Philosophy and Economics at good universities, where they become accustomed to having their judgments challenged and learn to create a logical argument.

Without that ability, which can be learned and refined with practice, would-be critics of the present day are often reminiscent of Samuel Pepys[610], who may have been a terrific diarist but was no critic. His diary entries on the works of Shakespeare, seldom much longer than the tweets of today, are masterpieces of incomprehension:

26 Sept 1662: "To the King's Theatre, where we saw *Midsummer Night's Dream,* which I have never seen before, nor shall ever again, for it is the most insipid, ridiculous play that ever I saw in my life."

1 March 1662: "To the Opera and there saw *Romeo and Juliet,* the first time it was ever acted, but it is a play, of itself, the worst that ever I heard, and the worst acted that ever I saw these people do, and I am resolved to go no more to see the first time of acting."

6 Jan, 1663: "To the Duke's House, and there saw *Twelfth-Night* acted well, though it be but a silly play, and not relating at all to the name or day."[611]

As Mark Shenton, theatre critic for the *Stage* says, "you mustn't just say something is good or bad – support it with why you think that."[612]

Jim Hoberman, longtime film critic for the *Village Voice*, puts the same idea another way: "Always ask yourself why you like what you like."

In this age of tweeting and instant comments on Facebook and assorted websites, the ability to construct a reasoned argument may no longer seem important, but it is.

Write Fast and Stick to your Guns

Not all critics need to be able to write at speed, but some newspapers demand instant reactions, and the *Daily Mail* was one of them. I enjoyed writing "overnight" reviews, especially if I was the first critic in the world to express an opinion. The demands of a very tight deadline gave a film a sense of occasion, an exhilarating sense of danger that previously I had encountered only when directing live on television.

Many critics avoid writing "overnight" reviews - they are certainly no rest cure and require a self-confidence that, secretly, some critics may not possess - but I always welcomed them. It's often said that "everyone's a critic," but the ability to write six hundred to a thousand words cogently in about half an hour is not granted to everyone.

The overnight critic is gambling with his reputation. His or her reactions have to be instantaneous – there's no time to check accuracy and references – and there's no rough first draft. Yet the first overnight review is likely to be quoted throughout the media, and that instant opinion (or kneejerk reaction) will still be there in fifty years time.

I well remember the pressure on critics who attended the first British preview of *Pearl Harbor,* a hugely expensive movie that had spent an enormous amount of money on wooing critics, even flying numerous American film-writers to publicity events that cost more than any British film could have mustered for its entire production budget. The word of mouth coming out of these events was excellent, and clips from the film had evoked enthusiastic responses.

Yet, as Michael Bay bombarded my senses, I was struck by how ludicrous the film was - not only banal, but to my mind exploitative of the suffering endured at this surprise Japanese attack on American ships. When I raced home in a taxi to record my thoughts for the next morning's edition, I had literally no idea if my reaction to the film was unique to me, and I knew that the preconception at the *Daily Mail,* for which I worked, was that *Pearl Harbor* would be an enormous hit.

So I was risking my career and reputation when I wrote a detailed - and, I hope, funny - account of the film's many shortcomings.[613] I was rewarded with an abusive phone call from the film's publicist, but I was gratified that my own review was merely the first of many to reveal that the film was, creatively if not commercially, a turkey.

Even more scary were the times when I *knew* that most other critics regarded such-and-such a film as brilliant - invariably from seeing it at some film festival that I had not attended - and yet, when I saw it for myself, I didn't like it at all.

I remember two cases in particular. Pedro Almodovar's *Women on the Verge of a Nervous Breakdown* (1988) was raved about by the vast majority of critics. Rita Kempley in the *Washington Post* called it a "glossy delight".[614] Jay Carr in the *Boston Globe* found it "sublime". [615] Virtually all my colleagues in the UK liked it as well.

I, on the other hand, found it laboured, unfunny and curiously offensive. I even went to see it a second time, in case I had suffered a sense of humour failure. I liked it even less. Although the film posed as a feminist comedy, it actually reinforced the Latin macho view of men as the centre of women's lives, and women as emotional cripples. Its gay view of women struck me as demeaning to women, even if some women - including the movie's star, Carmen Saura - didn't see it as such.

I could acknowledge its best aspect, the colourful design, which had a camp, tacky flamboyance. Overall, however, it struck me as being a creaky boulevard comedy in trendy wrappings. The plot was nonsensical, and the characterization thin.

At first I thought I was on my own. It won prizes at the Toronto and Venice film festivals. It was named best foreign film by the US industry's National Board of Review and by critics' associations in New York City and Los Angeles.

However, over the years I have found more and more writers who have agreed with me. It began with Mark Finch in the *Monthly Film Bulletin*, who remarked acerbically "the best to be said is that Almodovar makes a good interior decorator". John Elliot, in his *Guide to Films on Video* (1993) described the film as "without a jot of depth, with all the female characters being shown as poor creatures unhinged by their attraction to worthless men. A great disappointment despite the rave reviews it received from many critics upon release." And Simon Ross in his *Essential Film Guide* of 1993 agreed that it was "overrated, marred by a handful of extraordinary coincidences and nowhere near as funny as it thinks it is". [616]

So my advice is to stick to your guns, even if you think you're alone. Maybe others will come round to seeing the film in the same light that you did.

Another case in point was *The Piano* (1993). It arrived in Britain festooned with five-star reviews from those who had seen it at the Cannes Film Festival, where it had won the *Palme d'Or*. I fully expected to like it, since I had seen the promise in Jane Campion's first two films *Sweetie* (1989) and *An Angel at My Table* (1990).

However, after I sat through her third film I walked round Leicester Square three times to clear my head, wondering if the other critics were mad, or I was.

If you haven't seen it, the movie's heroine is Ada (Holly Hunter), a mute since the age of six, for reasons unexplained. She has borne an illegitimate daughter, now nine years old (Anna Paquin). This being the sexist nineteenth century, Ada has been sent off by her father to marry Stewart (Sam Neill), a man she has never met, on the other side of the world in New Zealand. The only ways she can express her feelings are through sign language, and by playing the piano. However, her new husband has no interest in her piano, and leaves it stranded on the beach where she landed. But a tattooed neighbour, Baines (Harvey Keitel), appreciates the beauty of her piano-playing and buys it. Baines uses it to get Ada into bed with him, paving the way for a romantic triangle and eventually a crisis, as the husband learns what is going on, through the child.

Though beautifully shot and intensely acted by Holly Hunter, this feminist fable didn't impress me. Its numerous admirers seemed more able than I to disregard its shambolic plot, failure to understand its period, and characters who were inconsistent, unsympathetic and puppetlike caricatures.

Although writer-director Campion went to great lengths to ensure authenticity of costume, she left out scenes crucial to a sense of social authenticity. Was it credible that no one would have pointed out to Ada a wife's marital obligations - around the house, if not in the marital bed? Everything Ada did, she seemed to do for herself, with no thought for her child's welfare, which struck me as anachronistic, as well as unsympathetic. Her sullen attitude had a strong whiff of 70s, women-as-victims feminism: the underlying notion was that the world owes women a loving. When suddenly she did change towards her husband - from hostility to, so far as I could tell, genuine lasciviousness - she did so without rhyme or reason.

But then none of the characters made much sense. At one moment, the little girl hated her new step-father; the next, she was informing him of her mother's adultery. One moment, Sam Neill's character was consumed by jealousy and hatred, brandishing an axe like Bluebeard; the next, he was reason personified. No sooner had Ada tried to commit suicide than she decided not to. Of course, humans are paradoxical and they do change; but in a drama, surely we're entitled to some clue as to why. In *The Piano*, the characters seemed like marionettes under the control of a whimsical puppet-mistress - and an absent-minded one. In one scene, Harvey Keitel's Baines told Ada he was illiterate; a few minutes letter, she was sending him a note to tell him she loved him.

The acting, too, struck me as immensely variable. To me, Keitel looked completely out of his depth: his accent, along with that of the little girl (who incomprehensibly won an Oscar), seemed to alter from scene to scene. But the actors had little chance to flesh out characters written in a politically correct shorthand: Ada's husband is cutting down the forest, so he can't be in touch with his emotions; Baines has gone native and wears Maori tattoos, so he must be all right. There were times when I longed for the relative subtlety of male characterization in a Jilly Cooper novel.

Feminists would doubtless smile knowingly at the way Ada was punished - it fitted in neatly with modern preconceptions that men will countenance no threat to phallic supremacy - and men might well marvel at Sam Neill's accuracy with an axe. Film students might admire the clarity - or the crashing obviousness - of the piano and axe symbolism throughout. They might commend the unusual camera viewpoints, and not mind the fact that these were more often gimmicky than revelatory. Even less would they be bothered that the direction gave no impression of space or distance, in a film whose early plot hinges on how far or not Stewart's house was from the beach where Ada lands.

The years have not been kind to Jane Campion's reputation. Her subsequent films - *The Portrait of a Lady* (1996), *Holy Smoke* (1999), *In*

The Cut (2003) and *Bright Star* (2009) - earned her a reputation for humourless feminism. Whether I was right or wrong about *The Piano*, I was reassured when some other leading critics turned out to share my misgivings and add a few of their own. I was especially relieved when a veteran reviewer I greatly respect, Stanley Kauffmann, dismissed it in America's *New Republic* as:

"an overwrought, hollowly symbolic glob of glutinous nonsense. The New Zealand writer-director Jane Campion, who made an appealing film of Janet Frame's autobiography *An Angel at My Table*, here reverts to the thick, self-conscious poeticizing of her first film, *Sweetie*... Every moment is upholstered with the suffocating high-mindedness that declines to connect symbols with comprehensible themes. I haven't seen a sillier film about a woman and a piano since John Huston's *The Unforgiven* (1960), a Western in which Lillian Gish had her piano carried out into the front yard so she could play Mozart to pacify attacking Indians."[617]

Like Kauffmann, John Simon in the *National Review* found the characterization thin and unconvincing:

"We never find out anything about Ada's background, her first husband, and how Stewart acquired her in marriage. Or why she gave up speaking... Why would a welcoming husband abandon his bride's beloved piano, her chief mode of self-expression, when there are enough porters to carry it; and why not at least move it out of the reach of the waves? Later, it is Stewart's less affluent partner, Baines - an Englishman gone native, who sports Maori tattoos on his face - who buys the piano from Stewart, and seems to have no problem hauling it to his homestead. That the piano should play perfectly after what it's been through is one of the film's most resounding lies... Jane Campion prides herself on leaving much unexplained. She has every right to be proud: at leaving things unexplained, Miss Campion is a champion... Flora's actions consistently make no sense, but she at least has the excuse of being a child. What the adults do would make sense only as the wet dream of an inane woman, which *The Piano*, apparently, is not meant to be."[618]

In the *Nation* Stuart Klawans described the characters as mere puppets:

"Campion's whim is the only law. You can't learn anything about the characters beyond what she chooses to tell you at the moment, because they are mere artifices - like Michael Nyman's music, which is neither convincing as a nineteenth-century imposture nor substantial enough to withstand scrutiny as part of our own era."[619]

Like most British newspapers, the *Guardian* had responded to *The Piano* on release with over-the-top enthusiasm. Derek Malcolm wrote:

"*The Piano* is certainly one of the best films of the year and proves without doubt, if we didn't know it already, after *Sweetie* and *An Angel At*

My Table, that Campion is now a major talent."[620]

In 2004, the new *Guardian* critic Peter Bradshaw saw it and wondered what all the fuss had been about. He called it "middlebrow, pseudo-literary cinema, which is shallow and prissy and genteel. Those self-regarding pretty-pretty compositions of Holly Hunter on the beach, drove me up the wall. She's mute: which manages to be such a smug passive-aggressive idea."

My point is not that I was right and my other critical colleagues wrong. Everyone is entitled to his or her opinion, especially if they can justify it. My argument is that if you write honestly about what you feel, and you can justify your reactions, the chances are that you will find out in the end that you are not as isolated as you thought you were. A weak critic goes with the fashionable flow; the good critic is willing to put his head above the parapet and take whatever contumely may come his way, for daring to say something different.

Let John Simon, a vitriolic critic who has drawn plenty of critical vitriol to himself, have the last word on the importance of critics to stick up for themselves:

"The critic strives to do his imperfect best. And part of that is explaining to his audience what his values are, where he stands; for though the critic and his readers need not stand on the same ground, the readers must know where the critic is standing and then make the necessary adjustments. You can read any map once you know its scale."[621]

THE FIFTH COMMANDMENT
Thou Shalt Avoid Excessive Egotism

Why Does Everybody Call Me Big Head?

All critics are, to a greater or lesser extent, egotists. Why else would you consider your own opinions to be important enough to inflict on others? George Bernard Shaw once said "The modest critic is lost." [622] Long before Shaw, Aristotle wrote of critics "they who are to be judges must also be performers".[623]

Film reviewer Judith Crist considered a healthy amount of conceit one of several essential requirements for the job:

"To be a critic, you have to have maybe three percent education, five percent intelligence, two percent style, and 90 percent gall and egomania in equal parts." [624]

At the same time, she said in a 1989 interview with the *Jerusalem Post,* a critic is merely "an individual voicing his or her own opinion. He's not the voice of God. In my reviews, I say what I think of a film and why, and my readers know my tastes by now. Some hate my taste, and so I'm reliable for them, too, since they know they'll like what I hate."[625]

On the other hand, the best critics don't only put across their own opinions; they weigh up alternative opinions, they try to work out what the artist was trying to achieve (and how far he has succeeded) and they appreciate the audience at which a particular work of art is aimed. They should also have the modesty to realise that their opinion is not law.

Stephen Sondheim once summed up the main qualities he looked for in a critic, and among these was humility:

"For me, a good critic is a good writer. A good critic is someone who recognises and acknowledges the artist's intentions and the work's aspirations, and judges the work by them, not by what his own objectives would have been. A good critic is so impassioned about his subject that he can persuade you to attend something you'd never have imagined going to. A good critic is an entertaining read. A good critic is hard to find."[626]

Why Even Honest Critics go Wrong

One reason professional critics are mistrusted is that they are frequently wrong. Professional critics have been complaining for years, with some reason, that the proliferation of unpaid critics on the internet has been undermining their authority.

However, the brutal truth is that the old guard of professional critics has often been slow to spot new talent - which is surely a primary justification for their existence.

One can only marvel at the obtuseness of the professional critic who wrote gravely of Kenneth Grahame's children's classic *The Wind in the Willows* that "as a contribution to natural history the work is negligible."[627]

It is equally easy to laugh at the idiocy of the 1940s review in *Field and Stream* of D.H. Lawrence's 1928 novel *Lady Chatterley's Lover*, about the steamy affair between an aristocratic lady and her gamekeeper:

"Unfortunately, one is obliged to wade through many pages of extraneous material in order to discover and savour sidelights on the management of a Midland estate, and in this reviewer's opinion the book cannot take the place of J.R.Miller's *Practical Gamekeeper*."[628]

Guess whose art exhibition the professional critics were panning here. Albert Wolff, editor of *Le Figaro,* wrote:

"Following upon the burning of the Opera-House, a new disaster has fallen upon the quarter. There has just opened at Mr Durand-Ruel's an exhibition of what is said to be painting... Five or six lunatics, one of them a woman - a collection of unfortunates tainted by the folly of ambition - have met here to exhibit their work. There are people who burst into laughter in front of these objects. Personally, I am saddened by them. What a terrifying spectacle is this of human vanity stretched to the verge of dementia." [629]

Henry Havard, the critic for *La Siecle,* wrote sarcastically:

"I confess humbly I do not see nature as they do, never having seen these skies fluffy with pink cotton, these opaque and moire waters, this multi-coloured foliage. Maybe they do exist. I do not know them."[630]

Yes, these critically panned artists were the Impressionists — including Pierre-Auguste Renoir, Claude Monet, Edouard Manet, Camille Pisarro and Alfred Sisley - and the reviews were of their 1874 exhibition in Paris, where some of the most talented artists who ever trod the earth were taken to task for being insufficiently realistic.

French art critics were not the only ones who could be slow to recognise quality. It is hard to imagine what the 19th century British art critic John Hunt was thinking when he wrote pompously about the upstart painter Rembrandt:

"Rembrandt is not to be compared in the painting of character with our extraordinarily gifted English artist, Mr Rippingille."[631]

Almost a century further on, here are a few examples of an American critical reaction to a foreign pop import:

"Not even their mothers would claim that they sing well." (*LA Times*)[632]

"Visually, they are a nightmare... Musically, they are a near disaster, guitars and drums slamming out a merciless beat that does way with secondary rhythms, harmony and melody. Their lyrics... are a catastrophe, a preposterous farrago of Valentine-card sentiments." (*Newsweek*)[633]

"They are god-awful. There so unbelievably, horribly, so appallingly unmusical, so dogmatically insensitive to the magic of the art that they qualify as crowned heads of anti-music." (*Boston Globe*)[634]

Especially if I tell you the year was 1964, you may guess that the group was the Beatles. One thing often forgotten about the Fab Four is how they were received by many rock critics in the United States. They were shockingly unfamiliar, too original, too new.

So bravo to all critics who depart from the consensus and can provide fresh, reasoned arguments for doing so.

I once wrote a book *The Critics' Film Guide*[635], which – among other things – looked back at films that had been undervalued by professional critics and tried to understand why. Certain films were critically unfashionable on release and had to wait years, sometimes decades, for those opinions to be reversed.

Singin' In the Rain is a revealing example of how critics can easily pre-judge films. On release, it was widely underrated for being studio-bound (unlike the recent hit *On The Town*, which was shot on location in New York) and unserious (unlike *An American in Paris*, which now looks a tad pretentious).

Critics queued up to say that *Singin' In the Rain* was pleasant enough, but just another product on the MGM conveyor-belt. Their snobbery now looks comical.[636]

Those mediocre reviews led to *Singin' In the Rain* being less of a hit than MGM would have wished. "I've made a lot of films that were bigger hits and made a lot more money," wrote Gene Kelly in 1977, "but now they look dated. This one, out of all my pictures, has a chance to last."[637]

The reason for its longterm success is, of course, that this is one of the most tuneful, brilliantly performed, wittily written and sensitively choreographed of all film musicals. Modern critics, with the benefit of hindsight, automatically give it a classic status that the original reviewers carefully withheld.

Another great film critically undervalued on release was *Casablanca*. C.A. Lejeune in the *Observer* described it as "a busy film with bright lines, a perfunctory romance and a dim message". *Variety* complained that "some of the characterisations are a bit on the overdone side". The *New Republic* dismissed it as "ineffectual but a pleasure of sorts".

Even after its release, critics have continued to find it lacking. The leading critic for the *Sunday Times* described it in 1945 as "overrated". As late as 1992, Derek Malcolm panned it in the *Guardian* as "gross sentimentality" and "schlock".[638]

One reason for *Casablanca*'s critical failure was its unfashionable politics: it was, and remains, pro-war propaganda. The hero's transformation from disinterested isolationist into an American prepared to kill for the right cause may have been just about acceptable against Nazis. It became much less "politically correct" during the Cold War, as the post-war liberal establishment argued that America had no right to police the planet.

Although the film is often dismissed as romantic or sentimental, its romanticism is not the kind beloved of liberals. Bogart - like Celia Johnson in another unfashionable but well-loved film, *Brief Encounter* - comes to realise that romantic love and personal fulfilment are not enough. Both films end with acts of self-sacrifice. *Casablanca* is not conventionally romantic at all, and is profoundly antipathetic towards the kind of emotional self-indulgence which resulted in permissiveness and the "me" generation.

The other reason why *Casablanca* has always failed to be intellectually fashionable is that the posher critics are often notoriously incapable of distinguishing between sentiment and sentimentality - a legacy, perhaps, of having American cinema try to tug on our heartstrings, week after week, with the subtlety of a gorilla wearing boxing gloves. Along with *It's a Wonderful Life* and *Les Misérables, Casablanca* is the most shameless tear-jerker of all time. If you don't blub when Bergman and Bogart meet in Rick's Café and during the final airport scene, there's something wrong with you. Whether you care to admit in print that you wept at a commercial Hollywood movie is another matter.

Casablanca is, as almost every non-critic knows instinctively, a masterpiece, a high point in cinema. The screenplay may be the result of last-minute rewrites and studio strife, but it ended up as a triumphant example of intricate plotting, subtle exposition and witty dialogue. It is high drama and not (as it's often accused of being) melodrama - for the simple reason that all the big scenes of emotion are thoroughly motivated by the writers and beautifully underplayed by the actors. Bogart, Bergman and Rains all give Oscar-worthy performances - though none of them won, and Bergman wasn't even nominated.

Technically, too, it's outstanding. Michael Curtiz's direction is unobtrusively excellent, and Arthur Edeson's Oscar-nominated cinematography bettered even his work on trendier classics such as *All Quiet on the Western Front* and *The Maltese Falcon*.

The other reason *Casablanca* was critically underrated for so long is that it was not made in the way some reviewers feel great pictures ought to be created. It constitutes eternal and uncomfortable proof that great films are often made not by *auteurs*, but by collaboration between craftsmen at uncomfortable speed, within an authoritarian studio system, and with a cavalier attitude to creative talent. At least eight writers, and probably twelve, contributed to the final screenplay.

The development of "*auteur* criticism" in the 1950s, led by Frenchmen such as Francois Truffaut, Jean Luc Godard and Claude Chabrol, was at first hugely beneficial to criticism. These critics had been brought up on films most traditional critics regarded as unimportant – American thrillers, gangster movies and westerns. They were anxious to prove that populist directors such as Alfred Hitchcock, Howard Hawks and John Ford were important film-makers, pursuing personal visions through genres such as the thriller and western. But the rise of *auteur* criticism had its bad aspects. As the eighteenth century critic Joseph Addison pointed out, "the best may err".[639] And even fine directors can make terrible mistakes, have an off day or discover their skills diminishing with age.

Auteurists often overestimated the role of the director and downgraded the writers, studios, actors, producers and craftspeople who contributed.

They also tended to overpraise movies by "*auteurs*" (many unworthy of the name) while downgrading films which were obviously the product of commercial studios. Even today, influenced by the *auteurist* tradition, some influential critics have a knee-jerk, adverse reaction to any Hollywood blockbuster; if it isn't "personal", they argue, how can it be any good?

The answer is, of course, that many of the very best movies have been commercially motivated, and have sought to do little more than entertain. Today we may be more prepared to recognise the merits of a *Singin' In The Rain* or a *Casablanca*; but many mere "entertainment" films remain despised, especially if they fall into a unfashionable category like "slasher movie" (Scorsese's *Cape Fear*), "monster movie" (Spielberg's *Jurassic Park*) or "action movie" (James Cameron's *Aliens*, Spielberg's *Raiders of the Lost Ark*, John McTiernan's *Die Hard*).

If I had a mission when I chose to become a film critic in the mid-80s, it was to try and make people realise that even the most respected *auteurs* are capable of making bad films, and that there is often more to entertainment or commercial movies than most people imagine. Nor is a film intrinsically better for being in a foreign language or designed for the "art house".

Similar sentiments inspired Cosmo Landesman and Julie Burchill, who were then married, to publish the *Modern Review* from 1991 to 1995. "Low culture for highbrows" was its catchphrase. It had a relatively small circulation, starting at around 5,000 copies and rising to a peak of 30,000 before falling away again. It was more talked about than read, but many of its brighter contributors were poached by mainstream newspapers, including Toby Young, Will Self, Nick Hornby and Anthony Quinn.

"The whole enterprise was driven by one fairly simple idea," says onetime Editor Toby Young, "and that was that critics had a responsibility to take the best popular culture as seriously as the best high culture. It doesn't sound remotely radical now, because the entire broadsheet press is stuffed with Oxbridge graduates writing about *The Terminator*. But in those days, it was a new idea."

Well, it passed for new. I remember regarding the *Modern Review* mob's claims of originality with a certain amount of cynicism. As the founders of the magazine fell out personally during the mid-90s, Julie Burchill's lesbian lover Charlotte Raven, who had replaced Toby Young as Editor, attempted to transform the magazine into something much more dogmatic and leftist - in Young's words, "a cross between *Spare Rib* and the *New Statesman*."[640] Unsurprisingly, hardly anyone bought it.

I imagine that most of the writers on *Modern Review* in its prime would have agreed with me that every film should be judged on its own merits, not on the past achievements of its director. But even today that is far from critical orthodoxy. Peter Greenaway, Derek Jarman, Terrence Malick and Jane Campion have all struck me as critics' darlings whose reputation has blinded some reviewers to glaring defects, especially with regard to storytelling and audience involvement.

Oddly enough, the pithiest comment on *auteurist* critics was made by Alexander Pope in his *Essay on Criticism*, way back in the eighteenth century:

"Some judge of authors' names, not works, and then nor praise nor blame the writings, but the men." [641]

Some classic comedies also received surprisingly sniffy reviews on release. Buster Keaton's *The General* and the Marx Brothers' *Duck Soup* were both severely criticised for trivialising warfare. To modern eyes, the criticism seems irrelevant. Both films are supremely well crafted and very funny.

Other masterpieces were condemned merely for being in a genre of which reviewers disapproved. Alfred Hitchcock's *Psycho*, the mother of all slasher films, opened to a virtually unanimous chorus of disapproval. One of Britain's leading critics, C.A. Lejeune of the *Observer*, grew "so sick and tired of the whole beastly business" that she walked out.[642]

Even the critics who stayed adopted a sternly moralistic line. Dwight Macdonald, a leading US critic, wrote that it was " a reflection of a most unpleasant mind, a mean, sadistic little mind". In the UK, the mid-market newspapers vied with each other to condemn it. Fred Majdalany in the *Daily Mail* said that Hitchcock had "scraped the bottom of the psychiatric barrel". Rene MacColl in the *Daily Express* called it "a sad prostitution of talent."[643]

The reason for their hatred is obvious. The film flew in the face of the critics' expectations. It was not one of Hitchcock's cool, glossy thrillers, but a venture into the most violent end of the then critically unfashionable horror genre. *Psycho* was both Hitchcock's first horror film, and the first of its kind to be aimed at the commercial mainstream.

I met Michael Powell when he accepted my invitation to address the Oxford Union on the future of British film, in late 1971. He was one of a panel of speakers, and though I knew he was a genius it became embarrassingly obvious from the fact that most of the questions were addressed to other panelists that, even though I'd given them a list of his credits, the vast majority of the audience didn't have a clue who he was. I kept on having to bring him into the discussion by asking for his comments.

Fortunately, his reputation rose in the next decades, and by his death he was acknowledged as one of the great British directors. Among his classics are *The Life and Death of Colonel Blimp* (1943), *I Know Where I'm Going* (1945), *Black Narcissus* (1946), *A Matter of Life and Death* (1946) and *The Red Shoes* (1948).

However, he was, as he put it to me, "unable to get arrested" after what he described as "a misadventure" in 1959. This was *Peeping Tom*, about a mad, voyeuristic serial killer who slaughtered women. "I was genuinely surprised by the vicious reaction", he said.

By modern standards, the film is not all that violent, but it was heartily disliked by virtually all the critics for seeming to revel in both the anti-hero's deeds and (even more tastelessly) the terror of his victims.

Derek Hill, in *Tribune*, wrote "The only really satisfactory way to dispose of *Peeping Tom* would be to shovel it up and flush it swiftly down the nearest sewer. Even then, the stench would remain." Isabel Quigly in the *Spectator* called it "the sickest and filthiest film I remember seeing."

Nina Hibbin, writing for the Communist *Daily Worker*, was no more impressed:

"Ugh! Obviously, Michael Powell made *Peeping Tom* in order to shock. In one sense he has succeeded. I was shocked to the core to find a director of his standing befouling the screen with such perverted nonsense. It wallows in the diseased urges of a homicidal pervert, and actually romanticizes his pornographic brutality. Sparing no tricks, it uses phoney cinema artifice and heavy orchestral music to whip up a debased atmosphere... From its slumbering mildly salacious beginning to its appallingly masochistic and depraved climax, it is wholly evil."

Leonard Mosley in the *Daily Express* despised the film even more lavishly:

"In the last three and half months... I have carted my travel-stained carcase to some of the filthiest and most festering slums in Asia. But nothing, nothing, nothing - neither the hopeless leper colonies of East Pakistan, the back streets of Bombay nor the gutters of Calcutta - has left me with such a feeling of nausea and depression as I got this week while sitting through a new British film called *Peeping Tom*. I am a glutton for punishment, and I never walk out of films or plays no matter how malodorous. But I must confess that I almost followed suit when I heard my distinguished colleague Miss Caroline Lejeune say: "I am sickened!" just before she made her indignant exit. Mr Michael Powell ought to be ashamed of himself. The acting is good. The photography is fine. But what is the result as I saw it on the screen? Sadism, sex, and the exploitation of human degradation."

With similar gusto, Alexander Walker denounced it in the *Evening Standard*:

"A clever but corrupt and empty exercise in shock tactics which displays a nervous fascination with the perversions it illustrates... Not only is it drivel, it is crude, unhealthy sensation at its worst. A sad discredit to a fine producer's reputation."

Even Dilys Powell in the *Sunday Times* failed to see any good in it:

"Perhaps one would not be so disagreeably affected by this exercise in the lower regions of the psychopathic were it handled in a more bluntly debased fashion. One does not, after all, waste much indignation on the Draculas and Mummies and Stranglers of the last few years; the tongue-chopping and blood-sucking, disgusting as they may be, can often be dismissed as risible. *Peeping Tom* is another matter. It is made by a director of skill and sensibility... He did not write *Peeping Tom*; but he cannot wash his hands of responsibility for this essentially vicious film."[644]

It is fashionable now to say that the critics' initial reaction was mistaken, and that *Peeping Tom* is a masterpiece. I'm not so sure that they were wrong; though cleverly made, this is a nasty, mean-spirited film.

However, the hatred the picture engendered was wildly disproportionate, and the damage the critics did to this hugely talented director's career was a great, great pity.

When I met him in 1971, Powell was trying to put together a film of William Shakespeare's play *The Tempest*. It was obvious that, like many creative artists towards the end of their careers, he identified intensely with Prospero, a magician in exile. I can't help suspecting Powell's film would have been much better than later attempts to shoot the play by Derek Jarman, Peter Greenaway and Julie Taymor. But Powell never got his project off the ground. Thanks to the critical reception given to *Peeping Tom*, Powell remained a Prospero in exile.

The most powerful American critic of her day, Pauline Kael was far from an isolated example of a professional reviewer who couldn't see the good in *Star Wars*. One of her fiercest critics agreed with her on George Lucas's film. "O dull new world!" snarled John Simon in *New York Magazine*. "It is all as exciting as last week's weather reports." A younger critic, Christopher Hitchens in Britain's leftist magazine the *New Statesman*, advised his readers that *Star Wars* was a turkey: "The film is simply a bore. So save your money."[645]

Needless to say, audiences ignored the critics - and rightly so. There was an enormous amount to like about *Star Wars*, and it was the professional critics' loss that they couldn't appreciate it.

Leading critics practically queued up to savage another science fiction classic, which today is recognised as having had a visionary power. Pauline Kael in the *New Yorker*, Richard Corliss in *Time*, Andrew Sarris in *Village Voice* and Tom Milne in the *Monthly Film Bulletin* all failed to see the point of *Blade Runner*.[646]

Alien ran foul of most professional critics because it occupied two genres that they have always found difficult to appreciate: horror and science fiction.

Frank Rich, in *New York Magazine*, noted that it didn't contain the ingredients that he looked for in a motion picture:

"*Alien* contains a couple of genuine jolts, a barrage of convincing special effects and enough gore to gross out children of all ages. What's missing is wit, imagination and the vaguest hint of human feeling."

Dave Kehr, in the *Chicago Reader*, felt that it insulted his intelligence, dismissing it as "an empty-headed horror movie, with nothing to recommend it beyond the disco-inspired art direction and some handsome, if gimmicky, cinematography... Instead of characters, the film has bodies."

Another of the more thinking American critics, David Denby of *New York Magazine*, disliked the way *Alien* made him feel: "The movie is terrifying, but not in a way that is remotely enjoyable."[647]

Some professional critics also find it difficult to see past the violence in a movie. A striking example of this was *Fight Club* (1999), now generally regarded as a classic. On release, it was savaged by some American reviewers as brutalizing, witless, infantile and fascistic.

Roger Ebert, the Pulitzer prize-winning critic of the *Chicago Sun-Times*, dismissed it as having no depth: "*Fight Club* is a thrill ride masquerading as philosophy."

Another veteran critic, Kenneth Turan of the *Los Angeles Times*, condemned it as "a witless mish-mash of whiny, infantile philosophising and bone-crunching violence... the delusional rantings of testosterone-addicted thugs. Aside from the protracted beatings, this film is so vacuous and empty it's more depressing than provocative."

One of British criticism's respected elder statesmen, Alexander Walker of the *Evening Standard*, denounced *Fight Club* as "not only anti-capitalism but anti-society, and, indeed, anti-God... an inadmissible assault on personal decency. And on society itself... It uncritically enshrines principles that once underpinned the politics of fascism, and ultimately sent millions of Jews to the death camps. It echoes propaganda that gave licence to the brutal activities of the SA and the SS. It resurrects the Führer principle. It promotes pain and suffering as the virtues of the strongest. It tramples every democratic decency underfoot... In any well-adjusted society, its stars would feel a backlash of public indignation well beyond the box-office."[648]

Well, it certainly proves the adage that no two people have the same experience while watching a film. For David Fincher's film struck me as witty, grown-up and extremely unlikely to brutalize anyone. I wrote at the time: "It has an original, funny, literate screenplay, contains three of the year's best performances, and is the most brilliantly directed picture since *Saving Private Ryan*. And, like Spielberg's film, it skilfully uses the shock of extreme violence to make points that are profound and revelatory about the human condition."[649]

Although I had the reputation of disliking violent films, I made *Fight Club* my film of 1999, just as I had made *Pulp Fiction* my film of 1994. Other "violent" films that I have praised include *Se7en* (1997), *Audition* (1999) and *Eden Lake* (2008).[650]

I would not wish to give the impression that all the older critics failed to grasp the fact that the film was not celebrating violence but condemning it. In the *Observer*, Philip French mounted a spirited defence of the film, calling it "a dazzling and disturbing fable about the discontent of men at the end of this terrible century."[651]

But, in the main, it was the younger generation who recognised what the movie was on about. In a rare foray into criticism, the novelist Bret Easton Ellis in *Gear Magazine* called it "a relentless, dizzying take on the male fear of losing power that's a wild, orgiastic pop masterpiece."

Andrew Johnston, in *Time Out New York*, wrote: "This is the first truly meaningful movie about (for want of a better term) the Generation X experience, and it arrives at a time when it's almost certain to be misunderstood."

A critique in *Rolling Stone* summed up the reason why David Fincher's film had incurred such critical wrath:

"How good is *Fight Club*? It's so fired up with explosive ideas and killing humour that the guardians of morality are yelling 'Danger - keep out!' That's how good."

Virtually every online critic leapt to the film's defence. The reliably intelligent online critic James Berardinelli described it as "a visual masterpiece... Also in play: a non-linear chronology, a voiceover by a narrator who might not be entirely reliable, frequent breaking of the fourth wall, and an occasional freeze-frame... When combined together, the satire, violence, and unpredictable narrative make a lasting and forceful statement about modern-day society."

Someone with the email address of *renshaw@inconnect.com* spotted that most of the professional critics hadn't been able to spot the ironies within the film: "Many critics and social conservatives have already offered up kill-the-messenger diatribes against the film's brutality and anarchist sub-plots, yet another depressing reminder that some people need their messages delivered to them in solemn 'isn't this a very, very bad thing' tones."[652]

Another film misunderstood by critics who couldn't see past the violence was *Starship Troopers*. I wouldn't make any great claims for the film's artistic merit, but if you read the professional critics' reviews after you have seen the picture, it is impossible to avoid the conclusion that most of them missed the central point, which is that it is a satire on gung-ho militarism, not a celebration of that kind of jingoism.

Roger Ebert failed to appreciate this and found the film "one-dimensional," a trivial nothing "pitched at 11-year-old science-fiction fans."[653] In the *New York Times*, Janet Maslin panned the "crazed, lurid spectacle" as "raunchiness tailor-made for teen-age boys."[654] Jeff Vice, in the *Deseret News*, called it "a nonstop splatterfest so devoid of taste and logic that it makes even the most brainless summer blockbuster look intelligent." [655]

Another misunderstood satire on violence was *Shoot 'Em Up* (2007), which also fell foul of the professional critics' refusal to see that it was a send-up. A.O. Scott in the *New York Times* deplored it as "a witless, soulless, heartless movie that mistakes noise for bravura and tastelessness for wit."[656]

Ty Burr in the *Boston Globe* also hated it "for its crunching ballet of flailing bodies and spinning cars, for its ghoulish black humour, and for its hopped-up, boys-only party vibe."[657]

Stephen McGarvey of *Crosswalk*, said that the movie "gives new meaning to the word 'wretched.'… a gratuitous spectacle of violence."[658]

Writing as I did for the *Daily Mail*, a newspaper which took a dim view of gratuitous violence, I took care to imply that, though I hugely enjoyed the film, those without a taste for black comedy might find it hard to take:

"This is so gruesome and joyously tasteless that it's not for everyone, but if you have a dark sense of humour, see it. The inspired action sequences are brilliantly staged and imaginatively shot; and at 86 minutes it doesn't outstay its welcome. If you enjoyed *Kiss Kiss Bang Bang* or *Lucky Number Slevin*, this one's for you."[659]

As so often, it was left to the much maligned internet critics to understand the ironic nature of the film. "*Shoot 'Em Up* is a thoroughly inventive and joyful piece of cinema, one of those films that is destined to become a cult classic" wrote Rick Mele in *The Cinema Source*.[660] To his credit, Tim Knight at *Reel.com* noticed the "sly jabs at American gun culture and 'family values.'" and called it "a rollicking hoot from start to finish".[661]

By way of contrast, history is riddled with "serious" films that were celebrated by professional critics on release but are now virtually forgotten.

Most of them were praised on release for being liberal – or, as we might say nowadays, politically correct. Among them are *The Searching Wind* (1946)[662], *Gentleman's Agreement*[663] (1947) and *The Rose Tattoo*[664] (1958).

Gentleman's Agreement starred Gregory Peck as a journalist who pretends to be Jewish in order to investigate racial discrimination. Elia Kazan's well-intentioned but facile tract against anti-Semitism won The New York Film Critics' Best Picture and Best Director awards, then went on to win three Oscars, including Best Film. Once considered courageous and powerful, now it looks terribly slow, preachy and melodramatic. It's evidence, if any were needed, that the "important" picture of today is the deservedly forgotten film of tomorrow.

Good critics should be aware that even they are, to some extent, affected by fashion and their own prejudices. As G.K. Chesterton once remarked:

"A great deal of contemporary criticism reads to me like a man saying 'Of course I do not like green cheese: I am very fond of brown sherry.'"[665]

How Tolkien Got Away With Mordor

The ultimate example of a work of art triumphing despite the professional critics is *The Lord of the Rings* – not so much the Peter Jackson films, which were almost unanimously praised by reviewers, but the original books, which were not.

Tolkien's fantasy did receive some acclaim, but mainly from fellow authors, such as W.H. Auden, Naomi Mitchison and Tolkien's friend and fellow fantasy-writer, C.S. Lewis. Only a small minority of professional critics agreed.

New York Times reviewer Judith Shulevitz disliked Tolkien's "pedantry" and said his "high-minded belief in the importance of his mission as a literary preservationist.... turns out to be death to literature itself."

Another American critic, Richard Jenkyns of the *New Republic* found the characters and the book itself to be "anemic" and "lacking in fibre".[666]

The most influential literary critic from the mid-1920s through to the 1960s, the American Edmund Wilson, who was a great advocate for modernism, hated the book. In 1956, he wrote a hatchet-job called *Ooh! Those Awful Orcs!* in which he called the book "juvenile trash", and said that it left him "let down, astonished, baffled". He predicted that it would have little impact on his side of the Atlantic. [667] How wrong he was.

Wilson's attack set the tone for most of the literary intelligentsia on both sides of the Atlantic. In 1961 the British Marxist critic Philip Toynbee described the novel in *The Observer* as "dull, ill-written, whimsical and childish". He wrote confidently that Tolkien's works had "passed into a merciful oblivion." Oops.[668]

More recently, that eternal stroppy teenager Germaine Greer – a feminist critic beloved of seemingly every BBC Arts producer - castigated a love of the book as *prima facie* evidence of being emotionally retarded. Actually, it's clear she hasn't bothered to read the book or see the film, as she describes them with characteristic inaccuracy as "Nazi propaganda full of Nordic Supermen".[669]

Leftist fantasy writer Michael Moorcock derided *The Lord of the Rings* as "*Winnie the Pooh* posing as an epic".[670] In 2011, he told the *Guardian* that Tolkien's masterpiece was no more than "a pernicious celebration of the values of a morally bankrupt middle class."[671]

The Marxist fantasy writer China Mieville has gone even further, dismissing his more successful forerunner Tolkien as "rural, petty bourgeois, conservative, anti-modernist, misanthropically Christian and anti-intellectual".[672]

John Yatt warned readers of the *Guardian* against exposing themselves to Tolkien's dangerous, politically incorrect ideology: "Strip away the archaic turns of phrase and you find a set of basic assumptions that are frankly unacceptable in 21st-century Britain."[673]

A few humourless feminist critics have condemned the book as prejudiced against women. In one such essay, hilariously entitled *No Sex, Please, We're Hobbits: The Construction of Female Sexuality in The Lord of the Rings*, an English teacher - one Brenda Partridge - blames Tolkien's allegedly chauvinistic view of women on the "Norse and Christian mythologies in which he was immersed".[674]

No matter that Eowyn is one of the most memorable "strong women" in the whole of English literature, or that the elf-queen Galadriel is portrayed as someone powerful enough to be a Sauron or Saruman. Of course, there is no getting away from the fact that the main protagonists in *The Lord of the Rings* are male; but as Peter Jackson and his two (female) co-writers discovered through a judicious raiding of the appendices, the love story between Aragorn and Arwen is a touching romance that contains within it more than a hint of sexuality.

The Lord of the Rings has succeeded over the years in uniting in condemnation all kinds of professional critics: modernists, post-modernists, Feminists, Marxists and the pompously politically correct. Tolkien would be proud.

Why do the commercial success of Tolkien's books and the high regard in which they are held by non-critics drive so many *literati* crazy? As Terry Pratchett once said, "stories of imagination tend to upset those without one". [675] And it shows that popular taste resolutely, bloodymindedly defies central planning and totalitarian diktats: the *literati* do not control, and have no right to control, what literature is.

Another reason why Professor Tolkien incenses those who regard themselves as a modernizing intelligentsia is that he was middle class and happy to be so. An Oxford academic with simple, homely tastes, he was completely uninterested in class alienation, and his hobbits represent a happy combination of the English middle and working classes.

Virtually alone of his literary generation, Tolkien saw no need to disguise himself as anything but bourgeois. He did not try to reinvent himself as working-class, non-English, or a beleaguered intellectual suffering exile within his own country. His best-loved book is a celebration of small people protecting the ordinary but beautiful aspects of family and home. As he once famously remarked, "I am, in fact, a hobbit".[676]

Tolkien had no ambition to be avant-garde - indeed, he is cheerfully reactionary in harking back to unfashionable myths and legends that he himself adored. Tolkien completely rejected the Modernist movement that has long been unquestioned orthodoxy among the literati. His priorities and themes were never those of the literary establishment. Plot, or story-telling, is the most compelling element in *The Lord of the Rings*.

Modernist novelists like to dwell on inner feelings and pick over minutiae, usually in a depressed and depressing way. But authors such as Tolkien and Mervyn Peake (writer of that other epic fantasy, the *Gormenghast* trilogy) had not only lived through but personally witnessed the greatest horrors of the twentieth century - Tolkien at the Somme, Peake at the concentration camps. Both turned to fantasy-writing as a way of dealing with their encounters with evil.

Tolkien bravely tackled the big themes of the twentieth century that many modernists couldn't or wouldn't handle: the trauma of war and genocide, the impact of industry on the environment, the burgeoning power but hidden fragility of totalitarianism. Most of his book was written during the rise of Nazi Germany and Stalinist expansionism; it is no accident that it chronicles the war against a Dark Lord whose mission is the domination of Middle-earth.

Moreover, Tolkien had no truck with modern miserabilism. The ultimate, empowering message of his greatest work is that one person, however insignificant, can make a difference.

There is a sense in which the true hero of *The Lord of The Rings* is not Frodo, Aragorn or Gandalf, but Sam Gamgee, a low-life, comic, subsidiary character who finds himself gradually elevated to an importance he could never have anticipated (and Tolkien probably didn't, either). He emerges as the unassuming moral centre of the book and indeed the films.

It is significant that, towards the end of *The Two Towers*, director-adapter Peter Jackson gives Sam the speech which encapsulates the Tolkien ethic, about the need to find and defend the good in the world, which incidentally is echoed in Richard Curtis's opening lines of *Love Actually*, another hit that hugely annoys modernist critics.

Tolkien's characters are also a good deal more complex than is usually acknowledged. They are not divided between Good and Bad, for underlying everything is a striking sense of how every one of us is corruptible.

In the films, the psychological disintegration of Frodo from brave little hobbit to deranged sociopath is movingly conveyed by Elijah Wood, in a performance that has been greatly undervalued. One masterstroke of Peter Jackson's co-writer Fran Walsh was to dramatize the schizophrenic nature of Smeagol/ Gollum, who emerges from the trilogy as one of literature's most imaginative and unique creations.

Underlying the critics' distaste for the book is, I think, a feeling that Tolkien is guilty of right-wing warmongering. He does indeed make a case for war as a regrettable but moral response to evil. King Theoden's change from weakling to warrior produces some of the most stirring moments in Peter Jackson's trilogy. And Aragorn's transition from alienated, disinterested outsider to involved, responsible leader is another major theme. Indeed, his character arc is similar to the one that may have troubled critics of that other classic movie *Casablanca*.

Yet no one could possibly come away from book or film without realising that Tolkien does not idealize war. Tolkien fought at the Somme in 1916. "One has indeed personally to come under the shadow of war to feel its oppression," he once wrote. "By 1918 all but one of my close friends were dead."[677]

Deep within his writing runs a profound sense of sadness at the losses, sacrifices and waste of war. In the wizard Gandalf's argument that the powerful but corrupting Ring be destroyed, rather than used as a weapon against Sauron, there is an unmistakable parallel with the scourge of nuclear weapons.

Tolkien's sympathies are clearly with the peace-loving hobbits and their pipe-weed, the horse-culture of the Rohirrim, the poetic beauty of the elves. It is only when these are threatened that Tolkien, like Gandalf, urges the need for self-defence.

Film director Peter Jackson was fortunate that after September 11th 2001 the zeitgeist was very much in Tolkien's favour: fighting back against senselessly malign evil became part of the spirit of our times. Several lines of dialogue in all three films have strong relevance to the war against terror, but all came directly from Tolkien; Jackson and his co-writers did not have to write them in to give the book contemporary relevance.

The intelligentsia were right to believe Tolkien was conservative. He was undoubtedly a reactionary in his deep hostility towards industrial progress. He gave up driving in 1939 after seeing what road building had done to his beloved English countryside, and even in the Seventies he never owned a television set or a washing machine. He famously sent a cheque to pay his taxes and wrote on the back, "Not a penny for Concorde".[678]

It is no accident that the dodgiest hobbit in the Shire is Sandeman the miller, for any reliance on machinery made a person suspect in Tolkien's eyes. So yes, he was eccentric; but to write a work so profoundly out-of-touch with literary convention and so likely to provoke derision from Tolkien's academic colleagues demanded a very large degree of eccentricity.

As with his attitude to war, an outlook that once might have seemed right-wing has now spread across the political spectrum. Tolkien's love of trees and the natural environment, once considered oddball, has become a political force. And Tolkien's disgust at humans who commit crimes against nature - such as the wizard Saruman's experiments in genetic engineering that produce the Uruk-Hai - seems all the more relevant in an age of human-genome research, cloning, and biotechnology.

Certain modern critics, such as Dr Stephen Shapiro, an American academic who teaches cultural studies at the University of Warwick in the UK, have tried to argue that Tolkien's book is racist:

"Tolkien's good guys are white and the bad guys are black, slant-eyed, unattractive, inarticulate and a psychologically undeveloped horde... Tolkien wrote *The Lord of the Rings* because he wanted to recreate a mythology for the English, which had been destroyed by foreign invasion."[679]

By extension, Dr Shapiro calls the films racist as well:

"For today's film fans, this older racial anxiety fuses with a current fear and hatred of Islam that supports a crusading war in the Middle East. The mass appeal of *The Lord of the Rings*, and the recent movies may well rest on racist codes."[680]

Such accusations rely on far too simplistic a reading of Tolkien's text and betray a lack of knowledge about Tolkien himself. True, there is no such thing in his work as a "good orc" or an "ignoble elf", but dwarves are a mixed bunch, and one of Tolkien's themes is of racial tolerance, as the dwarf Gimli and the elf Legolas overcome their racial conditioning to become fast friends.

The obviously white characters are far from uniformly good. Saruman, Wormtongue and the Numenoreans who became the Ringwraiths are anything but heroic. And if you look through the appendices, you will find numerous references to other fair-skinned peoples engaging in evil, including Elves and tribes of Northmen who ally themselves with Gondor's enemies.

Tolkien himself was anything but a racist. In his letters, he decries Apartheid in his birthplace of South Africa. He denounced the anti-semitism of his German publishers when they tried to find out if he was Aryan. And when someone wrote to ask whether his last name was Jewish, he replied that he "should consider it an honor if it were... I regret that I appear to have no ancestors of that gifted people." [681]

The Lord of the Rings celebrates racial diversity, not racial supremacy; and so did Tolkien, who was in his letters as critical of American globalization as he was of Soviet Communism.

Tolkien was not so much a bigoted Right-winger as a convinced anti-authoritarian. In 1943 he wrote to his son Christopher, "My political beliefs lean more and more to Anarchy (philosophically understood, meaning abolition of control not whiskered men with bombs)." [682] Unlike most intellectuals of his generation, he regarded socialism and statism as unworkable and inhuman.

Tolkien's marvellous central image, overlooked by far too many critics, is the Ring itself. It represents that ultimate power which is so tempting but must be resisted at all costs. For the ring, like power, appeals to those who want to do good; but then they start to cut corners, believe that the end justifies the means, and start to allow their belief in their cause to override their moral sense and humanity.

Instinctively, most readers know how wrong the critics have been about Tolkien. Three days after I saw *The Return of the King* in late 2003, *The Lord of the Rings* was - as widely expected - hailed as Britain's favourite novel by 750,000 viewers of BBC2, echoing a 1996 poll of 26,000 readers by Waterstone's bookstore, which crowned *The Lord of the Rings* "book of the century." Similar polls in Germany and Australia delivered similar results.

The Lord of the Rings shows just how important it is for a critic to approach works of art in an unprejudiced fashion. If you are determined to find a book racist, sexist and reactionary, you are likely to miss everything that conflicts with that view, and you'll blind yourself to the piece's merits. A good critic approaches everything not with a blank mind, but an open one.

Why Birdman Took Off

As someone who still goes to the movies in the hope of pleasure, I was astonished when, at the end of 2014, *Birdman* received near-universal critical acclaim. The only dissenting voices in the UK were Deborah Ross in the *Spectator* and David Edwards in the *Mirror*.

All the other UK papers and magazines ran uncritical raves. I looked in vain for any review of it at all on *Mail Online*, even though a very brief rave had appeared in my old newspaper, the *Daily Mail*. The *Mail Online* was content merely to report the film's success with critics and its nomination for awards.

The longest piece about the film was a discussion by Lucy Mapstone of the *Mail Online*, puffing the film without giving any evidence of having seen it but discussing in detail the clothing worn by Naomi Watts and Emma Stone when they were promoting the movie in New York: "Emma, 25, looked her usual stylish self in an effortlessly elegant monochrome ensemble, while 46-year-old Naomi exuded glamour in a retro-inspired dusky blue dress."

Daily Mail Australia contributed further to Associated Newspapers' impressive sartorial coverage: "She's usually seen dressed down, looking laid back and cycling her two boys to school or visiting some organic markets. But on Saturday night Naomi Watts couldn't have looked further from a school-gate mum. The Australian actress was dressed to the nines in a sheer grey embroidered gown for the Manhattan premier of her film *Birdman* at Alice Tully Hall. The long-sleeved dress hugged the athletic 46-year-old in all of the right places."

The point of the coverage becomes clearer if you scroll down to the following advertorial link: "If you want to channel Naomi's classic look, then take a leaf out her stylish book and plump for a maxi style. From Topshop's slinky grey number, to Forever Unique's embellished version. Naomi has sealed the deal on her chic look by opting for a dress with long sleeves, so if you want to do the same then make sure you check out the styles below from River Island and ASOS!"

As I couldn't find any British critic who saw the same film that I did, and the *Mail Online* was clearly no longer interested in reviewing one of the year's major releases, I penned the following critique for no financial reward and posted it on my own website:

Birdman has impressed a lot of people, especially critics, with its starry cast and air of importance. I came out of it with a feeling that it was about half as intelligent as it thought it was, that it was a shambolic mixture of styles and that it was fatally confused about what it was trying to say. I'd call it at its best an ambitious failure, at its worst a pretentious fraud.

The film is heavily indebted to Jean-Luc Godard, from its opening titles (a lift from Godard's 60s films, especially *Pierrot le Fou*) to its message that Hollywood films are pernicious garbage, via its use of actors in roles that reflect their careers in other films – notably *Alphaville*, starring Eddie Constantine, and all those films starring Godard's off-screen wife, Anna Karina.

Michael Keaton stars as Roggan Thomson, an actor who made his name in superhero movies but turned his back on them in order to find himself and create great art. He's now putting on a Broadway play based on a story by Raymond Carver, that he hopes will bring him respectability and make him a star again.

Critics have been keen to praise the courage of an actor willing to play a role so close to himself. Keaton famously decided to back out of the Batman franchise, although my recollection is that Keaton then chose not to make arty films or dedicate his life to the theatre, but to make a succession of films that ranged from the okay (such as *The Paper* and *Jackie Brown*) to the atrocious (*My Life, Multiplicity, Desperate Measures, Jack Frost, First Daughter, White Noise, Herbie: Fully Loaded* and *The Merry Gentleman*). Keaton's only stab at art was to play Dogberry, the comic watchman, in Kenneth Branagh's film of *Much Ado About Nothing*; but that was 22 years ago. All the same, Hollywood loves a comeback, which may be why this role won Keaton a Golden Globe and an Oscar nomination.

Critics also liked the film's central thesis, which is the uncontroversial one that Hollywood is now fixated on mindless superhero films which have little or nothing to do with art. One message clear from *Birdman* is that actors who appear in blockbusters are not required to do much acting; they are merely acquiring celebrity.

Any doubts that this is one of the movie's central messages are easily dispelled by the director's recent interview with *Deadline Hollywood*. Alejandro Inarritu describes superhero movies as "very right-wing", "poison" and "cultural genocide". "If you observe the mentality of most of those films," says Inarritu, "it's really about people who are rich, who have power, who will do the good, who will kill the bad. Philosophically, I just don't like them."[683]

In the film, this hatred of Hollywood is expressed most forcefully by a wildly implausible theatre critic (Lindsay Duncan) who confides to Keaton even before she sees his play that she will give him a terrible review, the nastiest of her career, because she can't stand what he represents: celebrity rather than acting, and movies rather than the theatre.

Of course, no real critic would ever admit to this, even if they were intending to do it, but the nature of this whole film is that characters say whatever's on their mind with no subtext, just like in a very bad soap opera. Apparently that's classier than the kind of dialogue that's in superhero movies, though I seem to recall some rather good dialogue in *Spider-Man 2* and the *Hellboy* films.

The whole film has a dated, hopelessly inaccurate view of the theatre. Lindsay Duncan as the *New York Times* critic claims to be able to "kill" a show, and the other characters agree. But no one has really had that power since Frank Rich laid down his critical pen in 2011 (and for the last years of his tenure he wasn't anything like the power he was in the 1980s). As if to emphasise this, there is *Phantom of the Opera* on just across the street from our hero's production; many of Andrew Lloyd Webber's shows have flourished despite poor reviews, and there's the famous example of the Queen musical *We Will Rock You* running in the West End for ten years despite universally terrible notices.

As in most films, the critic is portrayed as a chilly, unfeeling bitch. Keaton gets to put her down with an audience-pleasing speech about actors being concerned with Truth and Art, adding that critics don't create things, they only destroy. Since the critic is meant to be intelligent, it's hard to know why she doesn't point out that actors shelter behind roles, while critics put themselves on the line with their own opinions, week after week. Actors are interpreters. Critics such as William Hazlitt, John Ruskin and Oscar Wilde deserve to be treated with a lot more respect for their creativity than actors, especially bad actors.

Anyone who accepts the film's thesis that theatre is intrinsically more "artistic" than Hollywood movies hasn't been to some of the dodgy theatre productions I have, or any of the first-rate Hollywood movies. Inarritu is making a phoney dichotomy between two kinds of entertainment.

Hollywood insiders will enjoy some of the movie's in-jokes. I liked one line when Naomi Watts whinges "I wish I had more self-respect". To which fellow-thespian Andrea Riseborough replies, in a rare moment of self-knowledge, "You're an actress, honey." But nothing in Inarritu's films, which have included *Amores Perros, 21 Grams* and *Babel,* has shown any evidence of a sense of humour or lightness of touch. Regrettably, this is no exception.

Though many critics have called it a dark satire, really the movie is like some gigantic, therapeutic guilt trip for the actors, all playing roles not a million miles from themselves. Edward Norton, who plays a difficult, egotistical method actor who despises Hollywood, starred in a failed superhero movie, *The Incredible Hulk.*

Naomi Watts, who plays a film star making her Broadway debut, also chose to star in the notorious *Movie 43* and the awful Princess Di biopic, *Diana.*

Zach Galifianakis, who plays our hero's longsuffering manager, volunteered to appear in *The Hangover part II and III*, for God's sake.

They should all know about "selling out" to the movies, but they're on dodgy ground condemning actors who do. A good many of these, such as Michael Fassbender, Patrick Stewart, Ian McKellen and Robert Downey Jr, try to do artistic things in between the crowd-pleasers, and what's wrong with that? The two are not, as Inarritu seems to argue, incompatible.

Early on, there's a scene in which a bad actor is removed from our hero's play because he can't manage nuance and keeps going "over the top". What Inarritu doesn't seem to notice is that, for the rest of the movie, most of his actors do precisely the same, without punishment. The fact that Keaton is as hammy as anyone only adds to the confusion; is he meant to be great or mediocre? Whatever he is, it's hard to feel anything for a character who's so relentlessly self-absorbed.

For much of the movie, Inarritu seems to think his leading man is right to hate himself. Keaton is much given to grandiloquent self-love ("I am bigger and better than anyone else") and depths of self-loathing ("I look like a turkey with leukaemia"). It's clear that he desires fame above all else, and he has an *alter ego* in Birdman costume who wishes he would get back to making superhero movies that people will pay to see.

At other times, Inarritu bulds up the superhuman qualities of his protagonist. He can float in the air at will. He can move things by telekinesis. He can fly. At first, it seems as if his superhero powers are all in his mind, but confusingly there are other moments when other characters – even, in the end, his unimpressed daughter – appreciates that he is, indeed, superhuman.

The film's appeal to curmudgeonly critics may also be that it doesn't contain a single likeable character. All the actors are self-obsessed, but then the critic is too, and the hero's damaged daughter. This means that ordinary people will lack empathy for just about everyone, and start looking at their watches long before the end. I can't really discuss the last 30 minutes without giving too much away. Suffice it to say that the bombastic climax pretty much encapsulates the expression "on the nose".

The film is astonishingly sexist. When Watts objects to her co-star (Norton) raping her on stage, this is treated for laughs as an over-reaction. The movie goes on to suggest that she's secretly a lesbian, and that the man who attempted the rape is the sensitive and vulnerable one. He even gets to find love with a much younger woman who knows about the rape attempt but doesn't find this off-putting in the slightest.

Critics have also commended the film's style: a succession of long tracking shots. The camera seems always to be on the move, just as it was in *Russian Ark* and a lot of films by Resnais, Antonioni and Abbas Kiarostami that reached art-houses without making much impact on the general public.

I guess this is meant to signify that it is the opposite kind of film to anything created by Michael Bay: action films with the frenetic cutting of an MTV music video. But long takes are just one technique amongst many alternatives; and it's annoyingly unclear here whether they are meant to be realistic or expressionistic.

Some critics have compared the film to Darren Aronofsky's *Black Swan*, but that's unfair to the earlier film. *Black Swan* was consistently expressionistic, and pretty much everything was seen through the eyes of its psychologically disturbed central character. That's not true of *Birdman*. The camera keeps cutting away from Keaton for scenes with other characters that appear totally naturalistic, even when (as in the pivotal scene with the critic) no one is behaving remotely realistically. Every time Keaton's point of view is lost, the film loses impetus and focus.

As if to emphasize his own cleverness, Inarritu uses his music soundtrack conventionally for the most part but playfully inserts some moments when a percussionist appears in a scene with no explanation or rationale. What's this meant to be? A reminder that this is only a film? Is it yet another reference to Godard, who went in for this kind of thing in his prime? Hey, maybe it's a reference to *Blazing Saddles*, where Mel Brooks had an entire orchestra suddenly appear in a desert.

The film it really reminded me of was Bob Fosse's inventive but tiresome *All That Jazz*, though that at least had some decent singing and dancing in it. Both films were satirizing showbiz but were at least partly in love with its excesses. Both films end up, however unintentionally, as celebrations of overweening egotism.

Inarritu emerged as one of three Mexican directors who wowed critics with their early films. Alfonso Cuaron made the best-looking of the Harry Potter films and the recent blockbuster *Gravity*, while Guillermo del Toro has been responsible for such Hollywood films as the *Hellboy* movies and the underrated *Pacific Rim*. It's hard to see *Birdman* as much more than an envious, ill-judged sideswipe at his competitors.

The central joke in *Birdman* isn't the one that you might expect; it's that this attempt at a condemnation of Hollywood vacuity is, in fact, pretentious, overblown and sensationalist itself.

There's a memorable scene early on where Norton's insufferable Method actor accuses Keaton of overwriting and needless repetition, and suggest he cut away the flab to reveal the point of the piece. It's just as well Inarritu and his three co-writers didn't do that, or they'd have no film.

Birdman pleased the critics because it isn't the kind of pap they're used to. It's a different kind of pap altogether: pretentious, pointless and far too pleased with itself. I wasn't surprised when it won Best Picture at the Academy Awards, for the central character – a washed-up, once-talented guy who lamented that films weren't what they used to be – encapsulated perfectly with the prejudices of the elderly Oscars electorate. They could all identify with a guy like that.

Whether you share my doubts about the film or not, I hope you will agree that my review is an in-depth analysis, rather than a mere expression of delight at the picture's ambition, which I can appreciate was far greater than most other recent releases had – hence the surge of relief among critics whenever a film like this is released. I'm not saying that all the critics who wrote raves in favour of *Birdman* were dishonest, or fools. But their unanimity and reluctance actually to criticise was disturbing.

You may also notice that my piece is quite different from a discussion of what female celebrities wore to the premiere. My point is that, with the firing of intelligent, experienced critics (in whose ranks I presumptuously include myself), the dumbing down of our newspapers and magazines is continuing at breakneck speed.

I would like to be able to report that, by way of compensation in-depth analyses of *Birdman* appeared on the internet, written by eager young critics who could see through the hype of the mainstream coverage, but they didn't. It was left to the middle-aged and elderly to pipe up.

A long-established internet critic, Scott Tobias, wrote an intelligent piece, the tenor of which you'll be able to grasp from the following sentence: "Alejandro González Inarritu is a pretentious fraud, but it's taken some time to understand the precise nature of his fraudulence."[684]

Another veteran, Tony Macklin, a former film and literature professor at the University of Dayton and the former editor of the filmcrit magazine *Film Heritage*, also wrote honestly about the picture's faults: "*Birdman* is molted and motley. It coos and screeches. It's one of those films that keeps prattling about the truth, but it deals with it falsely. It smacks of pretension throughout... In *Birdman*, ignorance goes viral."[685]

Michelle Alexandria of the online entertainment magazine *Eclipse* didn't go for detailed analysis but was at least honest about her reaction to the script: "I'm not one who likes ambiguity. If I'm going on a 2 or 3-hour journey with you, I want to arrive at a destination and have some sort clarity at the end, otherwise it feels like lazy writing to me."[686]

Other middle-aged critics left cold by *Birdman* were Norman Wilner of *Now*, an alternative weekly based in Toronto, Canada, the caustic Walter Chaw of *Film Freak Central* (a rare Asian-American voice) and Edward Johnson-Ott of *NUVO News*, an alternative newsweekly operating out of Indianapolis.

Easily the most detailed analysis of the film's faults came in that mainstay of magazine culture, the *New Yorker*. Richard Brody mentioned the similarities to Godard and concluded "*Birdman* trades on facile, casual dichotomies of theatre versus cinema and art versus commerce. It's a white elephant of a movie that conceals a mouse of timid wisdom, a mighty and churning machine of virtuosity that delivers a work of utterly familiar and unoriginal drama. Of such things, too, can Oscar buzz be made."

Another decent stab at reviewing the film came from screenwriter/critic Mark Hughes, writing in the business magazine, *Forbes*: "*Birdman* exists in that realm of cinematic thought where condemning whatever is currently popular in mainstream film is considered intellectual bravery."

Veteran critic Peter Rainer also wrote a considered piece in the *Christian Science Monitor*, judging *Birdman* to be "a movie with ambitions as high-flying as its superhero but a success rate decidedly lower to the ground."

The Cautionary Tale of Pauline Kael

Was Pauline Kael the greatest of all film critics? The talented director George Cukor had a particular dislike of her. "Oh, fuck Pauline Kael, fuck her!" he once said. "And I don't use that language all the time. I don't care what she has to say. She's a bitch. She's spiteful, and she's wrong. Let's not talk about Pauline Kael."[687]

Kael didn't care much for Cukor either, finding his work laboured and uncinematic. She panned his classic *The Philadelphia Story* (1940) as "shiny and unfelt and smart-aleck-commercial".[688] Of his comedy *Born Yesterday* (1950), she wrote "the second half is pretty dreary... The movie is visually dead."[689] She called *A Star is Born* (1954) a terrible "orgy of self-pity and cynicism".[690]

Perhaps the feminist Kael never forgave Cukor for *The Women* (1939). She found the piece misogynistic, writing that "it confirms rich men's worst suspicions and fantasies of what women want (money) and what they're like when they're together (clawing beasties)."[691]

That's ironic since Cukor was renowned as a "woman's director". It's fair to say that Kael and Cukor were never on the same wavelength, and for my money Cukor's accomplishments have worn better than Kael's valuations of his work. Cukor had a point; Kael could be needlessly, and unfairly, mean-spirited and vituperative.

Renata Adler wrote a coruscating critique of Kael's collection of reviews *When The Lights Go Down* on August 14th 1980, in the *New York Review of Books*. Adler's 8,000-word diatribe was described by *Time Magazine* as "the New York literary Mafia's bloodiest case of assault and battery in years". Adler, a longtime colleague of Kael's on the *New Yorker* and a former film critic for the *New York Times* in 1968-9, dismissed Kael's reviews as "worthless" and was especially harsh about Kael's cavalier regard for the truth and her "strident knowingness":

"Whatever else you may think about her work, each column seemed more hectoringly to claim, she certainly does know about movies. And often, when the point appeared most knowing, it was factually false. Ms. Kael, for instance, berated George Roy Hill, at length and in particularly scornful, savvy terms, for having recorded the outdoor sequences of *Butch Cassidy and the Sundance Kid* indoors, in a studio. As it happens, Mr. Hill had insisted on recording outdoors, at great expense and over heavy objections from the studio, which had predicted (accurately, at least as regards Ms. Kael) that no one could tell the difference. When informed of such errors, Ms. Kael never acknowledged or rectified them; she tended rather to drag disparaging references to the work of filmmakers about whom she had been wrong into unrelated columns ever after."[692]

Adler set about dismantling Kael's taste in movies with forensic skill and no little passion:

"She has, in principle, four things she likes: *frissons* of horror; physical violence depicted in explicit detail; sex scenes, so long as they have an ingredient of cruelty and involve partners who know each other either casually or under perverse circumstances; and fantasies of invasion by, or subjugation of or by, apes, pods, teens, bodysnatchers, and extraterrestrials. Whether or not one shares these predilections - and whether they are in fact more than four, or only one - they do not really lend themselves to critical discussion. It turns out, however, that Ms. Kael does think of them as critical positions, and regards it as an act of courage, of moral courage, to subscribe to them. The reason one cannot simply dismiss them as *de gustibus*, or even as harmless aberration, is that they have become inseparable from the repertory of devices of which Ms. Kael's writing now, almost wall to wall, consists."[693]

Adler was especially cutting about her malign influence on others:

"Ms. Kael's quirks, mannerisms, tactics, and excesses have not only taken over her work so thoroughly that hardly anything else, nothing certainly of intelligence or sensibility, remains; they have also proved contagious, so that the content and level of critical discussion, of movies but also of other forms, have been altered astonishingly for the worse. To the spectacle of the staff critic as celebrity in frenzy, about to "do" something "to" a text, Ms. Kael has added an entirely new style of *ad hominem* brutality and intimidation; the substance of her work has become little more than an attempt, with an odd variant of flak advertising copy, to coerce, actually to force numb acquiescence, in the laying down of a remarkably trivial and authoritarian party line."[694]

In some respects, Adler's attack on Kael seems harsh. Kael could undoubtedly write well, and read today her film reviews are a good deal livelier than Ms Adler's. Kael could be sharp and witty. She also saw through some films that many other critics didn't - especially Stanley Kubrick's striking but unpleasantly exploitative A *Clockwork Orange* (1971), which she analyzed with wit and accuracy:

"The picture plays with violence in an intellectually seductive way — Alex's victims are twisted and incapable of suffering. Kubrick carefully estranges us from these victims so that we can enjoy the rapes and beatings. Alex [the anti-hero, played by Malcolm McDowell] alone suffers. And how he suffers! He's a male Little Nell."[695]

She also realised – against the run of critical fashion - that Terrence Malik's *Days of Heaven* (1978) was a vapid piece of work beneath its pretty exterior: "The film is an empty Christmas tree: you can hang all your dumb metaphors on it."[696]

But it is today an article of faith among many critics that Pauline Kael was the best of her kind. Some talk as though she should be canonized. I have often wondered whether they have really read her reviews.

She had a blind spot about many action movies. She never felt any excitement in *Raiders of the Lost Ark* ("there's no exhilaration"). She couldn't discern the point of *Star Wars* ("exhausting... it has no emotional grip").

Science fiction generally held little appeal. She never saw the good in *Robocop* ("the picture keeps telling you that its brutishness is a terrific turn-on, and maybe it is if you're hooked on Wagnerian sci-fi comic books"). She really hated Ridley Scott's visionary *Blade Runner* ("It hasn't been thought out in human terms. If anybody comes around with a test to detect humanoids, maybe Ridley Scott and his associates should hide.[697]")

She failed to see the point of Roman Polanski's horror classic *Repulsion,* writing in *Vogue* magazine that it was needlessly voyeuristic about mental breakdown - merely "horrors fondled for the camera... It is certainly relevant to our position in the audience to ask the simple, basic, 'Why was this movie made?'"[698]

She fulminated against Martin Scorsese's classic boxing biopic *Raging Bull* on the grounds that, for her, "it definitely isn't pleasurable[699]". Her political distaste for what she saw as the "fascism" of *Dirty Harry* meant that she wouldn't give that a good review either[700], and she never forgave Clint Eastwood for starring in it.[701]

She completely failed to notice that *The Little Mermaid* was a turning-point in high-quality animation, dismissing it as just more "Disney-style kitsch".[702] She was scathing about Woody Allen's Oscar-winning romantic comedy *Annie Hall* ("the neurotic's version of *Abie's Irish Rose*[703]") and frosty about the charms of *Big* ("a formula fantasy film... Everything has a tepid inevitability[704]")

As we've already seen, she obstinately refused to spot the merits of George Cukor's classics. But that's hardly surprising, as she was equally impervious to David Lean's moving *Brief Encounter* ("there's not a breath of air in it[705]"). She even felt a lofty distaste for *It's a Wonderful Life* ("Capra takes a serious tone here though there's no basis for the seriousness; this is doggerel trying to pass as art[706]").

Of all major critics, Pauline Kael was the most reliably wrong-headed. And, as she made a point of never seeing the same movie twice, she never revised her opinions. This is a big mistake, as even critics change – and mature. Another respected critic, Anthony Lane, has pointed out the importance of admitting this:

"What we feel about a movie – or, indeed, about any work of art, high or low – matters less than the rise and fall of our feelings over time. The *King Lear* that we see as sons and daughters (of Cordelia's age, say) can never be the same play that we attend as parents; the sound of paternal fury, and of the mortal fears that echo beyond it, will knock ever more insistently at our hearts. Weekly critics cannot do justice to that process; when we are asked to nominate our favourite films, all we can say is 'Well, just now I quite like *Citizen Kane* or *Police Academy 4*, but ask me again next year.'"[707]

Kael also allowed herself to become part of a clique. In 1972, after the Presidential election when Nixon retained power with a landslide majority over the liberal George McGovern (with 61% of the popular vote for Nixon, and only 38% for the Democrats), Kael showed a snooty kind of elitism all too common in New York: "I live in a rather special world. I only know one person who voted for Nixon."[708]

Part of Pauline Kael's problem was that she never ventured far from like-minded friends and (when she grew famous) acolytes, known to themselves and detractors alike as "Paulettes". This led to a hardening world-view that became rigidly exclusive of anything that might challenge her increasingly bizarre prejudices. She much preferred Brian De Palma to Alfred Hitchcock. She liked Barbra Streisand but detested Meryl Streep. She adored Marlon Brando but hated Clint Eastwood.

In her prime, Kael wielded enormous power and influence, via her growing band of acolytes, the Paulettes. British film critic Derek Malcolm says that "If a director was praised by Kael, he or she was generally allowed to work, since the money-men knew there would be similar approbation across a wide field of publications."[709]

Kael was even said to be able to prevent filmmakers from working. The eminent British director David Lean claimed that her criticism of his work kept him from making a movie for 14 years. Her disdain for the films of Alan Parker, whether good or bad, led the British director to describe her in 1990 as "the Rambo of film critics... a demented bag lady."[710]

The Australian critic Clive James adored Kael from afar, but didn't quite so much close up:

"When she was at the height of her fame, influence, and accomplishment as a film critic at the *New Yorker*, I thought the world of Pauline Kael. After I met her, I thought rather less of her, mainly because she seemed to nurse inexplicable hatreds that were bodied forth as voodoo spells."[711]

Even *Entertainment Weekly* reviewer Owen Gleiberman, a former Paulette, admits that she had faults: "She was a great, fascinating woman who had her dark side."[712]

Pauline Kael's own daughter Gina, delivered some surprisingly honest remarks at a memorial tribute that summed up Kael's personal and professional strengths and weaknesses:

"As a mother, Pauline was exactly what you would expect from reading her or knowing her. Taste, judgment, being right were crucial. Her inflexibility pleased her... Pauline's greatest weakness, her failure as a person, became her great strength, her liberation as a writer and critic. She truly believed that what she did was for everyone else's good, and that because she meant well, she had no negative effects. She refused any consideration of that possibility and she denied any motivations or personal needs... This lack of introspection, self-awareness, restraint, or hesitation gave Pauline supreme freedom to speak up, to speak her mind, to find her honest voice. She turned her lack of self-awareness into a triumph."[713]

But it was writer-director Woody Allen who, even when she was alive, summed up Kael's most glaring defect: "She has all the qualities of a great critic, except judgment."[714]

John Simon enlarged on this in 1982 when he wrote a scathing but highly perceptive review of Kael's latest collection of movie reviews, *Deeper Into Movies*:

"What emerges from collating these bits of ludicrous overpraise or pathetic true confessions is that the shoddy films Miss Kael extols all possess one or more of the following characteristics: they are reminiscent of the kind of movies she uncritically devoured in her early years; they exalt so-called healthy vulgarity as a way of life or filmmaking; they undermine the middle-class values which Miss Kael sometimes (though not consistently) wishes to feel liberated; and they feature a homely or butch heroine who nevertheless achieves romantic fulfillment. It is almost dotting the i's to point out that these are the hallmarks of filmgoing for purposes of wish fulfillment, escape, rebellion against parental authority, and nostalgia. They are all to a greater or lesser degree immature and neurotic, and though they perfectly validate movie-buff sentiments, they are not quite so satisfactory as critical apparatus."[715]

Simon's uncomplimentary conclusion is that Kael is not so much concerned with analyzing film as surrounding herself with like-minded people:

"Even more pronounced, however, is Miss Kael's social fallacy, her need to use film as a way to become part of a great, powerful, cozy, convivially laughing, crying and booing mass, The Audience, for whom she is filled with childish affection, maternal recriminations, and the shrill love-hate of an hysterical inamorata. There is hardly a page in this collection on which Miss Kael does not dispense accolades or spankings to her fellow moviegoers, does not agonize about why they loved some violent, brutal scenes, or rejoice at their lapping up something she herself cherished...

These, clearly, are the views of a loner yearning to become part of the community, of a person endowed with superior intelligence but gladly willing to sacrifice some (though not all) of it for the sake of warming herself at the bosom of the crowd. In this way, Pauline Kael strives to become, despite certain misgivings, the Great Pop Critic, and succeeds, not completely but alarmingly enough."[716]

And remember: Pauline Kael is the person most frequently held up as an example of a great critic. However brave and talented you may be at reviewing, be sure of one thing: you will not only discover that others disagree with you, you will make many enemies.

The Dangers of Subjectivity

Most critics approach art from a purely subjective angle. They think about whether it has any appeal for them, and then say whether it has or has not. That's fair enough, as a bare minimum. All criticism is necessarily subjective, and we all bring to art our own particular background, experience and emotions. However, the approach does have its limitations.

I was very struck by a piece that appeared in one of the Sunday papers a few years back, which described all the UK's national film critics, with one paragraph devoted to each. The thing that surprised me was how similar we all were in our backgrounds. All except two of us went to Oxford or Cambridge University. All but one had degrees in the humanities. All were white. All were middle-class. All lived in London.

I am not saying that these factors disqualified us from expressing an opinion. Part of a critic's job is to offer a subjective response and analysis – the more intelligent, mature, tasteful and well-informed, the better. If you're clever enough to get to Oxbridge, you'll probably be offered a job where you have to use your brain.

However, I do think that our backgrounds constitute an inbuilt bias. For example, films that have a high literary content – Jane Austen, say, or Shakespeare – get a considerably easier ride with critics steeped in English literature than they do with the general public.

There remains an imbalance between male and female critics. Research by the Centre for the Study of Women in Television and Film at San Diego State University in 2013 painted a disturbing picture. Surveying 2000 film reviews by 145 writers, it found the top male critics on the site aggregator *Rotten Tomatoes* wrote 82% of reviews. Women wrote a paltry 18%. Instead of levelling the playing field, the internet has amplified the imbalance.

Does this matter? I think so. Not only do female critics write as well as men, they also tend to prefer certain kinds of film that are despised by men – especially romantic comedies, or movies about family and community. In my experience, the same gender bias exists across the arts. I'm not sure if this is the result of discrimination, or merely a lack of editorial imagination and a reluctance to admit that these things matter. Well, they matter to me – and, I suspect, most women.

There is also the question of race. There are virtually no black or Asian critics among the members of the British Critics' Circle. This is not because of members' prejudice against them. They have simply not taken (or, perhaps, been offered) jobs that would have given them automatic membership, if they desired it.

The *Guardian's* Michael Billington feels especially strongly on this issue, but he admits to feelings of impotence:

"I'm not sure what you can do about this: you can't *will* critics into existence. But since we live in a vibrantly multi-cultural society and since black and Asian writers are increasingly making the theatrical running, it seems absurd that criticism should still be predominantly the white man or woman's burden."[717]

So, partly because of this largely unconscious discrimination and partly because I'm uncomfortably aware of being an educated white male in a country where such people are becoming a minority, I do try and broaden my approach beyond most critics.

For a start, I always attempt to understand what the film-makers were trying to achieve, and judge how well they have succeeded according to their own objectives.

And, because at the *Daily Mail* and *Mail Online* I was writing for over a hundred million readers worldwide, I also tried to advise readers of movies which I might not personally like but which might have an appeal or importance nonetheless.

THE SIXTH COMMANDMENT
Thou Shalt Develop a Style

Critics are Writers Too

One traditional defence of professional critics is that they write better than non-professionals.

"The main thing that people fail to grasp about criticism," restaurant critic Jay Rayner told me, "is that it is a writing job. And if you don't write well, you'll be sacked."[718]

But, as the irascible veteran critic John Simon pointed out in his book *Paradigms Lost,* not all reviewers are read for the quality of their writing. Simon took to task one of the most prominent critics in America. He dismantled Rex Reed's prose style with the relish of a university professor putting an arrogant undergraduate in his place:

"As you watch *Bugsy Malone*, Reed informs you, 'your heart is likely to hum with huggable good humour.' Have you ever tried to hug a humour, good or bad? And how does a heart hum good-humouredly: like an efficient workshop or like a contented theatergoer emerging from a tuneful musical? Elsewhere we read, 'The entire film shrieks with hypnotic tension,' although hypnotic tension does not shriek and doesn't even exist – under hypnosis one is relaxed."

Simon neatly exposes Reed's blundering attempts at metaphor:

"Brian De Palma, the director of *Obsession*, 'has a strong sense of the importance of atmosphere and coats the screen with a veneer of decaying doom.' Doom does not ordinarily come in veneers, still less is it decaying. But what I really want to know is this: when does De Palma shellac his screen – during the projection or before? And how many coats does he apply?"

Reed's attempts at alliteration also incur Simon's ridicule:

"*Network* 'is a combination of apocalypse and ambrosia that is mystifying.' Such a combination would indeed be mystifying, if only it were possible. Apocalypse is something revealed, ambrosia something eaten; the two have nothing in common beyond the alliterative initial."

Simon notes that Reed constantly bungles in the way he uses words:

"He refers to the Peter Finch character as part of the 'subplot' of *Network*, even though Finch is what the main plot revolves around; Reed thinks he is clever to coin the term 'morallegory,' blissfully unaware that allegory is always a moral or moralizing genre. Elsewhere there is talk of Bette Davis's 'masklike, map-lined face,' without understanding that that would mean a face lined with maps."

Simon concludes with a paragraph that neatly exposes how clumsy writing is usually evidence of a confused and unintelligent mind:

"I could go on quoting forever, but must conclude with an excerpt from Reed's review of *Providence*, where this 'often . . . confusing to comprehend (sic)' work is declared Resnais's 'most coherent and moving film. Pay attention to detail and allow it to wash over you like a warm surf and you'll be rewarded.' It takes singular obtuseness not to recognise that paying attention to detail is the exact opposite of letting something wash over you like warm surf, but at least there can be little doubt about which of those two approaches Reed takes in his criticism."

In Reed's defence, he can be an entertaining read and has come up with several one-liners about movies that help to explain his longevity as a critic. Having recently reread his reviews for the *New York Observer*, I would commend to you his debunking of Paul Thomas Anderson's *The Master* and Oliver Stone's *Savages*. Another review of 2012, his review of Christopher Nolan's fanboy favourite *The Dark Knight Rises*, is also a fine example of sustained invective.

But Reed didn't try very hard to understand David Lynch's movie *Mulholland Drive*, which he airily dismissed as "a load of moronic and incoherent garbage".[719] And his review of *Eternal Sunshine of the Spotless Mind* suggest that he didn't bend over backwards to understand that either.[720]

And, for sheer laziness, Reed's 2013 critique of *The Cabin in the Woods* deserves some kind of wooden spoon. He called the film, which in my opinion was among the best of its year, "a creepfest so stupid it makes trashy slash-and-burn epics like *Humans Versus Zombies* and *I Spit on Your Grave* seem like Molière and Proust."[721]

He's entitled to his opinion, but that doesn't mean he is entitled to misrepresent the content of the film. In his review, Reed describes events that simply never happen: "Vampires circle the moon and suck the hot stud's blood." Er, no they don't. Was this some kind of fervid dream Reed had while he was asleep? He mentions a "cellar of corpses", when there are no corpses in the cellar. He also misses events that do occur. "What they fail to notice is the hidden cameras," he writes about the characters, when in fact they do notice the hidden cameras.

Reed misunderstands the point of the movie, even though it is clearly expressed at its climax, and – while attempting to give away its resolution– wrongly describes it: "It's all part of an elaborate video game that allows paying customers to watch real people slaughtered according to the horror of choice. The five kids in the cabin are innocent pawns to test the mechanics of the game."

The trouble is – as everyone who has seen the movie will know - there is no such video game. There are no paying customers. Nor are the characters pawns testing the nonexistent video game's mechanics. On grounds of inaccuracy, this must be the worst example of film reviewing in the history of newspapers. Rex Reed is proof that not all leading professional critics are good writers; nor are they to be trusted as reliable reporters on the movies they have seen.

Be Concise

The most concise review of all time came in a London newspaper, about a show called *A Good Time*, which ran at the Duchess Theatre in the early 1900s. It consisted of one two-letter word: "No."[722]

Jim Hoberman, former film critic for the *Village Voice*, has good advice for aspiring reviewers: "Watch for excess words. If there's a shorter word, use it."

John Simon has argued that no review less than 1500 words long can really be considered criticism. However, many critics – including myself – are placed in the position of writing an in-depth analysis of the week's main film, but having to deal with other releases in a few sentences. Are the shorter reviews of less value than the long ones? Not necessarily. Length isn't everything.

Many of the best reviewers, including James Agee (who wrote for *Time Magazine* and *The Nation* in the 1940s) have been able to sum up a film brilliantly in a sentence, while some of those who have pontificated at length in *Cahiers du Cinema* or the *Monthly Film Bulletin* have had little worthwhile to say.

A good exercise when starting to compose a review is to try and sum a film up in a sentence. Indeed, some of my favourite one-liner reviews do just that.

9 1/2 Weeks was a piece of more-or-less plotless designer porn for the 1990s, with Mickey Rourke as a Wall Street fancier having a steamy affair with an employee of an art gallery (Kim Basinger). I always liked Simon Rose's one-line critique of *9 1/2 Weeks*: "It only seems that long."[723]

Logan's Run was a 1976 science fiction movie with wooden acting and laughable dialogue. Benny Green wrote in *Punch* that "it puts the future back two thousand years".[724]

And, although I admired the recent musical film of *Les Misérables*, I did smile at Anthony Lane's one-line parody of Herbert Kretzmer's lyric: "I screamed a scream as time went by."[725]

Of my own one-liners, I look back with most affection to one about *Puffball* (2007), which struck me as an unwatchably pretentious, tiresomely whimsical thriller by director Nicolas Roeg, poorly adapted by Fay Weldon's son Dan from her 1980 novel. I summed it up in the sentence: "This Fay Weldon is fey but not well done."

If you like bad puns, I would also offer you my one-line review of Pedro Almodovar's cutesy 1986 film about two serial killers, *Matador*, about which I wrote "Picador, and leave."[726]

One of my favourite reviews was by Woody Allen, disparaging one of the leading actresses in his own one and only musical, *Everyone Says I Love You*. Allen wrote "Drew Barrymore sings so badly, deaf people refuse to watch her lips move."[727]

Wit and Humour

We can't all be as talented as Woody Allen – or Oscar Wilde. He could be witty about virtually every subject, and that ability extended to his criticism. He wrote a memorably lethal one-liner about the novelist Henry James:

"Mr James writes fiction as if it were a painful duty."[728]

He caught everything that's wrong with Dickens in his wry comment on *The Old Curiosity Shop:*

"One must have a heart of stone to read the death of Little Nell without laughing."[729]

Wilde even tried his hand at theatre criticism:

"The first rule for a young playwright to follow is not to write like Henry Arthur Jones[730]... The second and third rules are the same."[731]

Samuel Johnson was the most prolific writer and critic of the eighteenth century. Centuries after his heyday, he is remembered most fondly not for his wisdom, but for his wit. To the writer of an unsolicited manuscript, he responded:

"Your manuscript is both good and original; but the part that is good is not original, and the part that is original is not good."[732]

Though not formally a restaurant critic, Johnson was well capable of a pithy judgment on food:

"A cucumber should be well sliced and dressed with pepper and vinegar, and then thrown out, as good for nothing."[733]

Even before he had written a play, George Bernard Shaw made himself a reputation as the wittiest music critic of his day. In March 1893 he wrote "The concert began with Schubert's unfinished symphony, which on this occasion ought to have been his uncommenced symphony".[734]

And on Franz Schubert's quartet, *Death and the Maiden:*

"By the time they came to variations on *Death and the Maiden*, I was reconciled to Death and indifferent to the Maiden."[735]

Dorothy Parker was one of the wittiest of all the American journalists who formed the Algonquin Round Table. She was for years a critic for such magazines as *Vogue, Vanity Fair* and the *New Yorker*, and her targets ranged from the theatrical ("*The House Beautiful* is the Play Lousy") to the literary ("This is not a book to be tossed aside lightly. It should be thrown with great force").

She had a particular horror of the twee, and vented her spleen against A.A.Milne in one of her most famous reviews. The breaking point for Parker was when Pooh reveals that he added the "tiddely pom" to his Outdoor Song which has To Be Sung In The Snow "to make it more hummy". Her caustic comment was "And it is that word 'hummy,' my darlings, that marks the first place in *The House at Pooh Corner* at which Tonstant Weader fwowed up."[736]

Of all the twentieth century critics, Kenneth Tynan had the most elegant turn of phrase: Of Anna Neagle in *The Glorious Days*, for example, he said that she shook her voice at the audience "like a tiny fist."[737] He was similarly cruel about Vivien Leigh's Cleopatra in *Antony and Cleopatra*:

"Taking a deep breath and resolutely focusing her periwinkle charm, she launches another of her careful readings; ably and passionlessly she picks her way among its great challenges, presenting a glibly mown lawn where her author had imagined a jungle."[738]

He was no kinder about her in another Shakespeare play:

"As Lavinia, Vivien Leigh (in *Titus Andronicus*) receives the news that she is about to be ravished on her husband's corpse with little more than the annoyance of one who would have preferred foam rubber". [739]

Philip Larkin is best known as a British poet, but he was an entertainingly witty, if conservative, critic of jazz for *The Listener* magazine. Here he lays into saxophonist John Coltrane:

"That reedy, catarrhal tone... that insolent egotism, leading to 45-minute versions of *My Favourite Things* until, at any rate in Britain, the audience walked out, no doubt wondering why they had ever walked in."[740]

Larkin particularly deplored Coltrane's pretentiousness and his "wilful and hideous distortion of tone that offered squeals, squawks, Bronx cheers and throttled slate-pencil noises for serious consideration."[741]

Larkin was equally uncomplimentary about Miles Davis:

"The fact that he can spend seven or eight minutes playing *Autumn Leaves* without my recognising or liking the tune confirms my view of him as a master of rebarbative boredom... I freely confess that there have been times recently, when almost anything - the shape of a patch on the ceiling, a recipe for rhubarb jam read upside down in the paper - has seems to me more interesting than the passionless creep of a Miles Davis trumpet solo."[742]

In the modern day, Martin Amis has often struck me as a wittier critic than he is a novelist. He has an excellent ear for lazy language, and even called a collection of his essays *The War Against Cliché*. One of his most memorable pieces is one where he dismembers Michael Crichton's best-selling novel *The Lost World*:

"Animals - especially, if not exclusively, velociraptors - are what he is good at. People are what he is bad at, and prose... The job of characterization has been delegated to two or three thrashed and downtrodden adverbs. 'Dodgson shook his head irritably'; 'Handle what?' Dodgson said irritably. So Dodgson is irritable. But 'I tell you it's fine,' Levine said irritably. 'Levine got up irritably.' So Levine is irritable too. 'Malcolm stared forward gloomily.' 'We shouldn't have the kids here,' said Malcolm gloomily.' Malcolm seems to own 'gloomily'; but then you instantly notice that Rossiter is behaving 'gloomily' too, and gloomily discover that Malcolm is behaving 'irritably'. Forget about 'tensely' and 'grimly' for now. And don't get me started on 'thoughtfully'."[743]

Another novelist-critic, A.N. Wilson, has a neat line in skewering other writers' prose style. Here he goes for Dan Brown's novel *Inferno*:

"*Inferno* reads less like a novel than a 'treatment' for a thriller film... To help unsophisticated readers, Brown writes like a tour guide, ever anxious to stress the fame of the places and art treasures we glimpse along the way. The prof and his doctor race past 'Florence's famed Cathedral,' and Vasari's 'famed Studio,' not forgetting the 'world-famous Uffizi Gallery.'"[744]

Clive James rarely turned his hand to film criticism, but on *Crouching Tiger, Hidden Dragon* in a Radio 4 essay he made some elegant, highly entertaining points about clichés of the oriental martial arts movie and the way movies sentimentalize violence:

"Many film critics, not all of them on medication, think that *Crouching Tiger, Hidden Dragon* is still the acme, apex and apotheosis of the Chinese meaningful violence martial arts movie, mainly because of the purportedly balletic beauty with which its featured personnel run up the sheer walls of the Forbidden City and along the treetops of the enchanted forest while slicing at each other with whirling swords made from fragments of a meteorite forged in the book-lined cave of a Confucian philosopher, with extra boiled rice..... If, after all that spinning, diving, somersaulting and grimacing, a sword a strikes home, it makes only a small neat puncture which in no way lessens the loser's capacity to speak that special dialogue that actually sounds more Chinese after it has been dubbed into English. "Your skills are great," says Falling Snow. 'Your sword was quick," says Rising Cloud. "Your quest is finished," says Passing Wind. Passing Wind is Rising Cloud's mentor. Passing Wind is old, older than the hills, visible in the background for purposes of comparison. Yet he, too, can fly. He's been flying since before the Wright Brothers. He's been flying since long before mainland China started turning out sword operas with flying people in them, and you probably remember him from the very first such epic that made an international hit: *Flying People, Flagrant Piffle*. He was a veteran even then, and by now he has run up every wall in China. All the young swordspersons fall to their knees before Passing Wind."[745]

After Jayne Torvill and Christopher Dean won a Gold Medal at the

1984 Olympics, Clive James wrote one of his most perceptive pieces, while elegantly acknowledging that he had little or no knowledge of ice-dancing. He began his review with the following, tongue-in-cheek paragraph about his own expertise:

"This might not be the only article on the subject in today's newspapers. But it will be the only article on the subject written by someone whose own talent for ice-dancing is beyond question. It was at Peterborough last year that I invented the difficult ice-dancing manoeuvre now generally known in the sport as 'landing on the money'. The rink was crowded and I was attempting to astonish my small daughter with sheer speed. Twenty-five years had gone by since I had last skated, but all the old style was still there - ankles touching the ice, nose level with the knees, arms flailing. Tripping over some young fool's training skate, I took off, sailed high, and fell with my body so perfectly arched that my upper thighs were the first part of it to hit the ice. The small change in my trouser pocket was driven through the flesh almost to the bone. The purple bruise could not only be seen for weeks afterwards, it could be read: ELIZABETH D.G. RED F.D. 1976. So what follows is essentially a tribute from a fellow-skater."[746]

James went on to give a brilliantly written, couch-potato's view of Torvill and Dean's dancing, ending up with an account of their dance to Ravel's *Bolero*:

"You see a delicious moment not long after the start, when they come towards you with his arms folded around her from behind. She is wrapped up in him, head bowed. Then she seems to wake, slowly spreading her arms wide, which opens his arms too, because they have been holding hands. While this is going on they are picking up speed. At such a moment, which turns out to be the precursor of an unbroken sequence of moments equally expressive, Torvill and Dean look like figments of a love-sick imagination."[747]

I doubt if the American humourist P.J. O'Rourke would make it into anyone's list of the world's great rock critics, but I've always liked his back-handed tribute to the left-wing activist and folk singer Pete Seeger:

"Pete Seeger is a modest, unassuming, cheerful, and kind-natured man. He's a good folk singer, if you can stand folk singing. And he's such an excellent banjo player that you almost don't wish you had a pair of wire cutters."[748]

Another consummate stylist is comic novelist and critic Howard Jacobson. Here he is writing in the *Independent* on a subject on which he has no particular expertise – the late paintings of Rembrandt, He does so with considerable style and insight:

"The outstanding work in this show is *Bathsheba at Her Bath*, a painting of such breathtakingly fleshly sumptuousness that one might say the person hasn't lived who hasn't seen it, and having seen it has no more living to do. But it is profoundly touching too – Bathsheba naked, lost between wondering and compunction, holding the proposal from King David which, if she acts on it, will make her an adulteress. If you want to see a conscience painted, then here it is. That her exquisiteness is what's got her into this, and that her conscience is therefore close fellow to her beauty, is the painting's subject. It is as though to paint the one is to paint the other. Bathsheba's very skin is infused with introspection."[749]

Because he's a funny, observant writer with his own voice, Jacobson can sound off about, well, just about anything. Here he lays into *Strictly Come Dancing* on television:

"As long as *Strictly Come Dancing* was about people discovering a gift for dancing they never knew they had – an unexpected grace, a fluidity of body and soul previously locked away inside them (think the human corkscrew which the twist told me I could become) – then it was engaging and at times even touching. But little by little the curse of light entertainment descended on the original conception, lightness begetting lightness as surely as ignorance begets ignorance. I say nothing of the lameness of Bruce Forsyth's jokes, which were apparently part of his charm – a subtlety lost on me – but which promise to continue anyway now he's gone. And nothing, either, of how celebrity has become so debased a concept as to mean somebody of whom no one has heard. More seriously objectionable is the way the judges, who once demonstrated knowledgeable criticism in action – this is what you're doing wrong, this is how you could do it better, these are the lines and shapes we want to see – have succumbed to the lure of celebrity and declined to pantomimic versions of themselves, gurning, preening, feigning lust, exchanging leers of suggestiveness and innuendo."[750]

Jacobson affects avuncular concern about the offscreen antics of the contestants:

"In the same collusive spirit we are asked to wonder, when teacher and learner are paired off, whether shenanigans are to be anticipated, whether the spouse seen smiling weakly in the audience as a dancer wraps her legs around the husband's waist, or the wife collapses in a panting heap into her partner's arms, is soon to be made a fool of. And so, ironically, it falls to me to speak up for dancing as an activity too intrinsically elegant to be demeaned, as movement whose subtle disciplines are worthy of serious respect, and as an art sufficiently sensual in itself not to be in need of low-brow sexing up. We accept today that Disney's cartoons of animals in tutus degraded them. Reader, humans can be degraded too."[751]

To write arresting criticism, a fresh eye and some talent are really all you need. Had he not been otherwise employed, Winston Churchill would have made an excellent critic, for he was eternally unafraid and had a wonderfully witty turn of phrase. As a young man, he was asked about a dinner he had attended the night before. "Well," he replied, "it would have been splendid... if the wine had been as cold as the soup, the beef as rare as the service, the brandy as old as the fish, and the maid as willing as the duchess."[752]

Jeremy Clarkson's criticism of cars often borders on the libellous, but does have a habit of making people smile. Here are three of his typically blokish but funny comments about cars he was reviewing:

About a Porsche Cayman S: "There are many things I'd rather be doing than driving it, including waiting for Bernard Manning to come off stage in a sweaty nightclub, and then licking his back clean."

About a Porsche Cayenne: "Honestly, I have seen more attractive gangrenous wounds than this. It has the sex appeal of a camel with gingivitis."

"The Suzuki Wagon R should be avoided like unprotected sex with an Ethiopian transvestite."[753]

Even the more intellectually respectable Dilys Powell made her name as Britain's premier film critic because she was a good writer with a gift for comedy. Towards the start of her career, she got into trouble with MGM for her review of *Gone With The Wind* (1939), in which she pithily expressed her reservations about Vivien Leigh:

"Miss Leigh gave a performance compact of vivacity, coquettishness and rigid egoism, extremely clever and well-trained and almost entirely without interest."[754]

MGM banned her for a year from all of their pictures, but Powell continued to be irreverent about Hollywood's attempts to make sophisticated cinema. Her hatchet job on the anachronisms and stylistic flaws of *Pride and Prejudice* (1940) was deftly administered:

"The manners of Meryton have, indeed, acquired a certain freedom since Jane Austen described them; for here is Mr Bingley leering agreeably over a sick-room screen at Jane, who ogles back as the doctor examines her uvula. Gatecrashing is, apparently, on the up and up; the invitation to the Netherfield party bears the postscript: 'Please bring this invitation with you.'... Perhaps there is an injustice in singling out the instances in which Hollywood has got the better of Hertfordshire... The film is a pleasant enough entertainment, and it remains only to commend the foresight of the character, I forget which, overheard playing a snatch of Mendelssohn."[755]

One of Powell's best jokes landed her in trouble with the distributors of *The Ten Commandments* (1956), when she made clear her lack of sympathy for Cecil B. DeMille's biblical epic:

"With the exception of a few spectacular crowd-scenes the film is visually dull. The details of action are excruciatingly obvious; if a child is seen toddling alone amidst the exodus, one knows with certainty that somebody, Moses probably, is about to carry it. And the whole experience (with an interval) lasts roughly four hours. I am afraid that long before the time was up I was silently imploring Mr DeMille (for a critic, too, can misquote Scripture for his purpose) to let his people go."[756]

However, Dilys Powell recognised in later life the danger of going for the easy laugh:

'"I suppose I began as most young people do, showing off and trying to make jokes... I did want to entertain and amuse my readers. I mean if you're a professional writer you want to be read and you want to be with your readers. And if people would sometimes enjoy a joke I'd made - well, I'd enjoy it myself, you know. [But] I hope I always thought I was being serious. Not only serious but truthful."[757]

TV critics, in particular, often seem to be less interested in reviewing programmes than in expressing witticisms or handing out insults. Whether you like or dislike them, writers such as Clive James, A.A. Gill and Victor Lewis-Smith all fall into this category. I felt James was generally fair in his criticism and didn't sacrifice truthfulness for an easy laugh; but many who followed him failed to live up to those standards, especially Victor Lewis-Smith, whom I regarded as an entertaining read but worthless as a judge of television.

In the years that I was TV critic for the *Sunday Telegraph*, I was aware of the need to entertain and make jokes, and did so. My favourite was a review of a mini-series called Monte Carlo, that starred an ageing Joan Collins singing in a night club, caked with far too many layers of make-up: "When she sings *The Last Time I Saw Paris*, she may well remind you of the last time you saw plaster of Paris."[758]

But I also felt a responsibility to programme-makers, partly because I was still working in television myself, directing shows such as *Network 7* and *After Dark* for Channel 4. Besides, I saw myself in another tradition - of writers such as Peter Black of the *Daily Mail* and Philip Purser, my predecessor at the *Sunday Telegraph* - in appreciating that television was not merely junk but, at least potentially, an emerging art-form.

The wittiest critic of the present day? I would nominate Craig Brown (the one who isn't a former Scottish football manager). Best known for his writing in *Private Eye*, he also has columns on the *Telegraph* and *Mail*. He has a wonderful gift for satirical insights, as well as a flair for parody. Some of his victims may find him cruel. Janet Street-Porter once booed him at an awards ceremony, which is an accolade, and Harold Pinter spotted him at a party and ostentatiously mimed throttling him. When the hostess asked Pinter "Do you want to punch him? The playwright replied "I wouldn't dirty my fists."[759]

Brown regards himself as responsible only to his readers. "The best critics," he says, "do not worry about what the author might think. That would be like a detective worrying about what a suspect might think. Instead, they treat the reader as an intelligent friend, and describe the book as honestly, and as entertainingly, as possible."[760]

His parodies are masterly when they expose the conceit of those he is parodying. He has a good nose for delusional celebrities, which may be why he has such fun writing from the point of view of Heather Mills McCartney. Here she is on why she identifies herself so passionately with Florence Nightingale:

"They try and make out she's only in it for the publicity. I was a nurse in the Crimea and believe me it's no easy job walking around with your lamp, tending to all those brave soldiers with blood spurting out of them, hearing their last words, wrapping them up in bandages and that."[761]

He also dislikes tweeness, and wrote my favourite critical sideswipe at the film of *The Sound of Music:*

"To this day, Julie Andrews insists on living by the rules set out in the song *Do-Re-Mi.* Thus, she never drinks a cup of tea without also consuming jam and bread, and whenever a Customs officer, tax inspector or policeman asks her what she calls herself, she always replies by singing the word 'Me!' Over the past half-century, this has resulted in several periods of incarceration for the plucky actress."[762]

He has a horror of overacting, born as he admits of traumatic exposure to the motel soap opera *Crossroads* as a child:

"My earliest prolonged exposure to the actor's art was watching the likes of Benny and Miss Diane in the TV series *Crossroads* for 25 minutes, five days a week, 52 weeks a year for a good ten years. The marvellous thing about *Crossroads* was that you always knew what was going on. If, for instance, Wee Shughie, the under-chef, suddenly spotted a spider on a blancmange, his facial expression would move within a split-second from easy-going enthusiasm to the utmost alarm. Ditto the busy-body, Amy Turtle. When Amy answered the motel telephone and her mouth shot open and her eyebrows shot up, you knew for sure that someone unsavoury was on the other end of the line. It may not have been very subtle, but at least we all knew where we were."[763]

Brown is equally worried by underacting:

"At the moment, I'm very much enjoying *Wolf Hall* on BBC2, but it can be a little hard to follow, largely because the acting is so subdued. If an actor in *Wolf Hall* looks blank, it means he has just heard some very bad news. If he raises an eyebrow, it means he's just heard his wife has had her head chopped off. And if he raises both eyebrows it means that his own head has just been chopped off."[764]

Last but not least, he has a splendidly developed gift for hilarious understatement, as in "By and large, the artistic establishment disapproved of Margaret Thatcher."[765] If you can write half as amusingly as Craig Brown, you have a bright future.

THE SEVENTH COMMANDMENT
Thou Shalt Have Perspective

The Dead Hand of Aristotle

There are grave dangers in being hidebound by the past.

It could be argued that the ancient Greek philosopher Aristotle was "the father of criticism"; but Aristotle never gave us a single appreciation of a book or play, let alone an author or playwright.[766] Instead, he laid down a number of arbitrary principles about theatre, that held sway among critics and dramatists for an extraordinarily long time.

The "classical unities" are rules for drama derived from a passage in Aristotle's *Poetics*. The first is unity of action: Aristotle argues that a play should have one main action that it follows, with no subplots, or very few. The second is unity of place: a play should cover a single physical space and should not attempt to compress geography, nor should the stage represent more than one place. The third is unity of time: the action in a play should take place over no more than 24 hours.[767]

Why? You may well ask. But sixteenth century Italian critics such as Lodovico Castelvetro and then 17th-century French critics, usually called the "neoclassicists", followed Aristotle's precepts to lay down laws about how all plays should be structured. French drama of the 17th century, particularly that of Corneille, Racine and Moliere did their best to adhere to Aristotelian rules.

English dramatists writing for the Elizabethan and Jacobean stage often acted as though unaware of Aristotle's precepts. Only two of Shakespeare's plays conform to the unities - *The Comedy of Errors* and *The Tempest*.

In the seventeenth century, John Dryden called Shakespeare "incomparable" precisely because of his disregard for regular convention:

"In most of the irregular Playes of Shakespeare or Fletcher (for Ben Johnson's are for the most part regular) there is a more masculine fancy and greater spirit in all the writing, than there is in any of the French."[768]

Dryden disliked the classic prejudice against mixing tragedy with comedy. He enjoyed the romantic extravagances of Shakespeare and noted that ancient Greek tastes in drama "would not satisfy an English audience." He refused to believe that ancient Greeks and Romans "were models for all time and in all languages." He wrote:

"It is not enough that Aristotle had said so, for Aristotle drew his models of tragedy from Sophocles and Euripides: and, if he had seen ours, might have changed his mind".[769]

Dryden's arguments did not carry weight with everyone. His contemporary, the critic Thomas Rhymer, continued to put forward neoclassicism as the only permissible set of rules in theatre. As late as 1728, Alexander Pope criticised all violations of the unities in his poem, *Dunciad*. Amazingly, the classical unities still carried weight in continental drama until Victor Hugo's *Hernani* (1830); the play raised huge controversy at its premiere with its shameless violation of Aristotle's precepts.

Influenced by Shakespeare, British dramatists were noticeably less hidebound. Samuel Johnson hailed Dryden as "the father of English criticism" and argued convincingly that ignoring the rules of the Greek critic had been liberating for Shakespeare and British drama in general:

"Whether Shakespeare knew the unities, and rejected them by design, or deviated from them by happy ignorance, it is, I think, impossible to decide, and useless to inquire. We may reasonably suppose, that, when he rose to notice, he did not want the counsels and admonitions of scholars and critics, and that he at last deliberately persisted in a practice, which he might have begun by chance. As nothing is essential to the fable, but unity of action, and as the unities of time and place arise evidently from false assumptions, and, by circumscribing the extent of the drama, lessen its variety, I cannot think it much to be lamented, that they were not known by him, or not observed: Nor, if such another poet could arise, should I very vehemently reproach him, that his first act passed at Venice, and his next in Cyprus. Such violations of rules... become the comprehensive genius of Shakespeare."[770]

Historical Perspective

Oscar Wilde was often accused of being a dilettante but he knew that good criticism demanded hard work:

"He who desires to understand Shakespeare truly must understand the relations in which Shakespeare stood to the Renaissance and Reformation, to the age of Elizabeth and the age of James; he must be familiar with the history of the struggle between the old classical forms and the new spirit of romance, between the school of Sidney, and Daniel, and Jonson, and the school of Marlowe and Marlowe's greater son; he must know the materials that were at Shakespeare's disposal, and the method in which he used them, and the conditions of theatric presentation in the sixteenth and seventeenth century, their limitations and their opportunities for freedom, and the literary criticism of Shakespeare's day, its aims and modes and canons, he must study the English language in its progress, and blank or rhymed verse in its various developments; he must study the Greek drama, and the connection between the art of the creator of the Agamemnon and the art of the creator of Macbeth; in a word, he must be able to bind Elizabethan

London to the Athens of Pericles, and to learn Shakespeare's true position in the history of European drama and the drama of the world."[771]

As a critical theorist, Wilde was strongly of the opinion that historical perspective was crucial to good criticism:

"For he to whom the present is the only thing that is present, knows nothing of the age in which he lives. To realise the nineteenth century, one must realise every century that has preceded it and that has contributed to its making. To know anything about oneself one must know all about others."[772]

One reason Martin Amis can write an intelligent review of James Joyce's *Ulysses* is that he has read Joyce's other stuff too, which gives him an informed perspective on the man's work:

"Throughout the course of his *oeuvre* one watches James Joyce steadily washing his hands of mere talent: the entirely approachable stories of *Dubliners*, the more or less comprehensible [of the *Artist as a Young Man*], then *Ulysses*, before Joyce girds himself for the ultimate reader-hostile, reader-nuking immolation of *Finnegan's Wake*, where every word is a multilingual pun. [Amis here is guilty of exaggeration.] The exemplary genius, he is also the exemplary Modern, fanatically prolix, innovative and recondite, and free of any obligation to please a reading public (in place of government grants or protective universities, Joyce had patronage). Unreined, unbound, he soared off to fulfil the destiny of his genius; or, if you prefer, he wrote to please himself. All writers do this, or want to do this, or would do this if they dared. Only Joyce did it with such crazed superbity."[773]

At the end of his essay, Amis admits that Joyce's super-elitist, self-centred approach has its drawbacks, a comment Amis is all the more entitled to make as someone who has himself made a living from novels:

"Joyce didn't love the reader, as you need to do. Well, he gave us *Ulysses,* incontestably the central modernist masterpiece; it is impossible to conceive of any future novel that might give the form such a violent evolutionary lurch. You can't help wondering, though. Joyce could have been the most popular boy in the school, the funniest, the cleverest, the kindest. He ended up with a more ambiguous distinction: he became the teacher's pet."[774]

In 2007, the film academic Ronald Bergan made an impassioned outcry in the *Guardian Online* for movie critics to find out more about the history of film. His beef was that reviewers seem to be selected for their writing ability than for their knowledge of cinema:

"There's a common fallacy that anyone can review a film. But how can you do it if you don't have the proper tools to 'read' a film?"[775]

Bergan argues that this has led to a deterioration in film criticism, which has become primarily descriptive, anecdotal and subjectively evaluative rather than analytical. Bergan recommends that all movie critics should have a degree in film studies:

"I believe that every film critic should know, say, the difference between a pan and a dolly shot, a fill and key light, direct and reflected sound, the signified and the signifier, diegetic and non-diegetic music, and how both a tracking shot and depth of field can be ideological."[776]

Bergan also believes they should know about more than Hollywood cinema:

"They should know their jidai-geki from their gendai-geki, be familiar with the Kuleshov Effect and Truffaut's *Une certain tendance du cinéma français*, know what the 180-degree rule is and the meaning of 'suture'. They should have read Sergei Eisenstein's *The Film Sense and Film Form* and the writings of Bela Balasz, André Bazin, Siegfried Kracauer, Roland Barthes, Christian Metz and Serge Daney. They should have seen Jean-Luc Godard's *Histoire du Cinema*, and every film by Carl Dreyer, Robert Bresson, Jean Renoir, Luis Buñuel and Ingmar Bergman, as well as those of Jean-Marie Straub and Danielle Huillet, and at least one by Germaine Dulac, Marcel L'Herbier, Mrinal Sen, Marguerite Duras, Mikio Naruse, Jean Eustache and Stan Brakhage. They should be well versed in Russian constructivism, German expressionism, Italian neo-realism, Cinema Novo, La Nouvelle Vague and the Dziga Vertov group."[777]

Really? Academic knowledge of that kind is all very well, but Bergan overstates his case – you hardly need to have seen a Robert Bresson film in order to understand a movie produced by Adam Sandler. And I could make a case for every film critic to work for a few years in the entertainment industry. It's been a great help to me as a critic that I have had to make films and TV programmes myself, and that kind of experience is not something you will learn on a film studies course.

However, it is all too easy to see that some critics haven't seen much that predates *Star Wars*, most have never seen an Ealing comedy, and virtually all are woefully ignorant of all but English-language movies. And if as a critic you're going to make airy statements about such and such a film being the "greatest" comedy or action movie of all time, it's a good idea if you have seen the major contenders for those accolades.

La La Land is a case in point. Misled by the critics, I went to it expecting a new *Singin' In The Rain* or the reinvention of the screen musical. I found only a slightly less annoying version of *Down With Love*.

Amateurish songs (and they weren't jazzy, so why would the leading man, supposedly a jazz enthusiast, want to express himself through them?) combined with sub-standard singing and dancing, even in the opening number where they had the whole pool of US talent to draw on, and a banal script that undermined its "follow your dream, and talent will succeed" message by showing us a couple "succeeding" with less talent than hundreds of singer-dancers slogging away in the real world for little reward.

What boggled my mind was that so many critics blithely compared *La La Land favourably* with top-rate musicals. Every Astaire-Rogers movie had superior songs, along with much better singing and dancing. The emotional weight and musical sophistication of every Rodgers and Hammerstein movie were in a different class (especially *Oklahoma, South Pacific, Carousel* and *The King and I*). And *West Side Story* had a jazz-influenced score that was light years ahead of this one. *La la Land* is more on the scale of a chamber musical, like *The Umbrellas of Cherbourg*, but even Demy's little film had a panache and catchiness that *La La Land* lacks.

I can see why some people, starved of style and sophistication, might find *La La Land* less depressing than most cinematic fare. At least it's on a human scale, unlike the blockbusters that have sent so many of us back to TV box sets. But when I read my erstwhile colleagues' five-star reviews, I was filled with optimism. After I'd seen the film, my mood was one of puzzlement and pessimism. I can't believe that the critics had really seen the great musicals to which they compared *La La Land*.

Good film criticism often involves making revealing comparisons. If you haven't seen Howard Hawks's movie *The Thing* (1951) or Edward L. Cahn's *It! The Terror From Beyond Space* (1958), the likelihood is that you will regard *Alien* as much more original than it truly is.

In order to appreciate *Star Wars* fully, it's a good idea to have seen Akira Kurosawa's *The Hidden Fortress*. Watching the anime classic *Ghost in the Shell* will help you make sense of the Wachowskis' film *The Matrix*.

And you are much more likely to tolerate the *longueurs* in Terrence Malick's film *The Thin Red Line* if you understand what critic Jonathan Rosenbaum said in his review, that those seemingly pointless cutaways are a homage to silent cinema:

"Malick's intimate acquaintance with the aesthetics of silent cinema reaches well past Murnau. The punctuating shots of nature in the midst of combat – a wounded bird, a riddled leaf, a hill of waving grass – are pure silent-movie syntax, as is the notion of a collective war hero (often found in films and fiction about World War I; William March's 1933 book *Company K* is one distinguished example). The poetic and philosophical internal monologues of Malick's various soldiers, often paired with a sustained and soulful close-up of the character, are the structural equivalent of intertitles in silent films of the teens and 20s. This is a precious legacy that most major filmmakers of the 90s (excepting Godard, Tarr, Tregenza, Manuel de Oliveira, and a handful of others who live outside the Oscars sweepstakes) have either forgotten or never discovered in the first place – a sensibility that frees images from the tyranny of the sound track, allowing them to register in all their primordial power – and the major achievements of *The Thin Red Line* would be unthinkable without it."[778]

Former *Sunday Times* film critic George Perry tells me that he was shocked when he discovered that the film critic of *Today* had never heard of the famous film critic turned director, Lindsay Anderson (of *If...* and *O Lucky Man!* fame). Ten years on, I suspect that hardly any young critics have heard of Lindsay Anderson. That's their loss, of course, but also their readers'.

Perry believes that the downgrading of knowledge as a qualification to become a film critic vanished long ago:

"I think wilful ignorance is the worst fault of professional critics, and it goes with the 'anyone can be a film critic' philosophy of many newspaper editors. One savours the absurdity of Penelope Mortimer, a superannuated novelist, suddenly parachuted into the *Observer* slot who referred to Hitchcock as purely a Hollywood director, totally unaware that he had enjoyed a substantial British career before *Rebecca*. What's even worse is that nobody on the *Ob*, and in those hot-metal days they still had an army of subs, spotted her howler."[779]

The best critics do tend to be well-informed. When Arnold Wesker's *Roots* was produced in 1959, a remarkable number of critics mistakenly hailed it as the first time the working class had been given a voice on stage. John Galsworthy's *Strife* was overlooked, not to mention Stanley Houghton's *Hindle Wakes* and Walter Greenwood's *Love on the Dole*. Virtually all the reviews lacked historical perspective.[780]

I remember that it used to annoy the theatre impresario Sir Donald Albery a good deal that the theatre critics had hailed Peter Brook's 1970 production of *A Midsummer Night's Dream* for the Royal Shakespeare Company, with actors performing acrobatic stunts in a brightly-lit, minimalist white box to the accompaniment of guitars, bongos, and tubular bells, as ground-breaking, original and revolutionary, when Sir Donald had seen foreign theatre productions that he felt Brook had plagiarized.[781]

Harold Hobson's 1964 review of Joe Orton's play *Entertaining Mr. Sloane* deliberately drew parallels with literary history that were guaranteed to annoy fellow-critics such as W.A. Darlington of the *Daily Telegraph* who had described it as so nasty that he felt "snakes had been writhing round my feet".[782]

Hobson's review three days later bravely but accurately compared Joe Orton to Jane Austen:

"Miss Austen had a keen eye for the absurdities of the fashionable fiction of her day; and so has Mr Orton. His *Entertaining Mr Sloane*, all proportions kept, is the *Northanger Abbey* of our contemporary stage."[783]

I was very struck, when I read the extraordinarily diverse reviews of my own Musical *Hard Times* at the Theatre Royal, Haymarket in London's

West End, how virtually all of the theatre reviewers who hated my show (a vociferous minority) had a view of Dickens' novel that was out of date by several decades. Although my show went on in 2000, their assumptions were rooted in attitudes expressed in the Sixties by F.R. Leavis in *Scrutiny* (which, bizarrely, treated Dickens' very stylized book as social realism). They took no account of scholarly examinations in the decades since then, by David Lodge and numerous others, which had revealed *Hard Times* to be primarily a domestic story, fairytale and allegory. Perhaps I shouldn't have had higher expectations of the theatre critics, but it was clear that – with more than a trace of arrogance - they regarded my approach to the book as old-fashioned, when really it was theirs that was more than thirty years behind the times.

It is a melancholy truth that many critics write not in order to express their own opinions but to join a club to which they wish to belong: a metropolitan elite handing down whatever opinions are currently popular or fashionable. That may sound like a harsh judgment, but I believe it covers many of those claiming to write "criticism" today.

The most celebrated and most vilified art critic of modern times, Brian Sewell of the *Evening Standard,* was outspoken in his condemnation of art critics who act this way. The targets of most of his writing were "the great and the good" of the art world.

His 2012 collection of reviews of English Contemporary Art, entitled *Naked Emperors* implicitly compared Sewell to the little boy in the Hans Andersen story who dares to point out the unwelcome truth, and has nothing but contempt for the cliquishness of those in authority over the art world:

"Successive governments in control of arts policy and purse-strings have been comatose in their contentment with the *status quo*, and the clique is more entrenched than ever, wholly in control of the institutions and the cash, the propaganda, the promotion and even of the attitude of broadcasters and the press. No one in the visual arts has ever been more securely established, more in control, than Nicholas Serota; with his multiplying Tates and satrapies from Newcastle to Margate, his influence on the Arts and British Councils, his Trojan Horses at the gates of the National Gallery and Royal Academy, his Tendency is everywhere. It is embodied in cronies, critics and curators (the collective noun for all is creep or crawl), theorists and academics, and expressed in obscurities of jargon that fro de haut en bas intellectually exclude the wider public, whether drawn to contemporary art in the spirit of enquiry and the hope of aesthetic reward or, as Hirst's flies to rotting flesh, drawn by the promise of exhibits freakish, grotesque, repugnant and bizarre, but aesthetically barren."[784]

There are at least as many film critics guilty of this creeping and crawling to the establishment - and some of them are familiar faces at national screenings. They are even more prevalent at evening screenings, those magnets for non-earning film critics, where sandwiches and access to films they can't afford tickets for frequently take the place of payment. My erstwhile colleague, Alan Frank of the *Daily Star*, was fond of remarking that if the supply of nibbles at evening screenings ever dried up, a good many people calling themselves film critics would be found rotting, uncared about and long dead of malnutrition, in their dingy bedsits.

Such critics are hardly likely to incur the wrath of publicists by badmouthing films; they are only too happy to toe the party line and see the good in everything while remaining tight-lipped on the film's defects - if, indeed, they are capable of spotting the film's defects, which is extremely doubtful.

Like me, the reviewer Irving Wardle (who was theatre critic for *The Times* and the *Independent on Sunday*) has a horror of what he calls "clubland reviewing" – the kind of criticism that reflects little more than the writer's anxiety to belong to a like-minded association of reviewers. Wardle believes this is how left-wing bias most often manifests itself:

"The habit of reviewing themes instead of plays... came in with the right-on liberal reviewers of my generation, who are apt to rely on the theatre for their political experience and respond with push-button reliability to such topics as apartheid, sexual prejudice, police corruption and the unalterable malevolence of the Tory Party. When a play happens to touch on one of these approved subjects, we undergo a string temptation to mark it up for good intentions, and turn a blind eye to its shortcomings in other respects The writer may show no talent for characterization, dialogue or story-telling, but at least he is handling something important."[785]

This orthodoxy of approach is especially rife at the BBC, where TV and radio producers alike seem to feel that any reviewing panel should consist of a token left-wing feminist (usually Germaine Greer), a token left-winger from a racial minority (often Bonnie Greer) and a left-wing gay man or woman (plenty to choose from). This, think the producers, will produce a balanced discussion. It produces the opposite, of course, which is why the ratings for such programmes are so low. Between them, the three token critics will cover all the bases of political correctness; but many viewers or listeners may wonder why they are being given no useful information on whether the play or film being discussed is worth the effort of seeing.

Wardle deplores the laziness of so-called "middle-distance writing", which avoids making a value judgment and affects a superiority on the part of the critic that is frequently groundless.

Wardle prefers a style of criticism that has both detail and perspective:

"Reviewing only comes to life when it opts for the alternatives of the close-up and long shot: the piercing detail that is its own justification, and the extended perspective that puts the show into a wider context."[786]

This is an echo of Soviet film-maker Sergei Eisenstein's view of reviewing. In his essay *A Close Up View*[787], he draws an analogy between the use of long shots, medium shot and close-up in film-making to three aspects of criticism. The long shot explores the ideological or moral correctness of a film. The medium shot, the view of most spectators, is primarily concerned with the "living play of emotions". The close-up involves breaking down a film, analysing its parts and the way in which they work or don't work. Eisenstein argued that all three approaches were necessary in criticism. No single one could justify accepting a work of art as good if the others are defective or absent. All three approaches deserve to be pursued.[788]

The British documentary-maker John Grierson laid the greatest emphasis on the long shot. In his view, film was most valuable when it had social responsibility. Although he admired the technique of Joseph Sternberg, he felt that the maker of *Shanghai Express* had become the maker of a vacuous film that was all about style, with no substance or purpose. For Grierson, *Shanghai Express* was "a masterpiece of the toilette". Grierson mused that "when a director dies, he becomes a photographer."[789]

Good critics, such as Michiko Kakutani, literary critic for the *New York Times*, do tend to have a multi-faceted approach to art, examining purpose, emotional impact and technique. Moreover, they can draw on a wealth of experience and use it to illuminate the place of phenomena such as Harry Potter in world literature. Here's Kakutani doing just that, in 2007:

"It is Ms. Rowling's achievement in this series that she manages to make Harry both a familiar adolescent — coping with the banal frustrations of school and dating — and an epic hero, kin to everyone from the young King Arthur to Spider-Man and Luke Skywalker. This same magpie talent has enabled her to create a narrative that effortlessly mixes up allusions to Homer, Milton, Shakespeare and Kafka, with silly kid jokes about vomit-flavoured candies, a narrative that fuses a plethora of genres (from the boarding-school novel to the detective story to the epic quest) into a story that could be Exhibit A in a Joseph Campbell survey of mythic archetypes. In doing so, J. K. Rowling has created a world as fully detailed as L. Frank Baum's Oz or J. R. R. Tolkien's Middle Earth, a world so minutely imagined in terms of its history and rituals and rules that it qualifies as an alternate universe, which may be one reason the 'Potter' books have spawned such a passionate following and such fervent exegesis... Ms. Rowling has fitted together the jigsaw-puzzle pieces of this long undertaking with Dickensian ingenuity and ardor."[790]

Another leading American critic, Harold Bloom, takes a beadier view of J.K. Rowling's work, though he only made it through to the end of her first novel. Under a one-star rating of the book and the headline "Can 350 million people be wrong?" he wrote an impassioned diatribe for the *Wall Street Journal*. He doesn't retract any of it:

"I could not believe what was in front of me. What I particularly could not bear was that it was just one cliché after another. In fact, I kept a little checklist on an envelope next to me, and every time any individuals were going, as you or I might say, to take a walk, they were going to 'stretch their legs.' At the fiftieth or sixtieth stretching of the legs, that was too much for me."[791]

Bloom's analysis of Harry Potter caused a furore, and anonymous readers piled in to call Bloom an "idiot", "an intellectual snob" and far, far worse:

"It is not an exaggeration to say that all hell indeed broke loose," says Bloom. "The editor called me ten days later and said, 'Harold, we've never seen anything like this before. We have received over four hundred letters denouncing your piece on Harry Potter. We've received one favourable letter, but we think you must have written it.' I said, 'No, I assure you.' It never stopped. The damn piece was reprinted all over the world, in all languages. I will never hear the end of it. But of course, the Harry Potter series is rubbish. Like all rubbish, it will eventually be rubbed down. Time will obliterate it. What can one say?"[792]

Both Bloom and Kakutani are entitled to their very divergent views of Harry Potter. Readers will form their own opinions on whether Bloom is right to say that "Rowling's mind is so governed by clichés and dead metaphors that she has no other style of writing."[793] Bloom is not so much a literary snob as a critic who prizes literary style over telling a story, which is why he also despises the popular author Stephen King. When King was awarded the National Book Foundation's 2003 medal for Distinguished Contribution to American Letters, Bloom called that decision "another low in the process of dumbing down our cultural life."[794]

The best critics don't always agree. The important thing is that they should be willing to explain why they believe what they do. After all, critics draw on their very different experiences of art and, indeed, life. Theatre critic Irving Wardle wrote generously in 1992 of his more right-wing contemporary, John Peter of the *Sunday Times:*

"Peter has every right to rend English playwrights limb from limb for their flirtations with Marxism; not because this viewpoint happens to coincide with that of the *Sunday Times* and its readers, but because, as a Hungarian emigre who witnessed the 1956 Russian invasion, he knows more about the realities of Marxism than the 'state of Britain' authors whose interest in revolutionary politics has yet to come between them and a hot dinner."[795]

In order to review TV soap opera, it's a good idea to have seen many soaps, so that you are able to make informed comparisons. Maureen Ryan of the *Chicago Tribune* had bothered to do this, which is why her review of *Grey's Anatomy* carried more weight than most:

"There's a trick to making a successful soap opera: The writers have to let the characters make mistakes and act poorly, but not screw up so badly that viewers don't much care if the lovelorn people on the show ever find happiness or contentment. For a while there, *Grey's Anatomy* had that balance right. Then it slid off a cliff during an annoyingly inconsistent, profoundly self-indulgent third season... It was especially dispiriting that most of the female characters had more or less been eviscerated. The women on the show started out as flawed but funny, intelligent professionals, but by the end of last season, they were a gang of mopey or vindictive whiners, each one obsessed, to an alarming degree, with their romantic travails at the expense of their friendships, self-esteem and careers."[796]

A.A. Gill had the self-confidence, born of long experience as a television critic, to draw wide conclusions from single episodes. Here he is on the TV adaptation of *Cranford:*

"I sat down to *Cranford* girded and gimlet-eyed, my modernist cudgel ready to bludgeon it to a silly pulp. Then, in the very first minute, Eileen Atkins gave me a look – just for a moment, a sideways look, more a glance, really, but it had such depth of character, such promise of interest and intimations of stories to come of hardship and parsimony, of steadfastness, piety, worldliness and a little kindness, all packed together in that one tiny gesture, like an apothecary's spice box – and I realised it was all up. I was hooked, gaffed, netted and filleted... Simply in terms of skill, range and honesty, television buries film at the moment. And we have a particularly strong cast of actresses who find themselves in their prime. The reason there are so many of them in *Cranford* is that the only people who will write decent parts for them are dead lady novelists, and that's not just a shame, it's a sinful waste of a great national resource."[797]

Sir Kenneth Clark (1903-1983) was much ridiculed by the intelligentsia for his 1969 TV series *Civilisation*, a neo-classicist account heavily biased in favour of European civilisation and reluctant to acknowledge much of the art that invigorated, say, Anglo-Saxon England or the Middle Ages.

Clark was routinely derided by many art experts as a snob and he certainly had his blind spots; but he was always articulate about why he was praising one thing and not another. Clark saw himself as defending a western idea of civilisation that was under threat. He was no "little Englander" not an instinctive conservative.

Underlying a good deal of his artistic criticism lay a contempt for totalitarianism, whether in its German nazi form or its Russian Stalinist identity. But he also had enthusiasm for modern architecture and for "the

once minor arts – textiles, pottery, photography, printing, advertisement",
which "all show evidence of real vitality". Such sentiments reflect Clark's
respect for the cohesive visual culture of the Renaissance, but also his
friendships with poster designers Edward McKnight Kauffer and Jack
Beddington, about both of whom Clark wrote appreciatively in his
autobiography.[798]

The depth of Clark's historical knowledge as an art critic could not be
doubted. And the way he used visual corroboration to back up his
arguments was exemplary.

John Berger's 1972 series *Ways of Seeing* was intended to be a
counterblast to Clark's denunciation of "the moral and intellectual failure of
Marxism". Berger's central argument was that "the art of any period tends
to serve the ideological interests of the ruling class." Again, Berger cleverly
used visual evidence to support his prejudices.

Robert Hughes' 1980 series *The Shock of the New* both celebrated
modern art and laid into leading practitioners of it, who according to
Hughes had succumbed to celebrity and the lure of the market-place. Andy
Warhol, Joseph Beuys, Robert Mapplethorpe, Jeff Koons, Marcel Duchamp,
Jean-Michel Basquiat, Julian Schnabel and Damien Hirst were, according
to Hughes, barely real artists at all but manipulators of the art market, and
all felt the lash of his scorn.

Hughes' critical prose was refreshingly free of art-world jargon. He
had a good turn of phrase that took no prisoners, writing that "Schnabel's
work is to painting what Stallone's is to acting: a lurching display of oily
pectorals"[799]; "The new job of art is to sit on the wall and get more
expensive"[800]; and "I am often viewed as a 'conservative' critic... When an
artist says that I am conservative, it means that I haven't praised him
recently." [801]

The art critic Matthew Collings has paid eloquent tribute to the
importance of *The Shock of the New:*

"What is great about what Hughes did was that he took an already
established story, which is the story of the isms of modern art, and he made
it into a gripping narrative. But that narrative wasn't just gripping because
of some abstract ability he had to make a story, but because he had high
aspirations. He gave you the feeling that he was genuinely depressed about
the noble aspirations of art no longer being there, that they had somehow
been lost, that the moment of modernism had past. He made you feel that
that thing that was lost was a tragic loss, and he found a voice to express
that so you could take it seriously. He wasn't a fuddy-duddy, he wasn't an
academic... He made that idea of modern art as something important that
was essential and that we needed. He made the passing of it seem like a
loss."[802]

All three of these art critics had their foibles and their prejudices, but there was no doubting their experience – or their ability to write and argue in an entertaining and inspirational manner.

Of all the art critics today, Andrew Graham-Dixon strikes me as having an exceptionally good eye and plenty of experience. His critical essays on the visual arts are the contributions to *The Culture Show* (BBC2) which consistently carry the most weight.

Historical perspective can also be found in the writing of the eternally controversial Brian Sewell, who became entertainingly incensed in 1997 when his predecessor as *Evening Standard* art critic, Richard Cork, compared modern artist Tony Cragg to one of the all-time-greats:

"Richard Cork, Arts Council panjandrum off and on for ever, so it seems, and one of the judges who award him the Turner Prize, has described the sculpture of Cragg in this exhibition as on a par with Michelangelo. It seems that critics specializing in contemporary art now have a historical perspective of no more than five years."[803]

Breadth of Perspective

The British theatre critic James Agate once wrote:

"It is an enormous advantage when theatre and film critics are authorities on something else besides plays and films. Though I place confidence in the judgments of Mr B. I should like to feel that he was also expert in aeronautics and water polo. I could wish that Mr C had been a flyweight boxer or ridden Derby winners."[804]

A fine example of a film critic with wide interests, Alistair Cooke (best known for his long-running series for BBC Radio 4, *Letter from America*) quoted Agate approvingly in his preface to an anthology of film criticism in the 1930s, *Garbo and the Night Watchmen*, adding that "yours truly is happy indeed that he gave only a little of his life to the movies and most of it to American politics, the landscape of the West, music, golf, fishing, and every known indoor game excepting only bridge."[805]

In 1994 Britain's foremost literary critic, George Steiner, interviewed by Ronald A. Sharp, lamented the decline of the critic with a broad perspective, the "man of letters":

"The man of letters represented a kind of consensus of taste and of interest in his society. People wanted to hear about literature, the arts, from a cultivated nonspecialist. Macaulay, Hazlitt — the ranking men of letters — almost made a book of a review; they were that long. There was time for that kind of publication. The man of letters might also write poetry and fiction, or biography, and in England the tradition has not died. We still have Michael Holroyd, my own student Richard Holmes who is now so acclaimed, we have Cyril Connolly, Pritchard, who is an exquisite short-story writer, a constant critic, a constant reviewer. And I'm not one who sneers about J.B. Priestley. The people who sneer about Priestley would give their eyeteeth to have had a jot of his talent. Critic, biographer, memorialist, in many ways Robert Graves, who was such a fine poet, was a supreme man of letters... The man of letters — and what was George Orwell, if he was not a man of letters, what was Edmund Wilson, whom I succeeded on *The New Yorker* twenty-seven years ago? — the man of letters has become very suspect."[806]

The best critics may not need to be "men of letters", but they should have the ability to draw unexpected comparisons and parallels. To become one of them, you need not only depth of perspective (in other words, a knowledge of history) but also breadth of perspective (knowing about areas other than your own). A lot of those reviewing unpaid on the internet can be described as film buffs, and many have an even more restricted vision than that. Some are enthusiasts for horror, or Hong Kong action films, or superhero movies. To be regarded as a first-rate film critic, you need to have a wide range of cultural and social reference points.

Cultivating an appreciation for other art forms will enhance your ability to write insightfully about film. Visit art galleries (you can't understand Peter Greenaway films unless you grasp that they are steeped in painting), read or see Shakespeare in the theatre (*Much Ado About Nothing* is the template for the modern romantic comedy), and listen to classical music (most symphonic composers of film scores are steeped in Wagner and Richard Strauss). It is even a good idea to read comic books or graphic novels, to see the differences between them on page and on screen.

Nathan Lee, ex-*Village Voice* Critic, thinks the biggest problem with film criticism today, particularly on the internet, is that it's too insular:

"To be a really good writer and film critic you need a range. You need to know what's going on in painting, you need to know what's going on in music, you need to read books, and get laid, and go to restaurants, you know what I mean? A lot of movie writing is very impassioned but it's very limited, very narrow. And I think good critics can put movies into a larger cultural and social perspective."[807]

Theatre critics, too, benefit from knowing about more than the stage. Here's an extract from Kenneth Tynan's review of N.F. Simpson's *A Resounding Tinkle*, in 1957. Note the way he takes pains to place it in its theatrical and non-theatrical tradition:

"About the highest tribute I can pay N.F. Simpson's *A Resounding Tinkle*, which was tried out at the Royal Court last Sunday, is to say that it does not belong in the English theatrical tradition at all. It derives from the best Benchley lectures, the wildest Thurber cartoons, and the cream of the Goon Shows. It has some affinities with the early revues of Robert Dhery and many more with the plays of M. Ionesco. In English drama, it is, so far as I know, unique. It is also astonishingly funny."[808]

Adrian (A.A.) Gill was widely known as both a TV and a restaurant critic, but when you read him you can see that he was not limited to those two areas. His TV review of *Kidnapped* for the *Times* showed not only that he had read the original novels, but also that he thought about the differences between novels and TV adaptations:

"There is one great, gaping flaw in the novel as far as television is concerned, and it's the thing that makes it so gripping: it's a first-person narrative. Davie is telling you the story. You never know much about him, so, as a reader, you impose your own character, which is brilliantly engaging — but on television, you have to be shown someone, which means you have a lead character who is a sort of underage Zelig. It's the same defect you get with *Treasure Island, Oliver Twist* and Pip in *Great Expectations*. In all of them, the supporting cast steal the show, are far more exciting and interesting. Making Davie an attractive, believable protagonist is the main task of an adaptation, and this latest attempt didn't just fail, it never really took a swing."[809]

A good critic should also have an eye for the social and political implications of a piece. Here's Gill on *Burn Up* (BBC2), a didactic drama on BBC2:

"Watching it was a bit like being manacled to the table at a Notting Hill dinner party, or being lectured by a vegan vitamin salesman. The finger-wagging about global warming was relentless and unabating... The goodies were witty, brilliant, sensitive, imaginative, attractive, sexy and great dancers - rather, I suspect, like the scriptwriters. The baddies were, well, they were all American. This was film-making from the Soviet school of political subtlety, a childishly black-and-white premise, delivered with a patronizing blog of a script, which overwhelmed the plot, pace, anything resembling a character and, finally, the audience's sympathy. Last week, George Monbiot, the *Guardian's* geography teacher, wrote that Channel 4 had done more environmental damage than any other organisation by showing its devil's-advocate documentary, *The Great Global Warming Swindle*. This was obviously before he'd seen this bloated, wasteful, gaseously hypocritical beached whale of a miniseries. Because it is this sort of toadying and special pleading that will poison the good intentions of the green movement. It's not the arguments or the facts or the science that are in doubt, it's the people doing the arguing. There is nothing like enough politically and socially committed fiction on television, but this dim, deaf drama was an object lesson in how not to make it; and the real inconvenient truth for the green movement is, as the old Jewish retail expression has it, in winning the argument they've lost the sale. They suffer the fatal flaw of being too smug to bear. There is a global resistance, not to the facts, but to environmentalists. It appears most of us would rather fry, drown or starve than be told what to do by a bearded git in sandals, and that's a rather comforting and cussedly human truth."[810]

It's important for a good arts critic to know who is subsidizing whom, and why. Brian Sewell made himself very unpopular in certain circles with his belief that the visual arts in Britain are riddled with corruption. This was Sewell on an Anthony Gormley exhibition at the Hayward Gallery, in 2007:

"The Department of Culture should investigate the benefits that accrue to the very few artists (and indirectly their dealers) who receive most of the patronage in promotion and cash doled out by Tate Modern and the Arts and British Councils, with the immediate consequence of the Turner Prize or an international exhibition a hefty increase in the prices asked (and got) for every scrap of work. Year after year, through these public agencies, public money is pumped into artists - Gormley, Kappor, Hirst foremost among them - who are millionaires supported by (and supporting) even richer dealers; yet neither the artists nor the dealers need these subsidies. I know this is not a clear-cut issue, that the public should be kept aware of major artists' recent work and that the country should be represented at great international events by the best artists that we have - but nothing of this is done without cost to the public and great benefit to the artist' there ought to be some kick-back to the public purse and, at the very least, the occasional gift by the artist of a significant work. At the moment, and for year past, the notorious artist and his dealer have by the rest of us been feather-bedded at enormous cost."[811]

On 5th January 1994, 35 leading figures from the art world signed a letter to the Evening Standard, attacking Sewell's "artistic prejudice", "demagogy", "formulaic insults", "homophobia", "hypocrisy", "misogyny" and "predictable scurrility".[812] A letter supporting Sewell from twenty other art-world signatories accused the first group of attempting to censor out of existence in order to promote "a relentless programme of neo-conceptual art in all the main London venues".[813] Two months later, he won the Press Award as Critic of the Year for the second time. No other art critic has won it even once.[814]

For my own part, I disagreed with Sewell on many points. He always seemed to underestimate photography as an art form irredeemably inferior to painting. And he was much given to entertainingly broad statements that did not stand up to close scrutiny.

For example, there is some truth in his observation that "the Sixties were the years in which the old indulged the young, and the young, not knowing what to do with the indulgence, frittered away their new freedoms."

However, the Sixties also saw the rise of the Beatles, who transformed pop music for the better and arguably have never been surpassed. And among the greatest films of the Sixties are *Psycho*, *Bonnie and Clyde* and *The Wild Bunch*. Are these examples of people frittering away their talent? I think not.

However, it is part of the job of any critic to express his opinions truthfully and persuasively. That is what Sewell did – and with considerable panache. He was unrepentant about his own perspective being at odds with conventional wisdom:

"Art criticism everywhere is now at a low ebb, intellectually corrupt, swamped in meaningless jargon, distorted by political correctitudes, anxiously addressed only to other critics and their ilk."[815]

There have always been bad critics, and some areas of criticism – notably, the visual arts – are notorious for attracting critics who wish themselves to rise up and become part of the bureaucratic hierarchy.

In a piece for *Prospect Magazine* in 2002,[816] Sewell wrote a staggeringly rude open letter, dated 24 February, to art critic Matthew Collings, famous for his TV appearances:

"In your way you perfectly represent the current state of art criticism. Twenty years ago I thought that the collective noun for art critics should be a creep or crawl, so evidently did they sing for their canapés and Chablis, so necessary to their incomes were the payments for their laudatory essays in dealers' catalogues. Twenty years ago, much in cash and kind was earned by compliant critics prepared to lick arse, but things have changed; the cash and carry aspect of the business has run down, the volume is much reduced and the *quid pro quo* much cheaper for the patron. The demand is less for services than for absolute loyalty to the tiny clique that now runs the visual arts in Britain. This means that those who are critical of Serota[817], for example, are excluded from the radio programmes of the BBC and all television channels. You do not belong to the generation of critics who benefited in kind, but you are very much the obedient contemporary critic, watching your back and never blotting your copybook."

Sewell wrote that the problem with critics was not so much that they were corrupt, but that they were idle:

"Critics are lazy. I read with dismaying frequency their rehashes of press releases. They are no better than the jurors in *Alice in Wonderland*, treating every word as if it were dictation. 'Your duty,' Marina Vaizey[818] lectured me for my failure to review an utterly trivial exhibition, 'is to signpost, not express your own opinion. Tell us it's there, describe it. That's all.' But it is not all... We need the Reithian view[819], always pitching above the heads of the ignorant so that we can draw them on (not below, so that they feel comfortable)."

Sewell expanded on his low opinion of modern art criticism in an interview with Naim Attalah, Chairman of Quartet Books, posted on 28 June 2013:

"Most critics are ill-informed; they have no practice either as painters or as art historians, so they come to the business of looking at pictures almost like strangers. There are other critics who can only be described as Vicars of Bray, in that whatever is stuck under their noses they feel bound to praise it. Richard Cork [art critic on *The Times*] is a very good example; it really doesn't matter what it is, as long as it has been vouched for, as long as it has a certificate of quality from the Tate Gallery or the Hayward or the Arts Council, he is prepared to say it is wonderful. There is yet another kind of critic who, thank God, is now in the decline – I'm thinking of people like Marina Vaizey. She believes in signposting; that it is her duty to say that something is there, and that that is enough. Well, it isn't enough. A critic should have some kind of bite on the subject with which his readers are not expected to agree. What he should be doing is providing an intellectual peg on which readers can hang their own arguments and their own judgements."[820]

Comedian and chat-show host Clive Anderson once described Sewell mischievously as "a man intent on keeping his Christmas card list nice and short".[821] The critic was resigned to his own unpopularity among his peers:

"I have been a lone voice in the world of art criticism – despised and rejected. There's an enormous amount of resentment because I am not a member of the club. Do I enjoy my notoriety? Absolutely not. I take a deep breath and get on with it."[822]

And Then There Was Nunn

Breadth of perspective is usually an asset in a critic. However, a critic who brings too much "baggage" to a piece of art may end up missing the point, and the strengths, of the work that is before him.

The original, 1980 production of *Nicholas Nickleby* by the Royal Shakespeare Company at the Aldwych Theatre is a case in point. I well remember attending previews and joining in the standing ovations for Trevor Nunn and John Caird's wonderful production. Had I been a critic - at the time I was a director in television - I would have written of it in glowing terms. So I was appalled at the notices it received.

Much later, in 2006, Michael Billington of the *Guardian* wrote, with a certain amount of selective amnesia:

"In 1980 I praised the RSC's production of *Nicholas Nickleby* for its skill while questioning whether it should have been done at all."[823]

Actually, his review was remarkably hostile and described the entire adaptation as "shapeless". He particularly disliked its richness, saying that it was "rather like being force-fed on peacock".[824] At the RSC's 50th birthday celebrations in 2011, an ironic reading of Michael Billington's original review was greeted with boos.[825]

Billington was far from alone in disliking *Nicholas Nickleby*. The critics *en masse* condemned it as a literary piece that should never have been adapted for the subsidised theatre, and chose to ignore the production's bravura theatricality.

There was a deeper, political explanation for their perversity. As all the critics knew, the production had come about because of a lack of funds for the Royal Shakespeare Company. The RSC had been faced with a drastic cut in Arts Council funding at the end of 1979. Instead of putting on two or three new productions in London in 1980 Trevor Nunn decided to put all the company's available resources into one spectacular production of "an intractable and labyrinthine and tentacular and epic work".

To Nunn's understandable dismay, the national critics chose to use the opening of *Nicholas Nickleby* not to review the show in front of them, but to bash the government for failing to support the arts financially.

Fortunately, *Times* columnist Bernard Levin, who had been a theatre critic at one time but hadn't been for some years – was prepared to be a dissident voice. Levin described *Nickleby* as "a ceaselessly entertaining...dramatic triumph" and openly despaired of his former colleagues.[826]

"Not for so many years," wrote Levin, "has London's theatre seen anything so richly joyous, so immoderately rife with pleasure, drama, colour and entertainment, so life enhancing, - in one word which embraces all these and more - so Dickensian. It is a celebration of love and justice that is true to the spirit of Dickens' belief that those are the fulcrums on which the universe is moved, and the consequence is that we come out not merely delighted but strengthened, not just entertained but uplifted, not only affected but changed."[827] Enthusiastic word of mouth from members of the audience and Levin's passionate defence turned *Nickleby* into the greatest commercial (and, in the end, critical) stage success of the 1980s.

Interestingly, even without a political axe to grind, several New York critics echoed the hostile views of the West End critics. Frank Rich in the *New York Times* described dull passages piling up as "dead weight".[828] John Simon in the *New York Magazine* felt that the work was a "middlebrow enterprise" doing "scant justice" to the novel.[829] However, the majority wrote raves, most of them writing variations on my own feeling, that it was "the theatrical experience of a lifetime". Ever since, even faced with productions far inferior to the original, the vast majority of critics have loved it.

Another revealing case is *Les Misérables*, also directed by Trevor Nunn and John Caird for the Royal Shakespeare Company. Five years after *Nicholas Nickleby*, this, too, received miserable reviews from most critics when it opened at the Barbican Theatre. Underlying the antagonistic reviews was old-fashioned cultural snobbery from critics who insisted that the RSC should be devoting itself to high art rather than populist musicals.

There was also a resentment that, should the piece be a success, directors who worked for a subsidized company would reap enormous dividends. Some thought Nunn was "using" the public's money for self-aggrandizing purposes. The grumblers noted that the production budget — the equivalent of about £1 million today — was far larger than those of other RSC productions. The *Sunday Times* began to investigate Nunn's personal finances, and found he was earning a great deal of money outside the company. That, thought some arts journalists, was a bad thing. Nunn sued the *Sunday Times* for libel, but the lawsuit resulted mostly in a correction of certain reported sums. It was hard to discern how much of the hostility towards Nunn was high-minded scruple and how much of it was mean-spirited envy.[830]

An additional factor was the fact that the lyrics had been written by a former critic, Herbert Kretzmer, a theatre and TV critic for the *Daily Mail*. Kretzmer recalls that he "didn't expect any mercy from my fellow critics when *Les Misérables*, for which I wrote the lyrics, opened, and I didn't get any from some of them."[831]

The *Sunday Telegraph's* Francis King described the show as "a lurid Victorian melodrama produced with Victorian lavishness... It stands in the same relation to the original as a singing telegram to an epic, the reduction of a literary mountain to a dramatic molehill".[832] Michael Ratcliffe in the *Observer* dubbed the show "a witless and synthetic entertainment".[833] Many condemned the project for converting classic literature into a musical.

The cruellest review of all came from Kretzmer's former colleague, Jack Tinker, in the *Daily Mail*, who called the show "The Glums" and said that trying to condense a 1,200-page novel into three and a half hours of stage time was "like attempting to pour the entire Channel through a china teapot".[834]

There were dissident voices. Michael Coveney, then of the *Financial Times*, found it "intriguing and most enjoyable," a show which "allies *Nickleby*-style qualities of superb ensemble presentation to a piece that really does deserve the label 'rock opera,' occupying brand new ground somewhere between Verdi and Andrew Lloyd Webber.'" Sheridan Morley of *Punch* woke up for long enough to acclaim it as "the musical of the half-decade," one which "soared out from the pit with blazing theatricality." *Time* and *Newsweek* came, saw, and predicted it would conquer. More importantly, so did the audiences.[835]

In 2010, Michael Billington looked back on his own distaste for the project and stuck to his guns, while admitting that the public may have different tastes from the critics:

"*Les Mis* succeeds because it is spectacular Victorian melodrama. Nothing wrong with that. What irked some of us back in 1985 was the claim by the original directors, Trevor Nunn and John Caird, that we were watching a piece of High Seriousness that required the resources of the RSC to stage. You could also argue, as I would, that *Les Mis*, by ditching spoken dialogue in favour of a through-composed score, led the musical down a false trail: away from the fun of wit, satire and romance towards the pomposities of pop-opera. But the fact is that audiences love *Les Mis*. What I find intriguing is that we think we live in a very cool, smart, cynical age. Yet, when the chips are down, what we really crave is a contest of good and evil, and lashings of spectacle. Just, in fact, like our Victorian ancestors. Plus ça change, plus c'est la meme show."[836]

Les Mis producer Cameron Mackintosh has grown resigned to the dichotomy between public and critics over the show, but he wasn't at first:

"It was a dagger in my heart when the reviews panned it. I'd rushed to buy the early-morning editions, and the first review I saw was Jack Tinker in the *Mail*, calling it The Glums. I had my usual post-production lunch with the team, and we all felt we'd been to a funeral. I rang the box office to gauge the reaction and the lines were jammed; they said they had never been so busy. The audiences had been euphoric. But that has been the story of *Les Misérables* ever since the novel was published: it sold in barrowloads, yet the critics hated it. I'm as surprised as anyone by its longevity; its strength lies in Hugo's observation of character, which crosses generations and cultures. And in Schönberg's music, one of the greatest musical scores ever written."[837]

What is it about *Les Mis* that alienates so many critics? Adam Feldman, theatre critic for *Time Out New York* and president of the New York Drama Critics Circle, was not surprised when even the lavish big-screen movie production drew mixed notices:

"The film version of *Les Misérables* is unabashed about its musicality, sincerity and sentiment. There is nothing in quotation marks. While it is very risky to go with that, it also can be very moving. It tells its story in a form that is very dramatically and musically direct, and it can make some people uncomfortable."[838]

The more intellectual critics, who pride themselves on being able to detect and analyze subtext, tend to become resentful when confronted with a show such as *Les Mis*, which says exactly what it has to say without apology. They tend to find it crude, bombastic and lowbrow, when really it is just being emotional and honest.

A Moral Perspective

Critics are often advised by their readers to be "objective". Nigel Andrews of the *Financial Times* claims he doesn't even know what "objective" means in the context of film criticism:

"There's no such thing as an objective response. As soon as you start feeling an emotion while watching a film, you're no longer objective. That doesn't mean your criticism won't be sound, if it's based also on reasoned argument, and the evidence of the film, and analyzing why it was good enough to elicit those emotions."[839]

Simon Price, former rock critic on the *Independent on Sunday*, thinks the notion of objectivity in criticism is simply wrong:

"Let's nuke, once and for all, the idea that a review should be 'objective'. Any response to art is personal by definition, and anyone who claims to write with a detached, oracular, objective, all-seeing all-knowing authority is a pompous, arrogant ass."[840]

Derek Malcolm of the *Guardian* and *Evening Standard* concurs:

"No such thing as objectivity, I'm afraid. We are all prey to our prejudices. Take Philip French and Westerns [He liked them]. And I have always hated feelgood movies."[841]

I take the view that critics should try to be fair but not objective. A critic with blind spots – not liking horror, say, or hating all musicals – is less likely to be reliable when it comes to spotting superior examples of their genre. And I would take with a large pinch of salt the views of someone who claimed that, say, all movies based on graphic novels are masterpieces.

All critics have different tastes. Each of us has a morality of some kind, whether it is Christian, Jewish, Muslim or so idiosyncratic that it may appear immoral or amoral. It is best to be honest about why a film, play or book leaves you cold or makes you angry. It allows your readers to evaluate what their own response may be.

I've steered clear so far of discussing video game reviewing, which is still very much in its infancy; but it's an exciting area of the arts, and evolving very rapidly.

In 2008 a British-produced game, *Grand Theft Auto IV*, became the most successful entertainment release in history. Within 24 hours of release, GTA IV had grossed $310m (£157m) – more than history's most successful book (*Harry Potter & The Deathly Hallows*, at $220m in 24 hours) and its most successful film (*Spider-Man 3* at $117m).

Interestingly, there's a healthy relationship between those reviewing games and those designing them – a sense of an art form in progress, as Lana Polansky has pointed out on the games website, *Medium Difficulty*:

"The games we love are improving all the time, and a lot of this is due to the fact that there is significant and extensive discourse taking place within design and development communities. And it gives me infinite joy to observe that the close reading seems to be gaining prominence too, particularly amongst game criticism blogs like *The Border House*, but even on larger sites like *Kotaku*. This is good news, because it means that some of the same highly complex, dense, subtle conversation taking place on more esoteric sites like *Electronic Book Review, Deep Fun* and *Game Studies* can finally be made palatable and accessible for a wider audience, as well as enhancing the level of inquiry by relatively untoward critical frameworks (for instance, literary ones like post-colonial or Marxist theory). It means we can take control of our media consumption by asking deeper, better questions about games, challenging game-makers to improve. We can start having honest, intelligent discussions about how games affect us, how we interpret specific games, and how we wish they were better. It may seem overwhelming, but to me, it's empowering."[842]

I agree with the Australian video critic Brendan Keogh, who wrote in the *New Statesman* in 2012:

"Videogames matter. That is beyond debate. As such, they demand critics equipped with a strong critical vocabulary in order to help players and non-players alike to understand the infinite experiences they are capable of delivering."[843]

If I were to offer one tip to an aspiring critic, it would be to become the first great reviewer of video games, because there isn't one at the moment. There are many websites where you can read in-depth critiques of video games. These include http://www.critical-distance.com, www.unwinnable.com and www.polygon.com.

However, most video game reviews that I have read have been (a) nerdy and (b) non-judgmental. Reviewers tend to concentrate on technical advances, whether it is multi-protagonist or not, and how it compares with previous video games in terms of looks and playability. The exceptions have tended to be when mainstream newspapers and magazines persuade critics from other areas to leave their day jobs and look at new gaming releases.

Here, for example, is rock critic James Delingpole commenting on a new video game in 2013, for the *Daily Mail*:

"Yesterday, in the process of robbing a bank, I beat up an elderly security guard before shooting dead perhaps 15 policemen, exulting in their murders with the flip dismissal: 'Shouldn't have been a cop.' After that, I stole a succession of fast cars, evading my pursuers by driving on the wrong side of the road, mowing down passers-by and killing more police by ramming straight into them. Then I went home for a change of clothes, a nap, a beer and a joint before getting into my stolen vehicle to wreak more mayhem, pausing briefly to enjoy the services of a prostitute. Had I kept going with this spree of orgiastic destruction and drug-fuelled violence, I would have got the chance to use much heavier weaponry, take stronger drugs, and not only murder people but torture them by pulling out their teeth with pliers, waterboarding them with flammable liquid, kneecapping them with a monkey wrench and making them scream with electric shocks. Welcome to the deeply disturbing world of the new computer game *Grand Theft Auto V*."[844]

Unsurprisingly, Delingpole had problems with the game's flippant amorality:

"It normalises extreme violence and cruelty, so the longer you play, the more you not only become inured to it, but start to find yourself gripped — and even sickly amused — by the action unfolding before your eyes. As a middle-aged parent, I like to think I'm mature enough to be able to appreciate the game's cartoonish, ugly, misogynistic, ultraviolent, pornographic worldview with a certain wry detachment. But whether the game's teenage target market is so readily capable of making such distinctions, I'm not nearly so sure. What troubles me about *Grand Theft Auto V* — which has an 18 rating that will be ignored by thousands of younger teenagers — is not just the message it sends out to youngsters (drugs are cool; crime pays; violence is fun), but what it says about the coarsening, the decadence and the hopelessness of our modern culture."[845]

Delingpole was hardly alone in finding the game ultra-violent and misogynistic. Yet on release it generated $800 million in worldwide revenue and immediately became the fifth-highest rated game on *Metacritic*. Reviewers differed over the power of its characterization; but *Edge* called it a "remarkable achievement" in open world design and storytelling. *Play* considered it "generation-defining" and "exceptional". Keza MacDonald of IGN called *Grand Theft Auto V* "one of the very best video games ever made".[846]

In my view, Delingpole is right to be concerned about the impact video games are having. Will they turn ordinary children into murderers? Of course not. But powerful points about their social effects have been put by experts such David Grossman, and never really answered. This former lieutenant commander and West Point psychology professor has pointed out that many games are murder simulators, training children in the use of guns and desensitising them to acts of murder.[847]

Mary Flanagan – a veteran game-designer and professor of digital humanities at Dartmouth College – prefers to accentuate the positive. She believes that video games can improve hand-eye coordination and foster better decision taking, problem solving and strategy under duress. In her book *Values at Play in Digital Games*, she explains how some video games can and do encourage honesty, cooperation and a sense of justice.

She can also see the emotional appeal, even to an adult, of games like *Grand Theft Auto*, as she reported to readers of the *Huffington Post*:

"Playing *GTA5*, I'm left with the awe that I can parkour across rooftops, leap into swimming pools, and go anywhere I please. The size of the world is immense. But I can also have sex with prostitutes and kill them to get my money back without any repercussions. I can run down characters with my SUV as a form of recreation. I can fire into crowds with an assault weapon. If I felt like it, I could do this for hours and hours, and days on end. And this is where the game moves from a transgressive game that explores human nature into something more than that: When you play violent games, a part of you know it's wrong - and enjoys that. Such experiences recall the controversial documentary *The Act of Killing* (2013), where Indonesian death squad leaders reenacted their crimes with surreal pleasure."[848]

Desensitising by constant exposure to violence is a controversial subject, and even now some people insist, counter-intuitively, that there are no harmful effects. I'm not one of them. There's plenty of research to show that playing violent video games encourages aggressive thoughts, feelings and behaviour.[849] It also seems pretty obvious to me that violent video games are likely to be more harmful than their TV or movie counterparts because they are interactive, and demand the player to identify with aggressive and even psychotic characters who have little or no morality.

Those who dismiss such concerns out of hand as "unproven", "kneejerk scaremongering" or "moral panic" are seeking to avoid some very awkward questions.

However, there are undoubtedly dangers for any reviewer in being moralistic. Those critics who took against Alfred Hitchcock's *Psycho* in 1960 because it was a violent slasher film now look old-fashioned and even foolish. Its artistic and storytelling strengths have come to be regarded as of more importance than its exploitative elements. And its approach to violence looks restrained by modern standards.

Similarly, *The Apartment* (also 1960) is now generally regarded as one of writer-director Billy Wilder's masterpieces – charming, brilliantly written and touchingly acted by Shirley MacLaine and Jack Lemmon. It was voted the best picture of 1960 not only at the Oscars, but also by the Directors' Guild of America, the British Film Academy, and the annual poll of reviewers and writers of the US trade publication *Film Daily*. Yet, on release, it was widely perceived as sleazy and immoral.

Ellen Fitzpatrick, in *Films in Review*, found herself out of sympathy with the Jack Lemmon character:

"I suppose a young clerk in a large insurance company might advance himself by lending his apartment to five of his superiors for their adulterous 'quickies,' but I don't think the idea is really very funny, or even interesting."

Dwight MacDonald asked "Where but in Hollywood would this situation be seen as comic material?"

Fred Majdalany, in the *Daily Mail*, also failed to see the humour in adultery:

"You don't get satire by treating the back alleys of infidelity with giggling facetiousness, periodically drenched by tears of bogus sentiment... As for Shirley MacLaine, it is tragic to see her great comic gifts butchered to prove that men are beasts and that she can also cry. A great disappointment."[850]

A victim of changing morality during the Sixties, Bosley Crowther lost his job as film critic of the *New York Times* because of his hostility to *Bonnie and Clyde* (1967). Crowther panned it as:

"A cheap piece of bald-faced slapstick comedy that treats the hideous depredations of that sleazy, moronic pair as though they were as full of fun and frolic as the jazz-age cut-ups in *Thoroughly Modern Millie*... This blending of farce with brutal killings is as pointless as it lacking in taste, since it makes no valid commentary upon the already travestied truth. And it leaves an astonished critic wondering just what purpose Mr Penn and Mr Beatty think they serve with this strangely antique, sentimental claptrap."

Crowther was far from alone in being troubled by the morality of *Bonnie and Clyde*, in which the audience is obviously meant to side with disaffected gangsters against the authorities. Over in Russia, V. Menshikov wrote hopefully in the Soviet newspaper *Pravda*:

"It is not just an exciting picture. It is part of a campaign to destroy the morals of Western youth."

John Simon took the moral high ground:

"The whole thing stinks in the manner of a carefully made-up, combed, and manicured corpse... What is basically wrong with the film is not so much violence as hero worship... To argue as they do that in periods of social injustice (which means anywhere this side of Utopia) the outlaw is clearly superior to the staid, plodding citizen is sentimental nonsense and moral truancy... The film's aestheticizing continually obtrudes on and obfuscates moral values. Thus, with one highly debatable exception, the crimes and killings performed by the Barrow gang are all picturesque, humorous, cozy or, at worst, matter-of-fact affairs. But the violence performed upon the gang is always made as harrowingly inhuman as possible. This is explained by the champions of the film as the outlaws' related awareness that death is real, and the grave their goal — in other words, a rude moral awakening. But, in fact, Clyde makes it clear, in an idyllic scene, that had he to do it over again, he would do exactly the same. He has learned nothing. Fair enough, if only the filmmakers did not so resoundingly applaud him for it."

Years later, in 1971, John Simon recognised that *Bonnie and Clyde* was a landmark in film criticism, not least because it made the up-and-coming Pauline Kael look more "modern" than Bosley Crowther and other more established critics:

"Kael's panegyric about *Bonnie and Clyde* runs sixteen and one-half tall octavo pages in rather fine print, and her enthusiasm for this American imitation-New Wave film epitomizes a sensibility that prefers trash to art, and plays, albeit more cleverly and guardedly, the same kind of games as the *auteur* critics to justify low-down cravings."[851]

Almost forty years on, the violence in *Bonnie and Clyde* now looks tame, if not downright prettified. It also looks like what it was, a film of its time. It was released just two months before the anti-Vietnam war march on the Pentagon in October 1967. It was Clyde's mysterious charisma as an outlaw that made him the darling of 1967, and the bloodiness of the two lovers' demise at the hands of uncomprehending lawmen made dissident audiences respond to it. If Lyndon Johnson's government was the law, then more and more young people knew they were outside it: outside its draft laws, outside the drug laws. For thousands and perhaps millions, *Bonnie and Clyde* reflected their own sense that they were becoming outlaws.

One danger of being moralistic is, of course, that morality changes. Take this hilariously outdated perspective on lesbianism in a 1962 movie review of William Wyler's *The Children's Hour* in *Films in Review*:

"Today, when every form of perversion except masturbation and bestiality have been shown on the screen [Lillian] Hellman, Wyler and the Mirisch Co. apparently thought a re-do of *The Children's Hour* would sell tickets if lesbianism were not only restored as the charge the evil child falsely brings, but also condoned... There is an explicit line of dialogue which asserts that those who choose to practise lesbianism are not destroyed by it – a claim disproved by the number of lesbians who become insane and/or commit suicide."[852]

I've often been accused of being too moralistic, but I remain unrepentant about my distaste for films that sexually exploit children, such as Adrian Lyne's *Lolita*, for movies that sell violence as manly and the only possible response to being hurt (there are too many of these to mention, but Sam Peckinpah's *Straw Dogs*, Oliver Stone's *Natural Born Killers* and the *Death Wish* series spring to mind) and indeed for most examples of torture porn. The *Hostel* and later *Saw* movies seem to me repellent in their obvious pleasure in the suffering of people, especially women. I don't enjoy them, and I think they're a form of environmental pollution.[853]

However, even the torture porn genre has its high points. One such was *Audition* (1999). This weirdest of horror films starts off as a relatively conventional romance, with a middle-aged widower (Ryo Ishibashi) trying to find a second wife by auditioning actresses for a non-existent feature film. His eye alights on a slender, submissive ex-ballerina (Eihi Shiina), and he's not unduly worried when she turns out to have lied about her professional experience. They date, and seem attracted.

There's one great shot when the whole mood changes. She is sitting on the floor of her apartment with the phone a little way from her, and what looks like a pile of blankets in the background. We realise she's been waiting obsessively for his call, not moving, for days. The phone rings, and we see a sinister smile of sensual triumph through the dark curtain of her hair. And the blankets in the background move. They're not blankets but a canvas sack, and there's something or someone in it, writhing and moaning in physical and psychological torment.

From that creepy moment, it's downhill all the way. Just as you think it may be turning into a classy, female revenge movie (a Japanese version of Clint Eastwood's *Play Misty For Me*), the female character turns from abused innocent into gloating sadist, and from there into a kind of erotic demon.

The film becomes a series of degrading mutilations. An immensely talented, stylish, unpleasant mess, *Audition* marked – as I wrote in 1999 - a new low in sadistic torture and amputation, allowed by the censors presumably because the sick acts of violence were carried out by a woman, and in a foreign language.

When I first saw it, I found *Audition* a film that was well nigh impossible to mark out of ten. The first time I saw it, I gave it 5/10, for it is both talented and repulsive.

However, the film has lingered in my mind ever since, and it would be churlish to deny its power to surprise and shock. There haven't been many parables about sexism that have had this kind of power. It's a genuine one-off and far creepier and more subtle than the torture porn films it doubtless helped to inspire. The two leading actors are also extraordinary, and no other films by Takashi Miike that I have seen come close to it in terms of atmosphere or quality.

So, ten years after I first saw it, I upped my mark considerably to 9/10. It's still a disgusting, unpleasant film, and I can understand those who walk out of it; but it is a masterpiece of horror, one of the most terrifying films ever. And that shot of the canvas sack is an all-time great, as is the sequence where we discover what's in it.

A Unique Perspective: Manny Farber

The film director Martin Scorsese has described Manny Farber (1917-2008) as "one of America's greatest film critics. Manny Farber's approach to movies was utterly unique - he saw elements and values that no one else saw, and he gave us the tools to see them, too."[854] Cultural commentator

Susan Sontag called him "the liveliest, smartest, most original film critic this country ever produced".[855] For film critic-turned-director Peter Bogdanovich, Farber was "razor-sharp in his perceptions" and "never less than brilliant as a writer."[856]

Yet very few people today seem to have read him, and he is nowhere near as highly esteemed as, say, Pauline Kael or Andrew Sarris.

One reason for the decline of Farber's reputation lies in his highly idiosyncratic judgments on some movies that are generally regarded as classics, but which he signally failed to appreciate. He slammed Frank Capra's masterpiece *It's a Wonderful Life* as just "the latest example of Capracorn."[857]

He couldn't see the point of the western usually considered the finest of its genre. He called *High Noon* "a deftly fouled-up western... Someone spent too much time over the drawing board conceiving dramatic camera shots to cover up the lack of a story."[858]

Another classic western, *Shane*, also failed to impress Farber. He dismissed it as "an incredibly slow Western with a Paul Bunyan type of hero, a pro-homesteaders theme, and the silliest of all child characters.[859]

Farber couldn't even see the good in *Casablanca*:

"Hollywood often uses its best players, writers and directors for its epic phonies... The *Casablanca* kind of hokum was good in its original context in other movies, but, lifted into *Casablanca* for the sake of its glitter and not incorporated into it, loses its meaning... Bogart's humanitarian killer, who was disillusioned apparently at his mother's breast, has to say some silly things and to play God too often to be as believably tough as he was in his last eight pictures."[860]

Farber's review of *The Third Man* was equally uncomplimentary:

"It bears the usual foreign trademarks... over-elaborated to the point of being a monsterpiece... *The Third Man's* murky, familiar mood springs chiefly from Graham Greene's script, which proves again that he is an uncinematic snob who has robbed the early Hitchcock of everything but his genius... Greene's story... is like a wheel-less freight train."[861]

Farber even disliked *Citizen Kane* – and for unusual reasons. He abused both director Orson Welles and cinematographer Gregg Toland for "arty" lighting and visual compositions.[862]

Many of Farber's opinions haven't passed the test of time; I can see why more people trusted the judgments of his fellow-critic James Agee, a fine writer and someone with a much firmer grasp on the tastes of the ordinary filmgoer. For the last twenty years of Farber's life, no one would employ him as a film critic, and he reverted to his first career as an artist.

Not many people will share Farber's lack of interest in narrative, characterization and audience involvement. His dislike of Hollywood led him to downgrade plenty of worthwhile mainstream product, while his sympathy for the low-budget underdog and underground bohemianism led him to overpraise movies just for being cheap and roughly made - "termite art" as he called it.

But he had a wonderful eye, formidable powers of description and the confidence to champion artists whose work he appreciated, some of whom went on to achieve great things. (He reminds me of John Peel's talent-spotting approach to being a disc jockey). These are formidable virtues in a critic. And he has the power to make you look at films in a different way, with the eyes of a painter - and that's no bad thing. You don't have to agree with a critic all the time to acknowledge he's telling you things you didn't know, and pointing out strengths that you hadn't spotted.

Farber "discovered" many filmmakers who went on to win acclaim as American masters: Budd Boetticher, Allan Dwan, Sam Fuller, Howard Hawks, Val Lewton, Anthony Mann, Preston Sturges, Raoul Walsh. He wrote lesser-known but perceptive essays, some written in collaboration with his wife, Patricia Patterson, on Robert Altman, Rainer Werner Fassbinder, Jean-Luc Godard, Werner Herzog and Martin Scorsese. He was also one of the first critics to give belated credit to animators such as Tex Avery and Chuck Jones.

His writing would enrage those who try and "score" critics' reviews today on the *Metacritic* website, or have to categorize all reviews as "fresh" or "rotten" for the website *Rotten Tomatoes*. Like the painter he was, Farber was often content to describe non-judgmentally.

I'm not sure I would advise any up-and-coming critic to emulate Manny Farber, for he was very much a product of his own background and milieu; but I would certainly advise any critic brought up in the literary tradition to be aware – as Farber was – of spectacle and visual composition.

Farber is perhaps the most extreme example of a major film critic who was obsessed with the visual. Fortunately, he was not alone. Here's his more popular contemporary, James Agee, showing that he too could approach a film visually, with his 1948 review of John Huston's *The Treasure of the Sierra Madre:*

"The camera is always where it ought to be, never imposes on or exploits or overdramatizes its subject, never for an instant shoves beauty or special meaning at you. This is one of the most visually alive and beautiful movies I have ever seen; there is a wonderful flow of fresh air, light, vigour, and liberty through every shot, and a fine athlete's litheness and absolute control and flexibility in every succession and series of shots."[863]

Agee was more alert than Farber to subtleties of acting, which he linked with the visual, as in his 1949 appreciation of Charlie Chaplin's 1931 film *City Lights:*

"At the end of *City Lights* the blind girl who has regained her sight, thanks to the Tramp, sees him for the first time. She has imagined and anticipated him as princely, to say the least; and it has never seriously occurred to him that he is inadequate. She recognises who he must be by his shy, confident, shining joy as he comes silently toward her. And he recognises himself, for the first time, through the terrible changes in her face. The camera just exchanges a few quiet close-ups of the emotions which shift and intensify in each face. It is enough to shrivel the heart to see, and it is the greatest piece of acting and the highest moment in movies."[864]

Farber did not have a monopoly of visual sensitivity. Take this evocative review by the talented British critic Dilys Powell of Michael Powell and Emeric Pressburger's *I Know Where I'm Going* (1945):

"It communicates an overpowering sense of place... The stark sudden hills, the dark waters, the island seen through veils of spray and mist - landscape and seascape here are handled as if they had personalities of their own; one feels the presence of wind and shore in a manner for which I can think of no English parallel except in Brian Desmond Hurst's early film of Synge's *Riders to the Sea*. The shots of the furious sea, the sullen curtain of the approaching storm, the whirlpool in whose gulf the little boat which plies between the islands is nearly lost, are as good as anything of their kind I can remember. And over and above the feeling of the physical setting there persists the feeling of a way of life too, remote and self-contained."[865]

Dilys Powell was a lot more perceptive than Farber in her reaction to *Citizen Kane*, which he dismissed as arty and self-indulgent, but she recognised as ground-breaking:

"There is no question here of experiment for experiment's sake; it is a question of a man with a problem of narrative to solve, using lighting setting, sound, camera angles and movement much as a genuine writer uses words, phrases, cadences, rhythms; using them with the ease and boldness and resource of one who controls and is not controlled by his medium... The camera moves, voices mingle and echo in caverns of space, with narrative purpose and not from exuberance; a face is shadowed not because it makes a beautiful individual shot, but because the character, the motives of the speaker are shadowed."[866]

Dilys Powell didn't care much for *Ben-Hur* or biblical epics in general, but she was still honest enough to commend the spectacle of Cecil B. DeMille's 1959 blockbuster on artistic grounds:

"If we must have films of this kind, this is the one to have. After all, the spectacular scenes remain: the sea-fight, the Triumph, a magnificent storm and, of course, the chariot-race - a scene superbly shot, superbly edited, superb in every way. I have never seen anything of its sort to touch it for excitement."[867]

Like Powell's hero Graham Greene, she appreciated that film has to be appreciated not as an offshoot of literature, but as a visual and sonic medium. Here she is in 1947, describing the masterly thriller *Odd Man Out*, in which a wounded IRA gunman (played by James Mason) goes on the run in Belfast:

"Carol Reed, who has more pace than any other director working in this country, has given to the scenes of chase a brilliance of action which dazzles... The fast-moving images are in themselves beautiful: erratic shadows spinning along lamp-lit walls, children playing in the shining dark night streets; but amid the poetry of light and shadow, the drama of the tumbling elaborate fights which Mr Reed handles so surely, the central movement is never lost from sight. Sound is used with unusual descriptive effect: the alarm bell, the dog yapping after the wounded man, the musty silence in the air-raid shelter with the children's voices shrilling in the distance and the small hollow thump as the little girl's ball bounces in. But again the whole complex of sound is directed towards a single narrative end: the clock striking the quarters, the ship hooting, delicately remind us of the shortening of time, the impossible margin for escape."[868]

Her review of Laurence Olivier's *Henry V* (1944) was another exemplary piece of criticism, for it recognised that its achievement was not primarily literary:

"When *Henry V* astonished the critics, it succeeded because, almost for the first time, colour had become an essential part of the narrative: the story was told, the characters were presented, in terms, not only of movement and dialogue, but of colour; colour gave edge to excitement, pointed contrast, accentuated rhythm. The dark Rembrandtesque tones of Olivier's face, turning his eyes as he thinks, deepened the mood of his great soliloquy in the camp at night. The brilliant blues and yellows and scarlets of the morning French army heightened the sense of relief from vigil, the sense of released action and fulfilled expectation. And all through this brilliant film the colour of the dresses against the soft neutral shades of the architectural background was so handled as to direct the spectator's attention; to guide his eye; in fact to narrate as the cinema should narrate."[869]

Another Unique Perspective: Lester Bangs

Frank Zappa once defined rock journalism as "people who can't write, interviewing people who can't talk, for people who can't read."[870]

Maybe he hadn't read Lester Bangs. Leslie Conway "Lester" Bangs wrote for *Creem* and *Rolling Stone* magazines, though in 1973 he was fired by *Rolling Stone* editor Jann Wenner for a splendidly disrespectful review of the group Canned Heat.[871] There were other well-known rock journalists of Bangs' era – such as Richard Meltzer, Nick Tosches, Dave Marsh and Jon Landau – but Bangs was by far the most acclaimed. He also had the good fortune to be immortalized on celluloid in former rock journalist Cameron Crowe's film *Almost Famous* – easily the most sympathetic portrayal of a critic in big-screen history.

In the film, Bangs mentors the leading character, a 15 year-old wannabe journalist, warning him not to get too close to the musicians he's commenting upon.

Philip Seymour Hoffman plays Bangs as an irascible but principled figure, determined to tell the truth without favouritism. Like Hoffman, Bangs died young (at 33), of an accidental drugs overdose.

Bangs was interesting as a rock critic partly because he was, unlike most reviewers, not afraid to alienate quite prominent performers:

"It seemed to me that the whole thing of interviewing as far as rock stars and that was just such a suck-up. It was grovelling obeisance to people who weren't that special, really. It's just a guy, just another person, so what?"[872]

He detested the narcissism of many rock performers, and this led him to castigate a variety of acts, from James Taylor to Led Zeppelin. His most famous description, however, is probably of Mick Jagger on stage:

"a spastic flap-lipped tornado writhing from here to a million steaming snatches and beyond in one undifferentiated erogenous mass, a mess and a spectacle all at the same time."[873]

Bangs made his name with two reviews in particular. One was his first ever *Rolling Stone* review in 1969, of the album *Kick Out the Jams* by MC-5:

"Musically the group is intentionally crude and aggressively raw. Which can make for powerful music except when it is used to conceal a paucity of ideas, as it is here. Most of the songs are barely distinguishable from each other in their primitive two-chord structures. You've heard all this before from such notables as the Seeds, Blue Cheer, Question Mark and the Mysterians, and the Kingsmen. The difference here, the difference which will sell several hundred thousand copies of this album, is in the hype, the thick overlay of teenage-revolution and total-energy-thing which conceals these scrapyard vistas of clichés and ugly noise."[874]

The other was a 1970 review of Black Sabbath's first album, which he derided as substandard Cream:

"Cream clichés that sound like the musicians learned them out of a book, grinding on and on with dogged persistence. Vocals are sparse, most of the album being filled with plodding bass lines over which the lead guitar dribbles wooden Claptonisms from the master's tiredest Cream days. They even have discordant jams with bass and guitar reeling like velocitized speedfreaks all over each other's musical perimeters yet never quite finding synch — just like Cream! But worse."[875]

Bangs' reviews occasionally descended into hyperbole, as when he wrote of Lou Reed's *Metal Machine Music* that it was "the greatest record ever made in the history of the human eardrum."[876]

But his writing was unusually literate for a contributor to the rock press, influenced for the better by Jack Kerouac and Charles Bukowski[877], and he used allusions to philosophy, politics and literature without apology. In his review of Van Morrison's album *Astral Weeks*, he even managed to quote the Spanish dramatist Gabriel Garcia Lorca.[878]

Bangs stands out as an unusually literate rock critic, and came up with some of my favourite quotations on rock music, such as:

"Nobody reads about rock 'n' roll because they're interested in music, all of us peruse this trash because we wanna know what lurid snivellers all our heroes are so we can gloat over them."[879]

"Don't ask me why I obsessively look to rock 'n' roll bands for some kind of model for a better society. I guess it's just that I glimpsed something beautiful in a flashbulb moment once, and perhaps mistaking it for prophecy have been seeking its fulfillment ever since."[880]

"Style is originality; fashion is fascism. The two are eternally and unalterably opposed."[881]

A new Bangs would be unlikely to gain a foothold in the rock press, which is too dependent on the music industry to tolerate someone of his prickliness and irreverence. That's our loss.

Contrarianism gone Mad? Armond White

Who is the most hated critic in the world? There have been occasions when I thought that might be me, but I would have to defer to the greater unpopularity of one man.

Armond White has always aroused strong feelings; and in 2014 he achieved lasting notoriety when he was expelled from the New York Film Critics Circle for heckling director Steve McQueen over the film *12 Years a Slave*.[882]

An Afro-American born in 1953, White attended Columbia University. A self-confessed "Paulette" (or follower of Pauline Kael), he was arts editor and critic for *The City Sun* between 1984 and 1996). He was lead film critic for the alternative weekly *New York Press* between 1997 and 2011, and editor of *CityArts* between 2011 and 2014. He currently writes for *National Review* and *Out*.[883]

He constantly bemoans the idiocy of other critics, saying "I don't read criticism for style (or jokes). I want information, erudition, judgment, and good taste. Too many snake-hipped word-slingers don't know what they're talking about."

He once told an interviewer that "Roger Ebert destroyed film criticism" and accused Ebert of "talking about movies as disconnected from social and moral issues, simply as entertainment".[884]

He has called *Village Voice* critic J. Hoberman "pathetic", "despotic", "traitorous" and "racist", describing him as "the scoundrel-czar of contemporary film criticism" whose malign "influence (as NYU instructor to the Times' Manohla Dargis and innumerable Internet clones) stretches from coast to coast, institution to institution"; he has described Hoberman's associates in the film community as "brownshirts", "fascists", and "backward children".[885]

White's strikingly deranged judgments of films include rave reviews for some disastrously unfunny movies by black film-makers, including *Norbit, Little Man* and *Dance Flick*. He is also that rarity among movie critics, an Adam Sandler fan, writing that "With *Bedtime Stories*, Sandler continues his winning streak of appealing and humane comedies". White even called one of Adam Sandler's most demeaning comedies, *I Now Pronounce You Chuck and Larry* (2007), "a classic".

Transformers – Revenge of the Fallen (2009) encouraged White to call the much-reviled director Michael Bay "a visionary" with "a great eye for scale and a gift for visceral amazement." He even wrote, seemingly without irony, that *G.I. Joe: The Rise of Cobra* (2009) "must be understood as an authentic measurement of our cultural values".

White angered the fanboys with his slating reviews of *District 9*, *Toy Story 3* and – most of all – *The Dark Knight Rises,* of which he said it "fabricates disaster simply to tease millennial death wish and psychosis."[886] Which seems fair enough to me.

The reason I would rather read Armond White than most other critics is not that I expect to agree with his opinions, which are frequently barmy, but that he has the courage to challenge the consensus.

I don't share his disgust for David Fincher's *The Social Network* but he is making a point that other critics didn't make – and one that contains some truth – when he writes that its lack of morality "is disguised by its topicality. It's really a movie excusing Hollywood ruthlessness."[887]

I admired the style of *Drive*, but I could see what White was driving at when he wrote "Fake toughness, fake sentimentality, fake style infected by Michael Mann. Brooding existential stuntman and petty criminal Ryan Gosling is so laconic and cool he's inadvertently comic."[888]

I have enjoyed most of the Pixar movies, but White's rave review for *The Lego Movie* did reflect a mistrust of corporatism that is healthy and justified:

"It is the totally unexpected political humour of *The Lego Movie* that makes up for its visual... shall we say, challenge. Any animated film that goes against the placid pretty perfectionism of Pixar has to be a work of political opposition and *The Lego Movie's* first two-thirds is a reminder how irreverent and nonpartisan political satire used to be: Millennial conformity is attacked in Emmet's anxious need for instruction – he seeks a manual for life that will confirm 'How to Fit In. Be Liked. Be Happy.' That cowardly affirmation could be the motto for film critics as well as Pixar drones."[889]

Armond White does believe in the value of informed criticism and he's unafraid to challenge the *status quo*. Here he is in an essay called *Do Movie Critics matter?* written on 19 March 2010, where he answers his own question resoundingly in the affirmative:

"Art appreciation, once a staple of a liberal-arts education that taught music, literature, and fine art, derives from knowledge of a form's history and standards, not simply its newest derivations or mutations... All opinions are not equal; the opinion most worth disseminating is the informed opinion, based on experience and learning. If criticism is to have a purpose beyond consumer advice, it is important that critics not follow trends but maintain cultural and emotional continuity 'a sense of mankind's personal history' in their reporting on the arts."[890]

Hardly anyone will agree with Armond White over most films, still less regard him as a reliable guide to the best that is on, but he does have his own unique perspective, and it's not an unintelligent one.

THE EIGHTH COMMANDMENT
Thou Shalt See What Isn't There

Hunt the Invisible

Kenneth Tynan was the *Observer*'s most distinguished theatre critic, and he said one thing that every critic should take to heart:

"A good drama critic perceives what is happening in the theatre of his time. A great drama critic also perceives what is *not* happening."[891]

Giles Coren agrees, and believes this applies equally to food criticism:

"A long time ago, ten years maybe, I repeatedly observed that restaurants were offering no information on the supply chain of their produce. Eventually, they listened, caught up, and restaurants, food suppliers and farmers have changed for the better as a result."[892]

Tynan followed his own precept when he came to the defence of a new play by a young female playwright from Salford at the Theatre Royal, Stratford, on 1 June, 1958. It was called *A Taste of Honey*.

Other critics slammed it for its naivety, and obvious failures of tone and technique. Alan Brien dismissed it in the *Spectator* as "a boozed, exaggerated, late-night anecdote of a play which slithers unsteadily between truth and fantasy, between farce and tragedy, between aphrodisiac and emetic... Twenty, ten or even five years ago, before a senile society began to fawn upon the youth which is about to devour it, such a play would have remained written in green longhand in a school exercise book on the top of the bedroom wardrobe."[893]

Milton Shulman was equally dismissive in the *Evening Standard*. He deplored Miss Delaney for knowing "as much about adult behaviour as she does about elephants" and suggested she read Shaw, Ibsen, O'Casey, Anouilh and Tennessee Williams.[894]

It was only Tynan who spotted that, for all its defects, the play had unfamiliar virtues:

"There are plenty of crudities in Miss Delaney's play: there is also, more importantly, the smell of living. When the theatre presents poor people as good, we call it 'sentimental'. When it presents them as wicked, we sniff and cry 'squalid'. Happily, Miss Delaney does not yet know about us and our squeamishness, which we think moral but is really social. She is too busy recording the wonder of life as she lives it. There is plenty of time for her to worry over words like 'form', which mean something, and concepts like 'vulgarity', which don't. She is nineteen years old: and a portent."[895]

Tynan spotted a quality in *A Taste of Honey* that was missing in the rest of the drama of his day. He was on to something most other critics hadn't noticed, for the film transferred to the West End and then to Broadway. It was also turned into a successful film.

Nigel Andrews, film critic of the *Financial Times*, strongly agrees with Tynan's claim that good critics need to spot what isn't before them:

"Yes. Absolutely. What's missing in the cinema today? What are people not doing? Why are there taboos or no-go areas? Or just plain lethargy zones because no one is pursuing themes or artistic possibilities they perhaps should be?"[896]

William Russell, former film critic of the *Glasgow Herald*, concurs:

"As well as seeing what is getting made one should be aware of the genre of films that are not getting made but which were once made. Why is this so? Does it matter?" [897]

A first-rate critic should be able to step back from a film far enough to think about its historical and socio-political context, and whether it is being fair and truthful. The reason I received a death threat from the IRA was because I pointed out an interesting truth: that every British film about the Troubles in Northern Ireland was from a Republican perspective, and not one of them reflected the views of the Protestant majority. This reflected a political bias at the BBC and Channel 4, that most other critics simply chose to ignore.

The one reliable exception was Alexander Walker, an Ulster Protestant, who was extremely voluble about this bias among British film-makers. He detected a left-wing establishment bias that he believed infected the commissioning process in Britain and had been stultifying the industry for decades.

When Walker's blood was up, he could be not only a formidable critic of the films that were set before him but also fully aware of the films that weren't. He was especially watchful about why certain films were subsidized into existence, while others were not. Walker was always worth reading for his fearlessness, which was admirable whether or not you always agreed with him.

One reason I found the 2005 Danish film, *King's Game*, so outstanding and unique was that it cruelly exposed the lack of films coming out of Britain, or indeed the rest of Europe, about the way we are governed, both nationally and by the European Union.

The reason is, of course, that film-makers are – however unconsciously - reluctant to bite the hand that feeds them, and the vast majority of European film-makers are heavily dependent upon state or EU subsidy. You don't have to be a member of UKIP to realise that's a bad thing.

Critics should not only see what is in a film, but notice the things that have been left out. Libby Gelman-Waxner (a.k.a. Paul Rudnick) noticed, for example, that Oliver Stone's film about the assassination of John F. Kennedy, *JFK*, was only convincing if you left quite a lot of the facts out:

"Oliver has told the press that whole much of the movie might not technically be true, it will serve as a countermyth to negate the Big Lie of the Warren Commission. I thought *JFK* was very absorbing, even though it claims that the military-industrial complex and just about everybody in America joined in a conspiracy to kill Kennedy before he could end the Vietnam War, because without a war nobody could make mopey selling helicopters. After seeing *JFK*, I got so paranoid that for a while I decided that I was involved in the conspiracy, but then I figured out the true culprit: the entertainment-industrial complex. Without Vietnam, there'd be no *Born on the Fourth of July*, no *China Beach*, no *Miss Saigon*, and Oliver would never have won an Oscar for *Platoon*. So let's reopen those government files: where was Oliver Stone on November 22, 1963, and, more crucially, where was his agent?"[898]

Do Your Homework

A good critic may need to do some homework in order to spot those important missing elements. I have already mentioned the historical distortions and omissions within the Oscar-winning film *Braveheart*.

A later history film with the real history left out was *The Patriot*, another star vehicle for Mel Gibson in the title role, Benjamin Martin. Most American critics responded enthusiastically to its gung-ho celebration of brave Americans rebelling against sneering, sadistic Brits. Harvey Karten of *Compuserve* called it "a spectacle that could cause its audience to rise up against the dull treatment of this marvelous episode from history teachers".[899] Donald Munro of the *Fresno Bee* stated that *The Patriot* "pays handsome tribute to the sacrifices of men who deserve to be remembered."[900]

To my surprise, hardly any critics bothered to check out the real identity of Benjamin Martin. I, with my usual pedantry/ attention to detail, did:

"The real model for Benjamin Martin - Francis Marion, nicknamed 'The Swamp Fox' - was an unrepentant slave-owner. The view [in the film] of black people in the South as cheery, loyal volunteer workers takes political correctness to ludicrous extremes. The true reasons for the American War of Independence are fudged, and it is presented as a straightforward struggle between aggrieved nice guys inhabiting a Garden of Eden avenging themselves against murderous Nazis with English accents. British annoyance is likely to be compounded by the fact that the director Roland Emmerich is himself from a nation that really did carry out such outrages. Atrocities committed by the Germans during the twentieth century have cynically been transposed two hundred years earlier to a different continent, and reallocated to the English... *The Patriot* is a nasty piece of work, calculated to make a fortune as a sentimental flagwaver on the Fourth of July. Hollywood should be ashamed of itself for telling lies about one of its most loyal allies to gullible American teenagers, but I don't expect it will be."[901]

Roland Emmerich was up to his old tricks again in *Anonymous*, which was greeted by many critics as a genuine attempt to rewrite history in line with the latest facts. Surprisingly few bothered to check out the true facts behind the film, though honorary mention must be made of the few who did, notably A.O. Scott of the *New York Times*, David Denby of the *New Yorker* and Philip French of the *Observer*. I weighed in with the most detailed account of its inaccuracies:

"Emmerich brings his usual inattention to detail to his latest project, an attempt to show that William Shakespeare (played by Rafe Spall as an illiterate buffoon) did not write Shakespeare's plays; their real author was Edward De Vere, 17th Earl of Oxford, played first by Jamie Campbell Bower and then, with a remarkable lack of aristocratic finesse, by Rhys Ifans. Unfortunately for this thesis, first propounded nearly a hundred years ago by the splendidly named Thomas Looney, the earl died in 1604, after which ten more of Shakespeare's plays continued to appear, until 1616, which – coincidentally or not - was when Shakespeare died. The film's central justification for a subterfuge by Oxford - that it would have been a disgrace for an earl to be associated with writing or the stage - hardly holds water, for the real earl held the lease of the Blackfriars Theatre in the mid-1580s, sponsored various theatrical and musical companies, and produced entertainments at court. He also published mediocre poems under his own name, which bear little similarity to Shakespeare's."[902]

I pointed out that chronology did not support Mr Emmerich's thesis:

"Emmerich and his American screenwriter John Orloff depict De Vere as a child prodigy who wrote and starred in a 1559 production of *A Midsummer Night's Dream*, usually considered a play of outstanding maturity written in the 1590s, at the grand old age of nine. According to Emmerich, Oxford wrote the part of Polonius in Hamlet as an insult to his former guardian, Sir William Cecil (David Thewlis), and Richard III as a satire on the ambitions of Sir William's son, Robert (Edward Hogg), There is no evidence for this. To fit in with Emmerich's conspiracy theory that Shakespeare was writing to support Essex's rebellion of 1601, *Richard III* is depicted as being performed, hot off the page in that year. In fact, it was *Richard II* that was performed in 1601. *Richard III* was written four years earlier. A pity, that... It is horribly apparent that the film-makers and actors have less knowledge of it than many literate thirteen year-olds."[903]

Another example of critics ignoring the real facts and swallowing the fictitious account of history in front of them is Richard Curtis's *The Boat That Rocked*, known in the USA as *Pirate Radio*. It purported to tell the story of governmental attempts to close down a free-spirited pirate radio station called Radio Rock – clearly an amalgamation of Radio Caroline and "Wonderful" Radio London.

Most critics disliked the film on the grounds that it wasn't very funny, and was often offensively sexist. However, they failed to spot that the movie failed most seriously in its central conflict, which lazily wasted a valuable opportunity to tell the truth about the demise of the pirate radio stations, a revealing moment in our political and cultural history.

Curtis presented a bog-standard, clichéd and dated portrait of stuffy authorities versus free-thinking youth that convinced Jules Brenner, film critic for *Cinema Signals*:

"Here's a story about a group of radicals defying their government that we can all get behind. All that's needed is a love of Rock and Roll and belief in the inevitability of music defeating its censors. Long live what these boys achieved in the 1960s."[904]

Chris Bumbray of *Jo Blo's Movie Emporium*, a Canadian website, was equally enthusiastic:

"I haven't the faintest idea why *The Boat That Rocked* flopped in the UK. The story's great - with pirate radio stations such as the one depicted in the film actually existing in the UK during the sixties.... I've got to ask - WTF people? This is a great flick."[905]

Those critics should have looked at the real events. Curtis was only 11 when the principal events of this movie took place, but that's no reason why he couldn't have done some research.

In real life, it was not the stuffy, reactionary Tories who shut down the pirates. It was Harold Wilson's technocratic Labour government. The two men charged with scuppering the pirates were not (as in the movie) stiff-backed, right-wing reactionaries called Dormandy and Twatt, but Edward Short, a machine-politician from Newcastle who rose to become Deputy Leader of the Labour Party, and that perennial darling of the Hard Left, Tony Benn.

As Postmaster-General in 1965, it was Benn who declared war on the pirates with the stark warning "the future does not exist for them."

The Labour government's official line was that broadcasting by pirate stations might interfere with emergency services, but if you read the speeches of the time, it's obvious that the ideologies that really drove them were anti-capitalist and anti-American. Curtis studiously ignored both phenomena.

Curtis makes the audience giggle at the idea of the snobby old BBC playing only 45 minutes of pop music per day, but neglects to explain that the reason why was not cultural or political conservatism, but restrictions imposed on broadcasters by the mighty Musicians' Union, which like most examples of socially conservative organised labour directly financed the Labour Party.

It struck me as interesting that even in a cheerfully lightweight, apparently apolitical film like *The Boat That Rocked*, history was carelessly rewritten in such a way as to disparage the conservatives who in reality were voices of progress. It was one of many disappointing aspects of this film. The fact that most critics couldn't be arsed to investigate the real history of British pirate radio thoroughly annoyed me.

Maybe my strength of feeling came from my having once been a historian, but it strikes me as awful that the laziness and/or mendacity of film-makers is so frequently unnoticed by the vast majority of professional and amateur critics. I would argue that it's enough to make an awful lot of professional critics look unprofessional.

Kenneth Tynan's adage still holds true, and it doesn't only apply to the theatre. To be a good critic, don't just look at what's in front of you. Be careful to check out what *isn't* there – and do your homework.

THE NINTH COMMANDMENT
THOU SHALT NOT DO IT FOR THE MONEY

Death of an Elite

Long gone are the days of "elitist" critics holding undue influence over what can and will find an audience. No longer does Frank Rich decide which shows will and won't run on Broadway, as he often did during his stint as chief theatre critic of the *New York Times* from 1980 to 1993.

Rich denied his own power, stating "critics don't close shows, producers do".[906] But there can be no doubt that his readers trusted him and regarded him as a reliable judge of good and bad in theatre. The impact of his adverse reviews earned him the nickname "the Butcher of Broadway".[907]

Rich wasn't always negative. In 1984 I saw Rich's power exerted to good effect, when I attended a Broadway preview of Stephen Sondheim's new musical about the pointillist painter Georges Seurat, *Sunday in the Park With George*. I eavesdropped on the audience in the bar at the interval. It was clear that, although the singing of Mandy Patinkin and Bernadette Peters was being appreciated, the show was not. The audience wasn't understanding or enjoying it at all.

I loved the show – especially the first act, which struck me as a brilliant exploration of the selfishness necessary in any great artist, and showed Sondheim at his most frankly autobiographical – but I could sense that for the general public the show was a baffling bore. Sondheim himself admits that during Broadway previews of the show, audiences were leaving in droves. It was only when a rave review by Frank Rich came out in the *New York Times* that the show started to win standing ovations. Thanks to reading Rich, the audience learned how to react to a new and challenging work.

Rich's power emanated partly from his gifts as a critic and partly from the prestige of the *New York Times*, but he also managed to reflect – even represent - the mindset and some would say prejudices of rich, Manhattan liberals. He has no modern equivalent in theatre criticism today, but that is partly because the audience on Broadway has fragmented and become more multicultural.

In the world of wine, Robert M. Parker has wielded the kind of formidable power that Rich once wielded over Broadway. Andrew Edgecliffe-Johnson of the *Financial Times* described Parker's as "the world's most prized palate".[908] *New York Times* wine critic Frank Prial acknowledges that "Robert M. Parker is the most influential wine critic in the world".[909]

Max Lalondrelle, fine wine buying director for Berry Bros & Rudd says: "Nobody sells wine like Robert Parker. If he turns around and says 2012 is the worst vintage I've tasted, nobody will buy it, but if he says it's the best, everybody will."[910]

Some critics, notably Jancis Robinson, have questioned his palate and the basis on which he scores wines out of 100. Others have questioned his preference for wines with a high alcohol content and strong tannin reds. And he is of limited usefulness when it comes to supermarket wines; he's principally interested in the "top end". He is certainly being caught up in popularity by other wine experts such as Jancis Robinson, Oz Clarke, Clive Coates, Andrew Jefford, John Livingstone-Learmonth and Stephen Spurrier. His influence is strongest in America.

According to *Guardian* food writer Tim Hayward, Frank Bruni – the *New York Times* restaurant critic from 2004 to 2009 - could shut down restaurants with one bad review. "There was a time when their [professional restaurant critics'] opinion was incredibly important," he says. "But the general public are eating out more these days and are more confident about what they like. Now the big-name critics are more like entertaining columnists."[911]

Bruni ascribes his diminished importance to the number of bloggers doing the same job that he is: "All the instant blog attention to new places can sometimes mean several things. Restaurants pay more attention to the way they come out of the gate than the way they'll mature and stabilize and endure through time. Restaurants that come out of the gate wobbly may never get a chance to recover: the naysaying and catcalling on a myriad of web sites threaten to do them in."[912]

In France, Francois Simon, restaurant critic of *Le Figaro* for more than two decades, was described in a *New York Times* profile of 2009 as "the most feared and most read figure in France's culinary world, an ordinary looking man with a fountain pen as razor-sharp as a butcher's slaughter knife."[913] He is reputed to have been the inspiration for Anton Ego, the pompous restaurant critic in the 2007 Pixar film *Ratatouille*.[914]

Simon is of the opinion that some chefs have become spoiled:

"Chefs are used to extremely excessive literary praise. They become insufferable, divas. They can't take the least criticism. But when you talk of them like they're Beethovens or Mozarts, you're lying."[915]

A favourable review from Simon can certainly fill any restaurant, and a series of derogatory comments about the Michelin three-star status of chef Bernard Loiseau was alleged to have led to Loiseau's suicide in 2003. Loiseau's widow Dominique denied this at the time, pointing out that Loiseau was a severe depressive and downgrading Simon's impact – "It's giving him too much importance".[916]

Ten years later, the truth emerged. A confidential memo from the Michelin Guide's then British Head Derek Brown (he is now director of Michelin) was leaked to the French newspaper *L'Express*. It said that Brown had spoken to Loiseau "of our concerns: irregularity, lack of soul, of recent character in the cuisine and readers' mail that is VERY mixed in terms of quality."[917]

Three months later, Loiseau shot himself with a hunting rifle. In 2013, Francois Simon told the *Daily Telegraph* that he had been treated "like a murderer" in the following years, but now felt vindicated: "Michelin did indeed envisage docking Bernard Loiseau a star. They wanted to pass me off as a killer, while Michelin exempted themselves of any responsibility."[918]

After the *L'Express* report, Oiseau's widow Dominique gave a passionate interview with the French weekly magazine *Le Point,* lashing out at François Simon for declaring his own vindication. At that point, she says, she "began to see things more clearly." Dominique revealed that the chef had indeed been "shaken" by Simon's 2003 article saying that the restaurant had been "legitimately threatened" by Michelin. "It's from this moment that his behaviour began to change, to become incomprehensible. We couldn't reason with him. He was convinced the media wanted his skin from now on," she says. She further blames Simon for refusing to explain his use of the word "legitimately," telling *Le Point*, "I am firmly convinced that if François Simon had a modicum of courage and uprightness to simply explain it with Bernard, maybe we wouldn't be here."[919]

Despite the menacing mystique surrounding Francois Simon, his panning reviews have not closed down thriving concerns. His description of the Paris restaurant Guy Savoy as "a three-star crucifixion" hasn't seemed to damage its popularity, and it still has three Michelin stars. Guy Savoy himself pooh-poohs Simon's significance: "Frankly, what he writes or says doesn't interest me. Life's too short."[920]

Simon calls the chef Marc Veyrat, well known for his use of organic and natural ingredients, a "clown" and "a fake peasant", but Veyrat's restaurants both rank three Michelin stars, and he remains the top-rated chef in the Gault-Millau guide.[921]

Similarly, Simon's fierce attacks on the cooking at top restaurants including La Tour d'Argent, Hélène Darroze, Le Procope, Allard, Maxim's and Brasserie Balzar have been relatively ineffective.[922]

Tracey Macleod, who reviews restaurants for the British newspaper *The Independent* and often appears as a judge on TV's *Masterchef*, doesn't believe she wields enormous power:

"In this country, we critics just aren't that important. We can't make or break restaurants. In 15 years of reviewing for *The Independent*, I've only once had a backlash from a chef I'd reviewed negatively; he phoned me a couple of times to take issue with me. Whether [Alexis] Gauthier was reacting to my underwhelming review of his restaurant or whether he just had a rush of blood to the head, I don't know. But if we give it out, it's only fair that we're ready to take it."[923]

Matthew Fort, best known nowadays for his appearances on *The Great British Menu* but formerly food and drink editor at the *Guardian*, agrees that the impact of individual food critics isn't all that great:

"I've lost count of the restaurants that I and other critics have praised to the skies, only for them to go into receivership shortly afterwards. In one memorable case the restaurant went into receivership before my review appeared. Equally numerous are the places given a right drubbing by the arbiters of restaurant taste, which are still doing a roaring trade years later."[924]

The age of one critic wielding make-or-break power is gone (even the authoritative Parker has significant competitors within the world of wine), and I wouldn't lament its passing. It is a good thing that more people have a chance to express their feelings about any wine, restaurant, work of art or entertainment.

Moaning about new technology leaning to a dumbing down of criticism is nothing new. According to quite a few eminent critics, criticism has been a dying art for at least 200 years.

Early in the twentieth century, the poet and critic T.S. Eliot lamented the proliferation of substandard reviewers:

"Criticism, far from being a simple and orderly field of beneficent activity, from which impostors can be readily ejected, is no better than a Sunday park of contending and contentious orators, who have not even arrived at the articulation of their differences."[925]

A century earlier, another poet-critic, Samuel Taylor Coleridge, warned of declining standards in criticism in his own era:

"Till reviews are conducted on far other principles, and with far other motives; till in the place of arbitrary dictation and petulant sneers, the reviewers support their decisions by reference to fixed canons of criticism, previously established and deduced from the nature of man; reflecting minds will pronounce it arrogance in them thus to announce themselves to men of letters, as the guides of their taste and judgment."[926]

In an essay of 1814, even progressive, democratically-minded William Hazlitt lamented the rise of the popular press, which had led to a dramatic, and to his mind disastrous, rise in the number of critics:

"The number of candidates for fame, and pretenders to criticism, is increased beyond all calculation, while the quantity of genius and feeling remain much the same as before; with these disadvantages, that the man of original genius is often lost among the crowd of competitors who would never have become such, but from encouragement and example, and that the voice of the few whom nature intended for judges, is apt to be drowned in the noisy and forward suffrages of shallow smatterers in taste. The principle of universal suffrage, however applicable to matters of government, which concern the common feelings and common interests of society, is by no means applicable to matters of taste, which can only be decided upon by the most refined understandings. It is throwing down the barriers which separate knowledge and feeling from ignorance and vulgarity, and proclaiming a Bartholomew-fair-show of the fine arts - 'And fools rush in where angels fear to tread'."[927]

The quotation, incidentally, is from Alexander Pope's *Essay on Criticism*, in which he tried to do what I have tried to do in this volume and lay down a few useful principles to guide those planning a career - or merely a dabble - in criticism. Pope wrote *An Essay on Criticism* when he was 22, but it's surprisingly full of wisdom about criticism in the age of the internet.

Among the still relevant aphorisms in the poem are "A little learning is a dangerous thing," "To err is human, to forgive divine" and "Fools rush in where angels fear to tread". All three are useful pieces of advice for anyone, especially would-be critics.

The Crisis in Professional Criticism

Professional critics rarely agree about anything, but they all recognise one thing: there is a crisis in criticism. Sarah Kent, art critic of the London listing magazine *Time Out*, reports that even within the print media:

"Critics are being replaced by feature writers who produce copy as bland as a press release or sycophantic interviews about the subject's celebrity status rather than their work, about which they seem to know almost nothing."

British music critic Norman LeBrecht observed in 2009 that

"In a borderless realm where anyone can tweet an uninformed response, reasoned criticism is under threat and undervalued. The arts are the first casualty of newspapers in retreat. Many US papers have sacked critics and abolished book sections."[928]

Former President of the British Critics' Circle Tom Sutcliffe noted in 2012:

"When the *Financial Times* created an arts page, thanks to Lord Drogheda, chairman of the Royal Opera House, also being the paper's managing director, it consisted entirely of reviews mainly of the live performing arts by respected critics. Andrew Porter, President of the Critics' Circle from 1971-73, devoted 8,000 words over two days to reviewing Britten's opera *The Turn of the Screw*. These days a review in the *FT* will rarely be longer than 350 words."[929]

In most newspapers today, a new opera production would be lucky to receive any reviews at all.I have lost count of the times I have been asked to sit on panels discussing the death of criticism or whether critics are still "relevant". I always refuse because, for me, such panels are invariably complacent and self-regarding. They consist mainly of critics congratulating themselves and their peers. They never include the editors and managing editors who are firing critics. And without them, you're never going to get so much as a hint of the grim reality.

In the last ten years, first in America and now everywhere, there has been a massive change of culture within newspapers, both tabloid and broadsheet, which are run much more by people with an eye to the bottom line (money) than to any notion of editorial quality.

It is no secret that most newspaper editors nowadays believe criticism is disposable because it is not reporting, which they regard as the core of journalism mainly because they came up through the news side themselves.

George Perry, former film editor of the *Sunday Times*, deplores this bias:

"Most editors, even of so-called 'quality' newspapers think that film critics in particular have a doddle of a job, and that it doesn't really require that much talent, as everybody goes to see films and can have an opinion. Far too often they think that all you need is a witty writer. Harry Evans was persuaded to remove a phalanx of elderly but distinguished critics in one go. They included Harold Hobson, Desmond Shawe-Taylor, Felix Aprahamanian and for film, Dilys Powell, an array that counted as the best in Fleet Street. It was utterly misguided. Dilys was replaced by Alan Brien who wrote wittily but was really a theatre man, and he reduced the stature of film criticism in the *Sunday Times* from which it has never recovered."[930]

Lazily, many editors assume that one opinion has about as much merit as another. They probably agree with novelist Will Self's piece for the *Guardian* in October 2013, in which he claimed that "the group amateur mind is indeed far more effective than the unitary perception of an individual critic".

The most recent proponent of this point of view is indie film-maker Kevin Smith. Smith's career sparked into life when critics liked his first two films, *Clerks* (1994) and *Chasing Amy* (1997). After that, his movies nosedived in quality. *Dogma* (1999) and *Jay and Silent Bob Strike Back* (2001) divided the critics; but five turkeys in a row - *Jersey Girl* (2004), *Clerks II* (2006), *Zack and Miri make a Porno* (2008), *Cop Out* (2010) and *Red State* (2011) - were poorly received by critics and audiences alike.

After *Cop-Out* received a near-universal thumbs-down, Smith went ballistic with an online rant against critics and the system in general:

"Whole system's upside down: so we let a bunch of people see it for free and they shit all over it? Meanwhile, people who'd REALLY like to see the flick for free are made to pay? Bullshit: from now on, any flick I'm ever involved with, I conduct critics screenings thusly: you wanna see it early to review it? Fine: pay like you would if you saw it next week. Like, why am I giving an arbitrary 500 people power over what I do at all, let alone for free? Next flick, I'd rather pick 500 randoms from Twitter feed and let THEM see it for free in advance, then post THEIR opinions, good AND bad. Same difference. Why's their opinion more valid? It's a backwards system. People are free to talk shit about ANY of my flicks, so long as they paid to see it."[931]

According to Smith, critics are irrelevant because "every dopey movie has its place" – a view that film reviewer Scott Weinberg questioned eloquently on the *Twitch* website:

"Some (even many) movies are churned out of the machine with little to nothing in the way of actual care or quality control. Smith cites *Juwanna Mann* as a lambasted film that he enjoyed, which is great, but what about *Epic Movie, Ringmaster*, or *The Love Guru*? Are all films simply deserving of blind praise, simply because they are completed films? This is a push towards conformity that would be scary if it came from anyone other than an independent filmmaker who hawks his wares like a used car salesman on speed. 'Every f*ckin' movie counts,' says Smith. This is one of the most childish things I've ever heard regarding film."[932]

Weinberg also took exception to Smith's claim that "If you use film criticism to become a filmmaker, then that's OK, but if you actually choose it for a career, and you love it, you're a passive observer who adds nothing to the equation":

"Let's clear this up right now, once and for all: FILM CRITICS ARE NOT FAILED FILMMAKERS. Speaking only for myself and a few dozen friends, I can say without fear of contradiction that this is the job we want. We love movies, we're good writers, and we have people who enjoy reading our opinions. Perhaps one day I will finish this witless screenplay I've written, but I do not fancy myself a screenwriter, a director, or any sort of filmmaker. They have their skill sets, and I have mine. Seems that if you want to use the position of film critic to become a director, Smith digs you, but if you actually love your job writing about film, you're a greedy stooge who cannot be trusted."[933]

Unfortunately, the Self/Smith analysis seems to be having the upper hand. Serious, analytical arts coverage is in headlong retreat. In most newspapers and magazines, there has been a move away from in-depth reviews and towards showbiz journalism and uncritical interviews, with reviews reduced to one-paragraph summaries of audience appeal - the more upbeat the better.

Even in America's most upmarket paper, the *New York Times*, the arts section now consists largely not of criticism but of features, and there are few reviews of theatre, opera, dance and classical music. Such reviews as there are far more likely to deal with TV, movies and pop music.

That reflects a general dumbing down of newspaper editors, the increasing fascination with celebrities - which has led to 'stars' (e.g. Jonathan Ross, Johnny Vaughan, disc jockey Steve Wright and broadcaster/serial dogger Paul Ross) being employed by some red-top tabloids instead of genuine critics. Slightly higher up the food chain, you'll find famous novelists, such as Will Self and Sebastian Faulks, being brought in to pontificate on film, about which they patently knew little or nothing.

The only good celebrity critic that I can think of is Denis Pratt. I realise he is hardly a household name, but you may know him better by his pseudonym, Quentin Crisp. He rose to prominence late in life because of the TV programme *The Naked Civil Servant*, in which John Hurt played him to perfection.

Though he spent most of his life as a nude male model and prostitute, Quentin Crisp was employed for a time as film critic for New York's leading gay magazine, *Christopher Street*. Doubtless, he was hired for his high celebrity profile and naughty reputation; but – against all the odds - his turned out to be an interesting new voice.

This was partly because he was elderly and had spent a lifetime watching movies, so he had a wider frame of reference than most professional critics.

He was also an accomplished writer, with a splendidly Edwardian turn of phrase. Many of his reviews were reminiscent of Oscar Wilde and Max Beerbohm in their elegance.

Crisp was refreshingly outspoken and didn't much care what others thought of him – excellent qualities in a critic. Here he sounds off about Diana, Princess of Wales:

"I always thought Diana was such trash and got what she deserved. She was Lady Diana before she was Princess Diana so she knew the racket. She knew that royal marriages have nothing to do with love. You marry a man and you stand beside him on public occasions and you wave and for that you never have a financial worry until the day you die."[934]

Ignoring her status as "the people's princess" and a gay icon, the politically incorrect Crisp blamed her death on her "fast and shallow" lifestyle:

"She could have been Queen of England – and she was swanning about Paris with Arabs. What disgraceful behaviour! Going about saying she wanted to be the queen of hearts. The vulgarity of it is so overpowering."[935]

Unsurprisingly, he had blind spots. He never saw anything to commend in *Star Wars:*

"Mr Guinness made a valiant attempt to bestow upon the movie a saintly, El Greco halo, but the story remained paralyzingly monotonous. I longed for its incessant, violent motion to cease."[936]

But he was entertainingly honest about some films that other critics were overkind:

"*The Big Chill* is an almost-perfect television play. It is very thoughtful but very slight. Without embarrassment, we can watch it with a cup of tea and a piece of toast beside us, while we file our toenails just as we do when listening to the depressing confidences of our friends... (The film) chooses to regard the sixties wistfully as a time of spiritual hope in which the young would suddenly bring peace to all mankind, when in fact they were all tottering about some campus or other weak with debauchery and senseless with drugs."[937]

Because of his own brushes with the constabulary, Crisp also had a fresh view of the New Orleans police thriller, *The Big Easy*:

"The copious literature that, as is customary before screenings, was handed to us by Columbia Pictures informed us that the film was made with the cooperation of the New Orleans police department. If this is true, then all its members are madmen as well as rogues. Every officer in sight, including Mr [Dennis] Quaid, is an extortionist and some are murderers, but more unsettling than any one instance of corruption over which we are allowed to gloat is the all-pervading contempt in which all policemen hold all civilians. It is this quality that makes *The Big Easy* so fascinating."[938]

Another dumb commissioning tendency is for editors to bring in "experts" to review certain movies. For example, because the central character in Darren Aronofsky's movie *Black Swan* was a ballerina, both the *Guardian* and Radio 4's *Today Programme* sent ballet dancers to review it. Unsurprisingly, they achieved near-perfect, wrong-headed unanimity in condemning it as an outrageously over-the-top collection of clichés about the ballet world, and a foul libel on their profession. Such a response was understandable but sublimely irrelevant to the film's merits and comically blinkered as to the director's achievement.

Asking dance professionals to review *Black Swan* for its realism was like inviting motel-owners to judge whether Alfred Hitchcock's *Psycho* is an accurate portrait of their own occupation, or polling inhabitants of New York's Gothic apartment block, the Dakota (notoriously used as a location for Roman Polanski's *Rosemary's Baby*), as to whether its inhabitants are really all Satanists. *Black Swan* was not a drama-documentary about ballerinas, nor did it set out to be; it was a deliberately stylised view of artistic obsession and descent into madness.

It was expressionistic in the same way as *Shutter Island, Fight Club* and *Repulsion*. All are examinations of a soul in torment. None is a fair representation of police detectives, office workers or attractive blonde Parisiennes living alone.

Richard Schickel, longtime critic for *Time Magazine*, believes that a major contributing factor to the decline of the film critic is a lowering of standards within the film industry:

"The current demise of film reviewing coincides with the ageing and death of the great foreign *auteurs* and with Hollywood's decision to concentrate on the production of blockbuster and tentpoles. I'm not saying that there are no interesting movies to review anymore, but I am saying that week-in, week-out there are very few of them that require the attentive interest of first-class critical intelligences... If American studio movies — the ones that (let's face it) most people are interested in — continue on their path to unreviewability (as I expect they will) that will diminish the need for, as well as the influence, of traditional reviewing."[939]

He also argues that the public has lost interest in serious criticism:

"The vast number of moviegoers — the people whose patronage make Judd Apatow movies or *Batman* sequels such huge international successes — need only know when one of those potential megahits is opening in a theatre near them; they really don't give a rat's ass that it has displeased those remaining critical sensibilities that are still aquiver with the desire — the need — for art."[940]

Schickel points to the important difference in culture between critics and their editors:

"Most of these people [editors] came up out of shoe-leather, reportorial journalism. They tolerated hoity-toity criticism when it seemed to support their needs, but mostly they never really liked us — or their music, art, dance, or book critics either, who are threatened species as well. Like most of their readers these editors wondered what right we had to our opinions, which were formed not by interviewing the masses, but by reporting exclusively on the state of our own minds, spirits, and historical knowledge. These people quite cheerfully believe that they are serving the needs of their readers by running star profiles, reports on visits to sets and, most important to them, the economic news from show biz."[941]

American reviewer James Bowman argued as long ago as 2003 that criticising many popular movies, such as *Austin Powers in Goldmember*, was a waste of time:

"Of *course* the thing amounts to what we movie critics call crap. That ought to go without saying. But then, did Mike Myers think it *wasn't* crap? I very much doubt it. In fact, I will go further and say that many of the worst movies being made today were intended by their makers to be just exactly as bad as they are. This creates rather a dilemma for the critic.

In critics' school they used to teach us that we were supposed to explore the gap between intention and achievement. What did the author intend, our beloved professor used to instruct us eager neophytes to ask ourselves, and how well did he succeed in realising his intention? Bad movies were movies that, it was assumed, were trying to be good movies and just not making it. The authors had made a mistake in putting scene A before scene B instead of vice versa, or in moving the camera in a distracting way, or in allowing incoherence to creep into the plot or the actors to overact and so spoil the effect they were trying to create. But Mr Myers and his colleagues were not trying to create any effect besides laughter. Accordingly, their movie consists of one joke after another, like a stand-up routine. Some of the jokes are good and some are not so good, but the main thing is that they keep coming — so that even if there are several duds in a row, it will never be long between laughs. And anyone who tried to treat such a movie as an artistic whole would be the butt of the biggest joke of all. In this as in other cases these days, to be critical is itself a critical lapse. It is to fail to 'get' the central and endlessly repeatable joke of post-modern movie-making, which is that the bad movie is bad because it is *supposed* to be bad."[942]

Concurrent with these developments has been the growth of multinational media groups which have interests in both newspapers and film studios. More and more newspapers and magazines are taken over by conglomerates that also have film-making interests. You won't find many hostile reviews of 20th Century Fox films in the Murdoch press or on Fox television.

Too many editors are to some extent dependent on advertising by the film industry. Especially in film and listing magazines, adverse criticism is stifled if a certain film has given that magazine a cover story.

There are some well-known film critics who seem to me to have given up trying to inform and instruct, because they are afraid of alienating their readers, their advertisers and/or their editors. That leads to a kind of appeasement of ignorance by people who ought to know better. They fear to show anything but enthusiasm for movies they know are going to be hits, whether they like them or not.

There are also political reasons why the cultural elite has come under attack. For the Right, especially the American Right, the notion of professional critics flags up warning signs. Critics are unelected, often left-of-centre politically and use their alleged expertise to override the mechanisms of the market and consumer choice. Why not do away with them completely, and free up the market?

The Left, naturally, dislikes the idea of an unelected elite. Many are happy to accept the view that one view is as good as another (except in politics, of course). Literature and the arts are merely a matter of personal taste. To say otherwise is to be a cultural snob.

Whether on the Left or Right, the press feels under attack from the internet, falling readerships and declining advertising. Why not sack critics who may alienate readers, advertisers or other hard-working arms of your newspaper's media empire, and install writers who will be more amenable, more willing simply to reflect what the public is buying, art that is popular, art that is inoffensive?

The short answer is, of course, that "popular" does not necessarily mean "good"; critics who have stood out against prevailing notions of good taste have often been proved to be right; and you're in danger of firing good critics and replacing them with bad, or not replacing them at all. Regrettably, that is happening on both sides of the Atlantic. Bad is driving out good. It's Darwinism stood on its head. It's the survival of the glibbest.

The most visible sign of the decline of print criticism has been the number of respected film critics who have been fired. In America, 2008 saw the professional demise of David Ansen, Nathan Lee of the *Village Voice*, Jack Mathews and Jami Bernard of the *New York Daily News*, Kevin Thomas of the *LA Times*, Jonathan Rosenbaum of the *Chicago Reader*, Michael Wilmington of the *Chicago Tribune*, Terry Lawson of the *Detroit Free Press* and Jan Stuart and Gene Seymour of *Newsday*.

For me, the employment of honest, incorruptible critics remains a vital sign of any journal's health. The culling of good critics by newspaper editors who should know better strikes me as a short-sighted policy that is removing one of the few things that make newspapers more worth reading than their internet equivalents: criticism that is knowledgeable, fair and based on experience, analytical skills and emotional intelligence.

There is a deep-rooted fallacy held by many at the top of newspapers, magazines and even – astonishingly – the BBC that one opinion is as good as any other, that the kind of critic they want is someone who sees with the eyes of the Average Man or Typical Reader (whoever that is) and can predict what their reaction will be. To this end, executives scrupulously avoid anyone who might be termed an expert or, worse still, elitist.

The late film critic Roger Ebert wrote back in 2008, when the cull of good critics was just beginning:

"A newspaper film critic is like a canary in a coal mine. When one croaks, get the hell out. The lengthening toll of former film critics acts as a poster child for the self-destruction of American newspapers, which once hoped to be more like the *New York Times* and now yearn to become more like the *National Enquirer*. We used to be the town crier. Now we are the neighbourhood gossip."[943]

Ebert blamed the cult of celebrity, which he argued had spread from the tabloids even to previously upmarket newspapers and magazines:

"As the CelebCult triumphs, major newspapers have been firing experienced film critics. They want to devote less of their space to considered prose, and more to ignorant gawking. What they require doesn't need to be paid for out of their payrolls... The age of film critics has come and gone."[944]

Ebert bravely blamed the dumbing down on the public:

"The celebrity culture is infantilising us. We are being trained not to think. It is not about the disappearance of film critics. We are the canaries. It is about the death of an intelligent and curious, readership, interested in significant things and able to think critically. It is about the failure of our educational system. It is not about dumbing-down. It is about snuffing out. The news is still big. It's the newspapers that got small."[945]

Charles Taylor, of the online magazine *Salon*, points out that the climate of fear affects the way print and online critics write:

"Publicly, film critics for established online publications will say that the Web has given a new home to film criticism. Off the record, many of those same critics will tell you their jobs depend on securing advertiser-pleasing hits by lavishing coverage on the worst of what's out there, especially the superhero and fantasy movies. Editors hope to attract hits by feeding into a movie's prerelease hoopla. What a critic actually thinks about the movie is often drowned in the ongoing publicity deluge. If a publication's critic declines to join in the publicist-generated excitement over *The Green Lantern* or the fifth *Pirates of the Caribbean*, the editor can always find a writer, usually a young one looking to get a byline, to whip up the mindless sort of 'Five Great Superhero Movies' list that guarantees traffic. Editors then point to the number of hits generated by this as proof that what the readers really want is coverage of the big movies — whether or not there's been coverage of anything else to choose from. All this deprives critics of one of the main functions of their job: to alert readers to different kinds of work. And because maintaining advertising dollars depends on keeping the clicks coming, it's easy for even good editors to make their publication a tool of the studio publicists."[946]

Not everyone regards the sacking of professional film critics as a bad thing. When in January 2012, J. Hoberman was axed from the *Village Voice*, Eileen Jones of the website *The Exiled* wrote: "old-school cineastes are rending their garments in grief and crying 'Oh the humanity!' Personally, I hate J. Hoberman and the film criticism he rode in on, and I only wish he'd tripped and broken his neck on the way out the door. Oh, all right, if that's too harsh, let's say I wish he'd broken his arm. His writing arm."[947]

Charming. In the UK, always about five years behind America, 2013 saw the culling of a massive number of leading critics. Philip French, veteran film critic for the *Observer*, may only just have retired in time. *The*

Independent on Sunday fired all its Arts critics including Jonathan Romney and Nicholas Barber (film), Tom Sutcliffe (TV), Kate Bassett (theatre), Charles Darwent (visual arts), Anna Picard and Simon Price (music). Other prominent firings included Anthony Quinn (film) from the *Independent*, Libby Purves (theatre) from the *Times*, Cosmo Landesman (film) from the *Sunday Times*, Derek Malcolm (film) from the *Evening Standard* and myself (film) from the *Daily Mail*, only a few months after being named Arts Reviewer of the Year at the London Press Club Awards. Charles Spencer took early retirement from the *Daily Telegraph*, and Jenny McCartney was sacked from being film critic of the *Sunday Telegraph*.

Not all these critics have been replaced – the *Independent on Sunday* merely publishes roundups of other people's reviews – and it is an open secret that those who have replaced outgoing critics have been not only younger but a lot cheaper. An enormous amount of experience and writing ability has been jettisoned, either for editorial or commercial reasons.

Nick James drew pessimistic conclusions in the November 2013 issue of *Sight and Sound* magazine:

"First, it seems many publishing outlets around the world have forgotten that their brands were built on the quality of their writers, and that if you remove quality writers to trim budgets, your brand will suffer. Second, the *Independent* group's policy on arts coverage seems not to understand why people read newspapers (in hand or online) so I'm led to ask if it's a deliberate act of self-destruction or a reach down-market."[948]

Stephanie Zacharek, an American film critic who left the online magazine *Salon* in 2010, takes a bleak view of paid film criticism:

"I don't believe film criticism overall is dying - it thrives, in many different forms and at many different levels of quality, on the Web. But the chances of being able to make a living at it are growing increasingly slim."[949]

Down under, too, the paid arts critic is a dying breed. Ben Eltham wrote *A Cultural Policy Blog* in 2009, and apparently the situation has worsened since then:

"In Australia, there hasn't been much in the way of reasoned criticism for some time. When I first started as a theatre and arts critic for *Brisbane's Courier-Mail* in 2001, that paper sustained a surprisingly serious commitment to the arts that belied its bucolic reputation. The paper gave regular work to a number of intelligent and well-qualified reviewers, corralled by an agile and feisty arts editor in Rosemary Sorensen. There was scope to write long features on important trends in contemporary culture, like the growth of turntables as a musical instrument or the popular success of electronic music. A glance at what passes for the arts section in today's bowdlerised tabloid *Courier-Mail* shows the extent of the cultural regress. Sorensen has moved on to greener pastures at *The Australian*, and her replacement, Suzannah Clarke, is more of an arts reporter, penning friendly but only marginally critical feature articles and employing a dwindling band of specialist reviewers to judge the vibrant culture of Australia's third-largest city. At the Fairfax newspapers, a similar story can be told. Although *The Age's* A2 section retains a certain commitment to surveying local books and literature, truly critical articles and reviews are hard to find. As with most newspaper arts coverage, the sycophantic interview and the PR puff piece are by-and-large the order of the day."[950]

In the British magazine *The Spectator* of January 2014, Elle Jay Smith noted that the arts coverage on BBC2's flagship programme *Newsnight* had descended into "a string of fawning advertorials":

"In the past six weeks, *Newsnight* has presented us with the following: an interview with Howard Hodgkin to coincide with his exhibition at the Alan Cristea Gallery, Mayfair; an interview with Michael Caine ahead of the release of his new movie Interstellar; curator Neil MacGregor giving us a 'virtual tour' of the British Museum's Germany exhibition; film director Mike Leigh, who has a film out on Turner, in conversation with Nicholas Serota of the Tate galleries, which is also exhibiting Turner; and there were the six back-to-back interviews with the shortlisted authors of the Booker Prize. The purpose of each of these was promotional. While it is expected that arts public relations and arts journalism will interact, you would think that a programme such as *Newsnight* would probe and push back just a little. It hasn't been."[951]

Smith points out that any notion of discovering new talent was on the back burner at *Newsnight*:

"The subjects on whom *Newsnight* has been lavishing its patronage do not, in the main, need it. Howard Hodgkin, Michael Caine, Mike Leigh, Germany – these are not breakthrough acts... The British Museum and Tate Modern must have snaffled up enough taxpayers' money over the years not to be in need of an indirect bung from the licence fee payer as well. Ian Katz, *Newsnight's* newish editor, was supposed to be ushering an edgier, more eclectic era for the programme. Instead he presents us with the same big establishment hippos splashing around in the same publicly-funded pool... The BBC, of course has to cover the arts, because it is a public service broadcaster and they are integral to the public sphere. But for that coverage to be worth anything it should critically engage with the artist's output, otherwise it's just advertising, which I always thought the BBC was not supposed to do."[952]

Nor is this tendency to puff confined to *Newsnight*. Arts coverage on BBC Radio 4's flagship programme *Today* consists of upbeat celebrity interviews and free advertising for upcoming shows, films and exhibitions. Arts coverage is treated as cheerful escapism from all the bad news in the real world, or a brief reminder of civilisation in an age of barbarism.

In a 2008 piece for the *Guardian*, art critic Adrian Searle tried to work out who was to blame for the prevailing anti-critic culture in newspapers and broadcast media:

"People blame the internet and the rise of the blogger. They blame the dumbing down of newspapers and the replacement of criticism with the sparkling-if-vapid preview featurette, and the artist-as-celebrity photo-opportunity profile. Who cares about the art or the concepts? They're just the MacGuffin. Tell us about the parties, the openings, the drugs and the dresses. Artists are creative and creative is sexy and good. Critics are a comedown. Some have hair sprouting from their ears. They're always complaining; they're untrustworthy; they're full of hate and spite and they make everything all so complicated, when all we're really trying to do is sell a lifestyle. Fuck 'em."[953]

In 2012 Dave Hickey, one of America's foremost art critics, retired, saying he – like other honest critics - no longer felt he had a worthwhile function:

"Art editors and critics – people like me – have become a courtier class. All we do is wander around the palace and advise very rich people. It's not worth my time."[954]

The 71 year-old Hickey was adamant that there was no way back. "What can I tell you? It's nasty and it's stupid. I'm an intellectual and I don't care if I'm not invited to the party. I quit."[955]

Andrew Grant, a freelance film critic and festival programmer based in Berlin, Germany, believes the decline of film criticism is principally a matter of diminished public demand:

"Film critics matter far less today than they did years ago. I grew up a child of the film industry, and can recall just how important those Friday reviews were. At one time, strong praise for an art-house film in *The New York Times* or *The New Yorker* almost guaranteed its success, whereas a pan would more than likely have a detrimental effect. Not anymore. Fewer people seek critical opinion, especially when they've been bludgeoned by aggressive (and effective, as it turns out) viral marketing campaigns that extend far beyond traditional means, and editors are conscious of this fact. Why pay salary and benefits for a single critic when you can hire three free-lancers for less money, and syndicate their 250-word minireviews to boot?"[956]

So here's a timely warning before you decide to try a career in criticism. Becoming a critic is not to be undertaken lightly. You're likely to be underpaid, and you're certain at some point to be fired. You're definitely going to be exploited.

Just before one critic was given the boot from his newspaper, he queried why journalists were not being paid for the use of their copy on the online version of the paper when that was bringing in more advertising revenue than the newspaper itself. He pointed out that, while journalists had been prepared to work for nothing when the online paper was running at a loss, it was unfair to expect journalists to work for nothing when it was quite obviously turning a profit and rewarding its executives with colossal pay rises. He never received a reply, although an Assistant Editor on his paper did try to assure him that the online version of the paper was still running at a loss - which was untrue. It had publicly announced that it was in profit the year before.

Another sign of the times is that Arianna Huffington sold the online newspaper the *Huffington Post* to AOL in 2011 for 315 million dollars, pocketing a fortune for herself without ever having paid its contributors for their blogs.[957] There seems to be plenty of money for some of those who exploit the internet, but not for the writers who supply the content.

Capitalism is often commended for its "trickle down" effect, not least by *Daily Mail* editor Paul Dacre. In 2002, he said of himself "I don't see how anybody can go to America, work there for six years and not be enthralled by the energy of the free market. America taught me the power of the free market, as opposed to the State, to improve the lives of the vast majority of ordinary people."[958]

Unfortunately, this benevolent capitalism has yet to make itself felt in online newspapers. In May 2014, *Mail Online* announced that it had increased its revenues by 45% to £28m in the six months to the end of March, more than offsetting the slight decline in sales and advertising at the *Daily Mail* and *Mail on Sunday*. *Mail Online's* growth meant that the combined business managed to keep revenues buoyant at £306m. Combined revenues from advertising were up 4%.

Stephen Daintith, finance director for the parent company Daily Mail and General Trust, announced that the profit per employee was up from £9,000 five years before to £29,000. "We are more focused, lean and efficient," he said.[959]

So why the need for firings? At the same time such organisations were "slimming down", the fat cats at the top were doing extraordinarily well. In the year ending September 2012, one Associated Newspapers executive, Kevin Beatty, received earnings of £1,133,000. *Daily Mail* editor Paul Dacre earned £1,780,000. In the year 2013-14, Dacre received a further inflation-busting pay rise of 5%, with annual pay of £2.412 million.[960] This revelation, on the 8th January 2014, came on the same day that a report from the High Pay Centre think tank revealed executive pay in Britain to have soared by 74% over the previous decade while workers' wages had remained flat. No trickle-down effect there, then.[961]

High Pay Centre director Deborah Hargreaves said: "While government figures confirm that wages for ordinary workers keep falling, it's clear that not everyone is feeling the pain. When bosses make hundreds of times as much money as the rest of the workforce, it creates a deep sense of unfairness."[962]

Private Eye editor Ian Hislop let a fat cat out of the bag in October 2013, when the BBC panel show *Have I Got News For You* debated the ongoing row between Ed Miliband and the *Daily Mail* over its claims that Ed's dad Ralph "hated Britain".

Hislop said of Ralph Miliband:

"This is the man that hated Britain on the evidence of one entry in a diary when he was sixteen when he'd just arrived as a refugee in this country. It was the most pathetic piece. What I think will be embarrassing for the *Mail*'s Editor is the *Mail* is owned by the Rothermere family. What did your Dad do? The current Lord Rothermere's father loved Great Britain so much he went to live in France as a tax exile. He then passed on the nom-dom status to his son who doesn't actually pay the normal amount of tax despite owning a newspaper that's owned through various tax companies in Bermuda."[963]

Jonathan Harmsworth, 4th Earl of Rothermere, has an estimated wealth of £720 million, according to the *Sunday Times* Rich List. As Hislop says, despite living with his family in a £40m neo-Palladian stately home in 220 acres of grounds in Wiltshire – plus a flat in London's Eaton Square - he has non-domicile tax status. A complex structure of trusts and offshore holdings mean that he pays almost no UK tax on his income, investments or wealth.[964]

I am not calling for the confiscation of inherited wealth or the overthrow of capitalism, but it's only fair to point out that capitalism has its downside, which is that it rewards greed, protects its sordid secrets and has very little interest in social justice.

If you haven't inherited a billion quid from your dad and you're clever and talented enough to be a good critic, you should consider carefully whether you are likely to be rewarded adequately for your talents. In the current economic climate, firing journalists is much more lucrative than being one.

Nor is this a recent phenomenon. Remember that the great British critic William Hazlitt, in many ways the founding father of criticism, died penniless.

George Bernard Shaw wrote an essay *How To Become a Music Critic* which – even though the sums of money have changed - rings as true today as when he wrote it in 1894:

"The emoluments of a music critic are not large. Newspaper proprietors offer men from a pound a week to five pounds a week for music criticism, the latter figure being very exceptional, and involving the delivery of a couple of thousand words of extra brilliant copy every week. And, except in the dead season, the critic must spend most of his afternoons and evenings, from three to midnight, in concert rooms or in the opera house. I need hardly say that it is about as feasible to obtain the services of a fully-qualified music critic on these terms as it would be to obtain a pound of fresh strawberries every day from January to December for five shillings a week. Consequently, to all the qualifications I have already suggested, I must insist on this further one - an independent income, and sufficient belief in the value of music criticism to sustain you in doing it for its own sake whilst its pecuniary profits are enjoyed by others. And since this condition is so improbable in any given case as to take my subject completely out of the range of the practicable, I may as well stop preaching, since my sermon ends, as all such sermons do, in a demonstration that our economic system fails miserably to provide the requisite incentive to the production of first-rate work."[965]

It is worth remembering that in her first 10 years of reviewing, the most acclaimed film critic of her generation, Pauline Kael, earned less than $2,000. To scrape a living, she had to work as a seamstress and cook, and she ghost-wrote textbooks. For years she broadcast without pay for the Pacifica radio-network. Her breakthrough came when, in 1965, she published *I Lost It at the Movies,* a selection of her past criticism. The book sold 150,000 copies and encouraged Kael to move to New York, where she wrote as a freelance for such large-circulation magazines as *Life, Holiday* and *McCall's.* Her hostile review in *McCall's* of *The Sound of Music,* which she described as a "sugar-coated lie", meant she was fired for her negativity.

On her next magazine, the *New Republic,* editors changed her copy without consulting her. After she resigned "in despair", she was fortunate that one of her reviews, a spirited defence of *Bonnie and Clyde,* found favour with William Shawn, editor of the *New Yorker,* who invited her to join his magazine. When at last she was offered a steady job (her stay at the *New Yorker* lasted until she retired in 1991), she was 49 years old.[966]

So don't expect criticism to be well paid, or a job for life. Do it because you want to. The age of professional critics earning six-figure salaries over a long period is over. If you want big money, there are other things you should do.

Internet Criticism at its Worst and Best

There's plenty of information and opinion on the Internet, but it may not always be reliable information or informed opinion. Hardly any of it undergoes the fact-checking or editorial input common in good print journalism.

Amazon reviews can be used to pursue personal vendettas and carry out dirty tricks. Professional writers R.J. Ellory[967], Orlando Figes[968], Johann

Hari[969] and Stephen Leather[970] have all been forced to confess that they have used fictitious names to extol their own work and slam competitors. John Locke, a successful self-publisher and author of *How I Sold One Million E-Books In Five Months*, has admitted to buying five-star reviews to boost his Amazon visibility.[971] In one week in 2013, the New York authorities fined 19 firms a total of $350,000 (£218,500) for posting fake reviews on websites.[972] You can rest assured that there are many more dodgy "reviewers" that haven't been caught out.

On October 11th, 2015, an undercover investigation by Robin Henry for the *Sunday Times* revealed what many people already knew: that fake reviewers using stolen identities could be hired for as little as £3 to promote books and other products into Amazon best-seller lists. [973]

One book, *Everything Bonsai!*, written over a weekend and full of mistakes, inaccuracies and illiteracies, managed with the outlay of only £56 to reach the top of the Gardening and Horticulture bestsellers category on Amazon's Kindle store. Four fake reviewers downloaded the book more than 200 times in five days by exploiting Amazon's free promotions, and then posting four- and five-star raves. Ironically, these reviews were accompanied by Amazon's "verified purchase" stamp, which is meant to show the reviews are genuine.

The *Sunday Times* also revealed that a best-selling chess guide on Amazon was written by an author with a false CV and with 100 laudatory reviews that were as fake as the author. Other dealers in fake reviews use Facebook "bookclubs" to sign up students to write paid-for "reviews". This is an incredibly widespread form of corruption that is misleading and fleecing thousands, perhaps even millions, of people who believe they are reading honest reviews.

Though I often read the amateur book reviews on Amazon, I wouldn't trust them - mainly because I don't (for example) share the majority belief that Dan Brown is a great writer. Expressing an opinion is not the same as having taste.

Anyone can write a book review on Amazon, blog about a film they have seen or simply tweet a kneejerk reaction. That doesn't mean they have anything coherent, informed or valuable to communicate – and there's so much of this material that it can easily drown out more informed comment.

Similarly, anyone can tweet. In a perceptive 2012 article for *Slate*, entitled *Against Enthusiasm*, Jacob Silverman argued convincingly that Twitter, at least for writers, had become a "mutual-admiration society":

"If you spend time in the literary Twitter- or blogospheres, you'll be positively besieged by amiability, by a relentless enthusiasm that might have you believing that all new books are wonderful and that every writer is every other writer's biggest fan."[974]

Silverman argued that this wasn't only superficial, it was fake. And the effect has been that fair, considered criticism is often regarded as unnecessarily harsh, like a slap to the face of a Prozac addict.

"Reviewers shouldn't be recommendation machines," Silverman concludes, "yet we have settled for that role, in part because the solicitous communalism of Twitter encourages it."

There really is a danger that great art and honest criticism will be drowned out by art calculated to appeal to the lowest common denominator, and tweets more concerned with achieving popularity than with telling the truth.

As film critic Philip French wrote in the *Observer* on 30th January 2011:

"The decline of print journalism and the ubiquity of the web may produce a cultural Gresham's law. Gresham declared that bad money drives good money out of circulation. It could be that bad criticism might have a similar effect on serious, considered writing."[975]

On the internet there is a very high degree of corruption. I don't mean financial corruption, though that undoubtedly exists; it's more often corruption by friendship. It's blatantly obvious with some books, for example, that friends and relatives have been hauled in to write raves about books that deserve at best one or two-star reviews.

Long before the arrival of the internet, novelist Anthony Trollope saw corruption by friendship – or enmity - as the most common cause of bad criticism:

"If the writer will tell us what he thinks, though his thoughts be absolutely vague and useless, we can forgive him; but when he tells us what he does not think, actuated either by friendship or by animosity, then there should be no pardon for him. This is the sin in modern English criticism of which there is most reason to complain. It is a lamentable fact that men and women lend themselves to this practice who are neither vindictive nor ordinarily dishonest. It has become 'the custom of the trade,' under the veil of which excuse so many tradesmen justify their malpractices!"[976]

Trollope explains why this kind of corruption is so seductive for its practitioners:

"Dishonesty begets dishonesty, till dishonesty seems to be beautiful. How nice to be good-natured! How glorious to assist struggling young authors, especially if the young author be also a pretty woman! How gracious to oblige a friend! Then the motive, though still pleasing, departs further from the border of what is good."[977]

Critic Tom Sutcliffe deplores the number of dishonest reviews on the internet:

"Many websites are springing up offering criticism at length by punter-reviewers being procured by promoters (and described as 'what you the people think')."[978]

Guy Dimond, food and drink editor at *Time Out*, believes his own area is infested with bad criticism:

"There's no shortage of not-very-credible guidebooks with their strings pulled by advertisers and PRs, or drivel written on the basis of freebies and advertorials... Our process is simple – we book under a false name, we eat there, we pay, we describe the experience. We don't meet PRs, go to launches, socialize with chefs or accept freebies. Our company pays the expenses. We usually visit once, sometimes twice, or three times."[979]

There is a particular kind of non-criticism that has grown up on the net, pretending to be criticism. In the world of film, so-called "fanboys" make up an extremely high proportion of those writing film reviews. Fanboys - who can be of either sex but are predominantly male and under 35 - praise almost every movie based on a comic strip, regardless of how terrible it is, and routinely insult any professional critics who disagree with them. If you want to wind them up, try writing a truthful review of a *Batman* movie.

Harry Knowles is the most famous fanboy in the world, even though he's now middle-aged and looks like a ginger Jabba the Hutt. In 1996, he set up the *Aint-It-Cool-News* website, a downmarket copy of an already existing website called *Coming Attractions*. "I was basically doing *comingattractions.com* but with a cult of personality behind it," Knowles admitted to *GQ* in 2003.[980] Knowles made his name by spreading gossip, true and untrue, about upcoming movies and published "reviews" that were effusive rants about how great most of these movies were. Hollywood studios rapidly realised that a splendid way to publicize film aimed at teenage boys and retarded adults was to get Harry Knowles to rave about them uncritically. This, Knowles was happy to do.

The result was a torrent of misinformation and poor judgment. In 1999, Knowles hailed the Robin Williams-plays-a-robot turkey *Bicentennial Man* as "a damn good film".[981] That's the movie Roger Ebert called "a letdown".[982] Peter Howell in the *Toronto Star* said it was "witless and lacks conviction".[983]

One of the two most critically panned turkeys of 2005 was the awful sci-fi adventure *Aeon Flux*, starring Charlize Theron. The *Guardian* proclaimed it "charmless and brainless".[984] Liza Schwarzbaum advised readers of *Entertainment Weekly* to "be prepared to collapse into a hoot and a howl of hilarity at all the wrong moments."[985]All Harry Knowles could say was that it was "a very accomplished film".[986]

Knowles even managed to pretend that Michael Bay's studio potboiler *Transformers 3: Dark Side of the Moon* (2011) was a masterpiece:

"Easily the best 3D since *AVATAR* – and in many respects I think it is superior. After I saw the film, my brain felt tired. Not from great thoughts, but from the experience of the film. It wore my brain out watching it. I found myself thinking about the set-ups Bay made to physically make this movie. The sheer volume of wow shots is spectacular. The action in this film is truly amazing work. Bay's talent for designing these shots is nothing short of amazing to watch. The physical look of everything is amazing."[987]

Knowles has been accused of all kinds of things – including theft,[988] nepotism[989] and body odour[990] – but one thing not in doubt is his execrable prose style, which is roughly that of a poorly educated, starstruck 13 year-old. His idea of a reasoned review of a *Pirates of the Caribbean* movie was to rave that "Johnny Depp is literally performing on another cosmic level of existence".[991]

Where other critics judged *G.I. Joe: The Rise of Cobra* (2009) to be worthless drivel, Knowles claimed it to be "a wild ride. Awesome. So much fun." [992] His equally predictable rave about the ultra-violent *The Expendables* (2010) climaxed with "a testicular masterpiece of mannish awesomery!!!... This is just a great fucking time."[993]

Four-letter words are a staple ingredient of Harry Knowles reviews and replace the need for appropriate adjectives. Note this rave about *Watchmen* (2009), which confirmed my belief that Zack Snyder's film would find its most appreciative audience among sad sociopaths, deranged pseudo-intellectuals and brutalized, immature men of all ages:

"This is a completely different experience. For the first time in my 22-23 year relationship with the characters and universe of *WATCHMEN*, there is something entirely new to dissect, talk about, argue about, get enraged over, get drunk over, fight over and to fucking love!... I WATCHED THE FUCKING *WATCHMEN* AND FUCKING LOVED IT! It isn't the perfect 5 hour wet dream that I always dreamt of, but I love it. I can't wait to see the dialogue you all have with this film, with each other and with us here at *AICN*. This was fucking awesome!"[994]

The quintessential Harry Knowles review, however, is this gushing panegyric to *Tron: Legacy* (2013), a film most critics found a cynical, soulless shambles:

"I live for films like *Tron*... The original helped me dream of the world I currently occupy. It's why I was ready those 14 years ago to create this site. I'd been waiting my whole life with a lot to say and I kinda knew that it'd be with a computer. That's why I took those typing classes... the keyboard could not be an obstruction between thought and expression. They needed to be effortless. That came from *Tron*... *Tron Legacy* – I've no idea how it'll play beyond the core. I am the core, it works wonderfully for me. Far better than I was hoping for. I laughed and cheered throughout – and after the screening, Father Geek, Quint, Merrick and Son Of Merrick were united in gleeful *Tron* geekery for a full hour... talking about what could happen next. What permanent actions had taken place. What's around Sam's neck exactly – and the notion of bringing... well, you should discover some of the questions on your own. It fucking kicked ass!... I'm a *TRON* geek for life!"[995]

Amazingly, there are numerous writers on the internet just as tragically illiterate and critically inept as Harry Knowles. One of the worst is someone calling himself "Michael" on *OnlineMoviesHut.com*. Here's his rave about, would you believe, the third *Big Momma's House* movie starring Martin Lawrence, *Big Mommas: Like Father Like Son* (2011):

"A great source of entertainment... a number of funny and hilarious events. Antics of the duo who had been dressed as females were funny and hilarious look at. Martin Lawrence and Brandon T. Jackson coming up giving life to main characters in this comedy flick appeared to have done a fine pieces [sic] of acting by coming up with believable pieces of acting to delight of comedy fans. Especially the former mentioned actor who is quite famous for his comedy acts had gone on to deliver another of his talented and skilled pieces which had been quite enjoyable in eyes of movie going crowds. Thus all and this [sic] had definitely been a most amazing and awesome one for delight of moviegoers who had been eager for this. *Big Mommas: Like Father, Like Son* movie review should also make it a point to mention that packed with incidents where satire and humour had been highlighted a one of a kind joyride this had gone on to be and viewers will surely keep this in their mind for a long time to come. Thus all and all it should be noted that those who had enjoyed this part of the comedy series will be looking forward to see the next installment of the series as well and the possibility another flick is pretty high."[996]

Fine writing, this is not. And it's a weirdly uncritical reaction to a movie that was comprehensively trashed by real critics. Derek Adams in *Time Out* wrote, "Quite how this flaccid, one-joke crime comedy franchise even got off the ground is a mystery."[997] Ryan Lambie, in *Den of Geek* (one of the better film websites, and not as geeky as its name suggests), described it as "a piece of neo-Dadaist art, a kind of anti- comedy that swirls in front of you like a black hole, sucking in any semblance of comedy in its vicinity. All you can do is stare, stupefied, into the cinematic void."[998] Peter Bradshaw in the *Guardian* said the film made him question the purpose of life: "If *Big Momma 4* comes out – well, that would be the time to make the booking with Dignitas and get the easyJet flights to Zurich."[999]

Robert Koehler, of *Variety*, is vitriolic about fanboy bloggers:

"Their diet of cinema is so restricted and codified, resulting in work that suffers enormously from a nearly complete lack of knowledge or interest in international film tendencies. They're of essentially the same ilk as junket and quote-whore critics who watch and write about little more than American blockbusters. Since they lack the ability to draw upon film history, and since they effectively write in a reinforcing echo chamber of bloggers and readers who maintain the same strict viewing habits, their writing has no chance of expansion, reflection, internal revolution — precisely the sort of dynamics necessary to a vital critical practice."[1000]

Even some bloggers, such as Mike D'Angelo, alias "The Man Who Viewed Too Much", wonder if the influence of the internet on criticism has been entirely beneficial:

"I do foresee a future in which the most gifted critics will wind up preaching primarily to a small, self-selected choir, while the average filmgoer — to the extent that he or she consults criticism at all — will simply check the aggregate results available on *Metacritic* and *Rotten Tomatoes*. It's inevitable that the more voices there are competing for your attention, the less valuable each individual voice becomes."[1001]

However, it would be a mistake to blame the internet alone for the demise of professional critics, and grossly unfair to pour scorn on everyone who writes on the internet. Despite evidence to the contrary, in the form of Harry Knowles and his kindred fanboys, there is no longer a clear demarcation in quality between print and online critics.

Lively reviewing of theatre is now being done on websites such as *Exeunt, Bellyflop, West End Whingers* and *A Younger Theatre*. A recent Ticketmaster survey, based on a sample of people who booked online, found that one in five theatregoers were writing reviews in some form using social media.

In the more densely populated world of film, journalists constantly move between print and web criticism. Matt Zoller Seitz combined being proprietor of *The House Next Door* (*www.thehousenextdooronline.com*) with working for the *New York Times*. Ed Gonzalez, Nick Pinkerton, Michael Joshua Rowin, Michael Sicinski and many others have moved between both areas. I operated my own website collection of movie reviews (*www.moviefilmreview.com*) at the same time I was reviewing for the *Daily Mail*.

Other print critics who have lost their film reviewing jobs – including Jonathan Rosenbaum (*www.Jonathanrosenbaum.com*) and Dave Kehr (*www.davekehr.com*) – still operate websites that showcase their critical talents.

I'm not sure there's any gulf in quality either, especially now that most of the experienced print critics have been culled. There is no guarantee that those currently working in print journalism know anything about film.

Many print critics do no research and have little if any experience of film technique. Still less do they have a deep knowledge of the history of cinema, and their interest in foreign-language films is painfully slight.

The same criticisms apply to many online critics, but there are intelligent, knowledgeable reviewers on the net, if you know where to find them. Online critics such as Eric D. Snider, Brad Brevet, Frank Swietek, Mary Ann Johanson, David Jenkins, Emma Dibdin and James Berardinelli are all writers of quality, and they are more capable than most professional print critics of constructing an argument to support their judgments.

Adrian Martin, of the Australian film website *Rouge*, is annoyed by the snobbery of print critics:

"This cult of professionalism — and the embattled defensive maneuvers that accompany it — seems to me a rather recent, and fairly puzzling, phenomenon. Did anyone reading Manny Farber's *Artforum* pieces on film in the 1960s bother to wonder whether he was a professional of the film-crit trade, or merely a gifted autodidact? What about the great French-Algerian critic Barthélemy Amengual (1919-2005), of whom it is said that he wrote about cinema, passionately and eruditely, for almost sixty years — without, in the vast majority of cases, being paid for it? it is the hard-to-budge professionals who (notable exceptions aside) appear to be the phonies, reactionaries, and blowhards of the scene."[1002]

Online reviewer Glenn Kenny, editor of the film magazine *Premiere* until it folded in 2007, believes online blogs can do things that print critics can't:

"The tools the Internet provides do make a difference — just the fact that it's easy to get screen grabs or put up clips is a huge thing. Shot-by-shot analyses are far more common on Web sites and blogs than in most periodical-published criticism for that reason, I think, and that certainly adds a new dimension."[1003]

Robert Koehler of *Variety* regards globalization as a blessing, and "surely the most misunderstood and absurdly demonized phenomenon of our time. Due to the Internet's global connections, the ways in which film lovers armed with a region-free DVD player (a beautiful product made in response to globalized demand, first spurred by fans of Asian/Hong Kong genre movies) can now access and purchase films from around the world in an instant — films that were either not accessible in a pre-DVD world (when the market demand prompting restoration and recovery of film titles didn't yet exist) and were virtually impossible to see in any form unless you lived in a major film centre — has affected both the culture and criticism."[1004]

Three film websites stand out. Girish Shambu's (*www.girishshambu.com*), David Bordwell's (*www.davidbordwell.net*) and GreenCine Daily (*www.daily.greencine.com*). The latter is especially worth discovering; David Hudson, who is based in Berlin, has spent long days and nights seeking out worthwhile cinema-related content, which he summarizes and links to the benefit of film buffs everywhere.

Some individual bloggers have outstanding specialized knowledge. Here I'm thinking especially of Michael E. Kerpan's *Roslindale Monogatari* for Asian films, and D. Copp's *My Gleanings*, on French film culture of the Fifties and Sixties.

Steve Erickson, of *Gay City News*, points out that such bloggers can serve a hugely useful purpose by alerting people to new (or old) talent. "Internet criticism has aided the rise of South Korean cinema and mumblecore. In the case of Korean cinema, *Filmbrain*'s blog, among others, hosted interesting debates on the films of Park Chan-wook, Kim Ki-duk, and Hong Sang-soo.... I'm not sure what Korean film and mumblecore have in common, although the parallels between the latter and the blogosphere are obvious, but I think bloggers like making discoveries they can claim as their own."[1005]

Erickson concludes with a statement that most of us would sign up to:

"I don't really care whether blog critics are professionals or amateurs as long as their writing is strong."

The Death of Criticism?

Back in 2007, *Time* film critic Richard Schickel foresaw the death of criticism. Looked at today, his essay is prophetic:

"Criticism - and its humble cousin, reviewing - is not a democratic activity. It is, or should be, an elite enterprise, ideally undertaken by individuals who bring something to the party beyond their hasty, instinctive opinions of a book (or any other cultural object). It is work that requires disciplined taste, historical and theoretical knowledge and a fairly deep sense of the author's (or filmmaker's or painter's) entire body of work, among other qualities. Opinion - thumbs up, thumbs down - is the least important aspect of reviewing. Very often, in the best reviews, opinion is conveyed without a judgmental word being spoken, because the review's highest business is to initiate intelligent dialogue about the work in question, beginning a discussion that, in some cases, will persist down the years, even down the centuries... Maybe most reviewing, whatever its venue, fails that ideal. But a purely 'democratic literary landscape' is truly a wasteland, without standards, without maps, without oases of intelligence or delight."[1006]

Martin Amis is sad but characteristically laid back about what he sees as the decline, if not the death, of literary criticism. He remembers the days, not long after he left Oxford in the early 1970s, when he worked for the *Times Literary Supplement*:

"My private life was middle-bohemian - hippyish and hedonistic, if not candidly debauched; but I was very moral when it came to literary criticism. I read it all the time, in the tub, on the tube; I always had about me my Edmund Wilson - or my William Empson. I took it seriously. We all did. We hung around the place talking about literary criticism. We sat in pubs and coffee bars talking about W.K. Wimsatt and G. Wilson Knight, about Richard Hoggart and Northrop Frye, about Richard Poirier, Tony Tanner and George Steiner. It might have been in such a locale that my friend and colleague Clive James first formulated his view that, while literary criticism is not essential to literature, both are essential to civilisation. Everyone concurred. Literature, we felt, was the core discipline; criticism explored and popularized the significance of that centrality, creating a space around literature and thereby further exalting it."[1007]

What brought about the demise of this literary idyll? Amis blames not the Internet, but the Organisation of the Petroleum Exporting Countries, OPEC:

"In the 60s, you could live on 10 shillings a week: you slept on people's floors and sponged off your friends and sang for your supper - about literary criticism. Then, abruptly, a bus fare cost 10 shillings. The oil hike, and inflation, and then stagflation, revealed literary criticism as one of the many leisure-class fripperies we would have to get along without."[1008]

Amis argues, however, that literary criticism was already doomed with the down-grading of literary talent:

"Explicitly or otherwise it had based itself on a structure of echelons and hierarchies; it was about the talent elite. And the structure atomized as soon as the forces of democratization gave their next concerted push. Those forces - incomparably the most potent in our culture - have gone on pushing. And they are now running up against a natural barrier. Some citadels, true, have proved stormable. You can become rich without having any talent (via the scratchcard and the rollover jackpot). You can become famous without having any talent (by abasing yourself on some TV nerd-othon: a clear improvement on the older method of simply killing a celebrity and inheriting the aura). But you cannot become talented without having any talent. Therefore, talent must go."[1009]

It's not only the mass media that are to blame, according to Amis, but academe. With the rise of post-modernism, deconstruction and kindred fashions in critical theory has come a downgrading of the artist and an upgrading of the critical amateur:

"Literary criticism, now almost entirely confined to the universities, moves against talent by moving against the canon. Academic preferment will not come from a respectful study of Wordsworth's poetics; it will come from a challenging study of his politics - his attitude to the poor, say, or his unconscious 'valourisation' of Napoleon; and it will come still faster if you ignore Wordsworth and elevate some (justly) neglected contemporary, by which process the canon may be quietly and steadily sapped. A brief consultation of the internet will show that meanwhile, at the other end of the business, everyone has become a literary critic - or at least a book-reviewer. Democratization has made one inalienable gain: equality of the sentiments. I think Gore Vidal said this first, and he said it, not quite with mockery, but with lively scepticism. He said that, nowadays, nobody's feelings are more authentic, and thus more important, than anybody else's. This is the new credo, the new privilege."[1010]

Much has been written in the past decade about The Death of Criticism. In his 2007 book with that title, Ronan McDonald – lecturer in English and American studies at Reading University – laments the demise of what he calls "the public critic", a writer "with the authority to shape public taste". Perhaps because he himself is an academic, he blames not the internet but academic influences – first the belief of Post-structuralists that good and bad are all relative and therefore valueless, and then the gurus of modern cultural studies, who claim that no one has the right to say what is good and what isn't.[1011]

He argues that the new academic orthodoxy is to use texts to reveal western biases towards logic, rationality, patriarchy and imperialism, and leave any other "quality" judgments out of the equation.

McDonald is surely right to call for a revival in English Literature departments of evaluative criticism, which is willing to look at works of literature both as aesthetic artifacts and as artistic expressions with a moral, social and political dimension. He argues in the tradition of Matthew Arnold that some degree of consensus can be reached about "the best that has been thought and written", without it becoming static, suffocating dogma.

He is also correct that there are too few taste-making intellectuals, and that the arts in newspapers, radio and television have been, and are being, dumbed down.

However, McDonald wildly overrates the importance of scholarly criticism. In my experience, few of those who review for newspapers and magazines are influenced at all by modern scholarly criticism. Almost none of them read it. If they are influenced by it at all, they are affected by the criticism they read at university.

Martin Amis seems to me to hit the coffin nail on the head when he points out that criticism has been killed by the misapprehension, encouraged by the growth of the internet, that everyone's opinion is of equal value. Informed or insightful criticism, the kind that is capable of constructing an argument and probing the ideas or values behind a work of art, is too often denounced - especially, in my experience, by those on the internet who can't spell or punctuate - as "snobbish", "out of touch" or (dreadful word) "judgmental".

It's true, of course, that tastes differ - and inevitably so. No two people see the same movie. Every one of us filters each piece of art we watch through our own tastes, backgrounds and moods. And no one can take away our right to our own opinion, however unpopular or out of step it may be with critical and intellectual fashion.

But when good critics write a review, they are not an unelected elite telling you what to think; they are exerting their democratic right to express their opinions, which you are perfectly at liberty to value, disagree with or disregard.

The old professional critical elite did have its merits. It was never a closed shop and became increasingly egalitarian. It did adhere to standards of justice and veracity. It was subject to quality control by editors. Though there have always been lazy and inept professional critics, most really do know a lot about the fields they cover.

The sentence of death on paid, professional reviewers is often encapsulated in that catchphrase "everyone's a critic". But the proliferation of critics does not mean that everyone's a good critic. Nor does it mean that everyone's opinion is equally valuable.

Film critic Mark Kermode, when promoting his book *Hatchet Job,* expressed his opinion of why professional critics are a sign of cultural health:

"I think informed opinion is important. Just because we've gone from print to digital, doesn't mean you have to dispense with values. Clearly some people thought, 'Why should we pay film critics? We can just get somebody off the web to do it.' Well the reason is, as the guy who was in charge of *The Chicago Sun-Times* said, 'quality journalism is not for free', and it isn't."[1012]

I remember making sympathetic noises to a talented colleague of mine, Anthony Quinn, when he was fired as film critic of the *Independent*, and he smiled and shrugged. "It's okay," he said. "The money was nice and I enjoyed doing it, but at least I'll have more time to write my novels."

The trouble with the decline of paid, "professional" criticism is that it means a lot of quality writers give up being critics. They have other options.

I was angry when I lost my job at the *Daily Mail*. But, like Quinn, I felt that I would have more time to write other things – and I have done. I haven't written a paid film review for over a year, nor have I been approached to do so. I've written six books, two musicals and a ballet instead.

The good news is that some film critics who have lost their paid jobs continue to blog about movies unpaid. The bad news is that these tend to be "film buffs", and there are numerous film buffs blogging about movies in any case. The very best writers tend not to be film buffs, for they have wider interests than film and other talents they can pursue if they're not wanted by newspaper editors. These are often the most valuable voices in criticism, and they are being silenced forever.

THE TENTH COMMANDMENT
Thou Shalt Remember Why Criticism is Important

Why Critics are Ignored

Along with being reviled and despised, every aspiring critic should expect to be ignored. The TV Critic on the *Huffington Post*, Maureen Ryan, admits that it can be a heart-breaking job:

"If you love television, you'll fall head over heels for shows that get low ratings. It's a fact. You will tell yourself not to get your hopes up for a *Terriers* or a *Men of a Certain Age*, but you will. Despite your best intentions, the rational part of your brain will reject the idea that these lovingly crafted gems could go away. But they will go away. And you'll be sad, because if you're doing this job right, you'll put part of your heart and soul into your work and watching something great die too soon can drag your spirit down."[1013]

The thing that keeps her going is the belief that critics can, occasionally make a difference:

"Sometimes fighting for shows works: Witness the five-year runs of *Friday Night Lights* and *Chuck* and the unlikely (but welcome) return of *Arrested Development*. And whatever bad TV I had to sit through, the last decade also brought us *The Shield, Veronica Mars, Lost, Battlestar Galactica, Mad Men, Deadwood, Parks and Recreation, Party Down* and so many other great shows."

The truth is, though, that ordinary people pay less and less respect to the pronouncements of critics. Even the film critic of the *New York Times*, A.O. Scott, admits he doesn't have much clout:

"I'm not convinced that film critics ever had much power over a film's immediate commercial fate, and plenty of moviegoers have always been happy to ignore what critics write."[1014]

In January 2015, restaurant critic Giles Coren wrote a piece in *Time Out* that encapsulated the mindset of fanboys and Hollywood producers who routinely take no notice of critics:

"I am rarely so out of kilter with prevailing cultural opinion as I am just now with the world's film critics, who have been brought collectively to the edge of suicide by the glut of superhero movies in whose midst we currently find ourselves. In recent years we have been through several sets of Bat, Super, Spider, Iron and X-Men. We've had Avengers, Daredevils, Green Lanterns and at least three different increasingly credible Hulks and yet, it seems, we have barely started. This year will see more Avengers, another crack at the Fantastic Four and the advent of a guy called

Ant-Man, who I can only assume has the superpower of being a bit itchy and knowing how to spoil a family picnic."[1015]

Coren believes that film critics are right to feel this makes them redundant:

"All this has led cultural commentators to declare the end of Hollywood. Indeed, the very End of Days. The studios have caved altogether to the lowest common denominator, they claim, and will no longer put real money into any production that does not involve secret identities, human flight, game-level CGI and a long history of success in comic form at either Marvel or DC. We, in turn, have lost our ability as an audience to process 'proper' films, and our attention spans have shrunk to the length of a teenage boy's orgasm, and because of this, serious filmmaking has come to an end. To which I can only shout 'hurrah!' I much prefer superhero films to worthy didactic historical costume crap and talky rubbish in black and white. I mean, who wouldn't swap *12 Years a Slave* for *12 Minutes an Amazonian Princess with a Star-Spangled Swimsuit and an Invisible Plane?*"

Coren takes the view that books are for serious culture, and films are for laughs:

"Serious writers on culture tend to insist that everything ever written can be boiled down to seven basic plots. But as a serious consumer of comics since the age of six or seven, I am here to tell you that there is only one plot that matters: 'You think I am me; but I am, in fact, a much more powerful and dangerous version of me. And if you don't show me some respect, the other me is going to rip your fucking head off.' Stories about anything else are just a waste of time."

Well, it's a point of view. But I suspect that not even Giles totally believes it, for in another column he has waxed lyrical about upmarket box sets and poured scorn on - guess what - popular culture:

"Popular culture is a grand delusion of idiocy and fake experience and I will have no part in it. I don't want to watch what other people are watching. Other people are idiots. To know that I am doing something that millions of others are doing at the same time is to cheapen that thing irredeemably. If I want communal activity, I'll go dogging."[1016]

When even critics pose as being contemptuous of other critics or seem disinclined to take popular culture seriously, it's unsurprising that audiences will pick up on the same vibe – although in Giles's case (he is, after all, an English graduate from Oxford with a first-class degree), I suspect he is more concerned with telling readers what he thinks they want to hear, than with telling the truth.

A classic example of the public showing contempt for critics was the Queen musical *We Will Rock You* in London's West End. Professional reviewers queued up to savage it. Mark Shenton in the *Sunday Express* called it a "grim spectacle" and "tacky, trashy tosh". Charles Spencer in the *Daily Telegraph* referred to a famous line in the song *Killer Queen* and wrote that it was unlikely to "blow your mind" but "guaranteed to bore you rigid". He added a dig at its likely audience: "this show is prole-feed at its worst." "Only hard-core Queen fans can save it from an early bath" was Old Etonian Robert Gore-Langton's confident forecast in the *Daily Express*.

There must have been a lot of hard-core Queen fans out there, because the show ran for more than ten years, and it won a special Audience Award at the Olivier Awards in a public vote for people's favourite show.

"Seldom has there been a bigger rebuke to the so-called power of the critics," admits Mark Shenton.[1017]

And then there's *Wicked*, a musical which had a very mixed response from the Broadway critics in 2003. Ben Brantley in the *New York Times* enjoyed the production values but panned the show, calling it a "sermon" with a "generic" score. He called it "a Wicked waste of talent."[1018]

When *Wicked* transferred to London's West End, it received even more dismissive reviews. Michael Billington in the *Guardian* said it was "more like a piece of industrial product than something that genuinely touches the heart or mind".[1019] For Charles Spencer of the *Daily Telegraph*, it was "a bit of a mess".[1020] Paul Taylor in the *Independent* was the most negative, calling it "melodramatic, incoherent and dreadfully superficial... overblown and empty".[1021]

Since then, the show has gone on to break box office records on Broadway, in the West End and around the world.

Every critic, sooner rather than later, must learn to suffer the indignity of seeing the paying public disregard his or her opinion. And some surprisingly influential people think it invalidates the whole idea of critics when, for example, the public obstinately flocks to see *The Hangover Part II* even when virtually every professional review has unanimously (and rightly) condemned it as far inferior to *The Hangover I*.

The truth, which may make some critics uncomfortable, is that many people who attend films, plays or art exhibitions have a well-justified scepticism about whether the critics are right, and wish to check out for themselves things they feel they might enjoy. That's the good news about our culture.

The bad news for anyone hoping to become a professional critic is that a lot of people have no taste and amazingly debased values, so they're likely to ignore you even if you're talking and writing good sense. Let's not forget that "vulgar" is a word derived from the Latin *vulgus*, meaning a crowd.

Some people proudly prefer junk food to *haut cuisine*, and who are we to say this is wrong? Maybe it's right – for them. Similarly, if they want to watch a mindless superhero movie or boogie on down to *Wicked* or *We Will Rock You*, they are free to enjoy it. Critics are offering advice, not issuing instructions.

I remember calling *The Hangover Part II* "the worst sequel of all time"[1022] and I wasn't alone in finding it despicable. America's leading critics were virtually unanimous in condemnation of the film, calling it "rancid",[1023] "botched"[1024] and "a headache-inducing, unapologetic money grab".[1025] *The New York Times* hailed the sequel as the worst kind of Hollywood landmark: "Someone has finally dared to make a mainstream American comedy in which nothing funny happens."[1026]

Even the young, desperately trendy internet critics didn't like it. One I know, who looks about 16, called it "tasteless, pointless, tactless and pretty much anything else you care to stick the suffix '-less' on."[1027]

The public couldn't have cared less. The film took $86 million (£53million) on its first weekend, a new record for a comedy.[1028]

It followed on from *Pirates Of The Caribbean 4*, which survived a critical mauling to make $346 million (£215million) on its opening weekend - the fourth largest global opening ever.[1029]

So does this obvious disparity between reviews and box office performance mean that critics are out of touch with the masses and no good to man or beast? The short answer is 'no'.

Critics are not tipsters. Unless they write for film industry papers, their function is not to guess whether or not the public is going to buy tickets. Critics are concerned with quality, not quantity.

The Hangover grossed fewer than $45 million (£28million) on its first weekend, but that does not mean it was only half as good as the sequel, which took almost double the amount.[1030]

The fact that the fourth *Pirates of the Caribbean* movie made five times as much money on its opening as the first is not evidence that it was five times as good as the original; it reflects the ready-made audience created by the success of its four predecessors.

It's all part of the Hollywood, assembly-line ethos, which is both the strength and the weakness of the American way - and the reason British films, with their one-off quirkiness, steal a disproportionate share of Oscars. At the box office in the short term, branding and publicity always carry more weight than the reviews. A *Pirates of the Caribbean* sequel will always outgun a *King's Speech* or a *Social Network*. That's not to say it should be more highly regarded – by critics or, in the longer term, audiences.

Mature, sophisticated audiences are likely to catch up with a film long after the first weekend. Some of the best films, such as *It's a Wonderful Life* or *Citizen Kane*, have had to wait years for commercial success. But they're often the ones that become much-loved classics.

Sequels backed by big studios dominate modern multiplexes, and that has a massive effect on the sale of tickets over a first weekend. If you look at the performance of the Harry Potter films, the box office figures "improved" even though the last but one, *Harry Potter And The Deathly Hallows Pt 1*, was not much good at all. The reason it did well at the box office was partly due to the fact that it started at 4,125 cinemas - unlike the first of the series, which opened on 500 screens fewer.[1031]

Sequels don't always make as much money as an original, but they are a safe bet at the box office because they are guaranteed to get massive promotion and to open on a large number of screens.

With poor-quality sequels, there is invariably a huge drop-off in audiences after the first week-end, but if a movie is opened "wide" enough - that means on enough screens - the sequel will have made back its costs before adverse word-of-mouth and damning reviews can take effect.

The Hangover Part II was massively inferior to the first movie, but audiences were always going to want to make up their own minds, not have critics tell them what to think of it. That strikes me as a healthily stroppy, anti-authoritarian reaction - and it's nothing new.

My job in reviewing it, however, was not to analyze its box office potential; it was to say what I thought of its quality, and - because I wrote for millions of readers - try to indicate the section of the population who might like it more than I did.

Arts critic Mark Lawson points out that critics and audiences have different priorities:

"Movies that appear in hundreds of reviewers' top 10s - such as Michael Haneke's *Hidden* and Noah Baumbach's *The Squid and the Whale* - are unlikely ever to appear in box-office charts. This is because critics are giving marks for originality, acting, photography and scripting, while mass audiences are more drawn to familiarity of genre, stars they would like to have sex with or plots that are more likely to make their dates have sex with them. Reviewers are doing their day's work, cinema-goers are escaping from theirs: this leads to an inevitable difference of response."[1032]

Lawson points out that book reviewers are just as out of touch with popular tastes as film critics, and confesses his own dislike of *The Da Vinci Code*:

"The Top 50 Bestseller list in Britain, based on bookshop sales, currently contains not a single work of fiction that has received significantly good reviews. Admittedly, the selection is slightly skewed by the presence of all four novels by Dan Brown - the extreme example of the difference between praise and sales - but the charts also feature numerous other popular novelists, such as Martina Cole and James Patterson, from whom it is scarcely worth the publishers sending out review copies since the books sell millions without any help from the pundits... My [panning] review of *The Da Vinci Code* as a book was not 'wrong', at least in my opinion; it simply applied values - of literacy, plausibility and characterisation - that are clearly not significant in the choices of beach and plane readers."[1033]

Lawson and I have both reviewed television, and he remembers, as I do, that the longrunning soap *EastEnders* was panned by TV critics in 1985. However, he does believe that TV critics can have their practical uses:

"Where television critics do have influence is in providing small-audience shows with a cachet that may lead to them being retained or recommissioned. The usual rule is that, in order to survive, a show needs the support of either the audience, an executive or reviewers. The latter are unlikely to be decisive alone but can trigger a death-row appeal."

Lawson agrees that the days of a single critic "killing" a show in the theatre are no more. He points to Julia Roberts' performance in *Three Days of Rain*, which was ridiculed by Broadway critics in 2006, but the show had sold out months previously. The same goes for Peter O' Toole's disastrous *Macbeth* in 1980, and Madonna's much derided starring performance in David Williamson's *Up For Grabs* (2002).

Lawson thinks he knows why they confounded the reviewers:

"The reason that such shows become critic-proof is economic: at best, 40-60,000 tickets might be available for a short theatre run by a major star and an audience of that size is available regardless of one person's judgment of its dramatic worth. As for *We Will Rock You*, musicals have always done better at generating greenbacks than newsprint. And, of course, the show's music was also already well-known. Indeed, all of the works that have proved commercially immune to derisive reviewers - The *Da Vinci Code* movie, Julia Roberts and Madonna on stage, the Queen musical in the West End - have one factor in common: an element - title, actor, songs - that was already exceptionally well-known."

Why Critics are Misquoted

However much the entertainment industry may affect to despise critics, it is always happy to use critics' names to advertise its wares. The cheekiest example of this was impresario David Merrick's wheeze after New York critics panned his 1961 Broadway musical *Subways Are For Sleeping*. Merrick managed to locate seven New Yorkers with the same names as the city's leading critics: John Chapman, Robert Coleman, Walter Kerr, John McClain, Norman Nadel, Howard Taubman and Richard Watts, Jr.

Merrick invited the seven to the musical and used their names and pictures in an advertisement under the heading "7 Out of 7 Are Ecstatically

Unanimous About *Subways Are For Sleeping*". The non-critics' raves included "A fabulous musical. I love it" and "One of the few great musical comedies of the last thirty years".

Unfortunately for Merrick, only one newspaper - the *New York Herald Tribune* - would publish the ad, and then in only one edition. All the same, the publicity generated enabled the musical to run for nearly six months. Merrick later admitted that he had dreamt up the scam years before but had had to wait for *New York Times* theatre critic Brooks Atkinson to retire, which he did in 1960. Merrick had never been able to find a non-critic with the same name.[1034]

Virtually every critic has a tale about being cynically abridged or quoted out of context.

Ads for the TV series *Lost* carried a rave from Mike Ryan, of *Vanity Fair*, calling it "the most addictively awesome television show of all time". Hardly anyone would have bothered to search out the original review, in which Ryan wrote the show was "the most confusing, asinine, ridiculous - yet somehow addictively awesome - television show of all time."[1035]

United Artists advertised their film *Hoodlum* with a single word from *LA Times* film critic Kenneth Turan's review, "Irresistible". This was taken from Turan's less than fulsome account of the film's merits: "Even Laurence Fishburne's incendiary performance can't ignite *Hoodlum*, a would-be gangster epic that generates less heat than a nickel cigar. Fishburne's 'Bumpy' is fierce, magnetic, irresistible even... But even this actor can only do so much."[1036]

The abject Eddie Murphy comedy *Norbit* was graced in its ads by Michael Wilmington's claim in the *Chicago Tribune* that "Eddie Murphy's comic skills are immense." They omitted to mention the rest of Wilmington's paragraph: "and *Dreamgirls* shows he's a fine straight dramatic actor too. So why does he want to make these huge, belching spectaculars, movies as swollen, monstrous and full of hot air as Rasputia herself — here misdirected by Brian Robbins of *Good Burger*, *Varsity Blues* and that lousy Shaggy Dog remake?"[1037]

After numerous protests from scandalized critics and members of the public, most reputable film companies now clear quotations from critics with the reviewer concerned. American studios also submit advertising materials such as newspaper ads and trailers to the Motion Picture Association of America for approval. But the MPAA is not concerned with the accuracy of the citations.

Rather more assertively, The European Union's Unfair Commercial Practices Directive condemns companies that "falsely claim accreditation" for their products in ways that are "not being true to the terms of the endorsement". It is enforced in the United Kingdom by the Office of Fair

Trading, and carries a maximum penalty of a £5,000 fine or two years imprisonment.

The truth is, however, that a critic's words can easily be twisted more-or-less legally into a use for which they were certainly not intended. Kenneth Tynan once complained to me that he wrote a heavily ironic review of a William Douglas Home comedy, full of insincere superlatives – only to find the superlatives hung outside the Cambridge Theatre as a massive, non-ironic recommendation.[1038]

Guardian critic Michael Hann was uncomplimentary about the rock musical *Rock of Ages*, writing "It's a very peculiar show indeed, with an unvarying and unpleasant tone of careless sexualisation. Rock'n'roll debauchery is presented as the pure and innocent way of dreamers."

Outside the theatre, however, hung a board proudly proclaiming that it was "rock'n'roll debauchery", as though this were a good thing.[1039]

Peter Bradshaw recalls being hung out to dry by the distributors of *The Fellowship of the Ring*. Instead of using one of the thousands of positive quotes from other critics, they decided to quote ultra-selectively.

"I didn't enjoy the first installment of the *Lord Of The Rings* trilogy, giving it only two stars," says Bradshaw, "but conceded that it was 'technically stunning'. Of course, on the poster, it simply read 'Stunning - The *Guardian*'. I was mildly irritated - it's cheeky."[1040]

Andy Dougan, of the *Glasgow Evening Times*, recalls an "absolutely dreadful" 1994 film called *Chasing the Deer*: "I wrote something like 'If this is the best that Scotland can produce, we're in a sorry state'. The production company quoted me in their prospectus as calling it 'the best that Scotland can produce'. I was furious that they were using me to persuade people to part with their hard earned money to finance yet another dire film and successfully took out an injunction, which legally barred them from using my quote."[1041]

Tim Robey of the *Daily Telegraph* had a similar experience over *Mrs Henderson Presents*, which – like *The Fellowship of the Ring* – attracted more than its fair share of critical acclaim. He had written that it was glitteringly funny for the first half an hour, but fell to pieces after that. "There was a big poster campaign on which I was quoted as calling it 'glitteringly funny'," recalls Robey. "But I was quite pleased to be on a poster campaign, so I really couldn't get too annoyed."[1042]

I have been misquoted out of context dozens of times, but never more outrageously than over a terrible British thriller called *Double X* (1992), improbably starring Norman Wisdom as a criminal mastermind and electronics genius. I was surprised when a PR release arrived, plugging the film's upcoming release on video and quoting just one critic, me, as writing "Unmissable... Has to be seen."

I turned to my original review, and sure enough it was a pan, calling it "a new low in British cinema". But then I spotted where they'd found those phrases. I had called the film "unmissably awful, a turkey to savour... The film has to be seen to be disbelieved for its deplorable direction, preposterous plotting, abysmal acting, catatonic cinematography, pathetic production values and kamikaze casting. I dread to think what the out-takes were like - if there were any."[1043]

I thought of complaining to the PRs, but there didn't seem much point. In a way, I admired their nerve. And how bad must the other reviews have been, if mine was the best?

No Statues For Critics?

Earlier in this volume, I listed most of the famous put-downs of critics, but I left one out. The Finnish composer Jean Sibelius (1865-1957) advised fellow composer Bengt von Tome: "Pay no attention to what critics say. A statue has never been erected in honour of a critic."[1044]

Sibelius was wrong then, and he's even more wrong now. For many centuries, there have been statues and busts in honour of Plato and Aristotle. Perhaps they are most renowned as philosophers, but they were also founders of criticism.

Paris hosts a memorial to literary critic Hippolyte Taine (1828-1893) in the Square d'Ajaccio in the 7eme district.[1045] Though now largely forgotten, Taine was a massive influence in his day. The 1911 *Encyclopaedia Britannica* asserted that "the tone which pervades the works of Zola, Bourget and Maupassant can be immediately attributed to the influence we call Taine's."[1046]

In the Luxembourg Gardens in Paris, you will find a statue to another French literary critic Charles Augustin Saint-Beuve (1804-1869)[1047] who was a champion of Victor Hugo - though Hugo fell out with the critic, not so much because he disliked one of his novels, but because Saint-Beuve had an affair with Hugo's wife.[1048]

Saint-Beuve coined one of the more memorable aphorisms about being a critic: "A critic is a man whose watch is five minutes ahead of other people's watches."[1049] But he is not as highly esteemed now as he was a hundred years ago. He was incorrigibly nosy and believed that it helps to know everything about the artist before analyzing what he has created - a theory that, as the novelist Milan Kundera observed, meant that he failed to appreciate most of the great writers of his age, including Balzac, Baudelaire and Stendhal.[1050] But at least he was awarded a statue.

In St Petersburg there is a statue of the Russian music critic Vladimir Stasov[1051] (1824-1906), who nurtured the careers of Tchaikowsky and Mussorgsky, though his popularity waned when he panned the influential ballet impresario Sergei Diaghilev, dismissing him as "a decadent cheerleader".

A bronze statue of the most famous critic of the eighteenth century, Samuel Johnson, (erected in 1910) stands near St Clement Dane's church.[1052] In the National Portrait gallery can be found Michael Rysbrack's bust of Alexander Pope,[1053] a poet but also writer of *An Essay Upon Criticism* (which, though in verse, really is an essay about criticism).

I don't know of any statues to such distinguished art critics as John Ruskin, Sir Kenneth Clark or Robert Hughes. But the Canadian artist Joe Fafard has made a statue of the American, Trotskyite art critic Clement Greenberg[1054], an indefatigable promoter of the abstract expressionist movement, especially Jackson Pollock and Mark Rothko.[1055]

In New York, there is no statue in honour of a critic, but two Broadway theatres have been named after two chief theatre reviewers for the *New York Times*. One was Brooks Atkinson[1056], who wrote for 35 years between 1925 and 1960 (with a short break during World War II, when he was a war correspondent). The other is Walter Kerr[1057], who was on the *New York Times* from 1966 for 17 years, and won a Pulitzer Prize in 1978 for his writings on the theatre, though the only review of his that is widely remembered is his verdict on Christopher Isherwood's *I Am a Camera*: "Me no Leica".[1058]

In 2014, their successor Frank Rich, who was theatre critic from 1980 to 1993, was inducted into Broadway's Theatre Hall of Fame for lifetime achievement in the American theatre.[1059]

When Roger Ebert died in 2013, President Obama issued an official tribute:

"Roger was the movies. When he didn't like a film, he was honest. When he did, he was effusive - capturing the unique power of movies to take us somewhere magical."[1060]

Roger even has a statue. In 2014, public subscriptions financed the creation by artist Rick Hamey of a life-size bronze of him in his famous "thumbs up" pose. It was placed outside the Virginia cinema in Champaign, Illinois, which hosts Ebertfest, the film festival that bears his name.[1061]

Even Tennyson's "louse in the locks of literature", the critic and academic John Churton Collins (1848-1908), has memorials to his name. Collins's friends and pupils founded Churton Collins prizes for the encouragement of English and classical study among university extension students of Oxford, Cambridge, and London. A Churton Collins memorial prize for the same subjects was also founded in the University of Birmingham. A portrait in oils by Mr. Thomas W. Holgate was placed in the Bodleian Library, and a water-colour portrait head by Mr. George Phoenix found its way to the upper library of Collins' home as an undergraduate, Balliol College, Oxford, together with a brass memorial tablet with Latin inscription by Dr. T. H. Warren. A brass memorial tablet was also set up in Oulton church, near the place he died - a Norfolk ditch, into which he fell while in a drugged sleep, and drowned.[1062] So even a critic who was condemned by a Poet Laureate and discovered dead in a ditch managed to find a measure of respectability after his demise.

Quite a few critics also went on to become recognised for their talents as creators. Even if you haven't read their criticism, the chances are that you will have experienced their work.

Giorgio Vasari (1511-1574) is often called the founder of art history and criticism, thanks to his seminal text *The Lives of the Most Excellent Painters, Sculptors, and Architects* (1550). He was, in fact, the first writer to use the term "Renaissance" (*rinascita*) in print. But he was also a considerable architect and painter. Today, his name is commemorated in one of his architectural creations, the Vasari corridor, an elevated passageway in Florence, that connects the Uffizi gallery with the Palazzo Pitti.[1063]

Critics such as Samuel Taylor Coleridge and T.S. Eliot became respected poets, others – such as Oscar Wilde and George Bernard Shaw – successful dramatists. Graham Greene was a fine film critic as well as a distinguished novelist.

P.G. Wodehouse started out as a theatre critic on *Vanity Fair* but became a skilled lyricist and librettist. In 1917, he had five shows running simultaneously on Broadway. In his spare time, he knocked out 93 novels, quite a few of them well received. He also wrote more than 50 stage works on Broadway and in the West End.

A couple of Wodehouse's friends also acquired respectability after careers in criticism. Wodehouse's stand-in theatre critic on *Vanity Fair*, Dorothy Parker, went on to become one of America's foremost poets, short story writers and wits of her age.

George S. Kaufman, for some years theatre critic of the *New York Tribune*, became the most famous playwright on Broadway and a celebrated Hollywood screenwriter. He wrote stage musicals and films for the Marx Brothers. He wrote two Pulitzer prizewinning shows: the play *You Can't Take It With You* and the musical *Of Thee I Sing* with songs by George and Ira Gershwin. Kaufman also directed the first stage productions of *The Front Page, Of Mice and Men* and Frank Loesser's celebrated Musical, *Guys and Dolls*.

In America, James Agee, the most prominent film critic of the 1940s, became a leading screenwriter. Among his works are *Night of the Hunter* and *The African Queen*.

French critics Claude Chabrol, Jean-Luc Godard, Jacques Rivette, Eric Rohmer and Francois Truffaut, started out as film critics on *Cahiers du Cinema*, founded in 1951 by the hugely influential Andre Bazin. For better and for worse, they championed the *auteur* theory, whereby the director was credited with the vision of a film, and raised the profile of numerous previously unfashionable film-makers including Robert Aldrich, Howard Hawks and Alfred Hitchcock. All went on to become famous film-makers in their own right.

In Britain, Lindsay Anderson and Karel Reisz turned from film critics into into talented directors. The TV critic Michael Frayn became a more than decent dramatist and novelist. And Stephen Sondheim, whose early works include film reviews, has managed to write a few good musicals.

All these and more probably deserved to have at least one statue erected in their honour, but statuary should not be the issue here. The question is: are any of these critics worth reading today? And, of course, they are.

The saddest thing about these critics is not that there are so few statues in honour of them; it is that so many are now out of print.

Why Better Critics are Needed

There remains a demand for good criticism, and it is hanging on in unlikely places. Turn on the television and you'll see critics of varying degrees of intellect and severity pronouncing opinions about dance (on *Strictly Come Dancing*), food (*Masterchef* and *The Great British Menu*), pop singers (*The X Factor*), cars (*Top Gear* and *The Grand Tour*) and football (*Match of the Day* and sundry other football programmes).

Every magazine - whether it be about gadgets, computer games or movies - contains reviews.

In America, the wine critic Robert M. Parker still has influence.

And it's not only professionals who are criticising. As we've seen, virtually everyone can be a critic. The internet has ensured that there are more people expressing opinions – whether about the Arts, hotels, restaurants or football – than ever before.

Oscar Wilde maintained that criticism was not parasitic upon the arts, it was itself an art:

"I am always amused by the silly vanity of those writers and artists of our day who seem to imagine that the primary function of the critic is to chatter about their second-rate work... The poor reviewers are apparently reduced to be the reporters of the police-court of literature, the chroniclers of the doings of the habitual criminals of art."[1064]

In 28 years as a professional critic, between 1985 and 2013, I didn't just see virtually every film that was released in Britain; in compiling my website of reviews under headings "pro", "anti" and "mixed",[1065] I read virtually everything that was written about those films. I gradually came to a most unfashionable realisation. There was more good writing *about* films than there was *in* them.

Critics are widely mocked as uncreative; yet the evidence to the contrary was before my eyes every week. Good criticism can be artistic, creative – and educational.

Criticism is often dismissed as a minor sub-genre within journalism, but it requires experience, expertise and talent, plus other qualities – the ability to see different points of view, appreciate technique and place art and entertainment in a sociopolitical context. These talents are far from common, and certainly not despicable.

This book makes no pretence of being a history of criticism, but let's remember that reviewing has a long and honourable tradition. Its roots go back as far as Aristotle's *Poetics*, though it really began to flourish during The Enlightenment. The Salon writings of French polymath Denis Diderot (1713–1784) are among the earliest examples of art criticism.

The German philosopher Immanuel Kant (1724–1804), evolved a sophisticated idea of critique in three of his works: the *Critique of Pure Reason* (1781), *the Critique of Practical Reason* (1788), and the *Critique of Judgment* (1790).

J.R.R. Tolkien may today be best known as a fantasy author, but he was also an academic and critic, whose best work in the area spanned over 30 years from the Thirties onwards and is mostly to be found in *The Monsters and the Critics* (1997). Not only did he champion such long-underrated pieces of literature as *Beowulf* and *Sir Gawain and the Green Knight*, he also made a spirited defence of fantasy fiction in *On Fairy Stories* (1939), which is one of the most perceptive critical essays ever.

Critics have often had a worthwhile role to play in opening audience's eyes to difficult or unfashionable art. Any list of critics who saved a stage play from early oblivion would have to include Harold Hobson on Pinter's *The Birthday Party* (25 May 1958, *Sunday Times*), Ronald Bryden on Tom Stoppard's *Rosencrantz and Guildenstern Are Dead* (28 Aug, 1966, *Observer*) and Cordelia Oliver on Peter Nichols's *A Day In The Death of Joe Egg* (May 1967, *Guardian*).

The kitchen sink dramas of the 1950s, Samuel Becket's *Waiting for Godot*, even the RSC's *Nicholas Nickleby* all owed their success to a minority of critics who spoke and wrote in their defence.

Music critic Simon Price is sure that criticism has helped many rock musicians to stand up to the "industry":

"In the past, bands knew they could not get away with releasing the same lazy shit over and over without someone calling them on it. Furthermore, by championing uncommercial but innovative music, critics have often pointed to the art's next step forward in a way which the industry could not. (Indeed, to do so was usually directly against the industry's interests.) If critics are taken out of the equation, and bad art goes unchallenged, ask yourself: who wins?... Only the major entertainment corporations... A world with uncriticised art gets the art it deserves."[1066]

No one would suggest that a reviewer who enumerates the shortcomings of a One Direction song or an Adam Sandler movie is being as brave as a Russian who dares to criticise Vladimir Putin. All the same, there is something at least mildly heroic about any critic who stands up to be counted, whether in support of something that's critically unfashionable or to celebrate new talent.

One of the things I liked most about *Ratatouille*, Pixar's animated movie from 2007, about a rat-turned-chef, was the final speech of food critic Anton Ego, who – as his name suggests - starts out as a villain. Gradually, however, he becomes close to the movie's moral centre. Here's his big speech on criticism:

"In many ways, the work of a critic is easy. We risk very little, yet enjoy a position over those who offer up their work and their selves to our judgment. We thrive on negative criticism, which is fun to write and to read. But the bitter truth we critics must face, is that in the grand scheme of things, the average piece of junk is probably more meaningful than our criticism designating it so. But there are times when a critic truly risks something, and that is in the discovery and defense of the new. The world is often unkind to new talent, new creations. The new needs friends. Last night, I experienced something new: an extraordinary meal from a singularly unexpected source. To say that both the meal and its maker have challenged my preconceptions about fine cooking is a gross understatement. They have rocked me to my core. In the past, I have made no secret of my disdain for Chef Gusteau's famous motto, 'Anyone can cook.' But I realise, only now do I truly understand what he meant. Not everyone can become a great artist; but a great artist can come from anywhere."

The critics I like best fall into two categories. Either they are *simpatico* – critics whom I trust because their tastes usually coincide with my own – or they write in a sufficiently entertaining or stimulating way to make me think.

Intelligent, well-informed criticism not only points you to things you might enjoy, it steers you away from things you certainly won't. It dissects analytically but then allows readers to arrive at judgments of their own.

Good criticism is not content to parrot production notes or press releases.

Good criticism does not follow a line laid down by editors pursuing a political or social agenda.

Good theatrical criticism, in particular, captures a moment that's unique and would otherwise be fleeting. When asked what his role was as a critic, Kenneth Tynan replied that it was "to give permanence to something impermanent".[1067]

Good critics are, in a way, teachers. As John Simon puts it:

"Good criticism of any kind – of movies, ballet, architecture, or whatever – makes us think, feel, respond; if we then agree or disagree is less important than the fact that our faculties have been engaged and stretched. Good criticism informs, interprets, and raises the ultimate questions, the unanswerable ones that everyone must try to answer none the less. This is teaching of the highest order."[1068]

Good critics refuse to be merely consumers; they examine, they consider and they express an opinion, regardless of the commercial consequences. As Pauline Kael wrote in 1974, "Criticism is all that stands between the public and advertising."[1069]

LaPresse columnist Pierre Foglia has written that "critiquing is a lot of things, but... it's first an act of resistance. Resistance to trends, to taking the easy way out, to ideologies, to patronizing lectures, to one's environment, to advertising."[1070]

Good critics are actively engaged with the things they are analysing. They don't only find fault, they commend and celebrate. They enable everyone who reads them to have the chance to become more involved and interested in the item under discussion.

Good critics and their appreciative readers are exactly the opposite of the passive consumers that many in positions of power and influence would like us to become.

Winston Churchill regarded criticism as a vital part of life:

"Criticism may not be agreeable, but it is necessary. It fulfils the same function as pain in the human body. It calls attention to an unhealthy state of things."[1071]

The Victorian critic Matthew Arnold expressed the purpose of criticism rather neatly, when he wrote that it is, or should be, "a disinterested endeavour to learn and propagate the best that is known and thought throughout the world."[1072]

Another reason criticism is of central importance to modern humanity is that it's very hard in many countries to be honest critics. In the relative safety of Britain and America, it's easy to be complacent about freedom of speech. But in many parts of the world, the life of a critic is anything but safe. Dissent is unpopular in all authoritarian societies, and in many of them speaking out is punishable by persecution, imprisonment and execution.

Christopher Hitchens wrote in 2001 that it is very easy to avoid making a stand:

"Be prepared in advance for the arguments you will hear (even in your own head) against such a mode of conduct [telling an unpopular truth]. Some of these are very seductive. What difference does it make, you may be asked (or ask yourself). There's no good answer to this question, as it happens. The universe may well be Absurd, and one's life is in any case certain to be a short one. However, this need not mean that we do not reserve the term 'absurd' for the self-evidently irrational or unjustifiable. You can't hope to change human nature or Human Nature; true enough again if slightly tautologous, because Nature is a given. But nobody accepts all human behaviour or human conduct as unalterable on that basis. Other invitations to passivity or acquiescence are more sly, some of them making an appeal to modesty. Who are you to be the judge? Who asked you? Anyway, is this the propitious time to be making a stand? Perhaps one should await a more propitious moment? And - aha! - Is there some danger of giving ammunition to the enemy?"[1073]

I would add one further familiar doubt in the mind of potential dissidents and critics: that by writing passionately against something, you are giving that something more publicity than it deserves. On that basis, it's always better to be silent.

Of course there will be people who will ask what right you have to express an unpopular or irreverent opinion. Just look at how FIFA deals with the investigative reporting, mostly in Britain, that has exposed its own corruption: essentially, by conducting bogus internal investigations and finding fault with their accusers. Dissidents are routinely described as self-appointed, elitist and arrogant.

The reason criticism is invaluable is that it teaches us to see things in a new way, or in an old way that's previously been hidden from us. Good criticism is like a flash of neural electricity, triggering a surge in our brain's activity, making us re-evaluate a little part of the world and, indeed, ourselves.

So if you want to be a critic, go ahead. But be a good one. Try to obey those ten commandments of criticism, which apply to just about every kind of critique, even social and political.

Above all, bear in mind the overarching law of criticism – and, indeed, of journalism as a whole. It was crisply expressed by Australian Prime Minister Julia Gillard in 2011, addressing the Australian National Press Club in Canberra:

"Don't write crap."[1074]

It's awfully good advice.

LAST WORDS

I have tried to avoid insulting the intelligence of my readers, so I haven't emphasized the importance of good grammar, correct spelling and presenting your opinions as clearly as possible. Clichés of all kind shouldbe used only with extreme wariness.

Nor have I emphasized such necessary virtues as punctuality and meeting your deadlines.

New Yorker film critic Anthony Lane lays down one final, practical tip for you to consider:

"Try to avoid the Lane technique of summer moviegoing... On a broiling day, I ran to a screening of *Contact*, the Jodie Foster flick about messages from another galaxy. I made it for the opening credits, and, panting heavily – which, with all due respect, is not something that I find myself doing that often in Jodie Foster films – I started taking notes. These went 'v. gloomy,' 'odd *noir* look for sci-fi,' 'creepy shadows in outdoor scene,' and so on. Only after three-quarters of an hour did I remember to remove my dark glasses." [1075]

ACKNOWLEDGEMENTS

I've consulted many other critics, and I'm grateful to all who have given me their views and reviews, either intentionally or unintentionally. I've had many conversations about criticism on both sides of the Atlantic, with such colleagues as Anne Billson, Peter Bradshaw, Roger Ebert, Angie Errigo, Henry Fitzherbert, Philip French, A.A. Gill, Dave Kehr, Mark Kermode, Cosmo Landesman, Mark Lawson, Jenny McCartney, Benedict Nightingale, Barry Norman, Dilys Powell, Peter Rainer, Jack Tinker and Alexander Walker. Reviewers who took the trouble to answer my lengthy questionnaire or communicate with me by phone or email included Nigel Andrews, Rupert Christiansen, Giles Coren, Quentin Falk, Alan Frank, Derek Malcolm, George Perry, Jay Rayner, William Russell, John Simon and James Cameron Wilson. Others have preferred to remain anonymous. I thank them all.

I am also grateful to critics I met as a young man, before I had any idea of reviewing as a career. As I wrote this book, I was often reminded of conversations I had long ago with Martin Amis, Christopher Hitchens, F.R. Leavis, Bernard Levin and Kenneth Tynan.

I have also discovered quite a lot of useful research material in my head, arising from chats I have had over the years with non-critics such as Donald Albery, Kingsley Amis, Stephen Daldry, Andrew Lloyd Webber, Cameron Mackintosh, Trevor Nunn and Michael Powell. Neither they nor I had a clue that some day I would write a book in defence of criticism, but all the same I thank them for their involuntary contributions. Needless to say, I take full responsibility for the conclusions I have drawn.

Finally, I'd like to thank all the practitioners in the world of film who have made time to talk to me. These include Gillian Anderson, Drew Barrymore, Halle Berry, Tim Burton, Steve Carell, Vincent Cassell, Geraldine Chaplin, Don Cheadle, Claire Daines, Guillermo del Toro, Catherine Deneuve, Julie Delpy, Johnny Depp, Michael Douglas, Kirsten Dunst, Nora Ephron, Julian Fellowes, 50 Cent, Albert Finney, Colin Firth, Harrison Ford, Terry Gilliam, Tom Hanks, Dustin Hoffman, John Hurt, Mathieu Kassovitz, Nicole Kidman, Christopher Lee, Emily Mortimer, Peter Mullan, Mike Nichols, Ron Perlman, Sam Raimi, Jim Sheridan, Will Smith, Sharon Stone, Audrey Tautou, Quentin Tarantino, Ray Winstone and Elijah Wood.

FOOTNOTES

[1] Alfonso Gumucio Dagron, *Jump Cut: A Review of Contemporary Media, no 26,* December 1981, p.68.

[2] Vladimir Putin (1952 -) was for 16 years an officer in the KGB, rising to the rank of Lieutenant Colonel before he retired to enter politics in his native Saint Petersburg in 1991. He moved to Moscow in 1996 and became Acting President on 31 December 1999 when President Boris Yeltsin unexpectedly resigned. Surviving widespread accusations of vote-rigging, Putin won the 2000 presidential election, and was reelected in 2004. Putin served as Prime Minister of Russia from 1999 to 2000 and again from 2008 to 2012. He has been President of Russia since 7 May 2012.

[3] Anna Politkovskaya (1958-2006) was a Russian journalist, writer, and human rights activist who opposed the Second Chechen War and Vladimir Putin. From 2000 onwards, she received numerous international awards for her work. In 2004, she published a personal account, *Putin's Russia.* On 7 October 2006 she was murdered in the lift of her block of flats. Eight years later, five men were jailed for the murder, but the identity of the person who ordered the contract killing was never clarified.

[4]   http://www.goodreads.com/quotes/14586-people-sometimes-pay-with-their-lives-for-saying-aloud-what

[5] https://www.goodreads.com/author/quotes/59019.Anna_Politkovskaya

[6] Alexander Valterovich Litvinenko (1962-2006) was a fugitive officer of the Russian FSB secret service who specialized in tackling organised crime. In November 1998, Litvinenko and other FSB officers publicly accused their superiors of ordering the assassination of the Russian tycoon and oligarch Boris Berezovsky. Litvinenko was arrested the following March on charges of exceeding the authority of his position. He was acquitted in November 1999 but re-arrested before the charges were again dismissed in 2000. In 2000, he fled to London with his family and was granted asylum. In the UK, he worked as a journalist, writer and consultant for the British intelligence services. In 2002 Litvinenko was convicted of "corruption" *in absentia* in Russia and given a three and a half-year jail sentence.

[7] http://en.wikipedia.org/wiki/Poisoning_of_Alexander_Litvinenko

[8] Robert Conquest   (1917 - 2015) was an Anglo-American   historian, novelist and poet who has specialized in the history of the Soviet Union and Russia, with particular attention to the excesses of Josef Stalin. His most famous books include *The Great Terror: Stalin's Purges of the 1930s* (1968), *Russia After Kruschev* (1965) and *Inside Stalin's Secret Police: NKVD Politics, 1936–1939* (1985).

[9] Robert Conquest, *Sunday Times*, 19 January 2007.

[10] Reported by Terrence McCoy, *Washington Post*, 28 January 2007.

[11] Boris Nemtsov (1959-2015) was a Russian politician and one of Vladimir Putin's most charismatic critics. Before Putin's accession to power, he had a successful political career in the 1990s under President Boris Yeltsin, and was credited with introducing capitalism into the Russian post-Soviet economy.

[12] Luke Harding, *Who Killed Boris Nemtsov? We will never know*, *Guardian*, 3 March 2015.

[13] *Russia opposition politician Boris Nemtsov shot dead*, BBC News, 27 February 2015.

[14] Luke Harding, *Who Killed Boris Nemtsov? We will never know*, *Guardian*, 3 March 2015.

[15] http://en.wikipedia.org/wiki/List_of_Chinese_dissidents

[16] http://en.wikipedia.org/wiki/List_of_Chinese_dissidents

[17] Ethan Gutmann, an award-winning China analyst and human-rights investigator, is the author of *Losing the New China: A Story of American Commerce, Desire and Betrayal*. He has written widely on China issues for publications such as the *Wall Street Journal Asia*, *Investor's Business Daily*, *Weekly Standard*, *National Review*, and *World Affairs* journal, and he has provided testimony and briefings to the United States Congress, the Central Intelligence Agency, the European Parliament, the International Society for Human Rights in Geneva, the United Nations, and the parliaments of Ottawa, Canberra, Dublin, Edinburgh, and London.

[18] Robert Park, *It's time to aid North Korea's Dissidents*, *www.worldaffairsjournal.org*

[19] *Jang Sung-taek's remaining family executed by Kim Jong-un*, Want China Times, 27 January 2014

[20] *Kim's uncle stripped of all posts, expelled from EWPK*, Xinhua News Agency, 9 December 2013.

[21] *Kim's uncle stripped of all posts, expelled from EWPK*, Xinhua News Agency, 9 December 2013.

[22] Mark Bowden, *Vanity Fair*, March 2015.

[23] Mark Bowden, *Vanity Fair*, March 2015.

[24] Mark Bowden, *Vanity Fair*, March 2015.

[25] Mark Bowden, *Vanity Fair*, March 2015.

[26] *Charlie Hebdo: Why Jihad came to Paris, Irish Times*, 10 January 2015.

[27] *Save Taslima Nasrin from Islamic Death Threat Fatwa in India*, www.islam-watch.org.

[28] Todd Herz, *Christianity Today*, 1 October 2002.

[29] http://en.wikipedia.org/wiki/Geert_Wilders

[30] Steve Hopkins, *Mail Online*, 5 January 201.

[31] *American atheist blogger hacked to death in Bangladesh, BBC News*, 2 March, 2015.

[32] Jason Burke and Said Hammadi, *Guardian*, 30 March 2015.

[33] Jason Burke and Said Hammadi, *Guardian*, 30 March 2015.

[34] David Keyes, *Our Ally Saudi Arabia Beheaded 10 People This Month, Daily Beast*, 18 January 2015.

[35] Debra Sweet, *The World Can't Wait: Stop the Crimes of Your Government*, 10 September 2014.

[36] Amnesty International Report, 2016/17.

[37] Amnesty International Report, 2016/17.

[38] Amnesty International Report, 2016/17.

[39] Robert Mugabe (1924 -) has been President of Zimbabwe since 31 December 1987. As a leading rebel against white minority rule, he was elected as Prime Minister in 1980, and served until 1987, when he became the country's first executive head of state. Mugabe set about creating a ZANU–PF-run one-party state, establishing a North Korean-trained security force, the Fifth Brigade, in August 1981 to deal with internal dissidents. The Fifth Brigade crushed an armed rebellion by fighters loyal to his rival Joshua Nkomo, leader of the minority Ndebele tribe, in the province of Matabeleland. Between 1982 and 1985 at least 20,000 people died in ethnic cleansing and were buried in mass graves. In 2008 Mugabe suffered a narrow defeat in the first round of a presidential election but won the run-off election in a landslide after his winning opponent Morgan Tsvangirai abruptly withdrew.

[40] Chris McGreal, *Zimbabwe dissidents pay price*, Guardian, 20 August 2001.

[41] Chris McGreal, *Zimbabwe dissidents pay price*, Guardian, 20 August 2001. Moven Mahachi (1948-2001) Ironically, Mahachi may have been murdered himself, by his own boss. On 26 May 2001 Mahachi died in a traffic "accident". On 30 July 2009 Mahachi's predecessor, Enos Nkala, claimed that Mahachi was assassinated on the orders of Robert Mugabe because he opposed the looting of diamonds in the Democratic Republic of the Congo.

[42] Chris McGreal, *Zimbabwe dissidents pay price*, Guardian, 20 August 2001.

[43] Huffington Post, 11 March 2017.

[44] A.A. Gill, *A.A. Gill is Away*, Weidenfeld & Nicholson, 2010.

[45] Sir Thomas Beecham (1879-1961) was an English conductor and impresario associated with the Liverpool Philharmonic, Hallé, London Philharmonic and Royal Philharmonic orchestras.

[46] Sir Thomas Beecham's view that critics deserve the death penalty is quoted on www.thelondoneconomic.com among the top 10 quotes of Sir Thomas Beecham.

[47] James M. Barrie (1860-1937) was a Scottish author and dramatist, whose most successful plays include *Mary Rose* and *Dear Brutus*. He is best remembered today as the writer who created *Peter Pan*.

[48] J.M.Barrie's remark is quoted by William Russell and Peter Cargin in *A Critical Century*, 2014. Page 12.

[49] Joseph L. Mankiewicz's 1950 film *All About Eve* starred Bette Davis as an ageing Broadway actress, Anne Baxter as the ambitious understudy who threatens her.

[50] George Jean Nathan (1882-1958) was an American drama critic and editor. He edited the literary magazine *The Smart Set*, and co-founded and edited *The American Mercury* and *The American Spectator*. Unlike Addison DeWitt (played by George Sanders), Nathan was not homosexual; instead, he tended to pursue young actresses.

[51] *Theatre of Blood* is a 1973 horror film starring Vincent Price and Diana Rigg.

[52] John Updike (1932 – 1979) is best known for his "Rabbit" series of novels, for which he twice won the Pulitzer Prize. He wrote regularly for *The*

New York Review of Books. His Bech stories, of which *Bech Noir* is one, were collated in *The Complete Henry Bech, Everyman's Library*, 2001.

[53] M. Night Shyamalan's *Lady in the Water* (2006) was widely ridiculed by critics. Shyamalan was pilloried for his self-regarding performance as a great but misunderstood writer. Joe Morgenstern in the *Wall Street Journal* wrote "This cloying piece of claptrap sets a high-water mark for pomposity, condescension, false profundity and true turgidity - no small accomplishment for the man whose last two features were the deadly duo *Signs* and *The Village*."

[54] M. Night Shyamalan's *The Village* (2004) received mixed reviews. I wrote in the *Daily Mail* that "because it's so original, I can easily forgive its flaws, especially its stilted dialogue, moments of portentousness and ponderous pacing. Some people will hate *The Village* and argue (with reason) that the main twist begs more questions than it answers; but this film is and does something different from the norm, and that's not easy to achieve." Others were not so kind. Rogert Ebert in the *Chicago Sun-Times* called it "a colossal miscalculation, a movie based on a premise that cannot support it, a premise so transparent it would be laughable were the movie not so deadly solemn."

[55] *After Earth* (2013) was a tedious sermon on Scientology and Dianetics, dressed up to look like a science fiction adventure. It was savaged by critics and a flop in America, but unexpectedly successful in foreign territories. Jordan Farley in *SFX Magazine* particularly disliked the leading character, played by Will Smith's son Jaden Smith: "The critical problem with *After Earth* is that Smith Jr's whiny character has all the likeability of an anal fissure."

[56] *The Last Airbender* (2010) was fantasy adventure film written, produced, and directed by M. Night Shyamalan. It was based on the first season of the Nickelodeon animated series *Avatar: The Last Airbender*. It received dreadful reviews, none worse than Roger Ebert's statement in the *Chicago Sun-Times* that "*The Last Airbender* is an agonizing experience in every category I can think of and others still waiting to be invented."

[57] *The Happening* (2008) was an American <u>supernatural</u> <u>thriller</u> film written, co-produced, and directed by <u>M. Night Shyamalan</u>. Mark Wahlberg gave a laughable performance as a man who realises that the biggest danger to humanity is, er, trees. I wrote in the *Daily Mail* that "paradoxically, for a movie which is about murderous maples, homicidal hornbeams and rampaging rhododendrons, our hero turns out to be the most scarily wooden thing in it."

[58] First for the *Sunday Telegraph* (1985-1993), then for the *Daily Mail* (1993-2013).

[59] From 1994 to 1998. I also produced and presented the Circle's annual awards ceremony in London, in aid of the NSPCC (National Society for the

Prevention of Cruelty to Children).

[60] By the London Press Club on 24 May 2013. Shortly afterwards, the *Daily Mail* discontinued my contract "for commercial reasons".

[61] When I was there, the *Daily Mail* had a circulation of over 2 million and a readership of about 4.3 million. They syndicated my reviews to newspapers around the world. I gather the *Mail Online*, for which I was the film critic, was the most successful online newspaper in the world and was viewed monthly by over 100 million people, though it's hard to estimate how many of those read the film reviews.

[62] In 2008, 16 year-old Charlie Lyne, blogger on his own website *UltraCulture*, unilaterally voted me Worst Critic in the World, although he was vague about his reasons. By 30 September 2009, however, I had (apparently) improved, as Lyne generously informed his readers that I was "not a bad film critic". However, there was no shortage of haters to take his place. On 12 September 2012, "some guy" asked on www.fark.com "Is the Daily Mail's Chris Tookey the most incompetent film critic of all time?" A person calling himself "master of the flying guillotine" replied "He's got terrible taste and is also incompetent". A gentleman called "Spiralmonkey" blamed the *Daily Mail* and its readership: "Yes, he is ridiculously inept with an astounding lack of judgement, but we're not talking a quality broadsheet here. He knows his audience, and they are mainly angry and ill-informed." Jonny17 wrote "Christopher Tookey is a disgrace to film journalism. A nasty, self-promoting man, who can't even write that well. In short. Fark Chris Tookey." Gameshowhost wrote "Chris Tookey doesn't understand the films he watches, and is likely suffering from autism". Stile4aly wrote "This man must die." I'm not sure if that was a death threat, or merely a statement of fact about mortality. Those quotations are from just one strand on one website. There are too many others to mention.

[63] Yes, I disliked *Watchmen* (2009), *Jonah Hex* (2010) and *R.I.P.D.* (2013) However, I have always liked good movies based on comic strips. My favourites include *Men in Black* (1997), *The Road to Perdition* (2002) and *Spider-Man 2* (2004).

[64] Okay, I panned *Sucker Punch* (2011), *Battleship* (2012) and *G.I. Joe: Retaliation* (2013). But I've admired hundreds of high-quality action movies, including *The Adventures of Robin Hood* (1938), *Die Hard* (1988) and *Skyfall* (2012).

[65] Of the 795 films that I have awarded scores of 8/10 or more, 707 are not in a foreign language – which would seem to indicate that I am not unduly prejudiced against films in the English language. 89% of my favourite movies are in the English language.

[66] The fact that 88 of my favourite 795 films are in a foreign language – that's 11% - would seem to indicate that I am not prejudiced against foreign-

language films either. I am perfectly happy to declare that *The Bicycle Thieves* (1949), *Tokyo Story* (1953) and *A Man Escaped* (1956) are all, in very different ways, masterpieces. Recent foreign-language films I have enjoyed include *Hidden* (2005), *King's Game* (2005) and *The Lives of Others* (2006).

[67] Someone calling himself "Bickle" made this claim on *Empire Online*, 29 June 2009: "The man is an idiot. He hates any film that doesn't promote wholesome, Christian moral values." The claim is groundless, and all the more surprising since I am an atheist. Films I have panned include *The Book of Eli* (2010), *Evan Almighty* (2010) and *The Nativity Story* (2006), all of which promoted Christian values – though that did not, regrettably, make any of them good films. Conversely, I can't detect the slightest promotion of "wholesome Christian values" in most of my favourite movies - *Fight Club, Psycho, The Apartment* and *Casablanca*, to name four out of hundreds. I am not prejudiced against Christian values; but they are hardly enough to make me give a bad film a good review.

[68] One of the weirdest accusations against me was darko18's claim on *www.empireonline.com* that "Unless the film he's reviewing is a Jane Austen adaptation starring Keira Knightley and some male lead who's made the jump from weekday TV to silver screen, it's blasphemous, youth-corrupting shit." I have no idea what he's on about here, and I've never accused any film of blasphemy. I did like *Pride and Prejudice*, starring Keira Knightley, but the idea that I don't like any other movies is patently absurd.

[69] In his 2010 autobiography *Straight Up*, Danny Dyer admitted his crack habit and recounted an epic drug binge before the performance of a Harold Pinter play on New York's Broadway in 2000. Dyer said he smoked so much crack the night before that he froze on stage. He said: "I fell in with a real canehead crowd and started to hit the crack pipe… Crack is like coke times 20. You get a massive rush and you feel like you could take on the world. It's like your blood has been removed and replaced with electricity. I took to it like a duck to water." This confession did not come as much of a shock to those of us who had suffered through his many abysmal performances in atrocious films.

[70] Mr Dyer's erroneous guess as to my sexual proclivities was, I've been told, on the commentary track for *Outlaw* (2017), though I've never bothered to listen to it myself. One viewing of *Outlaw* in the cinema was enough.

[71] The exact words in Dyer's *Ask Danny* column, in response to a letter from a 23-year-old reader – "Alex, Manchester" – asking for advice on how to get over his split from his girlfriend, was: "You've got nothing to worry about, son. I'd suggest going out on a rampage with the boys, getting on the booze and smashing anything that moves. Then, when some bird falls for you, you can turn the tables and break her heart. Of course, the other option is to cut your ex's face, and then no one will want her." This was quoted by Steve Busfield and Mark Sweeney in an article for the *Guardian* on 5 May 2010.

[72] These figures were quoted in the *Daily Mail, Radio Times* and *Daily Star* on 20 February 2012.

[73] It was announced in *Hello* magazine on 1 October 2013 that Dyer would join the cast of *EastEnders* as Mick Carter, landlord of the Queen Vic pub. And he did.

[74] Hundreds of bloggers, twitterers and facebook fiends weighed in. Their comments are all quoted on my website, *www.movie-film-review.com*, under my review of *Kick-Ass*.

[75] I'm afraid you'll have to take my word on this. Suffice it to say that the police have never invited me to assist them with their enquiries, and my relationship with my family's standard poodle Holly is platonic.

[76] My review of *Kick-Ass* appeared in the *Daily Mail* on 2 April, 2010

[77] These comments are all quoted on my website, www.movie-film-review.com, under my review of *Kick-Ass*. Unsurprisingly, after I quoted them, the comments disappeared from the internet, along with the YouTube clip that had inspired them.

[78] All these comments are quoted on my website, www.movie-film-review.com, under my review of *Kick-Ass*.

[79] Roger Ebert in the *Chicago Sun-Times* wrote "Shall I have feelings, or should I pretend to be cool? Will I seem hopelessly square if I find *Kick-Ass* morally reprehensible and will I appear to have missed the point? Let's say you're a big fan of the original comic book, and you think the movie does it justice. You know what? You inhabit a world I am so very not interested in. A movie camera makes a record of whatever is placed in front of it, and in this case, it shows deadly carnage dished out by an 11-year-old girl, after which an adult man brutally hammers her to within an inch of her life. Blood everywhere. Now tell me all about the context. The movie's premise is that ordinary people, including a high school kid, the 11-year-old and her father, try to become superheroes in order to punish evil men. The flaw in this premise is that the little girl does become a superhero. In one scene, she faces a hallway jammed with heavily armed gangsters and shoots, stabs and kicks them all to death, while flying through the air with such power, it's enough to make Jackie Chan take out an AARP membership. This isn't comic violence. These men, and many others in the film, are really stone-cold dead. And the 11-year-old apparently experiences no emotions about this. Many children that age would be, I dunno, affected somehow, don't you think, after killing eight or 12 men who were trying to kill her? I know, I know. This is a satire. But a satire of what?"

[80] Peter Rainer wrote in *The Christian Science Monitor*: "What can you say about a movie in which an 11-year-old girl slices and dices hordes of

hoodlums while mouthing choice obscenities that might give even a truck driver pause? Welcome to *Kick-Ass*, the latest and most egregious example of a comic book series-turned-movie. If we keep upping – or, to be accurate, lowering – the ante like this, pretty soon we'll be watching toddlers toting Uzis."

[81] Anthony Lane wrote in the *New Yorker:* "Kick-Ass is violence's answer to kiddie porn. You can see it in Hit Girl's outfit when she cons her way past security guards — white blouse, hair in pigtails, short tartan skirt — and in the winsome way that she pleads to be inculcated into grownup excess. That pleading is the dream of every pedophile... The standard defense of such material is that we are watching 'cartoon violence,' but, when filmmakers nudge a child into viewing savagery as slapstick, are we not allowing them to do what we condemn in the pornographer — that is, to coarsen and inflame?... If you find your enjoyment of *Kick-Ass* unclouded by such issues, good luck to you."

[82] Nigel Andrews wrote in the *Financial Times*: "Matthew Vaughn, former Guy Ritchie producer, co-wrote and directed, and on this evidence is all flash and no flair."

[83] Tim Robey wrote in the *Daily Telegraph* that *Kick-Ass* was "bratty and unpleasant, and needs to be argued with. Chloe Moretz's role as Hit Girl, a foul-mouthed 11 year-old vigilante in a purple wig, is ether a gift from geek heaven or a deeply icky fetish figure who should set all sorts of schoolgirl-porn alarm bells ringing: I know which side I'm on."

[84] Mike McCahill wrote in the *Sunday Telegraph*: "Much cold, unfelt violence: clearly, at the Methusalean age of 32, I fall outside the designated demographic, but then again I am old enough to remember plenty of films based on comic books that didn't so obviously resemble instructional videos for sociopaths."

[85] *Daily Mail*, 6 June 1997.

[86] Julian Petley and Mark Kermode, *Road Rage, Sight and Sound*, June 1997.

[87] Months before I saw *Crash*, let alone reviewed it, Alexander Walker weighed into it after seeing it at the Cannes Film Festival. He called it "vulnerable on almost every level: taste, seriousness, even the public-safety risk of promulgating such a perverted creed... A film that is immoral by any standard, unsafe at any speed." When, later, it received an 18 certificate from the British Board of Film Classification, Nigel Reynolds – again, quite independently of me - wrote in the *Daily Telegraph* that *Crash* was "morally vacuous, nasty, violent and little more than an excuse to string together one scene after another of sexual intercourse... Ban it? It barely deserves the notoriety. To bin it, would be a more sensible and honest way forward. The film has so little merit, so little reason, it adds so little to the sum of human knowledge, condition or even entertainment, that it is hard to see why David

Cronenberg, his financial backers and distributors have drawn breath to bring it before the public."

[88] Among the many film critics who disliked *Crash* intensely and had no connection with Associated Newspapers was Richard Corliss in *Time*, who wrote that it was "less a joyride than an endless traffic jam". Leah Rozen in *People* magazine called it "as repellent a film as has come down the pike in years". In the British leftist magazine the *New Statesman* Jonathan Coe pronounced that it was "numbingly boring. These are dull people with dulled emotions and dull obsessions, and this film registers this dullness with scrupulous fidelity."

[90] Ironically, several programmes I had directed for the ATV programme *Link* in the 1980s were commended within the disabled community for supporting the right of the disabled to have sex lives. So in claiming that I was prejudiced against them, Mr. Petley could hardly have been further from the truth.

[91] Mark Kermode, *Hatchet Job*, Picador, 2013.

[92] Reported by Vanessa Thorpe in *If Even Andrew Lloyd Webber fears bloggers, it is curtains for the critics?*, The Observer, 14 March 2010.

[93] Reported by Vanessa Thorpe in *If Even Andrew Lloyd Webber fears bloggers, it is curtains for the critics?*, The Observer, 14 March 2010.

[94] Reported by Vanessa Thorpe in *If Even Andrew Lloyd Webber fears bloggers, it is curtains for the critics?*, The Observer, 14 March 2010.

[95] Reported by Vanessa Thorpe in *If Even Andrew Lloyd Webber fears bloggers, it is curtains for the critics?*, The Observer, 14 March 2010.

[96] Reported by Vanessa Thorpe in *If Even Andrew Lloyd Webber fears bloggers, it is curtains for the critics?*, The Observer, 14 March 2010.

[97] John Simon, *Reverse Angle*, Potter, 1983.

[98] Howard Teichmann, *Smart Aleck: The Wit, World and Life of Alexander Woollcott*, 1976, p104.

[99] Quoted by A.A. Gill in the preface of his book *Table Talk: Sweet and Sour, Salt and Bitter*, Hachette, 2010.

[100] Quoted by Nicholas Grene in *The Politics of Irish Drama: Plays in Context from Boucicault to Friel*, Cambridge University Press, 1999 .

[101] Quoted in *Phillips' Treasury of Humorous Quotations*, edited by Bob Phillips, Tyndale House Publishers, 2015, p63.

[102] Answer to the author's questionnaire, 2015.

[103] Both Charles Spencer's *Daily Telegraph* review and Dame Judi Dench's response are quoted by William Russell and Peter Cargin, in *A Critical Century*, 2014. Page 42.

[104] Sir John Vincent Hurt CBE (1940-2017) was an English actor described by the American director David Lynch as "simply the greatest actor in the world" (the two had worked together on *The Elephant Man*). He won BAFTA and Golden Globe awards, and two Academy Award nominations. He is probably most fondly remembered, certainly by me, for his roles in *I Claudius* and *The Naked Civil Servant* on television, and (in the cinema) *A Man for All Seasons, 10 Rillington Place* and *Midnight Express.*

[105] Quoted by Sholto Byrnes in *John Hurt: I was abused, too, Independent*, 16 October 2005.

[106] Answer to the author's questionnaire, 2015.

[107] Quoted on www.quotespin.com.

[108] This was presumably in response to Coren's tweet from his Kentish Town home, in January 2010: "Next door have brought their 12-year-old son a drum kit. For f**k's sake! Do I kill him then burn it? Or do I f**k him, then kill him then burn it?" He followed this with: "Child for sale, charred and partially f**ked. Has own drum kit." Vivienne Pattison, the director of watchdog Mediawatch UK, condemned his tweet in the Evening Standard of 13 January 2010 as being in "very bad taste".

[109] Answer to author's questionnaire, 2015.

[110] Answer to author's questionnaire, 2015.

[111] Rupert Christiansen, *Rosenkavalier row: 'I stand by every word'*, *Daily Telegraph*, 21 May 2014.

[112] Answer to author's questionnaire, 2015.

[113] Libby Gelman-Waxner, *Ask Libby... Libby Gelman-Waxner answers your questions about the 'Citizen Kane' of male stripper movies, Entertainment News*, 18 January 2015.

[114] Quoted in www.forum.thefreedictionary.com.

[115] Answer to author's questionnaire, 2015.

[116] Quoted on www.onlyfamousquotes.com

[117] P.G. Wodehouse (1881 –1975) was an English comic novelist best known today for the Jeeves and Blandings novels and short stories. In addition to being drama critic for *Vanity Fair* in the 1910s, he was a playwright and lyricist who was part author and writer of 15 plays and 250 lyrics for 30 musical comedies, many of them produced in collaboration with Jerome Kern and Guy Bolton.

[118] Alexander Woollcott (1887 – 1943) was an American critic and commentator for *The New York Times* and *New Yorker* magazine, and a member of the Algonquin Round Table. He was the inspiration for Sheridan Whiteside, the main character in the play *The Man Who Came to Dinner* (1939) by George S. Kaufman and Moss Hart, and for the journalist character Waldo Lydecker in the film *Laura* (1944).

[119] George S. Kaufman (1889 – 1961) was drama editor for The New York Times from 1917 to 1930. He became a prolific playwright, theatre director and producer. He wrote several musicals, notably for the Marx Brothers. One play and one musical won the Pulitzer Prize for Drama: *You Can't Take It With You* (1937, with Moss Hart), and *Of Thee I Sing* (1932, with Morrie Ryskind and Ira Gershwin). He also won the Tony Award as a Director, for the musical *Guys and Dolls.*

[120] Dorothy Parker (1893 –1967) wrote theatre criticism for *Vanity Fair* from 1918, as P.G. Wodehouse's second-string. She became a literary critic for the New Yorker and was a founding member of the Algonquin Round Table, a collection of wits who met at the Algonquin Hotel, not far from Broadway. She became a poet, short story writer, satirist and screenwriter. Two screenplays she co-wrote, *A Star is Born* (1937) and *Smash-up, The Story of a Woman* (1947) received Oscar nominations.

[121] Quoted by Fred R. Shapiro in *The Yale Book of Quotations*, Yale University Press, 2006, p838.

[122] Kenneth Tynan (1927 –1980) was an English critic and writer. He made a big impact as a drama critic at *The Observer* (1954–58, 1960–63), though his film criticism was not as noteworthy. In 1963, Tynan was appointed as the new National Theatre Company's literary manager. After he used the F-word live on television, decency campaigner Mary Whitehouse wrote a letter to the Queen, suggesting that Tynan should be reprimanded by having "his bottom spanked". Her comment caused much laughter among those who knew of Tynan's notorious appetite for flagellation.

[123] Quoted in www.famous-quotes.com.

[124] G.B. Shaw, *Man and Superman*, 1903.

[125] Burt Reynolds (1936 -) is an American actor, director and producer, who became a star He has starred in many films, such as *Deliverance* (1972) and *Smokey and the Bandit* (1977), and won a Golden Globe Award as Best Supporting Actor for *Boogie Nights* (1997).

[126] Christopher Tookey, *The Critics' Film Guide*, Boxtree, 1994.

[127] John Barbour, in *Los Angeles*, quoted in Christopher Tookey, *The Critics' Film Guide*, Boxtree, 1994.

[128] Henrik Ibsen (1828 –1906) was a major 19th-century Norwegian playwright, and is the most frequently performed dramatist in the world after Shakespeare. His major works include *Brand*, *Peer Gynt*, *An Enemy of the People*, *A Doll's House*, *Hedda Gabler*, *Ghosts* and *The Master Builder*.

[129] George Bernard Shaw, *The Quintessence of Ibsenism*, Boston: Benjamin R. Tucker, 1891

[130] Wolfgang Amadeus Mozart (1756 – 1791) was quite a good composer.

[131] www.quotationspage.com.

[132] Walt Disney (1901 – 1966) co-founded The Walt Disney Company, which did well in movies, especially in the field of animation.

[133] www.justdisney.com.

[134] Alfred Tennyson, 1st Baron Tennyson (1809 –1892), was Poet Laureate of Great Britain and Ireland during most of Queen Victoria's reign. Among his best-known poems are *The Charge of the Light Brigade*, *Tears, Idle Tears* and *Idylls of the King*.

[135] www.thinkexist.com.

[136] David Mamet (1947 -) is best known as an American playwright, and won a Pulitzer Prize and received Tony nominations for *Glengarry Glen Ross* (1984) and *Speed-the-Plow* (1988). As a screenwriter, he has received Oscar nominations for *The Verdict* (1982) and *Wag the Dog* (1997). He is also an essayist and film director.

[137] Frank Rich, Jr. (1949 -) was a film critic for *Time* and the *New York Post*, and film critic and senior editor of *New Times Magazine*. From 1980 to 1993 he was chief theatre critic of the *New York Times*. In 1994, Rich became an op-ed columnist for the *New York Times*. *In* 2011, he left to become an essayist and editor-at-large for *New York* magazine.

[138] John Simon (1925 -) is an American author and literary, theatre and film critic. He was a winner of the George Polk Award for Film Criticism (1968) and the George Jean Nathan Award (1970). His reviews are notable for their

literacy, wit and aggression, though many have criticised him for being excessively personal.

[139] Quoted in Leslie Keane, *David Mamet in Conversation*, University of Michigan Press, 2001, p97.

[140] John Simon filled the position of *New York* magazine's theatre critic for 37 years, until he was fired in 2005, a few days before his 80th birthday. David Mamet wrote to broadwayworld.com commending his firing, on 12 May, 2005.

[141] David Mamet, *Why I Am No Longer a Brain-dead Liberal*, *Village Voice*, 11 March 2008.

[142] John Simon, *A Bad Business*, *New York Theater*, 2008.

[143] Elisabeth Vincentelli. *New York Post*, 7 December 2009.

[144] David Rooney, *Variety*, 7 December 2009.

[145] Brendan Lemon, *Financial Times*, 8 December 2009.

[146] John Simon, *Bloomberg*, 7 December 2009.

[147] John Simon, *Bloomberg*, 11 October 2009.

[148] Frank Rich, *New York Times*, 5 June 1981.

[149] Frank Rich, quoted by David Mamet in Preface to *Glengarry Glen Ross: A Play*, Avalon Travel Publishing, 1994.

[150] Frank Rich, *New York Times*, 4 May 1988.

[151] Frank Rich, quoted by David Mamet in Preface to *Oleanna: A Play*, Dramatists Play Service, Inc., 1998.

[152] Rosanna Arquette (1959 -) is an American actress, film director, and producer, best known for *Desperately Seeking Susan* (1985), *Silverado* (1985) and *Crash* (1996). She is currently on her fourth marriage, to an investment banker.

[153] www.litera.co.uk.

[154] Benjamin Disraeli (1804 – 1881) was a British Conservative Prime Minister who served two terms, one of nine months in 1868 and one of six years in 1874-1880. His own father, Isaac D'Israeli, was a literary critic.

[155] Benjamin Disraeli, *Lothair*, 1870. This is one of Disraeli's later novels, written after his first term as Prime Minister. Critics treated it less than

kindly. The *Quarterly Review* dismissed it as a bore: "So far as feeling is concerned *Lothair* is as dull as ditch-water and as flat as a flounder." *Macmillan's Magazine* said "A single conscientious perusal (without skipping) of *Lothair* would be a creditable feat: few will voluntarily attempt a second." After Disraeli's death, critics were kinder. Edmund Gosse called it a "superb ironic romance" and called it "unquestionably the greatest of his literary works". It remains, however, much less often read than Disraeli's more famous novels, *Sybil* (1845) and *Coningsby* (1844).

[156] Harry S. Truman (1884 –1972) was the 33rd President of the United States between 1945 and 1953. Truman controversially allowed the use of atomic weapons against Japan, though he resisted the temptation to order a nuclear strike on critics.

[157] Paul Hume (1915 – 2001) was fortunate that he had affronted a western leader rather than, say, Stalin. He survived Presidential disapproval intact and continued to flourish as music editor for the *Washington Post* from 1946 to 1982

[158] Margaret Truman (1924 –2008) was an American singer who wrote an acclaimed biography of her father, President Harry S. Truman. She also "wrote" successful thrillers, though these were allegedly ghost-written under her name by William Harrington and Donald Bain.

[159] Harry S. Truman's note to Paul Hume, 6 December 1950. The letter can be found at www.trumanlibrary.org.

[160] Alan Parker (1944 -) is an English film director and producer, who also writes screenplays. His most successful films include *Midnight Express* (1978), *Mississippi Burning* (1988), *Fame* (1980) and *The Commitments* (1991). His films have won nineteen BAFTA awards, ten Golden Globes and ten Academy Awards.

[161] http://alanparker.com/quotes/on-critics/

[162] http://alanparker.com/quotes/on-critics/

[163] http://alanparker.com/quotes/on-critics/

[164] Quoted in Simon Brew, *Are star ratings on movie reviews a good thing?*, *Den of Geek,* 11 February 2014.

[165] http://en.wikipedia.org/wiki/Michelin_Guide

[166] http://en.wikipedia.org/wiki/Star_(classification)

[167] http://en.wikipedia.org/wiki/Star_(classification)

[168] Jay Scott, *Jay Scott on Film: Introducing the death doughnut (or, this one rates a zero)*. *Toronto Globe and Mail,* 10 January 1992.

[169] www.insults.net.

[170] www.thefreelibrary.com.

[171] thinkexist.com.

[172] *Life and Letters of Berlioz* by Hector Berlioz, Daniel Bernard, H. Mainwaring Dunstan, Cambridge University Press, 2010, p300

[173] Quoted by Tom Service in *The Rite of Spring: 'The work of a madman',* *Guardian,* 12 February 2013.

[174] Quoted by Duncan Wu, *30 Great Myths about the Romantics,* John Wiley & Sons, 2015, p23.

[175] www.william-shakespeare.info.

[176] www.quotes.net.

[177] In March 1910, Gosse wrote to André Gide, whose expanded memoirs of Wilde had just appeared: "There has been a great deal of folly written about Wilde. I like the complete sanity of your picture. Of course he was not a 'great writer.' A languid romancier, a bad poet, a good (but not superlatively good) dramatist, - his works, taken without his life, present to a sane criticism, a mediocre figure." Quoted by Linette Brugmans, ed., *The Correspondence of André Gide and Edmund Gosse,* 1904-28 (1959).

[178] Arnold Bennett contributed a signed article to the *Evening Standard* on 30 June 1927, in which he stated "I think that Wilde's popular vogue is over... He made a few thousand pounds out of *The Importance of Being Earnest,* but the other plays, very inferior, did not do much."

[179] Quoted in Oscar Wilde, ed. Karl Beckson, Routledge, 2003. Henry James (1843 – 1916) was an American-British writer who spent most of his writing career in Britain. His famous works include *The Portrait of a Lady, What Maisie Knew* and *The Wings of the Dove.* His brother William James (1842 – 1910) was an American philosopher, psychologist and physician.

[180] Ambrose Bierce, *The Wasp,* March 31, 1882. Ambrose Bierce (1842-1914?) was a journalist, short story writer, and satirist. His most famous short story is *An Occurrence at Owl Creek Bridge,* but he is most often remembered for his satirical lexicon, *The Devil's Dictionary.* In 1913, Bierce traveled to Mexico to cover the Mexican Revolution. While traveling with rebel troops, he disappeared, so he probably died in 1913 or 1914.

[181] Marcel Proust (1871-1922) was a French novelist, critic, and essayist best known for his gigantic novel *À la recherche du temps perdu* (also known as *Remembrance of Things Past* or *In Search of Lost Time*), which was published in seven parts between 1913 and 1927. Proust self-published after the work had been turned down all over Paris by leading publishers.

[182] Evelyn Waugh (1903 – 1966) was a prolific English novelist, whose famous works include *Decline and Fall* (1928), *A Handful of Dust* (1934), *Brideshead Revisited* (1945), and the Second World War trilogy *Sword of Honour* (1952–61). He also wrote reviews, biographies and travel books.

[183] Quoted in *The Letters* of *Evelyn Waugh* edited by Mark Amory, Weidenfeld & Nicolson, 2010.

[184] Evelyn Waugh, 1951, writing of Spender's memoir *World Within World,* , reprinted in *Essays, Articles and Reviews*, ed Donat Gallagher, Little Brown, 1984, p. 394.

[185] Robert Graves (1895 – 1985) was an English poet, novelist, critic, and classicist. He was awarded the 1934 James Tait Black Memorial Prize for his two novels *I, Claudius* and *Claudius the God.*

[186] Dylan Thomas (1914 – 1953) was a Welsh poet and drunk, whose output included the radio play for voices *Under Milk Wood* and the poems *And death shall have no dominion* and *Do not go gentle into that good night.*

[187] Quoted by Nicolas Wroe, in a review (of *Dylan Thomas: A New Life* by Andrew Lycett) for the *Guardian,* 15 November 2003.

[188] James Joyce (1882 – 1941) was an Irish novelist and poet. His works include the short-story collection *Dubliners* (1914), and the novels *A Portrait of the Artist as a Young Man* (1916), *Ulysses* (1922)   and *Finnegans Wake* (1939)

[189] D.H. Lawrence (1885 – 1930) was an English novelist, poet, playwright, essayist, literary critic and painter. He was much praised by the literary critic F.R. Leavis, and his most famous works include the novels *Sons and Lovers* (1913), *The Rainbow* (1915), *Women in Love* (1920) and *Lady Chatterley's Lover* (1928) The last of these resulted in Penguin Books being prosecuted in 1960 under the Obscene Publications Act. The jury found the publishers not guilty. Notoriously, chief prosecutor Mervyn Griffith-Jones asked the jurors (three of whom were women) if it were the kind of book "you would wish your wife or servants to read".

[190] becketsbest.org.uk.

[191] Virginia Woolf (1882 – 1941) was a novelist, and central figure in the Bloomsbury Group of intellectuals. Her most famous works include the novels *Mrs Dalloway* (1925), *To the Lighthouse* (1927) and *Orlando* (1928),

and _A Room of One's Own_ (1929). She suffered from mental illness throughout her life and committed suicide by drowning.

[192] Museum of Foreign Literature, Science and Art, Volume 32, Google ebook.

[193] Noel Coward (1899 – 1973) was an English playwright, composer, director, actor and singer. His plays include _Hay Fever_, _Private Lives_, _Design for Living_, _Present Laughter_ and _Blithe Spirit_, and his most memorable songs include _Mad Dogs and Englishmen_, _I'll See You Again_ and _I Went to a Marvellous Party_. The Albery Theatre (originally the New Theatre) in London was renamed the Noël Coward Theatre in his honour in 2006.

[194] Irving Wardle, _Theatre Criticism_, Routledge, 1992.

[195] Gene Simmons (1949 -) is an Israeli-born American bass guitarist, singer-songwriter, record producer, entrepreneur, actor, and television personality. Known as The Demon, he is the bass guitarist/co-lead vocalist of Kiss, a rock band he co-founded in the early 1970s. With Kiss, Simmons has sold more than 100 million albums worldwide.

[196] Quoted by Charles M. Young, _Kiss: The Pagan Beasties of Teenage Rock_, _Rolling Stone_, 7 April 1977.

[197] Michael Coveney, _Criticism collapses on a wave of dissent and indifference_, _What's On Stage_, 30 July 2013.

[198] Alan Shearer (1970 -) is a retired footballer who played as a striker in the England national team and for Southampton, Blackburn Rovers and Newcastle United. He was both Newcastle's and the Premier League's record goalscorer. Since retiring as a player in 2006, Shearer has worked as a television pundit for the BBC. In 2009, he briefly left his BBC role to become Newcastle United's manager in the last eight games of their 2008–09 season, in an unsuccessful attempt to save them from relegation.

[199] Michael Owen (1979 -) is a retired footballer who played as a striker in the England national team and for Liverpool, Real Madrid, Newcastle United, Manchester United and Stoke City. He is a pundit on BT Sport football coverage and also appears on the BBC's _Match of the Day_. He is a successful racehorse breeder and owner.

[200] Alan Hansen (1955 -) is a retired Scottish football player who was a central defender for Partick Thistle, Liverpool and Scotland. He was a regular pundit on the BBC's _Match of the Day_ between 1992 and 2014, where he frequently criticised defences and revealed good knowledge of tactics. Notoriously, after Manchester United lost 1-3 to Aston Villa on the opening day of the 1995-56 Premiership season, he said "you can't win anything with kids". Manchester United proved him wrong by winning the

Premiership with an influx of youth players <u>Paul Scholes</u>, <u>David Beckham</u>, <u>Nicky Butt</u> and <u>Gary Neville</u> into the first team.

[201] Andy Gray (1955 -) is a Scottish retired <u>footballer</u> who played as a striker for his country and for Dundee United, Aston Villa, Wolverhampton Wanderers, Everton and West Bromwich Albion and Rangers. He was the lead football <u>pundit</u> for <u>Sky Sports</u>, revolutionizing coverage with his ability to criticise tactics and performances. He was dismissed in January 2011 following multiple allegations of <u>sexism</u>. Gray, along with former Sky Sports anchor <u>Richard Keys</u>, signed for <u>talkSPORT</u> in February 2011. They now both work for <u>beIN Sports</u> in <u>Doha, Qatar</u>.

[202] Gary Neville (1975 -) was <u>England</u>'s most-<u>capped</u> <u>right-back</u> and <u>Manchester United</u>'s <u>captain</u> for five years. He currently serves as a coach for the <u>England national football team</u>. Since retiring from football in the middle of the 2010–11 season, Neville has become a shrewd commentator for <u>Sky Sports</u>.

[203] Arsene Wenger (1949 -) is a <u>French</u> <u>football</u> <u>manager</u> famous for his development of promising young players such as Thierry Henry, Aaron Ramsey and Hector Bellerin. He has been the manager of <u>Arsenal</u> since 1996, where he has become the club's longest-serving manager, and the most successful in terms of major titles won. He revolutionised <u>football in England</u> in the late 1990s through changes in the training and diet of players. His playing career was undistinguished, owing to a lack of pace.

[204] Jose Mourinho (1963 -) is a Portuguese <u>football</u> <u>manager</u> and former football player who is currently manager of the English club <u>Chelsea</u>. His tactical acumen has enabled him to win league titles in Portugal, England, Italy, and Spain. He took Porto and Inter Milan to the highest honour in European club football, the <u>UEFA Champions League</u>. Mourinho began as a player in the <u>Portuguese Second Division</u>.

[205] Samuel Johnson, quoted in James Boswell's *The Life of Samuel Johnson*, 1791.

[206] Hans Keller (1919-1985) was an Austrian-born music critic, violinist and writer who held influential jobs at the BBC and wrote copiously for the *Listener* and *Spectator*.

[207] These works included Benjamin Britten's String Quartet No.3, Op. 94; Benjamin Frankel's String Quartet No.5, Op.43; David Matthews' Piano Trio No.1; and Buxton Orr's Piano Trio No.1.

[208] Jamie Bell thanked me at an awards ceremony in 2000 for my review of *Billy Elliot* (1999).

[209] Richard Curtis thanked me at an awards ceremony in, I think, 2004 for my reviews of *Four Weddings and a Funeral* (1994) and *Love Actually* (2003). He also admitted I was right not to have liked his co-written screenplay for *Bean* (1997).

[210] Stephen Daldry thanked me at an awards ceremony in 2000 for my review of *Billy Elliot* (1999).

[211] Julian Fellowes thanked me on several occasions for my review of *Separate Lies* (2005).

[212] Nicole Kidman thanked me at an awards ceremony for my reviews of her performances in *Dead Calm* (1988) and *To Die For* (1995), which she said had enabled her to be taken seriously as an actress.

[213] Mike Leigh thanked me at a couple of awards ceremonies for my reviews of *Secrets & Lies* (1996) and *Vera Drake* (2004).

[214] Sam Mendes thanked me at an awards ceremony for my review of *American Beauty* (1999).

[215] Peter Morgan took me out to lunch to thank me for my enthusiastic review of *Martha – Meet Frank, Daniel and Laurence* (1998). He went on to write films and plays including *The Queen*, *Frost/Nixon*, *The Damned United* and *Rush*.

[216] David Nicholls thanked me for my review of *Starter For 10* (2006).

[217] Rufus Sewell thanked me at a party for appreciating his performance in *Martha – Meet Frank, Daniel and Laurence* (1998).

[218] Quentin Tarantino thanked me in Toronto, Canada for persuading my fellow jurors to see and give an award to his first film, *Reservoir Dogs* (1992), at the Toronto Film Festival.

[219] Man Ray (1890 – 1976) was an American visual artist who spent most of his career in France. He contributed to the Dada and Surrealist movements. He was best known for his photography, and became a renowned fashion and portrait photographer.

[220] izquotes.com.

[221] Charles-Henry Hirsch (1870-1948) was a French poet, novelist, playwright and critic.

[222] Filippo Tommaso Marinetti (1876-1944) was an Italian poet, editor and playwright, who founded the Futurist movement with his *Futurist Manifesto*, written in 1909.

---

[223] *Futurism, An Anthology*, edited by Lawrence Rainey, Christine Poggi and Laura Whitman, Yale University Press, 2009.

[224] Quoted in Herschel B. Chipp, *Theories of Modern Art*, University of California Press, 1968. Page 287.

[225] Quoted in Herschel B. Chipp, *Theories of Modern Art*, University of California Press, 1968. Page 286.

[226] Peter Fuller, Theoria: Art and the Absence of Grace, Chatto & Windus, 1988. Page 177.

[227] Bernard Levin (1928 – 2004) was a journalist, critic, author and broadcaster. He reviewed television for the *Manchester Guardian*, was a political columnist on *The Spectator* and for the *Daily Mail* and *Times*. He reviewed theatre for the *Daily Express* and the *Daily Mail*. I knew him through my friendship with his onetime girlfriend, Arianna Stassinopoulos (later Huffington) who was President of the Cambridge Union at the same time as I was President of the Oxford Union.

[228] Desmond Leslie (1921 – 2001) was a British spitfire pilot in the RAF during World War II, and became a film maker, writer, and musician. He co-authored one of the first books on UFOs, *Flying Saucers Have Landed* (1953), with writer George Adamski. In the 1950s, he was also a pioneer in electronic music.

[229] Agnes Bernelle (1923 – 1999) was an actress and singer, whose performance in *An Evening of Savagery and Delight* attracted rave reviews at the Dublin Festival but lasted only three weeks at London's Duchess theatre. On the first night an usherette tipped a tray of hot coffee into Levin's lap, which may have jaundiced his view of the performance. Born Agnes Elizabeth Bernauer in Berlin, she was the OSS wartime Black Propaganda radio announcer codenamed Vicki, famous for demoralizing a German U-Boat Captain into surrendering with one of her targeted broadcasts.

[230] Ken Russell's screenplay for The Devils (1970) was based partially on the 1952 book *The Devils of Loudun* by Aldous Huxley, and partially on the 1960 play *The Devils* by John Whiting, also based on Huxley's book. Walker called *the film* "a garish glossary of sado-masochism... a taste for visual sensation that makes scene after scene look like the masturbatory fantasies of a Roman Catholic boyhood." In the UK it was banned by 17 local authorities. In 2002, for a *Sight and Sound* Top Ten Poll, published by the British Film Institute, the critic Mark Kermode called *The Devils* one of the ten most important films ever made.

[231] Ken Russell (1927 – 2011) was a film-maker obsessed with sex, music and the church. He is best known for his Oscar-winning film *Women in Love* (1969), *The Devils* (1971), The Who's *Tommy* (1975), and *Altered States* (1980). Unable to find work in his later years, Russell joined *Celebrity Big*

Brother in January 2007, at the start of the series, but left voluntarily within a week after an altercation with Jade Goody. On 11 January 2007, he told Natalie Clark of the Daily Mail "There used to be a word for such low-lifes - guttersnipes. I haven't used that word for more than 60 years - not until I met that girl and her mother."

[232] Quoted in Ken Russell's obituary by Xan Brooks in the *Guardian* on 28 November 2011.

[233] Martin Chilton, *Daily Telegraph*, 18 March 2015.

[234] www.dangerousminds.net

[235] This can be watched online at http://dangerousminds.net/comments/norman_mailer_and_gore_vidals_infa mous_televised_feud

[236] Boris Katchka, *Mr Tendentious, New York* magazine, 25 November 2007.

[237] Sylvia Miles (1932 -) is best known for her role as a hooker in *Midnight Cowboy* (1969), which earned her an Oscar nomination in 1969 for Best Supporting Actress. She received a second Oscar nomination as Best Supporting Actress for her role in *Farewell, My Lovely* (1975).

[238] The restaurant was called The Ginger Man. According to Roger Ebert, in an article of 20 April 1980, in the Chicago Sun-Times, the incident happened during the New York Film Festival.

[239] John Osborne's threat to Benedict Nightingale and Sheridan Morley is quoted by William Russell and Peter Cargin, in *A Critical Century*, 2014. Page 42.

[240] A.A. (Adrian Anthony) Gill (1954-2016) was a failed artist, dyslexic and alcoholic who reinvented himself as an award-winning TV critic and restaurant reviewer. He was reported to the Commission for Racial Equality in 1998 for describing the Welsh as "loquacious, dissemblers, immoral liars, stunted, bigoted, dark, ugly, pugnacious little trolls". The CRE decided not to prosecute Gill, on the grounds that he was not seeking to stir up racial hatred. Others he insulted included Clare Balding, Mary Beard and the inhabitants of the Isle of Man.

[241] Robert Kilroy's various bruising encounters are reported by Robert Chalmers, *The Independent on Sunday*, 6 June 2004.

[242] Steven Berkoff (1937 -) is an English actor, author, playwright and theatre director. As an actor, he is best known for villainous roles in *Rambo: First Blood Part II*, the James Bond film *Octopussy, Beverly Hills Cop* and the TV mini-series *War and Remembrance* (in which he played Adolf Hitler).

[243] www.movie-film-review.com. The review originally appeared in the *Daily Mail*.

[244] Craig Rosen, Creating the 'Berkovian' Aesthetic, Ph.D dissertation at the University of Colorado 2000.

[245] www.movie-film-review.com. The review originally appeared in the *Daily Mail*.

[246] Christopher Tookey, *Tookey's Turkeys*, *Matador*, 2015. The review originally appeared in the *Daily Mail*.

[247] The London Film Critics' Awards in 1999.

[248] www.movie-film-review.com. The review originally appeared in the *Daily Mail*.

[249] Giles Coren, January 2015, in an answer to a questionnaire I sent him.

[250] Giles Coren interviewed by Chloe Cann for *Xcity*, Spring 2013.

[251] Giles Coren, *Huffington Post*, 7 October 2014.

[252] Gordon Ramsay, *Why I Threw Out A.A.Gill*, *Independent*, 14 October 1998.

[253] *Metro*, 31 October 2007.

[254] William Langewiesche, *The Million-Dollar Nose*, *The Atlantic Monthly*, 2000.

[255] Craig Charles (1964 -) is an English actor, comedian, author, poet, television presenter and disc jockey. He is best known for playing Dave Lister in the British science fiction sitcom *Red Dwarf* and Lloyd Mullaney in *Coronation Street*. In June 2006, newspaper allegations of crack cocaine use resulted in Charles being suspended from *Coronation Street* and BBC Radio 6 Music. In August, Charles was arrested and released on bail pending further enquiries, and in September he accepted a caution for possession of a Class A drug.

[256] Victor Lewis-Smith, *Evening Standard*, 4 May 2004.

[257] Victor Lewis-Smith, *TV Reviews*, CreateSpace Independent Publishing Platform, 2012.

[258] Addison Cresswell (1960 – 2013) was described in Gavin Gaughan's obituary in the *Independent* as having "a public persona not unlike a Cockney villain". He also had the nickname "the Darth Vader of the Fringe".

In his Daily Telegraph obituary, other threats against journalists were recorded: "A gossip columnist once accused Cresswell of threatening to have him kneecapped, while the comedian Martin White has recalled: 'The first time I met Addison Cresswell, he put me in a headlock and threatened me with a broken champagne glass while screaming obscenities.' His agency, Off the Kerb, had a roster of British comedians including Jonathan Ross, Jack Dee, Mark Lamarr, Lee Evans, Jo Brand, Rich Hall, Jeremy Hardy, Michael McIntyre, Dara O' Briain, Alan Carr, Phil Jupitus and Marcus Brigstocke.

[259] Mark Kermode, *Hatchet Job*, Picador 2013.

[260] Barry Norman told me about this over lunch at Langan's Restaurant in the mid-1980s.

[261] Reported in The *Guardian*, 24 September 2013.

[262] Norman Sherry, *The Life of Graham Greene: 1955-1991*, Random House 2005.

[263] Sharon Osbourne (1952 -) is the wife of heavy metal singer-songwriter Ozzy Osbourne and has developed a reality TV career as an English television host, television talent competition judge, author, music manager, businesswoman, and promoter. Her first autobiography *Extreme* sold over two million copies and is the most successful female autobiography ever.

[264] As told to Martin Wainwright, *The Guardian*, 8 December 2006.

[265] Eliana Dockterman, *Time*, 17 July 2012.

[266] These events are recorded by Janielle Asselin in *It Happened to Me: I Received Rape Threats After Criticising a Comic Book*, 24 April 2014, on xojane.com.

[267] Lindy West, *What Happened When I confronted my cruellest troll*, *Guardian*, 2 February 2015.

[268] http://en.wikipedia.org/wiki/Anita_Sarkeesian

[269] Sir Winston Churchill (1874 –1965) was Prime Minister of the United Kingdom from 1940 to 1945 and again from 1951 to 1955. An inspirational wartime leader, Churchill was also an officer in the British Army, a historian, an author and an artist. He won the Nobel Prize in Literature, and was the first person to be made an honorary citizen of the United States.

[270] www.brainyquote.com

[271] Marcus Riley and B.J. Lutz, *Paige Wiser: "I'm Just Mortified"*, Nbcchicago.com, 10 June 2011.

[272] Robert Feder, *How a 'horrible decision' cost Wiser dream job at Chicago Sun-Times, Time Out Chicago,* 9 June 2011.

[273] Matthew Wright (1965 -) is an English television presenter and tabloid journalist, best known for formerly writing for *The Sun* and for being a gossip columnist for *The Daily Mirror.*

[274] Quoted by Lisa O'Carroll, *Guardian,* 11 December 2001.

[275] en.wikipedia.org/wiki/Matthew_Wright

[276] Elkan Allan (1922 –2006) was a British TV producer and print journalist. He is best remembered for his creation of the 1960s TV pop music show *Ready Steady Go!.* After 1968, he was for many years Television Editor of *The Sunday Times.* He wrote three film guides, and I forget in which one his gaffe appeared (I culled it in a clear-out of redundant books after a house movie). It was one of the following: *The Sunday Times Guide to Movies on Television* (1973), *The Sunday Times Guide to the Movies* (1977), or *The Virgin Video Guide* (1982).

[277] *Halliwell's Film Guide,* first published in 1977, was edited by Leslie Halliwell (1929 – 1989) until his death. First John Walker and then David Gritten took over as editors. It ceased publication in 2008.

[278] Stephen Sondheim, *Finishing the Hat,* Alfred A. Knopf, 2010.

[279] Stephen Sondheim, *Finishing the Hat,* Alfred A. Knopf, 2010.

[280] Stephen Sondheim, *Finishing the Hat,* Alfred A. Knopf, 2010.

[281] Stephen Sondheim, *Finishing the Hat,* Alfred A. Knopf, 2010.

[282] Answer to the author's questionnaire, 2015.

[283] Answer to the author's questionnaire, 2015.

[284] Rex Reed, *New York Observer,* 9 July 2013.

[285] Paul M. Rudnick (1957 -) is an American playwright, novelist, screenwriter and essayist. In 1988, he began producingsatirical film criticism for *Premiere Magazine* under the name Libby Gelman-Waxner, a daffy but opinionated Manhattan wife and mother. *Premiere* folded in 2007, but Libby resumed writing a monthly column for *Entertainment Weekly* in 2011. Rudnick's plays include *Jeffrey, The Naked Eye* and *I Hate Hamlet.* He wrote the screenplay for *Sister Act,* originally intended as a vehicle for Bette Midler; by the time it came out with Whoopi Goldberg in the lead, he refused to have his real name associated with it. He received sole writing

credit for *The Addams Family Values*, *In & Out*, and the screen version of his play *Jeffrey*. Other screenplays include *Isn't She Great* and the remake of *The Stepford Wives*.

[286] Libby Gelman-Waxner, *If You Ask Me*, Fawcett Columbine, 1994.

[287] Pauline Kael (1919 – 2001) was an American film critic who was at her best writing for the *New Yorker* magazine from 1968 to 1991.

[288] Herbert Biberman (1900 – 1971) was an American screenwriter and film director, who founded the Screen Directors Guild, which became the Directors' Guild of America. He may be best known for having been one of the "Hollywood Ten", film-makers who were cited for contempt of Congress and blacklisted after refusing to answer HUAC questions about their alleged involvement with the Communist Party. Biberman served six months at a federal institution at Texarkana, Texas.

[289] Paul Jarrico, *Paul Jarrico Reviews Pauline Kael on Salt of the Earth*, *Cineaste*, Fall 2007, Vol. 32 Issue 4, p34. Paul Jarrico was the film's producer.

[290] Bosley Crowther, *New York Times*, March 15, 1954.

[291] Steve Boisson, *Salt of the Earth: The Movie Hollywood Could Not Stop*, American History, February 2002. Kael wrote the review for *Sight and Sound*, in 1954.

[292] www.notable-quotes.com

[293] Richard Brinsley Sheridan (1751-1816) is an Irish-born writer responsible for three fine comedy plays in *The Rivals* (1775), *School For Scandal* (1777) and *The Critic* (1779). He was also a poet, owner of the London's Theatre Royal, Drury Lane until it burnt down, and for 32 years Whig member of parliament for Stafford (1780-1806)

[294] Mark Adams, *Sunday Mirror*, 22 February 2004.

[295] Catherine Shoard, *Sunday Telegraph*, 22 February 2004.

[296] David Gritten, *Daily Telegraph*, 20 February 2004.

[297] James Christopher, *Times*, 20 February 2004.

[298] Mark Adams, *Sunday Mirror*, 31 January 2010.

[299] Peter Bradshaw, *Guardian*, 5 February 2010.

[300] David Jenkins, *Time Out*, 5 February 2010.

[301] Mark Adams, *Sunday Mirror*, 13 December 2009.

[302] Nicholas Barber, *Independent on Sunday*, 5 January 2010.

[303] Robbie Collin, *News of the World*, 5 January 2010.

[304] Ray Bennett, *Hollywood Reporter*, 6 January 2010.

[305] Mark Adams, *Sunday Mirror*, 31 January 2010.

[306] Peter Bradshaw, *Guardian*, 5 February 2010.

[307] Dave Calhoun, *Time Out*, 5 February 2010.

[308] Mark Adams, *Sunday Mirror*, 13 July 2011.

[309] Henry Fitzherbert, *Sunday Express*, 25 June 2010.

[310] Peter Bradshaw, *Guardian*, 23 June 2010.

[311] Anthony Quinn, *Independent*, 24 June 2011.

[312] Mark Adams, *Sunday Mirror*, 7 February 2011.

[313] Manohla Dargis, *New York Times*, 11 February 2011.

[314] Roger Ebert, *Chicago Sun-Times*, 11 February 2011.

[315] Peter Bradshaw, *Guardian*, 16 February 2011.

[316] Mark Adams, *Sunday Mirror*, 26 June 2011.

[317] Michael Phillips, *Chicago Tribune*, 28 June 2011.

[318] Roger Ebert, *Chicago Sun-Times*, 28 June 2011.

[319] Christopher Tookey, *Daily Mail*, 1 April 2011.

[320] James Berardinelli, ReelViews, 26 March 2011.

[321] Mark Adams, *Sunday Mirror*, 27 March 2011.

[322] www.movie-film-review.com/devfilm.asp?rtype=1&id=1272

[323] www.movie-film-review.com/devfilm.asp?rtype=1&id=14710

[324] Baz Bamigboye, *Daily Mail*, 5 December 2007.

[325] http://www.movie-film-review.com/devqwentry.asp?id=85

[326] http://www.movie-film-review.com/devfilm.asp?rtype=1&id=14710

[327] http://www.movie-film-review.com/devFilm.asp?ID=14956

[328] http://www.movie-film-review.com/devFilm.asp?id=15524

[329] http://www.movie-film-review.com/devqwentry.asp?id=85

[330] Baz Bamigboye, *Daily Mail*, 2 September 2011.

[331] Christopher Tookey, *Daily Mail*, 20 January 2011.

[332] Philip French, *Observer*, 22 January 2012.

[333] Peter Bradshaw, *Guardian*, 19 January 2012.

[334] Robbie Collin, *Daily Telegraph*, 19 January 2012.

[335] Jonathan Ross's verdict was "Funny and very watchable... Tremendous moments... I thoroughly recommend *Striptease*." http://www.movie-film-review.com/devqwentry.asp?id=19

[336] About *Vanilla Sky*, Jonathan Ross opined "Cruise is great, Diaz is fabulous... Splendidly entertaining." http://www.movie-film-review.com/devqwentry.asp?id=19

[337] http://www.movie-film-review.com/devqwentry.asp?id=19

[338] Alexander Walker, *Evening Standard*, http://www.movie-film-review.com/devfilm.asp?rtype=3&id=12643

[339] Cosmo Landesman, *Sunday Times*, http://www.movie-film-review.com/devfilm.asp?rtype=3&id=12643

[340] Christopher Tookey, *Daily Mail*, 14 November 1998

[341] http://www.movie-film-review.com/devfilm.asp?rtype=1&id=15298

[342] James Christopher, *Times*, 19 March 2009.

[343] Philip French, *Observer*, 22 March 2009.

[344] Christopher Tookey, Daily Mail, 20 March 2009.

[345] Reply to the author's questionnaire, 2015.

[346] Tom Sutcliffe, *The Retiring President's Farewell, Critics' Circular*, Issue 9, 2012, p8.

[347] Tom Sutcliffe, *The Retiring President's Farewell, Critics' Circular*, Issue 9, 2012, p8.

[348] Brian Sewell (1931-2015) was a British art critic who most frequently wrote for the *Evening Standard* in London. He won many awards, and became a media celebrity because of his plummy voice and delight in controversy. He had an entertainingly bleak view of the Turner Prize, conceptual art and other art critics.

[349] Brian Sewell, *Evening Standard*, 31 October, 2003.

[350] Brian Dillon, *Fact*, 11 February 2005.

[351] Roger Ebert, *Chicago Sun-Times*, 2 February 1997.

[352] Jerry Roberts, *The Hollywood Scandal Almanac: 12 Months of Sinister, Salacious and Senseless History!*, The History Press, 2012.

[353] Sara Gaines, *Guardian*, 4 June 2001.

[354] *Robert W. Welkos, Sony Gets Caught in a Second Ad Blunder, Los Angeles Times*, 16 June 2001. Sony suspended Josh Goldstine, senior vice president of creative advertising, and Matthew Cramer, a director of creative advertising, in connection with the Manning scandal. Cramer reportedly used the name of an old college pal at USC when he came up with the name David Manning.

[355] Patrick Goldstein, *Studios' Web 'Plants' Lead to an Ethical Thicket, LA Times*, 1 October 2002.

[356] Patrick Goldstein, *Studios' Web 'Plants' Lead to an Ethical Thicket, LA Times*, 1 October 2002.

[357] Eric Childress, *Criticwatch – You Will Believe Warner Bros. will Use Junket Whores*, lwww.efilmcritic.com, 5 June 2013.

[358] Christopher Tookey, *Daily Mail*, June 1995. The review is included in Christopher Tookey, *Tookey's Talkies*, Matador, 2015.

[359] Mary Kenny described *Pulp Fiction* as "disgusting, violent, repellent, dangerous to young and unformed minds, childish, irrational, horrible, agonising, and distressingly like something out of a Nazi nightmare where human beings are subjected to every degradation just for the hell of it."

[360] www.movie-film-review.com/devFilm.asp?ID=4678

[361] http://www.movie-film-review.com/devFilm.asp?ID=15904

[362] In April 2012, Paul Field became editor of *Mail Plus*, a daily tablet edition of the newspaper, but he parted company with the *Mail* in December 2013. He is now a "boutique content strategy and digital publishing consultant".

[363] Answer to author's questionnaire, 2015.

[364] William Turvill, *Sacked Sunday Express critic tells of being told to change star ratings and get free theatre tickets for Desmond, Press Gazette,* 22 September 2014.

[365] Phone conversation with the author, 22 January 2015.

[366] Phone conversation with the author, 22 January 2015.

[367] Charles Spencer, *Daily Telegraph*, 2 November 2009.

[368] Jessica Elgot, *Despicable Me 2 Has Been Dragged Into the Daily Telegraph Advertising Scandal,* 19 February 2015.

[369] Tim Robey, *Daily Telegraph*, 28 September 2014.

[370] Jessica Elgot, *Despicable Me 2 Has Been Dragged Into the Daily Telegraph Advertising Scandal,* 19 February 2015.

[371] John Plunkett and Ben Quinn, *Telegraph's Peter Oborne resigns, saying HSBC coverage a 'fraud on readers', Guardian,* 18 February 2015.

[372] Guido Fawkes, *Media Guido,* 18 February 2015. www.Order-order.com.

[373] Robbie Collin, *Daily Telegraph*, 10 October 2014.

[374] David Gritten, *Daily Telegraph*, 9 October 2013,

[375] William Russell, reply to author's questionnaire, early 2015.

[376] Spiro T. Agnew (1918 – 1996) was the 39th Vice President of the United States, under Richard Nixon.

[377] www.politicaldictionary.com/words/nattering-nabobs-of-negativism. Agnew said this while speaking to the California Republican state convention on September 11, 1970. Though generally credited to Agnew, the line was actually written by White House speechwriter William Safire. Safire (1929 - 2009) was a public relations executive from 1955 to 1960 but became an author, columnist, journalist, and presidential speechwriter. In 1973, he joined the *New York Times* as a political columnist. Soon afterwards, he learned that he had been the target of "national security" wiretaps authorized by Nixon, and wrote with what he characterized as "restrained fury" that he had not worked for Nixon through a difficult decade

"to have him — or some lizard-lidded paranoid acting without his approval — eavesdropping on my conversations."

378 Maureen Ryan, *How To Be a TV Critic, Huffington Post*, 14 December 2011.

379 Mark Kermode, *Hatchet Job*, Picador, 2013.

380 Quoted by Guy Kelly, *Daily Telegraph*, 16 January 2015.

381 Quoted by Christopher Bray, Review of *I Found It At The Movies* by Philip French, *Observer Review*, 1 May 2011.

382 Quoted by Christopher Bray, Review of *I Found It At The Movies* by Philip French, *Observer Review*, 1 May 2011.

383 Howard Jacobson, *We have a right to be grumpy old people – there's much to be angry about nowadays, Independent*, 21 June 2013.

384 Quoted in Christopher Tookey, *Named and Shamed*, 2010, p197.

385 Joe Queenan, *Don't Get Cute, Guardian*, 24 December 2008.

386 Joe Queenan, *The Unkindest Cut: How a Hatchet-Man Critic Made His Own $7,000 Movie and Put It All on His Credit Card*, Hyperion Books, 1997.

387 Michael Billington, *Who Needs Critics? Why you do, Mr Sondheim, Guardian*, 23 November 2011.

388 Dwight Garner, *A Critic's Case for Critics Who Are Actually Critical, New York Times*, 15 August 2012.

389 Charlie Brooker, *Guardian*, 15 October 2010.

390 *Charie Brooker's Screenwipe*, quoted on www.tv.com.

391 Charlie Brooker, *Twilight's sulky vampires are less frightening than a knitted cushion, Guardian*, 12 July 2010.

392 Charlie Brooker, *A glance at the cinema listings proves Hollywood's imagination has crashed*, 3 August 2009.

393 Mark Kermode's rant against *Sex and the City 2* from 28 May 2010 can be heard and seen at
https://www.youtube.com/watch?v=daOfhAGGuo8 (part 1) and at
https://www.youtube.com/watch?v=MGsOxC2T6U8 (part 2).

[394] Lindy West, *Burkas and Birkins, The Stranger*, 27 May 2010.

[395] Libby Gelman-Waxner, *If You Ask Me*, Fawcett Columbine, 1994.

[396] Libby Gelman-Waxner, *If You Ask Me*, Fawcett Columbine, 1994.

[397] Roger Ebert was quoted by Marc Caro in the *Chicago Tribune* of 22 February 1999.

[398] Kira Cochrane, *Don't Mess with Michiko Kakutani, Guardian*, 1 May 2008.

[399] *Worst Book Reviews: Michiko Kakutani's 11 Meanest Reviews, Huffington Post*, 28 August 2012.

[400] Kira Cochrane, *Don't Mess with Michiko Kakutani, Guardian*, 1 May 2008.

[401] *Worst Book Reviews: Michiko Kakutani's 11 Meanest Reviews, Huffington Post*, 28 August 2012.

[402] Michiko Kautani reviewing Donna Tartt's *The Secret History* (1992), New York Times, 4 September 1992.

[403] Jay Rayner, *Beyond Belief, Observer*, 23 November 2008.

[404] Jay Rayner, *My Dining Hell: Twenty Ways to Have a Lousy Night Out*, Penguin, 25 May 2012.

[405] Jay Rayner, *My Dining Hell: Twenty Ways to Have a Lousy Night Out*, Penguin, 25 May 2012.

[406] Giles Coren quoted by James Weston in *Cherwell*, 11 February 2011.

[407] Giles Coren, *Potty-mouthed and proud, Spectator*, 1 October 2008.

[408] Giles Coren, *You Big Softie: Has Giles Coren put down his poison pen?. Evening Standard*, 24 May 2012.

[409] Quoted by Steven Baxter, *Yes, Giles Coren is absurdly thin-skinned, but aren't most writers?, New Statesman*, 28 August 2012.

[410] Giles Coren, *You Big Softie: Has Giles Coren put down his poison pen?. Evening Standard*, 24 May 2012.

[411] Giles Coren, *You Big Softie: Has Giles Coren put down his poison pen?. Evening Standard*, 24 May 2012.

[412] Anthony Burch, *Five Things I Didn't Get About Making Video Games (Until I Did It)*, www.kotaku.com.

[413] Martin Amis, *The War Against Cliché*, Vintage, 2001.

[414] Gore Vidal, *Literary Gangsters*, 1970 essay in *United States: Essays 1952-1992*, Abacus 1993.

[415] http://www.movie-film-review.com/devharsh.asp?act=2&param=623

[416] http://www.movie-film-review.com/devharsh.asp?act=2&param=887

[417] www.en.wikipedia.org/wiki/John_Simon_(critic)

[418] www.movie-film-review.com/devharsh.asp?act=2&param=792

[419] http://www.movie-film-review.com/devharsh.asp?act=2&param=840

[420] Simon Cowell (1959 -) is a music and television producer. He is known in the United Kingdom and United States for his role as a talent judge on TV shows such as *Pop Idol*, *The X Factor*, *Britain's Got Talent* and *American Idol*. He owns the television production and music publishing house Syco. In 2013, *TV Guide* named him #10 in their list of The 60 Nastiest Villains of All Time.

[421] Naomi Gordon, *17 of Simon Cowell's Best Insults*, www.digitalspy.co.uk, 7 October 2013.

[422] http://www.evancarmichael.com.

[423] http://www.evancarmichael.com.

[424] Luchina Fisher, *Obsessive Fan of Paula Abdul Commits Suicide*, ABC News, 13 November 2008.

[425] Jarett Wieselman, *New York Post*, 12 November 2008.

[426] *Mail Online*, 14 November 2008.

[427] Quoted by Michael Starr, *Simon 'appalled by self'*, New York Post, 4 March 2010.

[428] Joseph Addison, *Spectator*, No. 291, 1712.

[429] I first met Emma Watson (1990 -) when she was about ten, playing in our back garden in Alwyne Villas, Islington with my son Dan. Her father lived across the communal garden, in Alwyne Place.

[430] Camilla Long, *Richard Dawkins: God, is that your best shot?, Sunday Times*, 19 February 2012.

[431] Camilla Long, *Nigel Farage: Brimming over with bile and booze, Sunday Times*, 20 March 2010. Her arresting first line was "I'm quite relieved that Nigel Farage MEP has only one testicle."

[432] Gawain Towler, *Checking your facts – to every last detail*, blog at *journalism.co.uk*, 22 March 2010.

[433] Reply to the author's questionnaire, early 2015.

[434] Waldemar Januszczak wrote in the *Guardian* that Fuller was "unquestionably the most impressive art critic working in Britain... In terms of learning, range, perseverance, intellectual ambition, he is a lesson to us all... He displays a breadth of knowledge and an intellectual commitment to discovery which puts every other British art critic to shame."

[435] Peter Fuller, *Theoria: Art and the Absence of Grace*, Chatto & Windus, 1988. Page 3.

[436] Peter Fuller, *Theoria: Art and the Absence of Grace*, Chatto & Windus , 1988. Pages 3-4.

[437] Peter Fuller, *Theoria: Art and the Absence of Grace*, Chatto & Windus, 1988. Page 4.

[438] Clive James, *Whither the Hatchet Job?, New York Times*, 1 June 2013.

[439] *Omnivore* press release, www.hatchetjobof theyear.com, 16 December 2011.

[440] Adam Mars Jones, *Adam Mars-Jones: 'The only bad review is one whose writing is soggy', Observer*, 20 February 2012.

[441] Adam Mars Jones, *By Nightfall by Michael Cunningham – review, Observer*, 23 January 2011.

[442] Alison Flood, *Hatchet Job of the Year goes to assault on Rachel Cusk, Guardian*, 12 February 2013.

[443] Camilla Long, *Sunday Times*, 4 March 2012.

[444] Zoe Heller, *The Salman Rushdie Case, New York Review of Books*, 20 December 2012.

[445] Alison Flood, *Hatchet Job of the Year goes to AA Gill for Morrissey broadside, Guardian*, 11 February 2004.

[446] A.A. Gill, *Sunday Times*, 27 October 2013.

[447] Craig Brown, *Daily Mail*, 9 March 2013.

[448] Roy Greenslade, *The meaning of 'fruit': how the Daily Mirror libeled Liberace, Guardian*, 26 May 2009.

[449] *Liberace, the Daily Mirror, secret sixties gay London, and the mysterious death of a show business lawyer, Gay History*, 8 June 2013.

[450] *Liberace, the Daily Mirror, secret sixties gay London, and the mysterious death of a show business lawyer, Gay History*, 8 June 2013.

[451] *Liberace, the Daily Mirror, secret sixties gay London, and the mysterious death of a show business lawyer, Gay History*, 8 June 2013.

[452] Revel Barker, *Crying All The Way To The Bank*, Revel Barker, 2009.

[453] *Glasgow Herald*, 19 December 1985.

[454] Nina Myskow, *'Wally of the Week' column, Sunday People*, 1983.

[455] Tom Crone, *Law and the Media*, CRC Press, 2013

[456] Paul Magrath, *Law Report: 'Hideously ugly' tag could be defamatory, Independent*, 4 October 1996.

[457] Paul Magrath, *Law Report: 'Hideously ugly' tag could be defamatory, Independent*, 4 October 1996.

[458] http://mavrkydefamationcaselaw.blogspot.co.uk

[459] James Wilson, *An Ugly Affair*, New Law Journal, 2013. To be found at http://www.newlawjournal.co.uk

[460] Rex Reed, *New York Observer*, 5 February 2013.

[461] It would, however, be discourteous to name names, so I won't.

[462] Christopher Tookey, *Daily Mail*, 22 March 2013.

[463] Peter Bradshaw, *Guardian*, 22 March 2013.

[464] Rex Reed, *New York Observer,* 3 July 2014.

[465] Rex Reed, *New York Observer,* 3 July 2014.

[466] Charles Spencer (1955 -) was chief drama critic of the *Daily Telegraph* from 1991-2014. He suffered from alcoholism and long bouts of clinical depression, but won Critic of the Year at the 1999 British Press wards. His claim that Nicole Kidman's occasionally nude performance in the Blue Room at the Donmar Warehouse was "pure theatrical Viagra" earned him national fame, although I was sitting close to Charlie and didn't notice any evidence of arousal, though admittedly I wasn't really looking at him.

[467] Charles Spencer, *review of the Blue Room, Daily Telegraph,* 23 September 1998.

[468] Both Charles Spencer's *Daily Telegraph* review and Maureen Lipman's response are quoted by William Russell and Peter Cargin, in *A Critical Century,* 2014. Page 42.

[469] Chris Hastings, *Daily Telegraph,* 11 April 2009.

[470] *Glyndebourne opera critics spark 'sexism' row, BBC News,* 22 May 2014.

[471] *Glyndebourne opera critics spark 'sexism' row, BBC News,* 22 May 2014.

[472] Rupert Christiansen, *Daily Telegraph,* 21 May 2014.

[473] Rupert Christiansen, *Daily Telegraph,* 21 May 2014.

[474] Graham Greene, *Night and Day,* 29 July 1937.

[475] Shirley Temple (1928 – 2014) was a child star at the height of her fame between 1934 and 1938 in a string of hits including *Little Miss Marker* (1934), *Wee Willie Winkie* (1937) and *Rebecca of Sunnybrook Farm* (1938). Her chirpy performances were a big antidote to the economic times. "During this depression, when the spirit of the people is lower than at any other time, it is a splendid thing that, for just 15 cents, an American can go to a movie and look at the smiling face of a baby and forget his troubles," Franklin D Roosevelt stated in 1935. She later, as Shirley Temple Black, became a Republican politician and US ambassador to Czechoslovaka.

[476] Graham Greene, *Spectator,* 7 August 1936.

[477] Graham Greene, *Night and Day,* 28 October 1937.

[478] Andrew Johnson, *Shirley Temple scandal was real reason Graham Greene fled to Mexico, Independent,* 18 November 2007.

[479] Andrew Johnson, *Shirley Temple scandal was real reason Graham Greene fled to Mexico, Independent,* 18 November 2007.

[480] Shirley Temple, *Child Star: an autobiography*, McGraw Hill Book Co., 1988.

[481] Helen Dowd, *Men Who Made Judy a Monster, Daily Express,* 18 June 2008.

[482] Kael's review can be read in full in *Pauline Kael, When The Lights Go Down, Complete reviews 1965-80,* Marion Boyars, 1980

[483] http://www.movie-film-review.com/devharsh.asp?act=2&param=696

[484] Simon's review can be read in full in *John Simon on Film: Criticism 1973-2001,* Applause Theatre Book Publishers, 2005. My own feeling is that *Bugsy Malone* was an innocent pastiche which pointed up the clichés of the gangster genre and gently satirized the childishness of criminal behaviour. However, the sexualisation of children to which some critics took exception is there - especially in Jodie Foster's performance, which is knowing for her years. She was probably affected by her most recent role - as a child prostitute in Martin Scorsese's *Taxi Driver* (1976).

[485] Libby Gelman-Waxner, *If You Ask Me*, Fawcett Columbine, 1994.

[486] Libby Gelman-Waxner, *If You Ask Me*, Fawcett Columbine, 1994.

[487] Libby Gelman-Waxner, *If You Ask Me*, Fawcett Columbine, 1994.

[488] Ava Gardner, *Ava: My Story*, Bantam USA, 1990.

[489] Rod Liddle, *Sunday Times*, reported by Piers Morgan in *Don't You Know Who I Am?: Insider Diaries of Fame, Power and Naked Ambition*, Random House, 2012. P26.

[490] Charlie Brooker, *Guardian*, reported by Piers Morgan in *Don't You Know Who I Am?: Insider Diaries of Fame, Power and Naked Ambition*, Random House, 2012. P26.

[491] *Clive James: 30 Classic Quotes, Daily Telegraph*, 21 June 2012.

[492] Clive James, *Postcard From Los Angeles: 2,* June 17, 1979

[493] Sir Herbert Beerbohm Tree (1852 – 1917) was an English actor and theatre manager. He founded the Royal Academy of Dramatic Art in 1904 and was knighted, for his contributions to theatre, in 1909. His illegitimate children included film director Carol Reed, and a grandson was the actor Oliver Reed.

[494] www.insults.net.

[495] Cyril Connolly, *Sunday Times*, 29 September 1929.

[496] Christopher Tookey, *Named and Shamed*, Matador, 2010 , p73.

[497] James Agee, *Time*, 15 December, 1947.

[498] Christopher Tookey, *Daily Mail*, 11 April 2013.

[499] Sirhan Sirhan (1944 -) is a Palestinian of Jordanian citizenship who was convicted of the 1968 assassination of U.S. Senator Robert F. Kennedy. He is currently serving a life sentence in San Diego County, California.

[500] Ben Lewis, Sunday Times, 5 October 2008.

[501] Lynn Barber (1944 -) is an English journalist whose account of her early sex life was filmed as *An Education* (2009). While studying for her A levels, she had a two-year relationship with an older man, whom she knew as Simon Goldman, but who also called himself Simon Prewalski He was an associate of Peter Rachman, a notoriously exploitative and intimidating landlord in the Notting Hill area of London. In 2010 Barber confessed on *Desert Island Discs* that she had slept with "probably 50 men" during two terms at Oxford: " I was just jamming them in." she said. From 1967-74, she worked for the porn magazine *Penthouse*. From 1982-89 she was a feature writer on the *Sunday Express* magazine, and joined *The Independent on Sunday* before its launch in 1990. Now she writes mostly for the *Sunday Times*, where she became famous for abrasive interviews. After one of these, with the conceptual artists Jake and Dinos Chapman, the interviewees threatened to kill her if they ever met again. Barber was selected as Interviewer of the Year at the British Press Awards in 1985, 1986, 1990, 1996, 2002 and 2012.

[502] Quoted by Francis Wheen, *Financial Times*, 5 August 2011.

[503] Lynn Barber, *Daily Telegraph*, 1 November 2008.

[504] *Sarah Thornton – an apology, Daily Telegraph*, 26 September 2009.

[505] *Sarah Thornton – an apology, Daily Telegraph*, 26 September 2009.

[506] Joan Drutt, *The Reviewer who tried to kill the book*, http://joan-druett.blogspot.co.uk, 2 August 2011.

[507] Sarah Thornton, *My libel victory underlines the need for journalists to check their facts, Guardian,* 29 July 2011.

[508] *Sarah Thornton – an apology, Daily Telegraph,* 26 September 2009.

[509] Rob Sharp, *Has Lynn Barber killed the art of criticism?, Independent,* 28 July 2011.

[510] Quoted by Josh Halliday, *Guardian,* 26 July 2011.

[511] *Writer Sarah Thornton wins £65,000 damages over review, BBC News,* 27 July 2011.

[512] Lynn Barber, *Daily Telegraph,* 1 November 2008.

[513] Sarah Thornton, *My libel victory underlines the need for journalists to check their facts, Guardian,* 29 July 2011.

[514] Dame Zaha Mohammad Hadid (1950 - 2016) was an Iraqi-British architect. She received the Pritzker Architecture Prize in 2004 — the first woman to do so — and the Stirling Prize in 2010 and 2011.

[515] Martin Filler, *The Insolence of Architecture, New York Review of Books,* 5 June 2014.

[516] Anna Kats, Zaha Hadid's Trials and Tribulations, ww.blouartinfo.com, 26 August 2014

[517] Joanna Walters, *New York Review of Books critic 'regrets error' in Zaha Hadid article, Guardian,* 26 August 2014.

[518] Anna Kats, Zaha Hadid's Trials and Tribulations, ww.blouartinfo.com, 26 August 2014

[519] Paul Goldberger, *Vanity Fair,* 27 August 2014.

[520] Anna Kats, Zaha Hadid's Trials and Tribulations, ww.blouartinfo.com, 26 August 2014

[521] Jay Rayner, *My Dining Hell: Twenty Ways To Have A Lousy Night Out,* Penguin, 2012.

[522] Jay Rayner, *McDonald's, Guardian,* 22 June 2003.

[523] http://www.shortnews.com/start.cfm?id=31135

[524] http://www.freerepublic.com/focus/f-news/920911/posts

[525] Jay Rayner, *McDonald's, Guardian*, 22 June 2003.

[526] Valentine Low, *Critic threatened with legal action, Evening Standard*, 11 April 2015.

[527] http://forums.egullet.org/topic/36035-critic-sued-by-restaurant

[528] Caroline Workman, *Irish News*, 26 August 2000.

[529] Quoted by Maev Kennedy, *Critics bite back after restaurant reviewer sued for calling chicken too sweet, Observer*, 20 February.

[530] *Appeal overturns food review case*, BBC News, 10 March 2008.

[531] Sean Megehan, *The Porcini was praiseworthy. But a Lawsuit was Served Next, New York Times*, 23 August 2004.

[532] Walter Olson, *Update: Dallas paper agrees to second restaurant review, overlawyered.com*, 3 January 2006.

[533] Nancy Nichols, *Where is Dotty Griffith?, www.sidedish.dmagazine.com*, 8 August 2008.

[534] Quoted in *Philafoodie, Adventures in food and wine in Philadelphia*, 27 February 2007.

[535] Adam Liptak, *Serving You Tonight Will Be Our Lawyer, New York Times*, 7 March 2007.

[536] *An Update on the Chops v Leban Lawsuit, Philafoodie, Adventures in food and wine in Philadelphia*, 18 June 2007.

[537] Michael Klein, *Chops steak houses are closing, Philly.com*, 28 June 2013.

[538] Adam Liptak, *Serving You Tonight Will Be Our Lawyer, New York Times*, 7 March 2007.

[539] Richard Ackland, *When judges judge critics, the results can taste a bit like reflux, Sydney Morning Herald*, 2 December 2011.

[540] Richard Ackland, *When judges judge critics, the results can taste a bit like reflux, Sydney Morning Herald*, 2 December 2011.

[541] Lema Samandar, *Former reviewer Matthew Evans, who cost Fairfax $600,000, has turned to farming and television, Australian Daily Telegraph*, 10 June 2014.

[542] Christopher Tookey, *Tookey's Turkeys*, Matador, 2015.

[543] Caryn James, *New York Times*, 24 May 1995.

[544] www.movie-film-review.com/devfilm.asp?rtype=1&id=2236

[545] Roger Ebert, *Chicago Sun-Times*, 24 May 1995.

[546] Peter Bradshaw, Guardian, 7 March 2004.

[547] Roger Ebert, *Chicago Sun-Times*, I October 2004.

[548] Martin Amis (1949 -) is best-known for the novels *The Rachel Papers*, Penguin (his 1973 debut, which won the Somerset Maugham Award), *Money*, Vintage (1984) and *London Fields*, Vintage (1989). He received the James Tait Black Memorial Prize for his memoir *Experience*, Vintage. Fond of depicting the sordid and debauched, he is often regarded as a master of what the *New York Times* called "the new unpleasantness".

[549] Julian Barnes (1946 -) had three of his earlier books shortlisted for the Booker Prize: *Flaubert's Parrot*, Vintage (1984), *England, England*, Vintage (1998), and *Arthur & George*, Vintage (2005). He eventually won the Man Booker Prize for his book *The Sense of an Ending*, Vintage (2011). Other honours include the Somerset Maugham Award and the Geoffrey Faber Memorial Prize. In 2004 he became a Commandeur of L'Ordre des Arts et des Lettres. From 1979 to 1986 he worked as a television critic, first for the *New Statesman* and then for *The Observer*, succeeding Clive James.

[550] Christopher Hitchens (1949 - 2011) was an author, literary critic and journalist who produced over thirty books, including five collections of essays, mostly on politics, literature and religion. He won numerous awards and became a noted critic of religion and such public figures as Mother Teresa, Bill Clinton and Pope Benedict XVI. Though he was often described as "neo-conservative", especially after 9/11, he was never as right-wing as his younger brother, columnist Peter Hitchens; Chris continued to describe himself as a socialist and Marxist, and was, instinctively, anti-totalitarian.

[551] Craig Raine (1944 -) was a fellow of New College, Oxford from 1991 to 2010 and is now emeritus professor. He has been the editor of *Areté* since 1999. He is best known as a "Martian poet", with a tendency to see old things in unfamiliar ways, and his works include several poetry collections: *The Onion, Memory*, Oxford University Press (1978), *A Martian Sends a Postcard Home*, Oxford University Press (1979), *A Free Translation*, Salamander (1981), *Rich*, Faber and Faber (1984), *History: The Home Movie*, Penguin (1994), and *Clay. Whereabouts Unknown*, Penguin (1996). His reviews and essays are collected in two anthologies: *Haydn and the Valve Trumpet*, Faber and Faber (1990) and *In Defence of T. S. Eliot*, Picador (2000).

[552] Preface to *The War on Cliché* by Martin Amis, Vintage, 2002.

[553] I knew them best in the years 1969-73, when I was an undergraduate at Exeter College, Oxford. Martin Amis, who was thinking about writing a novel, was a year ahead of me at Exeter and despite his lack of height at 5'4" a distinct hit with the ladies. Craig Raine was an English lecturer at Exeter College and an aspiring poet. Chris Hitchens was a firebrand of the student left, who went to work at the *Times Higher Education Supplement* in 1971, where he served as social science correspondent until he was fired. Future novelist Julian Barnes had recently graduated from Magdalen College, Oxford, and was working at the Oxford University Press as a lexicographer for the Oxford English Dictionary supplement. Julian lived in a house in east Oxford with my friend, the poet Christopher Reid (also at Exeter College), who went on to become the leading "Martian poet" along with Craig Raine. The boozy Buddy Holly evening in question, which took place at some point during 1971, did not include Chris Hitchens, who must have been drinking somewhere else that night.

[554] Charles Hardin Holley (1936 – 1959), better known as Buddy Holly, was an American musician and singer-songwriter, whose biggest hits included *That'll Be the Day* and *Peggy Sue*. He died in a plane crash, along with Ritchie Valens and J.P. "Big Bopper" Richardson, inspiring Don Maclean's classic tribute song *American Pie*.

[555] Quoted in Robert Hughes, *The Shock of the New*, 1980. Page 95. Alexander Rodchenko (1891-1956) was a Russian artist, sculptor, photographer and graphic designer. He was a founding father of constructivism and became famous for his photographs of Soviet sporting achievements and military parades.

[556] Peter Fuller, *Theoria: Art, and the Absence of Grace*, Chatto & Windus, 1988. Page 177. Louis Aragon (1897-1982) was a French poet, novelist and editor. He was a longtime member of the Communist Party, until his death.

[557] George Steiner (1929 -) is an American literary critic, philosopher, novelist and educator. Steiner was Professor of English and Comparative Literature at the University of Geneva (1974–94), Professor of Comparative Literature and Fellow at the University of Oxford (1994–95) and Professor of Poetry at Harvard University (2001–02). He lives in Cambridge, England, where he has been Extraordinary Fellow at Churchill College since 1969.

[558] George Steiner interviewed in Autumn 1994 by Ronald A. Sharp, *The Paris Review*, Winter 1995.

[559] Harold Bloom (1930 -) is an American literary critic and Sterling Professor of Humanities at Yale University. Bloom has written more than 20

books of literary criticism, several books discussing religion, and a novel. His books have been translated into more than 40 languages.

560 Harold Bloom, *Ranting Against Cant, Atlantic Unbound*, 16 June 2003.

561 Harold Bloom, *Ranting Against Cant, Atlantic Unbound*, 16 June 2003.

562 Harold Bloom, *Ranting Against Cant, Atlantic Unbound*, 16 June 2003.

563 Geoff Dyer (1958 -) Geoff Dyer is the English author of four novels and seven books of non-fiction, which have won a number of literary awards and been translated into 24 languages.

564 Geoff Dyer, *Out of Sheer Rage: In The Shadow of D.H. Lawrence*, Abacus, *1998*

565 Roger Scruton (1944 -) is an English philosopher, a conservative and an expert on aesthetics.

566 Roger Scruton, in an interview with Spencer Case for *The College Fix, University of Colorado Boulder*, 14 March 2014.

567 Roger Scruton, in an interview with Spencer Case for *The College Fix, University of Colorado Boulder*, 14 March 2014.

568 Roger Scruton, in an interview with Spencer Case for *The College Fix, University of Colorado Boulder*, 14 March 2014.

569 Roger Scruton, in an interview with Spencer Case for *The College Fix, University of Colorado Boulder*, 14 March 2014.

570 Roger Scruton, in an interview with Spencer Case for *The College Fix, University of Colorado Boulder*, 14 March 2014.

571 Antonio Gramsci (1891 – 1937) was an Italian Marxist theoretician and politician who wrote on political theory, sociology and linguistics. He was a founding member and one-time leader of the Communist Party of Italy and was imprisoned by Benito Mussolini's Fascist regime. Gramsci evolved a theory of cultural hegemony, which describes how states use cultural institutions to maintain power in capitalist societies.

572 Gyorgy Lukács (1885 – 1971) was a Hungarian Marxist philosopher, aesthetician, literary historian, and critic. He was one of the founders of Western Marxism, which departed from the Marxist orthodoxies of the USSR.

573 Herbert Marcuse (1898 – 1979) was a German-American philosopher, sociologist, and political theorist. In his written works, he criticised

capitalism, technology, historical materialism and entertainment culture, arguing that they represent new forms of social control.

[574] Quoted in Robin Phillips, *The Illusionist: How Herbert Marcuse Convinced a Generation that Censorship Is Tolerance & Other Politically Correct Tricks*, *Salvo* magazine, Spring 2012.

[575] Robin Phillips, *The Illusionist: How Herbert Marcuse Convinced a Generation that Censorship Is Tolerance & Other Politically Correct Tricks*, *Salvo* magazine, Spring 2012.

[576] Daniel J. Flynn, *Intellectual Morons: How Ideology Makes Smart People Fall for Stupid Ideas*, Crown Forum, 2004.

[577] Colleen Flaherty, *Doing Themselves In?*, *www.insidehighered.com*, 20 October 2014.

[578] Roger Scruton, *What Ever Happened to Reason?*, *City Journal*, Spring 1999.

[579] Roger Scruton, *Islam and the West: Lines of Demarcation*, *Azure no 35*, Winter 2009.

[580] Abraham Lincoln (1809 – 1865) was the 15th president of the United States, serving from 1861 until his assassination in 1865. He led the United States through its Civil War, abolished slavery and went some way towards modernizing the economy.

[581] thinkexist.com

[582] Ralph Waldo Emerson, *Journals*, 1847.

[583] George Perry, *The Dilys Powell Film Reader*, Carcanet, 1991.

[584] Irving Wardle, *Theatre Criticism*, Routledge, 1992.

[585] Irving Wardle, *Theatre Criticism*, Routledge, 1992.

[586] Stephen Potter (1900 – 1969) was a British author best known for his comic self-help books including *The Theory and Practice of Gamesmanship: Or the Art of Winning Games Without Actually Cheating*. Several of his books were adapted for the cinema in the 1960s and for television in the 1970s.

[587] Stephen Potter is quoted on Goodreads.com and the website of the Los Angeles Review of Books.

[588] Stephen Fry (1957 -) (born 24 August 1957) is an English comedian,

actor, writer, presenter and activist. After being expelled from two schools and spending three months in prison for credit card fraud, Fry studied English literature at Queens' College, Cambridge, gaining a second-class degree,   and became involved with the Cambridge Footlights and long-time collaborator Hugh Laurie. As half of the comic double act Fry and Laurie, he co-wrote and co-starred in *A Bit of Fry & Laurie*, and took the role of Jeeves in *Jeeves and Wooster*. Though cast in Simon Gray's 1995 play *Cell Mates*, he left three days into the West End run, claiming stage fright. He is also the long-time host of the BBC television quiz show *QI*. He wrote and presented the Emmy Award–winning *Stephen Fry: The Secret Life of the Manic Depressive*, which explored his own mental illness.

[589] Christopher Tookey, *Daily Mail*, 30 November 2007.

[590] Christopher Tookey, *Daily Mail*, 24 August, 2011.

[591] Nigel Andrews, answering the author's questionnaire, January 2015.

[592] William Hazlitt, *On Criticism*, in *Table Talk, Essays on Men and Manners*, 1822.

[593] William Hazlitt, *On the Works of Hogarth &c, Lectures on the English comic writers*, 1819.

[594] William Hazlitt, *On Gusto* from The Round Table, 1817.

[595] William Hazlitt, *Characters of Shakespeare's Plays*, 1854.

[596] William Hazlitt, *Mrs Siddons' Lady Macbeth*, in *A View of the English Stage: or, a series of dramatic criticisms, etc.*, 1818.

[597] William Hazlitt, *The Spirit of the Age, or Contemporary Portraits*, 1825.

[598] William Hazlitt, *The Spirit of the Age, or Contemporary Portraits*, 1825.

[599] William Hazlitt, *The Spirit of the Age, or Contemporary Portraits*, 1825.

[600] William Carew Hazlitt, *Memoirs of William Hazlitt: With Portions of His Correspondence, Volume 2*, 1867.

[601]   Arnold Hauser, *Social History of Art, Volume 4: Naturalism, Impressionism, The Film Age*, 1999.

[602] John Ruskin, *The Library Edition of the Works of John Ruskin*, edited by E.T. Cook and Alexander Wedderburn, 1903-12. Volume V, Page 425.

[603] When asked to visit Keble, Ruskin replied "No! If it is new, it is hideous." Quoted in Ruskin's *Letters to H.G. and M.G.*, 1903. Page 28.

[604] Peter Fuller, *Theoria: Art, and the Absence of Grace*, Chatto & Windus, 1988. Page 107.

[605] John Ruskin, *Modern Painters, Volume 1*, 1873. Page 325.

[606] Oscar Wilde, *The Critic as Artist*, 1890, in *The Critic as Artist: With Some Remarks on the Importance of Doing Nothing*, CreateSpace, 2014.

[607] Francois Mauriac, *A Critique of Criticism*, 1961. Mauriac (1885 -1970) was a French author, member of the *Académie française* and laureate of the Nobel Prize in Literature (1952). He was awarded the Grand Cross of the *Légion d'honneur* in 1958.

[608] Giles Coren, in answer to the author's questionnaire, 2015.

[609] Joseph Addison, *Literary Criticism, Spectator no 291*, 2 February 1712)

[610] Samuel Pepys (1633 – 1703) is Britain's most famous diarist, though in his lifetime he was better known as a reforming naval administrator and member of parliament.

[611] Samuel Pepys, *The Diaries of Samuel Pepys – A Selection*, Penguin Classics, 2008.

[612] Mark Shenton, *Advice to a Younger Theatre Critic, The Stage*, 6 February 2013.

[613] Christopher Tookey, *Tookey's Turkeys*, Matador, 2015, p334.

[614] Rita Kempley, *Washington Post*, 22 December 1988.

[615] Jay Carr, *Boston Globe*, 23 December 1988.

[616] http://www.movie-film-review.com/devfilm.asp?rtype=3&id=12083

[617] Stanley Kauffmann, *New Republic*, 10 December 1993.

[618] John Simon, *Praise Jack, Shoot the Piano, National Review*, vol 45, No 25, 27 December 1993, pp65-67.

[619] Stuart Klawans, *The Nation*, vol 257, no 19, 6 December 1993.

[620] Derek Malcolm, *The Guardian*, 28 October 1993.

[621] John Simon, *Reverse Angle*, Potter, 1982.

[622] Shaw is quoted in Michael Holroyd, *Bernard Shaw*, 2012. Page 140.

[623] Aristotle, *Poetics*, 4th century BC.

[624] Crist is quoted in John Robert Colombo, Popcorn in paradise: the wit and wisdom of Hollywood, 1980. Page 159.

[625] Dennis McLellan, Judith Crist obituary, *Los Angeles Times*, 8 August 2012.

[626] Stephen Sondheim, *Look, I Made A Hat*, Virgin Books, 2011.

[627] Quoted by Tess Coslett, *Talking Animals in British Children's Fiction, 1786-1914*, 2006.

[628] Quoted by Ned Sherrin, *Oxford Dictionary of Humorous Quotations*, 2008.

[629] Albert Wolff, *Le Figaro*, 3 April 1876.

[630] Quoted in Charles S. Moffett, *New Painting, Impressionism, 1874-1886*, 1986.

[631] Quoted by Matthew Parris, *Scorn with Extra Bile*, 1998. Page 223.

[632] *Los Angeles Times*, 1964.

[633] *Newsweek*, 1964.

[634] *Boston Globe*, 1964.

[635] Christopher Tookey, *The Critic's Film Guide*, Box Tree, 1994.

[636] Campbell Dixon of the *Daily Telegraph* declared that "with just a little wit the film might have ranked high among its kind." Penelope Houston in *Monthly Film Bulletin* compared it to *On The Town* and said it was "less completely successful". Catherine de la Roche of *Picture Post* compared it with *An American in Paris* and said that *Singin' In The Rain* was not on the same high level.

[637] www.movie-film-review.com/devFilm.asp?ID=9947

[638] www.movie-film-review.com/devfilm.asp?rtype=2&id=2637

[639] Joseph Addison, *Cato, A Tragedy in Five Acts*, Act V, Kessenger, 2004.

[640] John Harris, *'I Supplied talent and drugs'*, *Observer*, 29 May 2005

[641] Alexander Pope, *An Essay on Criticism*, 1811.

[642] C.A. Lejeune, *Observer*, 7 August 1960.

[643] www.movie-film-review.com/devfilm.asp?rtype=3&id=8926

[644] www.movie-film-review.com/devfilm.asp?rtype=3&id=8555

[645] www.movie-film-review.com/devfilm.asp?rtype=3&id=10325

[646] www.movie-film-review.com/devfilm.asp?rtype=3&id=1821.

[647] www.movie-film-review.com/devfilm.asp?rtype=3&id=387

[648] www.movie-film-review.com/devfilm.asp?rtype=3&id=12660

[649] Christopher Tookey, *Tookey's Talkies*, Matador, 2015.

[650] My reviews of all of these are in Christopher Tookey, *Tookey's Talkies*, Matador, 2015.

[651] Philip French, *Observer*, 14 November 1999.

[652] www.movie-film-review.com/devfilm.asp?rtype=1&id=12660

[653] Roger Ebert, Chicago Sun-Times, 1 January 2000.

[654] Janet Maslin, *New York Times*, 1 January 2000.

[655] Jeff Vice, *Deseret News,* 1 January 2000.

[656] A.O. Scott, *New York Times,* 7 September 2007.

[657] Ty Burr, *Boston Globe,* 7 September 2007.

[658] Stephen McGarvey, *Crosswalk,* 7 September 1977.

[659] Christopher Tookey, *Daily Mail*, 14 September 2007.

[660] Rick Mele, *The Cinema Source*, 7 September 1977.

[661] Tim Knight, *Reel.com*, 7 September 1977.

[662] www.imdb.com/title/tt0038915

[663] www.movie-film-review.com/devFilm.asp?ID=4761

[664] www.movie-film-review.com/devFilm.asp?ID=9407

665 G.K. Chesterton, *All I Survey*, Methuen, 1933.

666

https://answers.yahoo.com/question/index?qid=20070411154249AAf86hX

667 Edmund Wilson, *'Oo, Those Awful Orcs!' Nation*, April 14 1956

668   https://ajcarlisle.wordpress.com/tag/philip-toynbee-lord-of-the-rings-critique

669   http://www.thetolkienforum.com/index.php?threads/lotr-nazi-propaganda-germaine-greer.11791

670 https://ajcarlisle.wordpress.com/tag/michael-moorcock-lord-of-the-rings-critique

671 Michael Moorcock, *Wizardry and Wild Romance,* 1987.

672 Quoted by John Newsinger in interview with China Mieville for the International Socialism Journal, Autumn 2000.

673 John Yatt , *Guardian,* December 2, 2002

674 Brenda Partridge, *No Sex, Please, We're Hobbits: The Construction of Female Sexuality in The Lord of the Rings,* an essay in *J.R.R. Tolkien: This Far Land*, edited by Robert Giddings, *1983*. Page 179.

675 Terry Pratchett is quoted on *www.goodreads.com.*

676 Tolkien is quoted by Perry C. Bramlett in *I Am In Fact a Hobbit: An Introduction to the Life and Work of J.R.R. Tolkien*, 2003.

677 Tolkien is quoted by John Garth, in *J.R.R. Tolkien Encyclopedia: Scholarship and Critical Assessment*, edited by Michael D.C. Drout, 2006.

678   Tolkien is quoted by Humphrey Carpenter in *J.R.R. Tolkien: A Biography*, Houghton Miffin, 2014.

679 Steven Shapiro, *The Scotsman*, 14 December 2002.

680 Steven Shapiro, *The Scotsman*, 14 December 2002.

681   Tolkien is quoted by Michael D.C. Drout, in *J.R.R. Tolkien Encyclopedia: Scholarship and Critical Assessment*, edited by Michael D.C. Drout, 2006.

682 Tolkien is quoted by Mark Home in his biography, *J.R.R. Tolkien*, 2011, Page 124.

[683] Mike Fleming Jr, *Alejandro G. Inarritu and Birdman, Deadline Hollywood*, 15 October 2014.

[684] Scott Tobias, *The Dissolve*, 16 October 2014.

[685] Tony Macklin, *tonymacklin.net*, 29 October 2014.

[686] Michelle Alexandria, *Eclipse Magazine*, 13 December 2014.

[687] Colin Jarman, *The Book of Poisonous Quotes*, Contemporary Books, 1993.

[688] http://www.geocities.ws/paulinekaelreviews/p3.html

[689] http://www.geocities.ws/paulinekaelreviews/b7.html

[690] http://www.geocities.ws/paulinekaelreviews/s8.html

[691] http://www.geocities.ws/paulinekaelreviews/w4.html

[692] Renata Adler, *review of When The Lights Go Down, New York Review of Books*, August 14th 1980.

[693] Renata Adler, *review of When The Lights Go Down, New York Review of Books*, August 14th 1980.

[694] Renata Adler, *review of When The Lights Go Down, New York Review of Books*, August 14th 1980.

[695] Pauline Kael, *Stanley Strangelove, New Yorker*, January 1972.

[696] Pauline Kael, *5001 Nights at the Movies*, Henry Holt, *1991*.

[697] Pauline Kael, *Taking It All In*, Rinehart and Winston, 1984.

[698] Pauline Kael, *Vogue*, December 1965.

[699] Pauline Kael, *5001 Nights at the Movies, Henry Holt, 1991.*

[700]   http://unobtainium13.com/2012/09/26/film-review-dirty-harry-dir-by-don-siegel/

[701]   http://thinkexist.com/quotation/pauline-kael-never-forgave-clint-eastwood-for/518537.html

[702]   http://ghiblicon.blogspot.co.uk/2006/06/pauline-kael-on-little-mermaid.html

[703] http://alexsheremet.com/pauline-kael-one-films-worst-ridiculous-critics/

[704] http://www.geocities.ws/paulinekaelreviews/b4.html

[705] http://articles.latimes.com/2014/mar/08/entertainment/la-et-mn-turan-on-film-20140309

[706] http://www.reelviews.net/reelviews/it-s-a-wonderful-life

[707] Anthony Lane, *Nobody's Perfect,* Pan Macmillan, 2003, p535.

[708] Gwynn Nettler, *Social Concerns,* McGraw-Hill, 1975.

[709] Emily Smith, *The Brian De Palma Handbook*, Emereo Publishing, 2013.

[710] Alan Parker, *Film Yearbook,* 1990.

[711] Clive James, *A Critic and a Poet, The Atlantic,* 22 August 2012.

[712] Philip Lopate, *Pauline Kael: A Life in the Dark review (Extended), Film Comment,* November/December 2011.

[713] *Roaring at the Screen with Pauline Kael, New York Times,* 27 October 2011.

[714] Elaine Showalter, *Times Literary Supplement*, 11 April 2012.

[715] John Simon, *Reverse Angle*, Potter, 1982.

[716] John Simon, *Reverse Angle*, Potter, 1982.

[717] Michael Billington is quoted in William Russell and Peter Cargin's *A Critical Century* (2014). Page 73.

[718] Phone conversation with the author, 22 January 2015.

[719] Rex Reed, *New York Observer*, 5 October 2001

[720] http://flavorwire.com/403308/its-time-to-fire-rex-reed

[721] Rex Reed, *New York Observer*, 10 April 2012.

[722] Laura Ward, *Book of Put-Downs,* Robson, p153.

[723] Christopher Tookey, *Named and Shamed*, Matador, 2010, p177.

[724] Christopher Tookey, *Named and Shamed*, Matador, 2010, p7.

[725] Anthony Lane, New Yorker, 7 January 2013.

[726] Christopher Tookey, *Named and Shamed*, Matador, 2010, p5.

[727] Christopher Tookey, *Named and Shamed*, Matador, 2010, p16.

[728] Bruce Bashford, *Oscar Wilde: The Critic as Humanist*, Farleigh Dickinson University Press, 1999.

[729] Joseph Pearce, *The Unmasking of Oscar Wilde*, Ignatius Press, p45.

[730] Doris Arthur Jones , *Taking The Curtain Call: The Life and Letters of Henry Arthur Jones,* Macmillan, 1930.

[731] Henry Arthur Jones (1851 – 1929) was an English playwright whose first success was *The Silver King* (1882), a melodrama written with Henry Herman, produced at the Princess's Theatre, London. Other hits included *Saints and Sinners* (1884), *The Middleman* (1889) and *Judah* (1890). His style was realist and conservative, and lacked the depth of his contemporary, Henrik Ibsen whose fame outlasted his.

[732] www.brainyquote.com/quotes/quotes/s/samueljohn161407.html

[733] James Boswell, *The Life of Samuel Johnson,* Carter, Hendee & Co, 1832, p425.

[734] George Bernard Shaw, *The Great Composers: Reviews and Bombardments,* University of California Press, 1978.

[735] George Bernard Shaw, *Shaw's Music*, Max Reinhardt, Bodley Head, 1981.

[736] Dorothy Parker, book review of A.A. Milne's *The House at Pooh Corner*, for *The New Yorker*, October 20, 1928

[737] Godfrey Smith, *Critic Kenneth Tynan Has Mellowed But Is Still England's Stingingest Gadfly*, New York Times, 9 January 1966.

[738] Kenneth Tynan, John Lahr, *The Diaries of Kenneth Tynan*, A & C Black, p12.

[739] Samantha Ellis, *Peter Brook's Titus Andronicus, August 1955, Guardian,* 25 June 2003.

[740] Clive James, *Reliable Essays: The Best of Clive James,* Pan Macmillan, 2009.

[741] Clive James, *Reliable Essays: The Best of Clive James,* Pan Macmillan, 2009.

[742] Clive James, *Reliable Essays: The Best of Clive James*, Pan Macmillan, 2009.

[743] Martin Amis, *The War Against Cliché*, Vintage, 2001.

[744] A.N. Wilson, *Dan Brown Inferno Review: Bilge but a hell of a page turner, Daily Mail*, 13 May 2013.

[745] Clive James, *A Point of View*, Pan Macmillan, 2011.

[746] Clive James, *Reliable Essays: The Best of Clive James*, Pan Macmillan, 2009.

[747] Clive James, *Reliable Essays: The Best of Clive James*, Pan Macmillan, 2009.

[748] pjorourkeonline.blogspot.com/2009/10/red-warbler.html

[749] Howard Jacobson, *Independent*, 5 December 2014.

[750] Howard Jacobson, *Independent*, 12 September 2014.

[751] Howard Jacobson, *Independent*, 12 September 2014.

[752] Quoted in Jay Rayner, *My Dining Hell*, Penguin, 2012.

[753] All these Jeremy Clarkson quotations and more can be found at http://www.thefloatingfrog.co.uk/fun/jeremy-clarksons-50-best-quotes-of-all-time/

[754] www.movie-film-review.com/devfilm.asp?rtype=3&id=4932

[755] http://www.movie-film-review.com/devrasp.asp?act=2&param=314

[756] George Perry, *The Golden Screen: Fifty Years at the Films*, Pavilion, 1989

[757] Dilys Powell obituary, *Independent*, 5 June 1995.

[758] Christopher Tookey, *Sunday Telegraph*, 1986.

[759] Craig Brown, *Guardian*, 2 October 2010.

[760] Craig Brown, *Daily Mail*, 15 January 2014.

[761] Craig Brown, *The Lost Diaries*, Fourth Estate, 2011.

[762] Craig Brown, *The Lost Diaries*, Fourth Estate, 2011.

[763] Craig Brown, *Daily Mail*, 2 February 2015.

[764] Craig Brown, *Daily Mail*, 2 February 2015.

[765] Craig Brown, *Daily Mail*, 15 April 2013.

[766] George Saintsbury, *A History of English Criticism*, Atlantic, 2013 (first published in 1911).

[767] Aristotle, George Whalley, John Baxter, Patrick Atherton, *Aristotle's Poetics*, McGill-Queen's Press – MQUP, 1997.

[768] John Dryden, *The Works of John Dryden now first collected*, W. Miller, 1808.

[769] John Dryden, *The Works of John Dryden now first collected*, W. Miller, 1808.

[770] Samuel Johnson, *Preface to Shakespeare*, IndyPublish.com, 2007.

[771] Oscar Wilde, *The Critic as Artist*, CreateSpace Independent Publishing Platform, 2012.

[772] Oscar Wilde, *The Critic as Artist*, CreateSpace Independent Publishing Platform, 2012.

[773] Martin Amis, *The War Against Cliché*, Vintage, 2001.

[774] Martin Amis, *The War Against Cliché*, Vintage, 2001.

[775] Ronald Bergan, *What Every Film Critic Should Know*, Guardian, 26 March 2007.

[776] Ronald Bergan, *What Every Film Critic Should Know*, Guardian, 26 March 2007.

[777] Ronald Bergan, *What Every Film Critic Should Know*, Guardian, 26 March 2007.

[778] Jonathan Rosenbaum, *Chicago Reader*, 15 January 1999.

[779] George Perry, reply to author's questionnaire, early 2015.

[780] Gareth & Barbara Lloyd Evans, *Plays in Review 1956-1980*, Batsford, 1985.

[781] Based on conversations I had with Sir Donald Albery in the early 1970s.

[782] W.A. Darlington, *Daily Telegraph*, 7 May 1964.

[783] Harold Hobson, *Sunday Times*, 10 May 1964.

[784] Brian Sewell, *Naked Emperors,* Quartet 2012.

[785] Irving Wardle, *Theatre Criticism*, Routledge, 1992.

[786] Irving Wardle, *Theatre Criticism*, Routledge, 1992.

[787] Sergei Eisenstein, *A Close-Up View*, 1945, reprinted in *Film Essays and a Lecture*, ed. Jay Leyda, Princeton University Press, 1982, p.152.

[788] Andrew Tudor, *Theories of Film*, Secker & Warburg, 1974, p49.

[789] Andrew Tudor, *Theories of Film*, Secker & Warburg, 1974, p64.

[790] Michiko Kakutani, *New York Times*, 19 July 2007.

[791] Harold Bloom, *Boston Globe*, 24 September 2003.

[792] Harold Bloom, *Ranting Against Cant, Atlantic Unbound*, 16 July 2003.

[793] Harold Bloom, *Boston Globe*, 24 September 2003.

[794] Harold Bloom, *Dumbing Down American Readers, Boston Globe*, 24 September 2003.

[795] Irving Wardle, *Theatre Criticism*, Routledge, 1992.

[796] Maureen Ryan, *Chicago Tribune,* 11 October 2007.

[797] https://books.google.co.uk/books?isbn=0297857517

[798] Kenneth Clark, *Another Part of the Wood: A Self-Portrait,* John Murray, 1974

[799] poy.time.com/2012/12/19/tributes-to-those-we-lost.../robert-hughes/

[800] Robert Hughes obituary, *Daily Telegraph*, 7 August 2012.

[801] artfcity.com/2012/08/07/outspoken-critic-robert-hughes-dies-aged-74/

[802] http://www.abc.net.au/rn/legacy/programs/sunmorn/stories/s1509883.htm

[803] Brian Sewell, *Evening Standard*, 23 January 1997.

[804] Quoted on the website *Neil Young's Film Lounge*, 6 July 2009.

[805] Alastair Cooke, preface to *Garbo and the Night Watchmen*, McGraw-Hill, 1937

[806] George Steiner interviewed by Ronald A. Sharp, *The Paris Review*, Autumn 1994.

[807] http://www.moviezeal.com/10-ways-to-become-a-better-film-critic-part-1/

[808] Kenneth Tynan, *Observer*, 8 December, 1957

[809] homepage.eircom.net/~odyssey/Quotes/Popular/TV/TV_Reviews.html

[810] blogs.news.com.au/dailytelegraph/timblair/index.php/.../dioxide_drama/

[811] Brian Sewell, *Evening Standard*, 25 June 2007

[812] www.outsidersinlondon.org/Outsiders_in_London/25.html

[813] britainisnocountryforoldmen.blogspot.com/.../britain-is-still-country-for-...

[814] Brian Sewell, *The Reviews That Caused the Rumpus and other pieces*, Bloomsbury, 1994.

[815] http://www.art-quotes.com/auth_search.php?authid=2027#.VS0RbqadxG4

[816] Brian Sewell, *Are young British artists nincompoops and Frauds?*, *Prospect*, April 2002.

[817] Sir Nicholas Andrew Serota (1946-) is director of the Tate art museums and galleries. He was director of the Whitechapel Gallery, London, and The Museum of Modern Art, Oxford, before becoming in 1988 director of the Tate, the United Kingdom's national gallery of modern and British art. He has also been chairman of the Turner Prize jury.

[818] Marina Vaizey (1938 -) is an American art critic, curator and author based in the United Kingdom. She has been Art Critic for the *Financial Times* and *Sunday Times* and editor of the *Art Quarterly and Review*. She was a founding Trustee of the Geffrye Museum and has also been a trustee of the Imperial War Museum and the South Bank. She has also been a judge for the Turner Prize. She was one of thirty-five prominent members of the art establishment who wrote to the editor of the *Evening Standard*, demanding that its art critic Brian Sewell be sacked.

[819] The word "Reithian", conveying a vision of broadcasting and journalism as a means of educating the masses, is derived from John Charles Walsham Reith, 1st Baron Reith, (1889 – 1971) who In 1922 became general manager

of the BBC. In 1927 became the BBC's . In 1975, excerpts from Reith's diary were published which revealed his pro-fascist opinions, On 9 March 1933, he wrote in his diary: "I am pretty certain... that the Nazis will clean things up and put Germany on the way to being a real power in Europe again. They are being ruthless and most determined." After the July 1934 Night of the Long Knives, in which the Nazis exterminated their internal dissidents, Reith wrote: "I really admire the way Hitler has cleaned up what looked like an incipient revolt. I really admire the drastic actions taken, which were obviously badly needed." After Hitler invaded Czechoslovakia in 1939 he wrote: "Hitler continues his magnificent efficiency." Reith also praised the Italian fascist Benito Mussolini. Reith's daughter, Marista Leishman, has written that her father in the 1930s did everything possible to keep Winston Churchill and other anti-appeasement Conservatives off the airwaves. It's good to know that public service broadcasting was in such safe hands.

[820]   https://quartetbooks.wordpress.com/2013/06/28/brian-sewell-the-orwell-essays/

[821] http://en.wikipedia.org/wiki/Brian_Sewell

[822] Brian Sewell interviewed by Angela Wintle, *Daily Telegraph*, 14 June 2012.

[823] Michael Billington, *Guardian*, 21 June 2006.

[824] http://literature.britishcouncil.org/david-edgar

[825]

http://www.illuminationsmedia.co.uk/blog/index.cfm?start=2&news_id=1140

[826] Bernard Levin, *Times*, 8 July 1980.

[827] Bernard Levin, *Times*, 8 July 1980.

[828] Frank Rich, *New York Times*, 5 October 1981.

[829] John Simon, *New York*, 5 October 1981.

[830] Michelle Dean, *Without Public Arts Funding, We Wouldn't Have Les Misérables, The Nation,* 17 January 2013.

[831] Herbert Kretzmer's report on his fellow critics is quoted by William Russell and Peter Cargin, in *A Critical Century*, 2014. Page 63.

[832] Francis King, *Sunday Telegraph*, 13 October 1985.

[833] Michael Ratcliffe, *Observer*, 13 October 1985.

[834] Jack Tinker, *Daily Mail*, 9 October 1985.

[835] Benedict Nightingale, *Les Misérables is reborn as a lavish rock opera*, *New York Times*, 30 March 1986.

[836] Michael Billington, *Twenty-five years on, they ask me if I was wrong about Les Misérables*, *Guardian*, 21 September 2010.

[837] Cameron Mackintosh interviewed by Anna Tims, *How We Made Les Misérables*, *Guardian*, 19 February 2013.

[838] Susan Wlosczyna, *USA Today*, 24 January 2013.

[839] Reply to the author's questionnaire, early 2015.

[840] Simon Price, *A Parasitic But Necessary Art: Simon Price on the Role of the Critic*, *The Quietus*, 18 October 2013.

[841] Reply to the author's questionnaire, early 2015.

[842] http://www.mediumdifficulty.com/tag/lana-polansky/

[843] Brendan Keogh is quoted in Helen Lewis, *Where to find good videogames criticism*, *New Statesman*, 3 Decmber 2012.

[844] James Delingpole, *Daily Mail*, 17 September 2013.

[845] James Delingpole, *Daily Mail*, 17 September 2013.

[846] http://en.wikipedia.org/wiki/Grand_Theft_Auto_V

[847] David Grossman has written two pertinent books about violence in the media, *On Killing* (1996) and *Stop Teaching Our Kids to Kill* (1999).

[848] Mary Flanagan, *Huffington Post*, 30 September 2014.

[849] If you want an overview, read for example Chapter 3, in W. Warburton & D. Braunstein (Eds.) *Growing Up Fast and Furious: Reviewing the Impacts of Violent and Sexualised Media on Children*, Annandale, NSW, Australia: The Federation Press. Also worth reading is Douglas A. Gentile and Craig A. Anderson's *Violent Video Games: The Effects on Youth, and Public Policy Implications*, a chapter in N.Dowd, D.G. Singer and R.F.Wilson (Eds.) *Handbook of Children, Culture and Violence*, Thousand Oaks, 2006.

[850] All these hostile reviews and more can be found at *http://www.movie-film-review.com/devfilm.asp?rtype=3&id=749*

[851] http://www.movie-film-review.com/devfilm.asp?rtype=3&id=2093

[852] Quoted in Ardis Gillick and Michael McCormick, *The Critics Were Wrong*, Citadel Press 1996. P200.

[853] My reviews of all of these can be found in *Tookey's Turkeys*, Matador, 2015.

[854] http://www.loa.org/volume.jsp?RequestID=312

[855] http://en.wikipedia.org/wiki/Manny_Farber

[856] Manny Farber, *Farber on Film: The Complete Writings of Manny Farber*, Library of America, 2009.

[857] Manny Farber, *Farber on Film: The Complete Writings of Manny Farber*, Library of America, 2009.

[858] Manny Farber, *Farber on Film: The Complete Writings of Manny Farber*, Library of America, 2009.

[859] Manny Farber, *Farber on Film: The Complete Writings of Manny Farber*, Library of America, 2009.

[860] Manny Farber, *Farber on Film: The Complete Writings of Manny Farber*, Library of America, 2009.

[861] Manny Farber, *Farber on Film: The Complete Writings of Manny Farber*, Library of America, 2009.

[862] Manny Farber, *Farber on Film: The Complete Writings of Manny Farber*, Library of America, 2009.

[863] James Agee, *The Nation*, 31 January 1948.

[864] James Agee, *Life*, 3 September 1949.

[865] Dilys Powell, *Sunday Times*, 18 November 1945.

[866] Dilys Powell, *Sunday Times*, October 1941.

[867] Dilys Powell, *Sunday Times*, December 1959.

[868] Dilys Powell, *Sunday Times*, February 1947.

[869] Dilys Powell, *Sunday Times*, 18 December 1955.

[870] http://www.brainyquote.com/quotes/quotes/f/frankzappa128284.html

[871] Jim DeRogatis, *A Final Chat With Lester Bangs*, November 1999.

[872] Jim DeRogatis, *A Final Chat With Lester Bangs*, November 1999.

[873] Maria Bustillos, *Lester Bangs: Truth-Teller, New Yorker*, 21 August 2012.

[874] Lester Bangs, *Rolling Stone*, April 5, 1969

[875] Lester Bangs, *Rolling Stone*, 17 September 1970.

[876] http://kuoi.asui.uidaho.edu/~kamikaze/Audio/review_mmm.php

[877] Jim DeRogatis, *A Final Chat With Lester Bangs*, November 1999.

[878] Lester Bangs, *Astral Weeks, Stranded*, 1979.

[879] http://www.jimdero.com/Bangs/bangsisms.htm

[880] http://www.jimdero.com/Bangs/bangsisms.htm

[881] http://www.jimdero.com/Bangs/bangsisms.htm

[882] White was expelled on 13 January, 2013. He had twice been chairman of the New York Critics' Circle.

[883] http://en.wikipedia.org/wiki/Armond_White

[884] David Chen, *Armond White: "I Do Think It Is Fair To Say That Roger Ebert Destroyed Film Criticism", /Film*, 20 July 2010.

[885] Armond White, *My Greenberg Problem – and Yours, New York Press*, 17 March 2010.

[886] Quoted in Mark Jacobson, *No Kiss Kiss, All Bang Bang, New York*, 15 February 1009.

[887] Armond White, quoted in *Neal Gabler, Everyone's a Critic Now, Observer*, 6 February 2011.

[888] Armond White, *Now Playing, City Arts*, 14 November 2011.

[889] Armond White, *A Piece of Resistance, City Arts*, 7 February 2014.

[890] Armond White, *Do Movie Critics Matter?, First Things*, 19 March 2010.

[891] Jonathan Law, *The Methuen Drama Dictionary of the Theatre*, A&C Black, 2013.

[892] Reply to author's questionnaire, early 2015.

[893] Alan Brien, *Spectator*, 6 June 1958.

[894] Quoted by Samantha Ellis, *A Taste of Honey*, 10 September 2003.

[895] Kenneth Tynan, *Observer*, 1 June 1958.

[896] Reply to author's questionnaire, early 2015.

[897] Reply to author's questionnaire, early 2015.

[898] Libby Gelman-Waxner, *If You Ask Me*, Fawcett Columbine, 1994.

[899] Harvey S. Karten, *Compuserve*, 1 January 2000.

[900] Donald Munro, *Fresno Bee*, 1 January 2000.

[901] Christopher Tookey, *Tookey's Turkeys*, Matador, 2015.

[902] Christopher Tookey, *Tookey's Turkeys*, Matador, 2015.

[903] Christopher Tookey, *Tookey's Turkeys*, Matador, 2015.

[904] Jules Brenner, *Cinema Signals,* 16 November 2009.

[905] Chris Bumbray, *Jo Blo's Movie Emporium,* 16 November 2009.

[906] Quoted by Charles Wright in his review of Frank Rich's memoir *Ghost Light* in *Theatermania*, 22 November 2000.

[907] Quoted by Charles Wright in his review of Frank Rich's memoir *Ghost Light* in *Theatermania*, 22 November 2000.

[908] Andrew Edgecliffe-Johnson, *Robert Parker, the American Bacchus*, *Financial Times*, 14 December 2012.

[909] Frank J. Prial, *Decantations: Reflections on wine by the New York Times wine critic,* St Martin's Press, 2001.

[910] Andrew Edgecliffe-Johnson, *Robert Parker, the American Bacchus*, *Financial Times*, 14 December 2012.

[911] *What Does It Take to be a good restaurant critic?*, *BBC News*, 28 April 2010.

[912] http://www.eater.com/2010/7/20/6725953/frank-bruni-blogs-have-made-dining-out-more-faddish

[913] *Food critic goes through the looking-glass, New York Times,* 4 January 2009.

[914] *Food critic goes through the looking-glass, New York Times,* 4 January 2009. In *Ratatouille* (2007), a rat becomes a brilliant chef, even impressing Paris's most unforgiving food critic, Anton Ego.

[915] *Food critic goes through the looking-glass, New York Times,* 4 January 2009.

[916] Elaine Sciolino, *In Paris, A Critic Criticised, New York Times,* 13 January 2009.

[917] Simon Tomlinson, *Michelin Guide accused of cover-up over death of top French chef, Daily Mail,* 24 January 2013

[918] *Daily Telegraph,* 23 January 2014

[919] Amy McKeever, *Bernard Loiseau's widow Accuses French Paper of Manipulation, Blames Media for His Suicide, www.eater.com,* 7 March 2013.

[920] *Food critic goes through the looking-glass, New York Times,* 4 January 2009.

[921] Elaine Sciolino, *In Paris, A Critic Criticised, New York Times,* 13 January 2009.

[922] Elaine Sciolino, *In Paris, A Critic Criticised, New York Times,* 13 January 2009.

[923] Tracey MacLeod: *Chefs turn sour on food critics who criticise, Independent,* 18 November 2011.

[924] Matthew Fort interviewed by Chloe Cann for *Xcity,* Spring 2013.

[925] http://blog.bestamericanpoetry.com/the_best_american_poetry/2011/07/t-s-eliot-criticises-the-critics.html

[926] http://thefloatinglibrary.com/2010/04/04/arts-criticism/

[927] http://archive.org/stream/essaysonfineart00hazlgoog/essaysonfineart00hazlgoog_djvu.txt

[928] http://www.theage.com.au/news/entertainment/arts/how-to-prolong-a-critical-condition/2009/12/06/1260034218468.html?page=fullpage

[929] Tom Sutcliffe is quoted by William Russell and Peter Cargin's *A Critical Century* (2014). Page 78.

[930] Reply to author's questionnaire, early 2015.

[931] www.frontrowreviews.com, 25 March 2010.

[932] Scott Weinberg, *Twitch*, 17 July 2012

[933] Scott Weinberg, *Twitch*, 17 July 2012

[934] Quoted by Tim Fountain, in *Resident Alien: Quentin Crisp Explains It All*, Nick Hern Books,1999. p. 20.

[935] Quoted by Tim Fountain, in *Resident Alien: Quentin Crisp Explains It All*, Nick Hern Books,1999. p. 20.

[936] Quentin Crisp, *How To Go To The Movies,* St Martin's Press, 1989, p31.

[937] Quentin Crisp, *How To Go To The Movies,* St Martin's Press, 1989. p142-3.

[938] Quentin Crisp, *How To Go To The Movies,* St Martin's Press, 1989, p191.

[939]   http://www.cineaste.com/articles/film-criticism-in-the-age-of-the-internet.htm

[940]   http://www.cineaste.com/articles/film-criticism-in-the-age-of-the-internet.htm

[941]   http://www.cineaste.com/articles/film-criticism-in-the-age-of-the-internet.htm

[942] James Bowman, *The Death of Criticism, American Spectator*, 7 January 2003.

[943] Roger Ebert, *Death to critics! Hail to the CelebCult!*, *www.rogerebert.com*, 26 November 2008.

[944] Roger Ebert, *Death to critics! Hail to the CelebCult!*, *www.rogerebert.com*, 26 November 2008.

[945] Roger Ebert, *Death to critics! Hail to the CelebCult!*, *www.rogerebert.com*, 26 November 2008.

[946] *The Problem With Film Criticism, Dissent Magazine*, Fall 2011.

[947] Eileen Jones, *Exiled*, 5 January 2012

[948] Nick James, *Sight and Sound,* November 2013.

[949] Stephanie Zacharek, *The Fall of the Professional Critic, Continued*, 24 July 2008.

[950] Ben Eltham, *Where Have All The Arts Critics Gone?*, www.newmatilda.com, 24 December 2009.

[951] Elle Jay Smith, *Spectator*, January 2014.

[952] Elle Jay Smith, *Spectator*, January 2014.

[953] Adrian Searle, *Critical Condition: Has big money replaced the pundit in the art world?*, *Guardian*, 18 March 2008

[954] Edward Helmore and Paul Gallagher, *Doyen of American critics turns his back on the 'nasty, stupid' world of modern art*, *Observer*, 28 October 2012.

[955] Edward Helmore and Paul Gallagher, *Doyen of American critics turns his back on the 'nasty, stupid' world of modern art*, *Observer*, 28 October 2012.

[956] *Film Criticism in the age of the internet: A Symposium*, www.cineaste.com, Fall 2008.

[957] Richard Adams, *Huffington Post to be sold to AOL for $315m*, *Guardian*, 7 February 2011.

[958] Bill Hagerty, *Interview with Paul Dacre, editor of the Daily Mail*, *Guardian*, 9 September 2002.

[959] Mark Sweeney, *Mail Online's soaring revenues offset publisher's print ad decline*, *Guardian*, 22 May 2014.

[960] *Guardian*, 8 January 2014.

[961] *Huffington Post*, 8 January 2014.

[962] *Pay divide UK: UK bosses earn 143 times more than employees*, *Sydney Morning Herald*, 19 August 2014.

[963] *Ian Hislop lets rip at Daily Mail and Rothermere family*, *Daily Mirror*, 4 October 2013.

[964] *Jonathan Harmsworth, 4th Lord Rothermere*, netlibrary.net.

[965] George Bernard Shaw, *How To Become a Music Critic, 1894.*

[966] *En.wikipedia.org/wiki/Pauline Kael.*

[967] *R.J. Ellory's secret Amazon reviews anger rivals*, *Guardian*, 3 September 2012.

[968] *Orlando Figes to pay fake Amazon review damages, BBC News*, 17 July 2010.

[969] Jeremy Duns, *Johann Hari is still lying to you*, www.jeremy-duns.co.uk, 7 September 2012

[970] *Sock puppetry and fake reviews: publish and be damned, Guardian*, 4 September 2012.

[971] *R.J.Ellory, Author, caught writing fake reviews, Huffington Post*, 4 September 2012.

[972] *Fake online reviews crackdown in New York, Guardian*, 23 September 2013.

[973] Robin Henry, *Our little book roots out the Amazon chart cheats, Sunday Times*, October 11th, 2015.

[974] Jacob Silverman, *Against Enthusiasm, Slate*, 4 August 2012.

[975] Philip French, *Observer*, 30 January 2011.

[976] Anthony Trollope, *Autobiography of Anthony Trollope*, CSP Classic Texts.

[977] Anthony Trollope, *Autobiography of Anthony Trollope*, CSP Classic Texts.

[978] Tom Sutcliffe, *The Retiring President's Farewell, Critics' Circular*, Issue 9, 2012.

[979] Guy Dimond, interviewed by Chloe Cann for *Xcity*, Spring 2013.

[980] Harry Knowles interviewed by Sanjiv Bhattacharya in GQ, 2003.

[981] Harry Knowles, *Ain't It Cool movie reviews*, 9 December 1999.

[982] Roger Ebert, *Chicago Sun-Times*, 17 December 1999.

[983] Peter Howell, *Toronto Star*, 17 December 1999.

[984] Peter Bradshaw, *Guardian*, 16 February 2006.

[985] Liza Schwarzbaum, *Entertainment Weekly*, 1 December 2005.

[986] Harry Knowles, *Ain't It Cool Movie Reviews*, 2 December 2005.

[987] Harry Knowles, *Ain't It Cool Movie Reviews*, 27 June 2011.

[988] http://en.wikipedia.org/wiki/Harry_Knowles

[989] *BONEHEAD OF THE MONTH 1: Harry Knowles Must Go!*, www.efilmcritic.com, 15 April 2003.

[990] *What Happened to Harry Knowles?*, CHUD.com, 5 December 2010.

[991] Harry Knowles, *Ain't It Cool Movie Reviews*, 8 July 2003.

[992] Harry Knowles, *Ain't It Cool Movie Reviews*, 20 July 2009.

[993] Harry Knowles, *Ain't It Cool Movie Reviews*, 7 August 2010.

[994] Harry Knowles, *Ain't It Cool Movie Reviews*, 24 February 2009.

[995] Harry Knowles, *Ain't It Cool Movie Reviews*, 9 January 2011.

[996] http://www.movie-film-review.com/devfilm.asp?rtype=1&id=15776

[997] Derek Adams, *Time Out*, 15 February 2011.

[998] Ryan Lambie, *Den of Geek*, 15 February 2011.

[999] Peter Bradshaw, *Guardian*, 17 February 2011.

[1000] *Film Criticism in the Age of the Internet: A Critical Symposium*, www.cineaste.com, Fall 2008.

[1001] *Film Criticism in the Age of the Internet: A Critical Symposium*, www.cineaste.com, Fall 2008.

[1002] *Film Criticism in the Age of the Internet: A Critical Symposium*, www.cineaste.com, Fall 2008.

[1003] *Film Criticism in the Age of the Internet: A Critical Symposium*, www.cineaste.com, Fall 2008.

[1004] *Film Criticism in the Age of the Internet: A Critical Symposium*, www.cineaste.com, Fall 2008.

[1005] *Film Criticism in the Age of the Internet: A Critical Symposium*, www.cineaste.com, Fall 2008.

[1006] Richard Schickel, *Time*, 20 May 2007.

[1007] Martin Amis, *The War Against Cliché*, Vintage, 2002.

[1008] Martin Amis, *The War Against Cliché*, Vintage, 2002.

[1009] Martin Amis, *The War Against Cliché*, Vintage, 2002.

[1010] Martin Amis, *The War Against Cliché*, Vintage, 2002.

[1011] Ronan McDonald, *The Death of the Critic*, Continuum, 2007.

[1012] Mark Kermode, interviewed by Stephen Carty on *List Film*, 25 October 2013.

[1013] Maureen Ryan, *How to be a TV Critic, Huffington Post*, 14 December 2011.

[1014] Quoted in *Whither Film Criticism in the age of Rotten Tomatoes?, Toronto Globe and Mail*, 11 September 2014.

[1015] Giles Coren, *Serious film-making has come to an end. Hurrah!, Time Out*, 13 January 2015.

[1016] Giles Coren, *How the DVD Boxset changed TV, Esquire*, 26 September 2013.

[1017] The critics' quotes and Mark Shenton's conclusion are all drawn from William Russell and Peter Cargin's *A Critical Century* (2014). Page 73.

[1018] Ben Brantley, *New York Times*, 31 October 2003.

[1019] Michael Billington, *Guardian*, 28 September 2006.

[1020] Charles Spencer, *Daily Telegraph*, 28 September 2006.

[1021] Paul Taylor, *Independent*, 28 September 2006.

[1022] Christopher Tookey, *Daily Mail*, 27 May 2011.

[1023] Joe Morgenstern, *Wall Street Journal*, 27 May 2011.

[1024] Mick LaSalle, *San Francisco Chronicle*, 26 May 2011.

[1025] Betsy Sharkey, *Los Angeles Times*, 27 May 1011.

[1026] Manohla Dargis, *New York Times*, 25 May 2011.

[1027] Charlie Lyne, *Ultra Culture*, 26 May 2011.

[1028] *Hollywood Reporter*, 30 May 2011.

[1029] *Hollywood Reporter*, 22 May 2011.

[1030] *Box office Mojo*, 30 May 2011.

[1031] Statistics on screens are from *imdb.com.*

[1032] Mark Lawson, *Who cares what the reviews say?*, *Guardian*, 24 May 2006.

[1033] Mark Lawson, *Who cares what the reviews say?*, *Guardian*, 24 May 2006.

[1034] www.hoaxes.org/ archive/permalink/subways_are_for_sleeping

[1035] https://community.qlikview.com/blogs/theqlikviewblog/2013/08/01/conte xtomy-no-more

[1036] www.motherjones.com/politics/1997/11/not-such-thriller

[1037] http://www.gelfmagazine.com/archives/eddie_murphys_huge_belching_s pectacular.php

[1038] This is based on a conversation I had with Kenneth Tynan at a dinner to commemorate the 150th anniversary of the Oxford Union, in 1973. I'm not sure which of Douglas Home's numerous plays Tynan meant. He made me aware that he had disliked all of them.

[1039] Michael Hann, *Warning: review quotes can be very misleading*, *Guardian*, 8 May 2012.

[1040] Andrea Hubert, *Hold the front page!*, *Guardian*, 18 August 2008.

[1041] Andrea Hubert, *Hold the front page!*, *Guardian*, 18 August 2008.

[1042] Andrea Hubert, *Hold the front page!*, *Guardian*, 18 August 2008.

[1043] www.movie-film-review.com/devFilm.asp?ID=3793

[1044] https://books.google.co.uk/books?isbn=3110157659

[1045] http://vdujardin.com/blog/paris-taine-gouraud/

[1046] en.wikipedia.org/wiki/Hippolyte_Taine

[1047] http://commons.wikimedia.org/wiki/File:Statue_of_Charles_Augustin_Sa inte-Beuve,_Luxembourg_Gardens,_Paris_2013.jpg

[1048] en.wikipedia.org/wiki/Charles_Augustin_Sainte-Beuve

[1049] https://books.google.co.uk/books?isbn=8170997062

[1050] Howard Jacobson, *Whatever It Is, I Don't Like It*, Bloomsbury 2011, p229.

[1051] Alex Ross, *Statues of critics*, *www.therestisnoise.com*, 19 March 2006.

[1052] www.thehistoryoflondon.co.uk/dr-samuel-johnson/

[1053] www.npg.org.uk › Collections

[1054] Alex Ross, *Statues of critics*, *www.therestisnoise.com*, 19 March 2006.

[1055] www.visual-arts-cork.com/history-of-art/abstract-expressionism.htm

[1056] en.wikipedia.org/wiki/Brooks_Atkinson_Theatre

[1057] http://en.wikipedia.org/wiki/Walter_Kerr_Theatre

[1058] www.playbill.com/features/article/quotable-critics-150427

[1059] en.wikipedia.org/wiki/American_Theater_Hall_of_Fame

[1060] *Obama: 'Ebert was the movies'*, *USA Today*, 4 April 2013.

[1061] *Roger Ebert Statue unveiled outside Illinois theater*, *Time*, 25 April 2014.

[1062] http://en.wikisource.org/wiki/Collins,_John_Churton_(DNB12)

[1063] insideinferno.com/en/florence/locations/vasari-corridor

[1064] Oscar Wilde, *The Critic as Artist, Collected Works of Oscar Wilde*, Wordsworth, 2007, p983.

[1065] www.movie-film-review.com

[1066] Simon Price, *A Parasitic But Necessary Art: Simon Price on the Role of the Critic*, *The Quietus*, 18 October 2013.

[1067] Quoted by Irving Wardle, *Confessions of an honest thief*, *Independent*, 12 July 1992.

[1068] John Simon, *Private Screenings*, Macmillan, 1967.

[1069] http://www.firstthings.com/article/2010/04/do-movie-critics-matter

[1070] Quoted in Sylvain Verstricht, *The Death of Popular Criticism*, *www.localgestures.com*, 19 November 2011.

[1071] www.brainyquote.com/quotes/quotes/w/winstonchu103863.html

[1072] Quoted in Ryan Call, *A Different notion of the critic*, 5 August 2009.

[1073] Christopher Hitchens, *Letters to a Young Contrarian*, Basic Books, 2001.

[1074] Shane Wright and Nick Butterly, *Gillard tells journos to 'cut the crap'*, *West Australian*, 15 July 2011.

[1075] Anthony Lane, in his introduction to *Nobody's Perfect: Writings from The New Yorker*, Picador, 2002, page xx.

Lightning Source UK Ltd.
Milton Keynes UK
UKOW06f0246190717
305596UK00001B/39/P